# Illustrated Guide to the Catholic Churches in the Diocese of Plymouth

Published by Sally Woodhead
Hatchwell, Widecombe-in-the-Moor,
Devon. TQ13 7UB

Copyright © Sally Woodhead 1992

ISBN 0 9520381 0 2

All rights reserved. No part of
this work may be reproduced by
any means without permission.

Location maps are reproduced by
permission of Ordnance Survey.
© crown copyright.

Extensive reference has been made
to "The Oxford Dictionary of Saints"
edited by D. H. Farmer (3rd ed. 1992)
by permission of Oxford University Press.

Printed at Al Ghurair Printing Press, Dubai

# Illustrated Guide to the Catholic Churches in the Diocese of Plymouth

**SALLY WOODHEAD**

**Illustrated by Christopher Woodhead**

**FORWARD**

**By the Bishop of the Diocese of Plymouth**

September 1992.

Vescourt, Hartley Road, Plymouth, Devon, PL3 5LR

It gives me great pleasure to recommend this 'Illustrated Guide to the Catholic Churches in the Diocese of Plymouth' by Sally Woodhead. It is a good guide for to-day's visitor. It is also provides valuable historical information about our churches and is a readable account of how the Catholic church developed in Cornwall, Devon and Dorset both before and after the canonical foundation of the diocese in 1850.

This book also puts into our hands an appreciation of the work of those who have gone before us, and enables us to become among the treasures, both artistic and religious, which are to be found in our churches.

I hope it will be widely used.

✝Christopher Budd

# CONTENTS

*page* 8 Introduction.
11 Acknowledgements.
12 Map of the Diocese of Plymouth.

14 **ASHBURTON** *Our Lady of Lourdes & St. Petrock.*
16 **AXMINSTER** *St. Mary.*
18 **BARNSTAPLE** *St. Mary's.*
20 **BEAMINSTER** *St. John.*
22 **BIDEFORD** *The Sacred Heart.*
24 **BISHOPSTEIGNTON** *St. Mary Magdalene.*
26 **BLANDFORD FORUM** *Our Lady of Lourdes & St. Cecilia.*
28 **BODMIN** *St. Mary's Abbey.*
30 **BOURNEMOUTH** *Christ the King.*
32 **BOURNEMOUTH** *Our Lady of Victories & St. Bernadette.*
34 **BOVEY TRACEY** *Holy Ghost.*
36 **BRAUNTON** *St. Brannoc.*
38 **BRIDPORT** *SS. Mary & Catherine.*
40 **BRIXHAM** *Our Lady Star of the Sea.*
42 **BUCKFAST** *Buckfast Abbey.*
48 **BUCKFASTLEIGH** *St. Benedict.*
50 **BUDE** *St. Peter.*
52 **BUDLEIGH SALTERTON** *St. Peter Prince of the Apostles.*
54 **CALLINGTON** *Our Lady of Victories.*
56 **CAMBORNE** *St. John the Baptist.*
58 **CHAGFORD** *The Holy Family.*
60 **CHIDEOCK** *Our Lady Queen of Martyrs & St. Ignatius.*
64 **CHULMLEIGH** *Our Lady & St. Bernard.*
66 **COMBE MARTIN** *St. Mary.*
68 **CREDITON** *St. Boniface.*
70 **CROYDE** *The Barn.*
72 **CULLOMPTON** *St. Boniface.*
74 **DARTMOUTH** *St. John the Baptist.*
76 **DAWLISH** *St. Agatha.*
78 **DORCHESTER** *Holy Trinity.*
80 **EXETER** *Blessed Sacrament.*
82 **EXETER** *Sacred Heart.*
86 **EXETER** *St. Thomas of Canterbury.*
88 **EXETER** *Holy Cross.*
90 **EXMOUTH** *Holy Ghost.*
92 **FALMOUTH** *St. Mary Immaculate.*
94 **GERMOE** *St. Mary.*
96 **GILLINGHAM** *St. Benedict.*
98 **GUNNISLAKE** *St. Joseph.*
100 **HARTLAND** *Our Lady & St. Nectan.*
102 **HAYLE** *St. Joseph.*

| page | | |
|---|---|---|
| 104 | **HELSTON** | *St. Mary.* |
| 106 | **HEMYOCK** | *St. Joseph.* |
| 108 | **HOLSWORTHY** | *St. Cuthbert Mayne.* |
| 110 | **HONITON** | *The Holy Family.* |
| 114 | **ILFRACOMBE** | *Our Lady of Ilfracombe Star of the Sea.* |
| 116 | **IPPLEPEN** | *St. Mary.* |
| 118 | **IVYBRIDGE** | *St. Austin's Priory.* |
| 120 | **KINGSBRIDGE** | *Sacred Heart.* |
| 122 | **KINGSKERSWELL** | *St. Gregory.* |
| 124 | **KINGSTEIGNTON** | *St. Columba's Hall.* |
| 126 | **LANHERNE** | *SS. Joseph & Anne.* |
| 128 | **LAUNCESTON** | *St. Cuthbert Mayne.* |
| 132 | **LISKEARD** | *Our Lady & St. Neot.* |
| 134 | **LOOE** | *Our Lady & St. Nicholas.* |
| 136 | **LYME REGIS** | *SS. Michael & George.* |
| 138 | **LYMPSTONE** | *St. Boniface.* |
| 140 | **LYNTON** | *The Most Holy Saviour.* |
| 142 | **MARNHULL** | *Our Lady.* |
| 144 | **MAWNAN SMITH** | *St. Edward.* |
| 146 | **MODBURY** | *St. Monica.* |
| 148 | **MULLION** | *St. Michael Archangel.* |
| 150 | **NEWQUAY** | *Most Holy Trinity.* |
| 152 | **NEWTON ABBOT** | *St. Joseph.* |
| 154 | **OKEHAMPTON** | *St. Boniface.* |
| 156 | **OTTERY St.MARY** | *St. Anthony.* |
| 158 | **PADSTOW** | *St. Saviour & St. Petroc.* |
| 160 | **PAIGNTON** | *Sacred Heart & St. Teresa.* |
| 164 | **PENZANCE** | *The Immaculate Conception of Our Lady.* |
| 166 | **PERRANPORTH** | *Christ the King.* |
| 168 | **PLYMOUTH** | *Cathedral.* |
| 172 | **PLYMOUTH** | *Christ Church.* |
| 174 | **PLYMOUTH** | *Christ the King.* |
| 176 | **PLYMOUTH** | *Holy Cross.* |
| 178 | **PLYMOUTH** | *Our Lady of Lourdes.* |
| 180 | **PLYMOUTH** | *Our Lady of Mount Carmel.* |
| 182 | **PLYMOUTH** | *Our Most Holy Redeemer.* |
| 184 | **PLYMOUTH** | *St. Edward the Confessor.* |
| 186 | **PLYMOUTH** | *St. Joseph.* |
| 188 | **PLYMOUTH** | *St. Margaret Mary.* |
| 190 | **PLYMOUTH** | *St. Paul.* |
| 192 | **PLYMOUTH** | *St. Peter.* |
| 194 | **PLYMOUTH** | *St. Teresa.* |
| 196 | **PLYMOUTH** | *St. Thomas More.* |
| 198 | **PLYMOUTH** | *The Holy Family.* |
| 200 | **POOLE** | *St. Anthony of Padua.* |
| 202 | **POOLE** | *SS. Joseph & Walburga.* |
| 204 | **POOLE** | *St. Mary.* |

| | | |
|---|---|---|
| page 206 | **POOLE** | *Our Lady of Fatima.* |
| 208 | **PORTLAND** | *Our Lady & St. Andrew.* |
| 210 | **PRESTON** | *Our Lady.* |
| 212 | **REDRUTH** | *The Assumption.* |
| 214 | **St. AGNES** | *Our Lady Star of the Sea.* |
| 216 | **St. AUSTELL** | *St. Augustine of Hippo.* |
| 220 | **St. IVES** | *Sacred Heart & St. Ia.* |
| 222 | **St. MAWES** | *Our Lady Star of the Sea & St. Anthony.* |
| 224 | **SALCOMBE** | *Our Lady Star of the Sea.* |
| 226 | **SALTASH** | *Our Lady of Perpetual Succour.* |
| 228 | **SCLERDER ABBEY** | *Our Lady of Light.* |
| 232 | **SEATON** | *St. Augustine.* |
| 234 | **SHAFTESBURY** | *The Holy Name & St. Edward the Martyr.* |
| 236 | **SHALDON** | *St. Ignatius of Loyola.* |
| 240 | **SHERBORNE** | *Sacred Heart & St. Aldhelm.* |
| 242 | **SIDMOUTH** | *Most Precious Blood.* |
| 244 | **SOUTH BRENT** | *St. Dunstan.* |
| 246 | **SOUTH MOLTON** | *St. Joseph.* |
| 248 | **SWANAGE** | *The Holy Spirit & St. Edward.* |
| 252 | **TAVISTOCK** | *Our Lady of the Assumption.* |
| 254 | **TEIGNMOUTH** | *Our Lady & St. Patrick.* |
| 256 | **TINTAGEL** | *St. Paul.* |
| 258 | **TIVERTON** | *St. James.* |
| 260 | **TIVERTON** | *St. John.* |
| 262 | **TORPOINT** | *St. Joan of Arc.* |
| 264 | **TORQUAY** | *Holy Angels.* |
| 266 | **TORQUAY** | *Our Lady Help of Christians & St. Denis.* |
| 268 | **TORQUAY** | *Our Lady of the Assumption.* |
| 270 | **TORQUAY** | *SS. John Fisher & Thomas More.* |
| 272 | **TORQUAY** | *St. Vincent.* |
| 274 | **TORRINGTON** | *The Holy Family.* |
| 276 | **TOTNES** | *St. Mary & St. George.* |
| 278 | **TRURO** | *Our Lady of the Portal & St. Piran.* |
| 280 | **UPWEY** | *The Holy Family.* |
| 282 | **WADEBRIDGE** | *St. Michael.* |
| 284 | **WAREHAM** | *St. Edward the Martyr.* |
| 286 | **WEST MOORS** | *St. Anthony.* |
| 288 | **WEYMOUTH** | *St. Augustine of Canterbury.* |
| 290 | **WEYMOUTH** | *St. Joseph.* |
| 292 | **WIMBORNE** | *St. Catherine.* |
| 294 | **WITHYCOMBE** | *St. Anne.* |
| 296 | **WOOL** | *St. Joseph.* |
| 298 | **WYKE REGIS** | *St. Charles.* |
| 300 | **YELVERTON** | *Holy Cross.* |
| | | |
| 302 | **List of colour plates** | |
| 303 | **Further reading** | |

## INTRODUCTION

This book started off in 1988 as a guide for new residents in the Diocese or the holiday visitor, and, hopefully, may also provide for parishoners the means to make an armchair pilgrimage to the other churches in their Diocese. Having moved to Devon in mid '86 after many years abroad in the Vicariate of Arabia I was anxious to feel at home again in the Catholic Church in England. It is not always easy to adjust to life in another location away from familiar buildings and customs. Many Catholic Churches appear anonymous in their surroundings and can be hard to find. Prior to 1986 I knew the South West only as a venue for holidays, and finding a church was sometimes quite a challange. To find them all was the first simple objective of the book. However, in the search for answers to intriguing questions suggested by the churches, the Diocese revealed itself as an incredibly exciting place, past and present. We have, indeed, a rich Christian heritage in the South West, providing the first century setting for the legend of Joseph of Arimathea and the Holy Grail, followed later by the establishment of Celtic Christianity. By and during the Middle Ages, many beautiful churches and abbeys existed or were founded. Sadly, the reign of King Henry VIII brought about the dissolution of the monasteries in 1539, the confiscation of churches and land, and the abolition of the "Catholic" dioceses. The last of the Marian bishops expired in 1585.

Nearly a hundred years later, in 1688, during the reign of the Catholic King James II, Pope Innocent XI (1676-1689) approved the setting up of three new bishops for the Church in England to aid His (Solitary) Lordship Dr. Leyburn.
England and Wales were divided into "Four Districts", each with its own Vicar Apostolic: Northern District, Midland District, London District and Western District. Our very first Vicar Apostolic of the Western District was Bishop Philip Michael Ellis O.S.B.

In 1829 the Catholic Emancipation Act was passed, and so began an exciting building programme for the Catholic Church in England, and especially in our own corner in the South West.

On 29th September 1850, the feast of St. Michael the Archangel, Pope Pius IX (1846-1878) restored the Hierarchy in England and Wales. The Metropolitan See was fixed at Westminster and there were twelve Suffragan Sees. The pre-Reformation titles for the various Dioceses, such as Exeter, York and Winchester were not used. The South West became the "Diocese of Plymouth", consisting of the counties of Dorset (west of the original county border), Devon, Cornwall, and the Isles of Scilly.

Bishop George Errington was consecrated as first Bishop of Plymouth on 25th July 1851, the feast of St. James. His successors were Bishop William Vaughan (1855-1902), Bishop Charles Graham (1902-1911), Bishop John Keily (1911-1928); Bishop John P. Barrett (1929-1946), Bishop Francis Joseph Grimshaw (1947-1954), and Bishop Cyril E. Restieaux (1955-1985). Bishop Christopher Budd is Plymouth's eighth Bishop, consecrated in 1986.

As the Diocese grew, there were many unsung heroes: Missionaries, emigre French priests, Religious Orders in exile from France, from Spain, and "ordinary" Diocesan priests (so many not named here) who planned and saved and bargained and put up with all sorts of discomfort for the sake of Christ and His Church in the South West.

In 1992 the Diocese can be proud of its fine Cathedral designed by Joseph and Charles Hansom, also the famous Monastery that re-emerged like a phoenix from the ashes out of the dust of centuries beside the River Dart, the various Retreat Centres including St. Rita's at Honiton, Holy Trinity House at Newquay, St. Mary's Abbey Buckfast, the Shrine of the Dorset Martyrs at Chideock, the Shrine of St. Cuthbert Mayne at Launceston, and the National Shrine of St. Boniface (our Diocesan Patron) at Crediton. We are fortunate too to be able to share in the spirituality of several Enclosed Orders by using Parish Churches adjacent to their monasteries: at Lanherne (the oldest Carmel in England), at Sclerder (also Carmelite) and at Lynton (Poor Clares).

There is something to suit all tastes and ages in the Diocese: exciting modern churches at Wool and St. Austell, traditional buildings such as Our Lady Help Of Christians & St. Denis at Torquay, converted stables at Ottery St. Mary, and the "Barn" at Croyde. There are two resplendent family chapels on private estates which have played an important role in the Catholic history of the South West, one at Lulworth in Dorset (the home of the Weld Family), the other at Ugbrooke in Devon (the home of the Clifford Family).

The search for the link between the church and its dedication in each case became particularly interesting, and is noted where found. Where a direct link was not discovered, it is hoped that other information noted about the dedication may be of interest. The heroism of the various patrons, and especially the martyrs of the South West, is overwhelming.

The illustrations relate directly to the church in each case, and record a personal memory, an attempt to define the essence of each.
I must add that many of the clergy who answered the questionnaire in 1988 subsequently moved to other parishes, so most will find that some material included about their present church was furnished by a predecessor!

The search for information has led to an interesting liturgical experience. One can celebrate the Eucharist in a very quiet way, or listen and become one with 4 part choral polyphony, one can sing folk or "modern" or join in hymns of ecumenical flavour and tradition. In some parts of the Diocese there is the spontaneous shared joy of Taize and in others the timeless, unhurried quality and peace of Gregorian chant. The buildings are equally diverse.

The plan of any Catholic Church is a simple arrangement. and all the Churches illustrated follow the prescribed form. However, no two are the same, or even similar in character, except for that shared quality of prayerfulness exuded by buildings which have witnessed continual prayer.

Each building has come about through the determination of individuals or groups, sometimes through the generosity of benefactors, but often by financial sacrifice and struggle. Some emulated the splendors of ancient basilicas. In other places the first Mass, following appropriate precedents "happened" in a barn or small upper room.

Over the four years duration of intermittent visits to all the churches in the Diocese, revisiting has, in some cases, revealed great changes of refurnishing and reordering. Some Churches have disappeared in that time, and a new one has opened. As a record, therefore, the book glimpses a stretched moment in time.
A sucession of visits to every church in a diocese is an experience shared perhaps only by a bishop and the writer of a guide book. The journey revealed a Church not only rooted deep in its pre-Reformation convictions, but one with a lively response to change and diversity.

**May God Bless our Plymouth Diocese.**

ACKNOWLEDGEMENTS

There are many people I would like to thank, first of all, His Lordship Bishop Christopher Budd, for his interest when I went to see him with a few sketches and ideas in 1988. He provided me with an initial letter of support which proved most helpful when visiting the various churches . If there was any doubt about my intent or purpose, the Bishop's letter acted as a reference. He kindly updated the "old" letter in 1991.

My thanks to the Diocesan Archivist, Fr. Christopher Smith, for the loan of many past Diocesan Year Books, answers to "odd" queries and help through the Diocesan History Group Meetings.

Many thanks to the priests of the whole Diocese of Plymouth who kindly answered the questionnaires sent out in 1988 and gave me some time when I visited their Parishes, provided keys for locked Churches and Chapels of Ease, provided access to past records and sent me further information through the post or by telephone.

Many thanks to parishioners throughout the Diocese who helped me by unlocking more churches, spent time chatting about the history of their Parish and sent me all sorts of details by Post.

Thanks to my family who have put up with my many moments of silent scribbling, thinking, reading and, ultimately the pounding of the typewriter or word processor....!

My thanks especially to Christopher, my husband, who has been my photographer, illustrator, proof reader, patient helper and financier!

Finally, thanks to the Holy Spirit for the idea for this book. I did not realise how many moments of sheer joy would permeate the toil of research. The following words have so often been true:

*"I rejoiced when I heard them say*
*Let us go to God's house ..." (Psalm 121.)*

S.B.W.

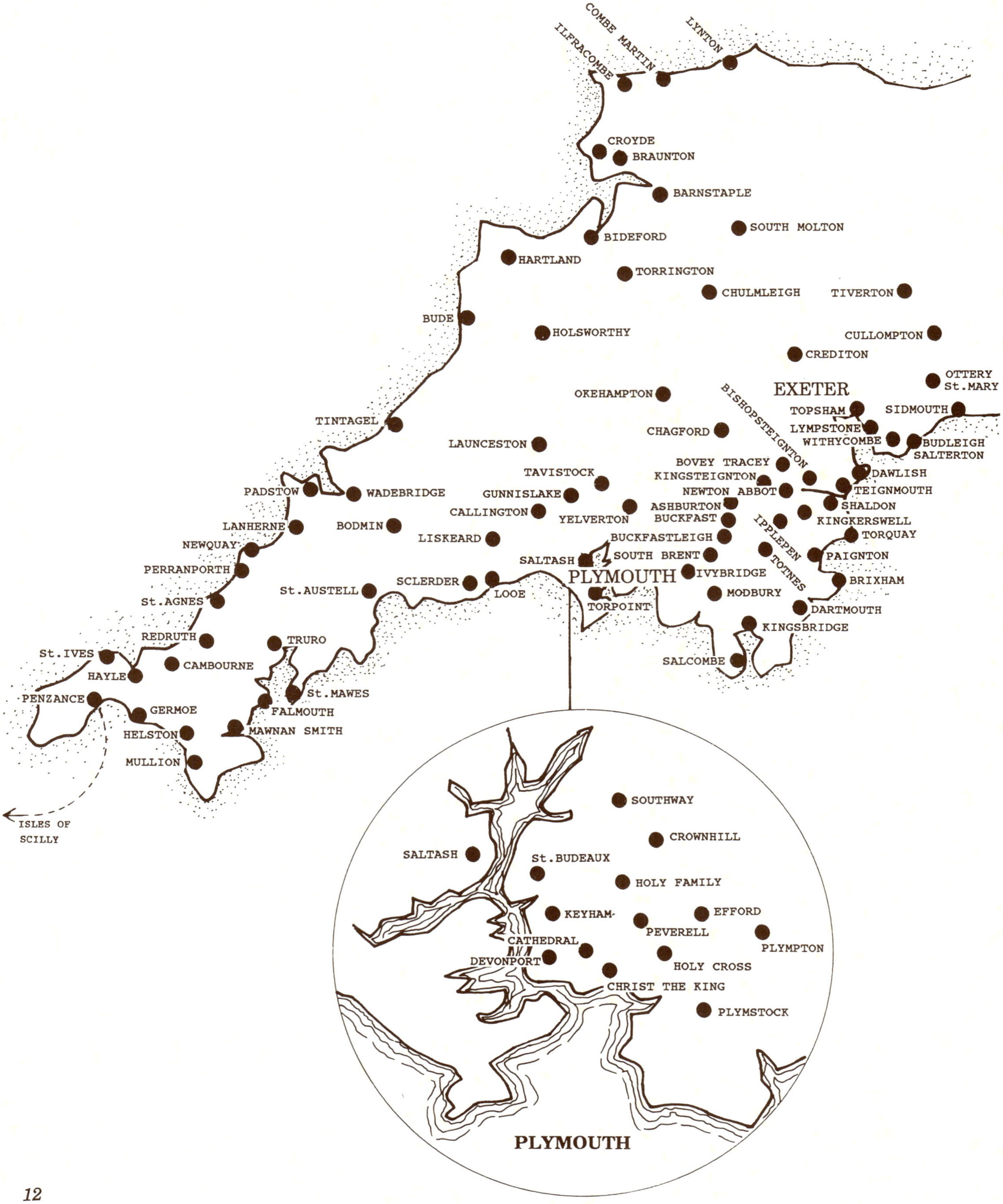

COMBE MARTIN
LYNTON
ILFRACOMBE
CROYDE
BRAUNTON
BARNSTAPLE
SOUTH MOLTON
BIDEFORD
HARTLAND
TORRINGTON
CHULMLEIGH
TIVERTON
BUDE
HOLSWORTHY
CULLOMPTON
CREDITON
OKEHAMPTON
BISHOPSTEIGNTON
EXETER
OTTERY St.MARY
TOPSHAM
SIDMOUTH
TINTAGEL
CHAGFORD
LYMPSTONE
WITHYCOMBE
BUDLEIGH SALTERTON
LAUNCESTON
BOVEY TRACEY
DAWLISH
TAVISTOCK
KINGSTEIGNTON
PADSTOW
WADEBRIDGE
GUNNISLAKE
NEWTON ABBOT
TEIGNMOUTH
CALLINGTON
ASHBURTON
SHALDON
LANHERNE
BODMIN
YELVERTON
BUCKFAST
KINGKERSWELL
NEWQUAY
LISKEARD
BUCKFASTLEIGH
IPPLEPEN
TORQUAY
SALTASH
SOUTH BRENT
PAIGNTON
PERRANPORTH
PLYMOUTH
IVYBRIDGE
TOTNES
SCLERDER
BRIXHAM
St.AUSTELL
LOOE
MODBURY
St.AGNES
TORPOINT
DARTMOUTH
REDRUTH
KINGSBRIDGE
TRURO
St.IVES
CAMBOURNE
SALCOMBE
HAYLE
St.MAWES
PENZANCE
GERMOE
FALMOUTH
HELSTON
MAWNAN SMITH
MULLION
ISLES OF SCILLY
SOUTHWAY
CROWNHILL
SALTASH
St.BUDEAUX
HOLY FAMILY
KEYHAM
EFFORD
PEVERELL
PLYMPTON
CATHEDRAL
DEVONPORT
HOLY CROSS
CHRIST THE KING
PLYMSTOCK
PLYMOUTH

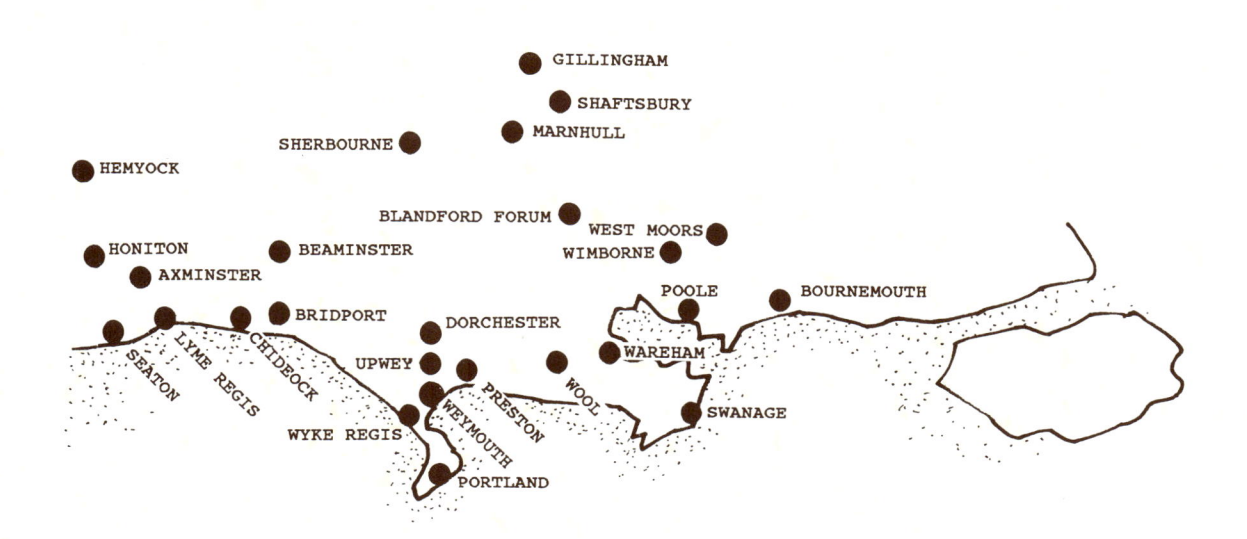

# The Diocese of Plymouth

Map locations:
- HEMYOCK
- HONITON
- AXMINSTER
- SEATON
- LYME REGIS
- CHIDEOCK
- SHERBOURNE
- BEAMINSTER
- BRIDPORT
- UPWEY
- WYKE REGIS
- WEYMOUTH
- PRESTON
- PORTLAND
- GILLINGHAM
- SHAFTSBURY
- MARNHULL
- BLANDFORD FORUM
- WEST MOORS
- WIMBORNE
- DORCHESTER
- WOOL
- POOLE
- WAREHAM
- SWANAGE
- BOURNEMOUTH

# Ashburton

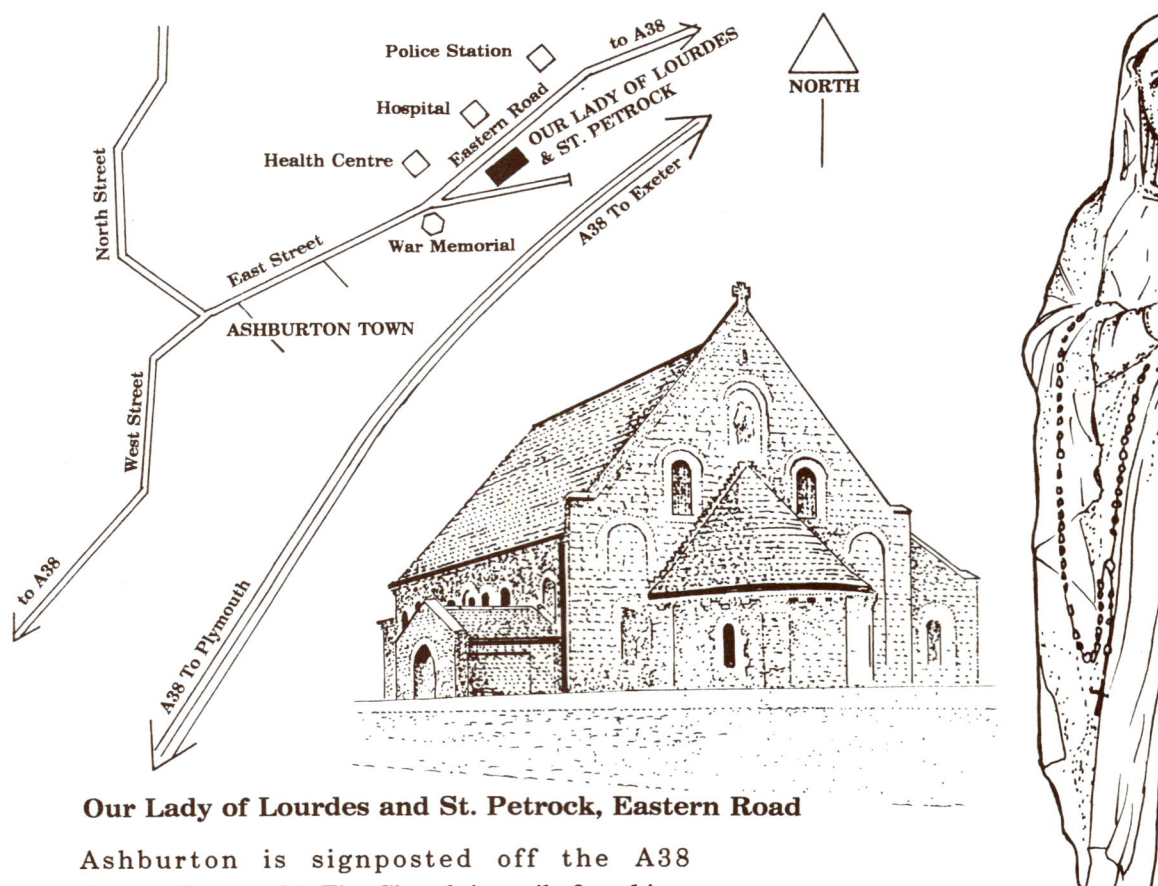

**Our Lady of Lourdes and St. Petrock, Eastern Road**

Ashburton is signposted off the A38 (Exeter-Plymouth). The Church is easily found in Eastern Road (the continuation of East Street), just past the War Memorial and opposite Ashburton Health Centre. There is a local bus service to and from Plymouth and Exeter and the neighbouring towns. Car Parking is available within the Church grounds or nearby.

The Church is dedicated to Our Lady of Lourdes and the famous sixth century Cornish man, Saint Petrock. There seem to be many legends and varied accounts of Petrock's existence. Some say he went to Rome and then to Jerusalem and India and on his return to Britain slew a dragon! Petrock came from Wales but made his way to Devon and Cornwall to preach the Gospel. He founded several monasteries, one at (Petrockstowe) Padstow. Later he became a hermit and lived on Bodmin Moor. He died at Treravel and was buried at Padstow. Many churches have been dedicated to him in Devon and Cornwall, South Wales and Brittany. There are various feast days in his memory including June 4th. The feast of Our Lady of Lourdes is kept on 11th February each year.

# Our Lady of Lourdes and St. Petrock

In 1882, when the Benedictine monks came to Buckfast, there was not one Catholic in Ashburton to greet them. Two decades later, however, the situation was different and it was then that Abbot Boniface Natter decided to revive Catholic life in the vicinity. The Mass was restored in 1911 in a temporary chapel in a barn in Roborough Lane. Three years later a hut, transported all the way from Launceston, was carefully erected on the other side of the road. It was transformed into a small church. In 1919 Dom. John Stephan, a monk of Buckfast, became the first Parish Priest. The present site in Eastern Road was acquired in 1933 and in November 1935 the Church of Our Lady and St Petrock was opened. The building was not totally completed. At the end of 1976 work began on the Sanctuary. Bishop Cyril Restieaux presided over the solemn opening of the finished church and the consecration of the new altar just before Christmas 1977.

Contact address of Priest: St. Mary's Abbey, Buckfast, Devon. TQ11 OEE. Tel: (0364) 43301.

# Axminster St. Mary,

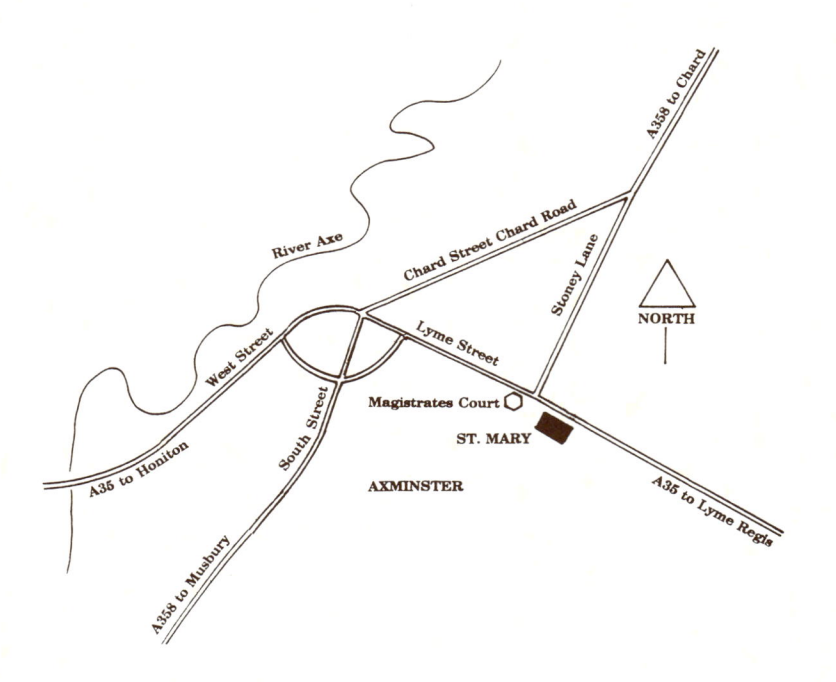

**St. Mary, Lyme Road**

From Honiton take the A35 east, from Dorchester/Bridport the A35 west, from Musbury the A358 north, from Chard the A358 south into Axminster. St Mary's Catholic Church, built of local stone in Gothic style, is situated on the right hand side of the road 600 yards out of the centre of town, on the A35 going towards Dorchester, not far from the Magistrate's Court. Car parking is available at the Church. Axminster lies on the train route - London (Waterloo) to Exeter.

The Church is dedicated to Our Blessed Lady. Axminster has had a tradition of Marian devotion for centuries: the pre-Reformation Church in the centre (C.of E.) is also dedicated to Mary (and St. John the Evangelist). Mary leads us by her example to Christ. Scripture does not recall any great or marvellous works of the Holy Virgin except her total commitment to God. Mary's life on earth, and now, in heaven, simply directs us towards Him.

St. Mary's Church was opened for `public worship' on Ascension Day, May 29th 1862. It replaced a former chapel, dedicated to Our Lady, which had been in use since the feast of the Assumption, August 15th 1831.

A sculptured stone calvary is built into the exterior wall at the west end of the church. There is an inscription recording deaths of the Knights', eminent Catholics, who worked hard to restore Catholicism to Axminster: "Per crucem et passionem tuam, libera nos, Domine".

Some beautiful stained glass can be seen inside the Church: at the west end a "rose" window representing the Last Judgement, memorial windows along the nave, and, at the east end, the Annuncation, the Angel Gabriel with Mary, the handmaid of the Lord.

Contact address of Priest:
The Presbytery, Lyme Road,
Axminster,
Devon. EX13 5BE.
Telephone: (0297) 32135.

# Barnstaple

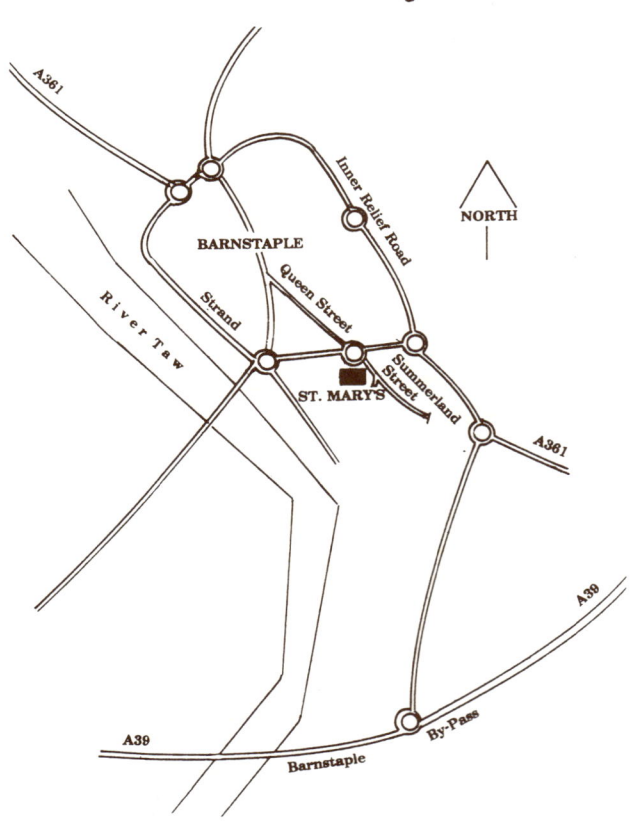

**St. Mary's, Higher Church Street.**

Many roads meet at Barnstaple: A39 from Lynton, A39 from Bideford, A377 from Exeter, A361 from Ilfracombe, A361 from South Molton. The modern Church of St Mary Immaculate Mother of God overlooks a main roundabout in the town centre. It has a prominent white spire and is adjacent to the old, Romanesque style, church. From Queen Street (G.P.O. on the corner), continue straight into Summerland Street. Turn right into Higher Church Street. There are several car parks nearby. Buses run from Exeter, Bideford and neighbouring towns.

The Church is dedicated to St. Mary Immaculate Mother of God, thus continuing an association with the old Church of the Immaculate Conception. Mary was the first of the redeemed. Mary, holy and spotless, lived and lives through love in His Presence. She was the chosen Mother of Christ and is the mother of us all. The feast of the Immaculate Conception is kept on 8th December each year.

Contact address of Priest:
The Presbytery, Higher Church Street, Barnstaple, North Devon. EX32 8JE.
Telephone: (0271) 43312.

# St. Mary, Immaculate Mother of God

This Church was built in 1984/5 as a replacement for the old one, which, in spite of its historic interest had become far too small and dilapidated for continued use. The former Church came about through Sir Bouchier Palk Wrey of Tawstock Court who married a Catholic widow, Lady Weld. They had their own private chapel in 1832. When Lady Weld died her husband bought land in Barnstaple and built the Church of the Immaculate Conception. It may be interesting to note that this church's foundation in 1844 preceded (by 7 years) the establishment of the Plymouth diocese. The Church was consecrated in 1855. It is possible that the original design was prepared by A.W. Pugin although he was not the site architect.

The foundation stone in honour of St. Mary Immaculate Mother of God was blessed by the Rt. Rev. Cyril Restieaux on 19th November 1984. The Rite of Dedication occurred on the Feast of the Visitation, 31st May 1985. The Church is built of local Exeter brick throughout. It has a sloping slated roof and a "latern tower topped by a fibre glass fleche, surmounted by a gilded cross". The altar, ambo and font are made of Somerset Doulting Stone. At the northern end of the Church there is a stained glass window (made at Buckfast Abbey) depicting the Risen Christ. There are four smaller side windows of adoring angels. The Stations of the Cross were made by a local artist and parishioner, Nancy Kelly.

The church is built to conform to the decree of the Vatican Council on Liturgy and Worship.

The Parish extends over a large area from western Exmoor and South Molton to Chulmleigh in the south. Just to the east of Barnstaple is Shirwell, where St. Cuthbert Mayne (Protomartyr of the English Seminaries abroad) was baptized in St. Peter's Church on 20th March 1544. St. Cuthbert Mayne probably attended Barnstaple Grammar School. He was the first "seminary priest" from Douai to die for the faith. He was martyred in the barbarous custom of the day in Launceston Market Place on 30th November 1577.

# Beaminster

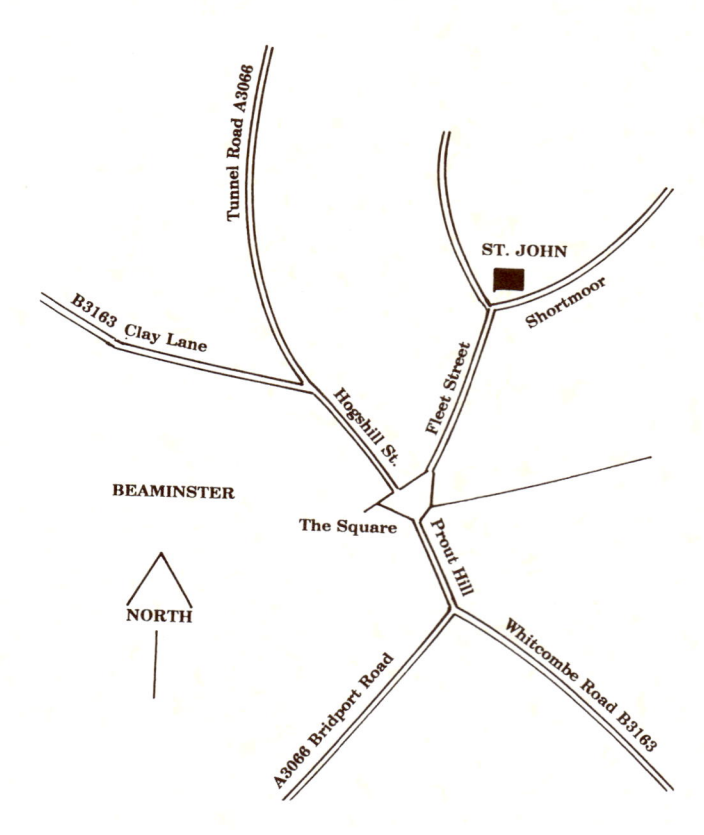

The dedication is to St. John the Apostle and Evangelist, the son of Zebedee, the brother of James, possibly one of the youngest of Christ's apostles. He witnessed The Transfiguration, went with Peter to prepare The Last Supper, followed Christ even after the betrayal, into the palace of Caiphas, a "Solitary Apostle" at the foot of the Cross, with the Holy Mother, throughout the trauma of Calvary. He is traditionally the writer of the Fourth Gospel. St. John left Jerusalem some 12 years after The Ascension and went to Asia Minor to Ephesus where he led the Early Christian Church. He endured persecution, exile in Patmos, but lived to a ripe old age to die eventually at Ephesus. His feast is celebrated on 27th December.

**St. John, Shortmoor.**

From the north leave the M5 at Taunton. Beaminster is situated off the A3066 (which links A35 Bridport to A30 Honiton/Yeovil) and the B3163 (which links the B3164 at Broadwindsor to the A356 Maiden Newton/ Crewkerne). From The Square in Beaminster turn into Fleet Street. Continue straight until the sign for Shortmoor only, turn right. The entrance to St. John's is about 100 yards on the left. The Church, a pleasing modern structure of Minster stone, is set back in its own grounds, enhanced by a little rose garden, and has ample parking facilities.

The construction of this little church, set in the heart of Dorset, began in May 1966. It was blessed and officially opened by the Rt. Rev. Bishop Cyril Restieaux on 17th March 1967.

# St. John

The interior was enriched a few years ago by the addition of two engraved windows, of St. John the Evangelist and Blessed John Munden, on either side of the Altar - the work of two local artists.

Blessed John Munden was a schoolmaster at Netherbury in the Beaminster parish. 1985 recorded the fourth century of his martyrdom. He was born at Mapperton, educated at Winchester and Oxford, then later ordained a seminary priest abroad. Unfortunately, on his return to England he was arrested and interrogated by the Secretary of State, Sir Francis Walsingham.

He was sent to prison in the awesome Tower of London and after a year of incarceration, on 5th February 1585, taken to Tyburn to be hanged, drawn and quartered together with five other priests.

There is a memorial to Blessed John Munden at the back of the Church and also a picture of 14 of the 136 English martyrs beatified by Pope Pius X1 (1922-1939) on 15th December 1929.

Contact address of Priest:
St. John's Presbytery, Shortmoor, Beaminster, Dorset. DT8 3EL.
Telephone: (0308) 862741.

# Bideford

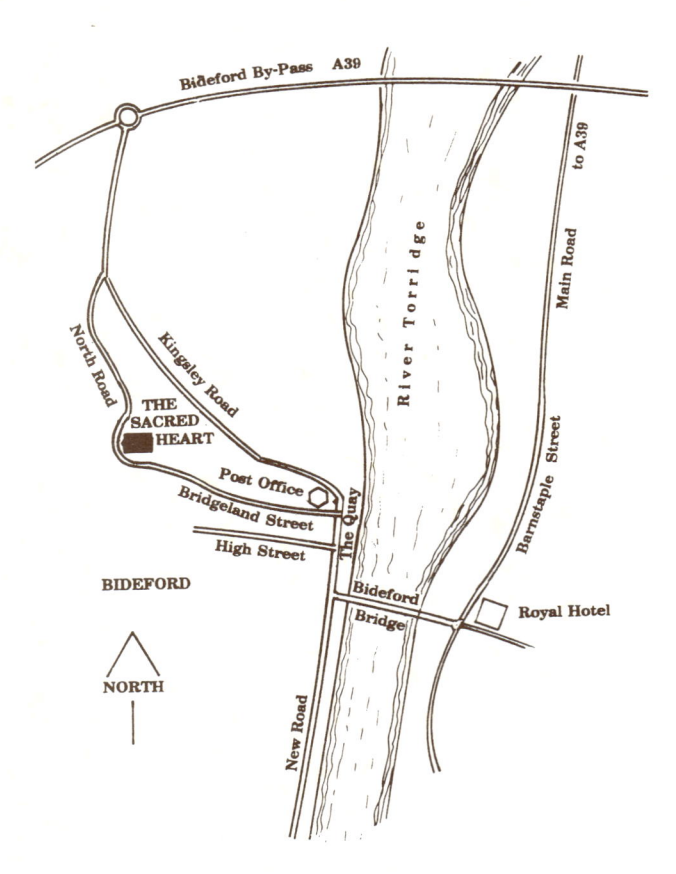

**The Sacred Heart    North Road**

From Barnstaple take the A39 south west, from Bude the A39 north east, from Okehampton the A386 north, from Holsworthy the A388 north to Bideford. Once in the centre find "The Quay". Near the Post Office and pedestrian traffic lights turn into Bridgeland Street/North Road, and continue to the stop sign. The Church of the Sacred Heart is situated on the right, on a long bend which used to be part of the main and only road from Bideford to Appledore and Westward Ho. There is a small car park near the church, free parking on Sundays.

The dedication honours The Sacred Heart and a devotion that has existed for at least nine centuries. It is always the same Jesus Christ that we honour no matter under what title. Devotion to the Sacred Heart is devotion to the Person of Jesus Himself. The Sacred Heart pierced for us is a symbol of Jesus' great love for us and His mercy towards us. The feast of The Sacred Heart is celebrated on the Friday after the 2nd Sunday after Pentecost.

# The Sacred Heart

In 1882 a Catholic Mission started in Bideford served from Barnstaple. Two rooms were hired in a public building in Bridgeland Street and converted into a Chapel. Mass was celebrated there on 15th August for the first time, it was the feast of the Assumption of Our Lady. Over the years as the congregation increased the Chapel facilities became inadequate. In May 1891 "Woodland Cottage" came up for sale. It was purchased for use as a presbytery with the garden as a site for a Church. On 18th July 1892 work commenced on levelling the ground west of the new presbytery ready for building. On 4th August 1892 Bishop Graham laid the foundation stone and four months later on 15th December the Church of The Sacred Heart was solemnly opened.

On the Sanctuary wall hangs a carved wood crucifix, the work of the artist who made the Calvary for Brompton Oratory - the late Miss Blyton Smith.

One of the Benedictine monks of Farnborough Abbey made the carved wood, painted statue of the Madonna and Child in the Lady Chapel.

There is an unusual feature in the Baptistry added to the Church in 1907 by Canon Middleton. The design of this turret which incorporates circles of coloured glass set in concrete was copied from a Byzantine source, the Crusader Church of St. Anne beside St. Stephen's Gate in Jerusalem (near the Pool of Bethsaida where Jesus healed the cripple). The turret over the Baptistry is crowned with a copper cupola and there also is the Church bell with "Ave Maria 1893" inscribed on it.

Contact address of Priest:
The Presbytery, North Road,
Bideford, Devon. EX39 2NW.
Telephone: (0237) 472519.

# Bishopsteignton

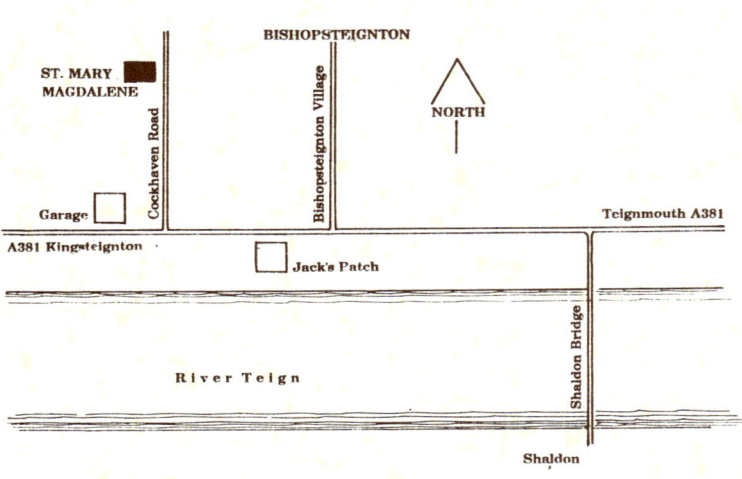

### St. Mary Magdalene, Cockhaven Road

Take the road out of Teignmouth along the dual carriageway to Shaldon Bridge. Continue straight on the A381 for about 3 miles. Go on past the Garden Centre (Jack's Patch) on your left. About a quarter of a mile further on turn right at the garage into Cockhaven Road. St. Mary Magdalene's Church, set back off the road in its own garden, is about 100 yards up on the left. The nearest railway stations to Bishopsteignton are Newton Abbot or Teignmouth. A 187 bus runs from Exeter to Newton Abbot. No Parish car park exists, but parking is allowed down Cockhaven Road.

The Church is dedicated to Mary Magdalene the patron saint of repentant sinners and also the Contemplative life. Mary's surname may have been due to her birthplace, Magdala, a town near Tiberias on the shores of Galilee. Mary Magdalene was freed from "seven devils" by Christ. She followed Him with loyal devotion as He went through the villages preaching and teaching, forgiving sins and healing. She stood at the last at the foot of the Cross on Calvary together with Mary Our Blessed Mother and St. John. At the tomb on the first Easter morning Mary Magdalene was privileged to be one of the first to see the Risen Christ. Her feast day is kept on 22nd July each year.

# St. Mary Magdalene

St. Mary Magdalene's is a small country church built and opened in 1937 as a Chapel of Ease for Teignmouth. It is one of a number of churches built in the 1930's by the Misses Robinson in Bishop Barrett's time. It is a real gem of a place to pray in, set apart from the hustle and bustle of towns and traffic. Stained glass in vivid richness on either side of the Sanctuary depicts the praise of angels: "Gloria in Excelsis" / "Te Deum Laudamus". A fresco on the Sanctuary wall above the tabernacle portrays a devout and artistic impression of the Mass, the Sacrifice of Calvary, to the glory of God. It is quite powerful.

A modern altar decorated with a carved relief shows the scene of The Last Supper. Small but magnificently intense castings, pictures of the Way to Golgotha, set around the Church, reveal the humanity yet divinity, the tragedy yet triumph of the Cross!

Contact address of Priest:
The Presbytery, Glendaragh Road,
Teignmouth, Devon. TQ14 8PH.
Telephone: (0626) 774640.

# Blandford Forum

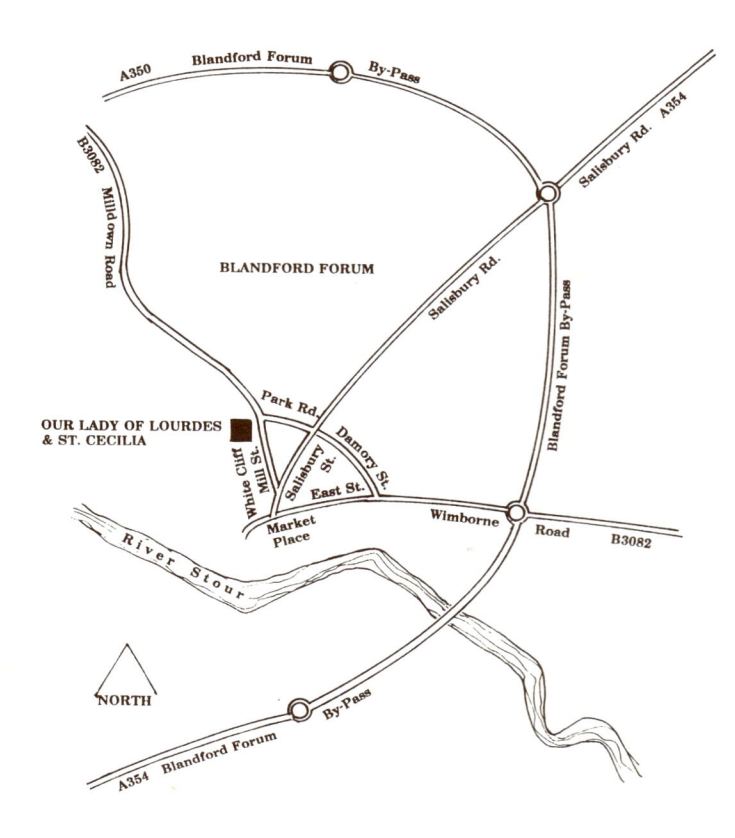

**Our Lady of Lourdes & St. Cecilia, White Cliff Mill Street.**

The A354 Dorchester/Salisbury, A350 Shaftsbury/Poole and B3082 Wimborne roads lead into Blandford Forum. The Catholic Church is easily found following the one way system from the centre of the town. Go down East Street into Market Place and follow on right into Salisbury Street. Bear left as the road forks going into White Cliff Mill Street. The Church is on the left handside, gable to road, a red brick building with a small stone cross on the roof.

The dedication is to Our Lady of Lourdes and St. Cecilia. The young Roman martyr, Cecilia, allegedly lived during the second or third century. According to legend she was forced to marry a pagan nobleman. She converted him to Christianity and he was subsequently martyred for his Faith together with his brother. Cecilia was arrested soon afterwards for refusing to sacrifice to pagan gods. Six centuries later her incorrupt remains were thought to be found during the transfer of martyrs' relics from the catacombs of St. Callistus on the orders of Pope Pascal 1 (817-824). In 1599 the ancient body of Cecilia was rediscovered during Church building alterations for one of the Cardinals. The renowned sculptor, Stefano Maderna, created a marble effigy of the saint. A life-size replica now rests in a tomb in the catacombs of St. Callistus in Rome. Since the sixteenth century St. Cecilia has been favoured patron of church music, of all musicians and singers, of organ builders and poets! Her feast is celebrated on 22nd November.

Contact address of Priest:
The Presbytery, White Cliff Mill Street, Blandford Forum, Dorset. DT11 7BN.
Telephone: (0258) 452051.

# Our Lady of Lourdes and St. Cecilia

# Bodmin

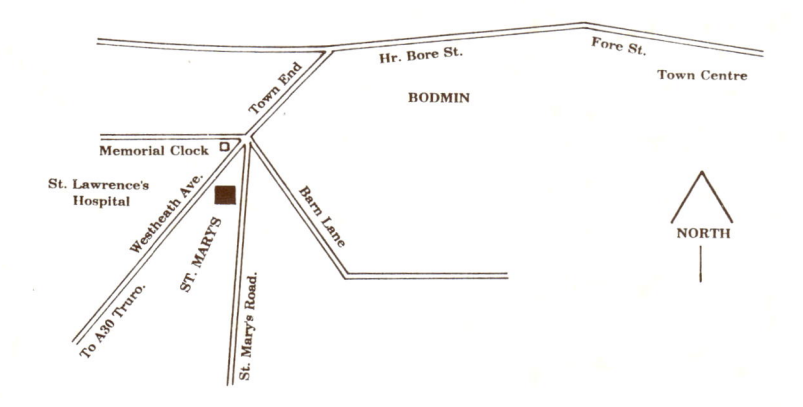

**St. Mary's, St. Mary's Road.**

St. Mary's Abbey Church is located on the A30, at the apex of Westheath Avenue (A30 to Truro) and St. Mary's Road. Helpful landmarks include a Memorial Clock opposite the Abbey Church and St. Lawrence's Hospital nearby.

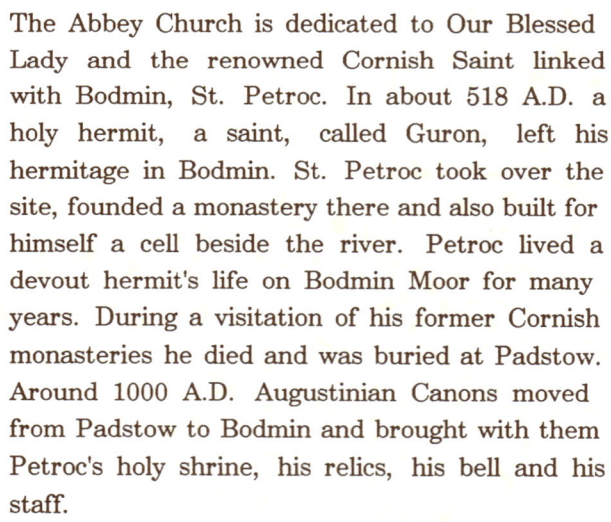

The Abbey Church is dedicated to Our Blessed Lady and the renowned Cornish Saint linked with Bodmin, St. Petroc. In about 518 A.D. a holy hermit, a saint, called Guron, left his hermitage in Bodmin. St. Petroc took over the site, founded a monastery there and also built for himself a cell beside the river. Petroc lived a devout hermit's life on Bodmin Moor for many years. During a visitation of his former Cornish monasteries he died and was buried at Padstow. Around 1000 A.D. Augustinian Canons moved from Padstow to Bodmin and brought with them Petroc's holy shrine, his relics, his bell and his staff.

About 117 years later a discontented religious pinched Petroc's bones and disappeared to Brittany! Other relics vanished in the Reformation. They may have once been at Rialton, the summer residence of a pre-Reformation Prior of Bodmin, but it is not really known. An ivory casket which once contained some relics of St. Petroc may be seen inside the Anglican Church.

# St. Mary's Church

The Canons Regular of the Lateran returned to Bodmin on the feast of St. John the Baptist, June 24th 1881. Mass was celebrated on that day for the first time since the suppression of the monastery by King Henry VIII in 1539. Before the Reformation the Canons were at the other end of the town - adjoining the present Anglican Church, known as the Priory. On the 56th anniversary of the Canons Regular coming back to Bodmin, June 24th 1937, the foundation stone of the new church was laid by Bishop John Barrett. The plan was to create a conventual church on the lines of a pre-Reformation Cornish Church, that is, with a nave, side aisles and tower, but with the "east" end and ambulatory serving as a Lady Chapel. Construction work was abandoned during the war and for 14 years after that. Then, new plans were made. The present Church, built of local stone, was blessed and opened by Bishop Restieaux on June 24th 1965.

The bare, stone walls of the interior, enhanced only by a glorious depth of colour from Buckfast Abbey stained glass, evoke a sense of timelessness, like the quality of prayer. The width, the geometric sections, hint at classical tradition and spaciousness. Austerity, simplicity, tranquility exist here.

The statue in the Lady Chapel was found in a well in the old Priory Grounds (now the Council Offices). The statue has been restored.

Contact adddress of Priest:
The Presbytery, 21, West Heath Avenue,
Bodmin, Cornwall. PL31 1QH.
Telephone: (0208) 75802.

# Bournemouth

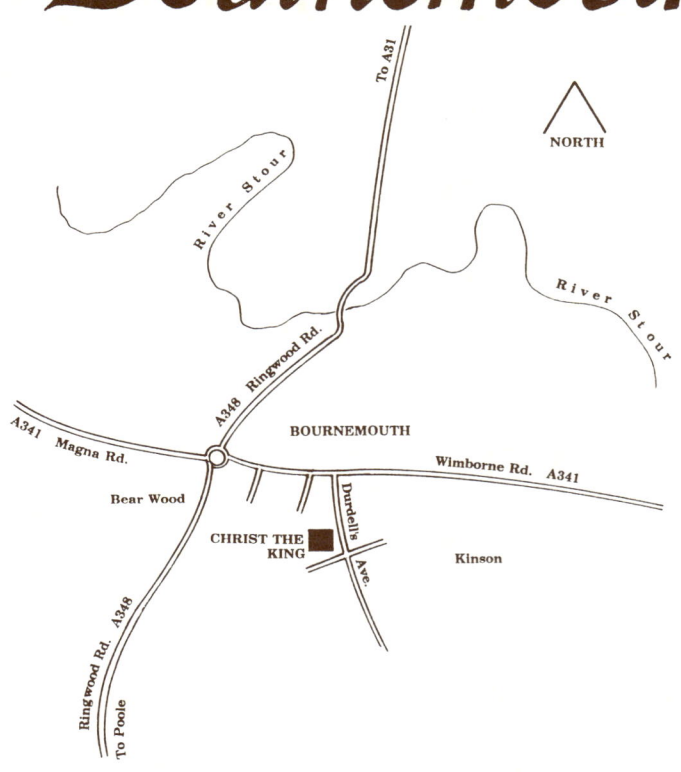

**Christ the King, Durdell's Ave.**

Heading south down A31 from Southampton/West Moors, follow the signs to Bournemouth, signs for A348 and signs for A341. The A348 is the Ringwood Road from Poole which joins after Ferndown the A31 to become the M3. Turn at Bear Cross (on A348) into Wimborne Road (A341). Continue straight. Take the third turning on the right into Durdell's Avenue. The tower and cross of Christ the King make the Church readily identifiable. There is a Lourdes Grotto within the garden. Car parking is possible in front of the Church.

The Kingship of Christ is mentioned in several parts of the Old Testament; in the prophesies of Isaiah, Ezechiel and Jeremias. In the New Testament, in the Gospels, we have the very words of Christ, the prisoner before Pontius Pilate, acknowledging His Kingship to rule over a spiritual kingdom not of this world, one of grace and justice, holiness and truth, love and peace. The feast of Christ the King is celebrated on the last Sunday of the liturgical year.

# Christ the King

The beginning of the Church and school at Kinson probably goes back to the purchase of a four and a half acre plot of "countryside" in the 1930's. At one time Mass was said at the Dolphin Hotel in Wimborne Road, then a converted Scout hut was in use as a church. In 1950 a new church was built, opened by the late Archbishop Grimshaw, dedicated to St. Theresa. But still there was need for another church! In 1963 a kind benefactor, Mrs Margaret Wells, left a legacy which helped to ease ecclesiastical finance. The foundation stone, in vivid display on the external wall of the church, now set beneath a large bronze statue of Christ the King, was blessed by Bishop Cyril Restieaux on 8th August 1965. The solemn opening occurred on June 30th 1966 and the Consecration on May 29th 1979.

The building is approximately one hundred feet long, fifty two feet wide and twenty five feet high. The interior is lofty and full of light. In contrast, there is a very private side chapel, in somewhat lesser light, and separated from the sanctuary by a grille. Above the holy water stoop in the entrance foyer is situated an interesting miniature carving of the Crucifixion scene. An article in the Diocesan Year Book of 1980 reports "The Universe" description of this building as *"the Benjamin Church of Bournemouth"*.

Contact address of Priest:
The Presbytery, 46, Durdell's Avenue, Kinson, Bournemouth, Dorset. BH11 9EH.
Telephone: (0202) 572939.

# Bournemouth

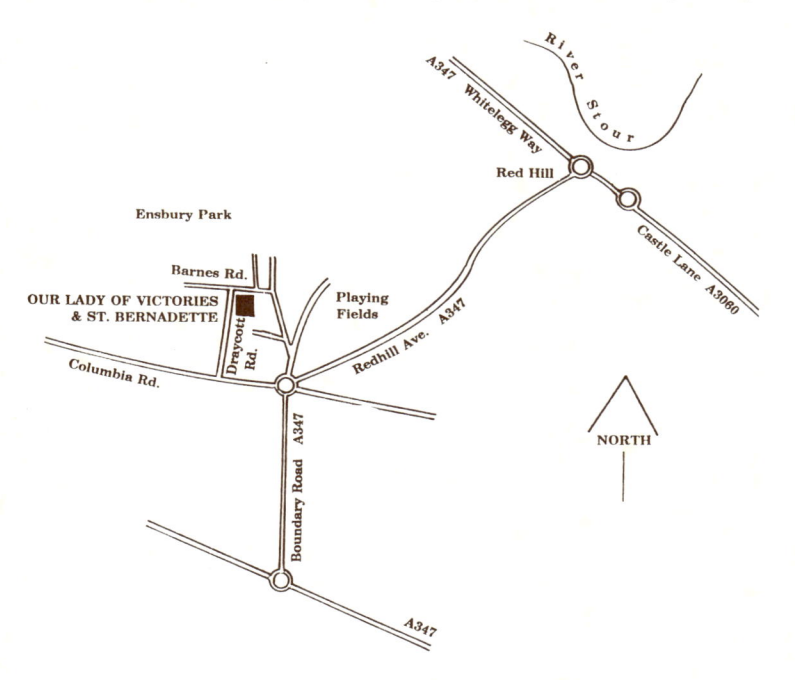

**Our Lady of Victories & St. Bernadette, Draycott Road.**

Arriving in the north of Bournemouth follow directions for Ensbury Park. From picturesque tree bordered Redhill Avenue (A347), (Redhill Park adjacent), continue straight to the roundabout and turn at the third exit into Columbia Road. There is a signpost giving directions to the Catholic Church in Draycott Road. This unusual brick church stands at the end of its own drive. Car parking is available within the grounds.

The dedication is twofold: honouring the patronage of the Virgin of Victory and St. Bernadette. There are many fascinating records of the powerful intercession of Our Lady of Victory, including the following. At the time of the fourth Crusade, that is, at the beginning of the thirteenth century, the Venetians took from Constantinople an ancient Byzantine icon of the Mother of God. Early in the seventeenth century this icon was put on the Marian altar in St. Mark's Basilica. In 1630 when Venice was severely troubled with The Plague both people and rulers requested the prayers of their Madonna, the Virgin of Victory. Accordingly, everyone's devotions intensified. For fifteen Saturday evenings the icon was solemnly carried around the Piazza, accompanied by the people, in procession, piously chanting the Litany of the Blessed Virgin. The Doge even founded another new Church in thanksgiving for the favour hoped for! Then in 1631 the opportunity came for a special Mass of thanksgiving. Venice was delivered from The Plague, the Venetians convinced that their victory over the disease had been brought about by the grace of God and the intercession of Our Lady of Victory!

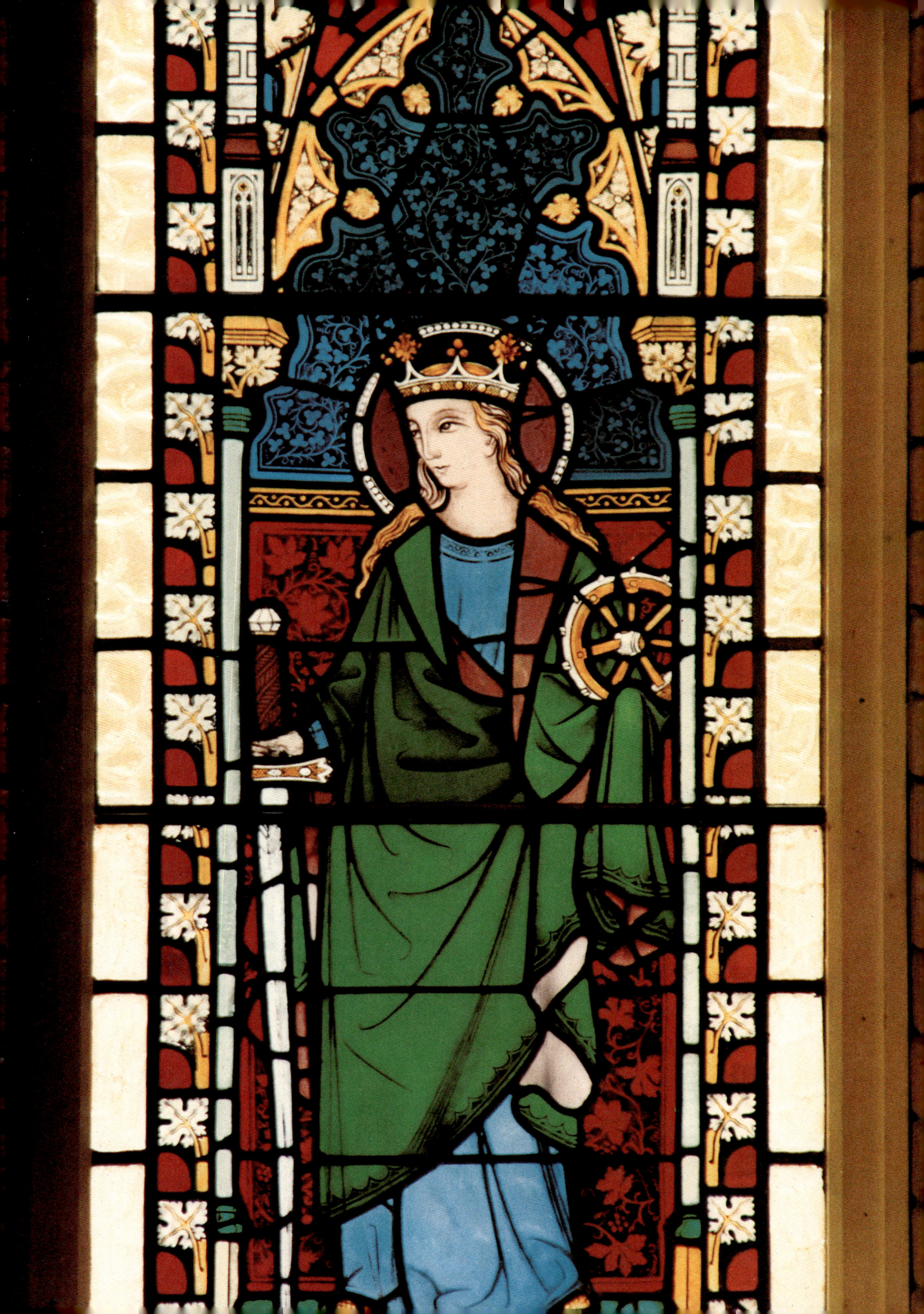

# Our Lady of Victories and St. Bernadette

This parish is one of certain renown because it is the first in the world to be dedicated to St. Bernadette. There is a Lourdes Grotto within the grounds and over the Church entrance is a large Portland stone statue of the saint, the work of Bernard Davis. The image is not the usual one of a meek shepherdess, but of Sister Marie-Bernard, of the Convent of Saint Gildard in Nevers, France.

A special feature of the interior of the building is a tiny ivory statue of St. Bernadette presented to the Parish on December 8th 1933 by His Holiness Pope Pius X1 (1922-1939) to commemorate the first dedication of its kind.

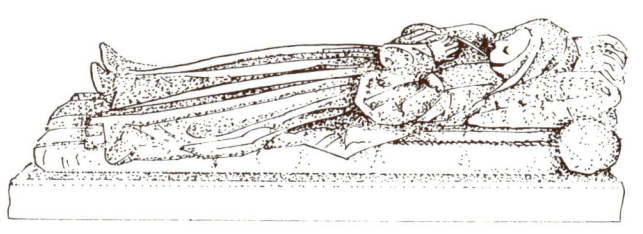

Contact address of Priest:
The Presbytery, 46, Draycott Road, Ensbury Park, Bournemouth, Dorset. BH10 5AR.
Telephone: (0202) 529202.

# Bovey Tracey

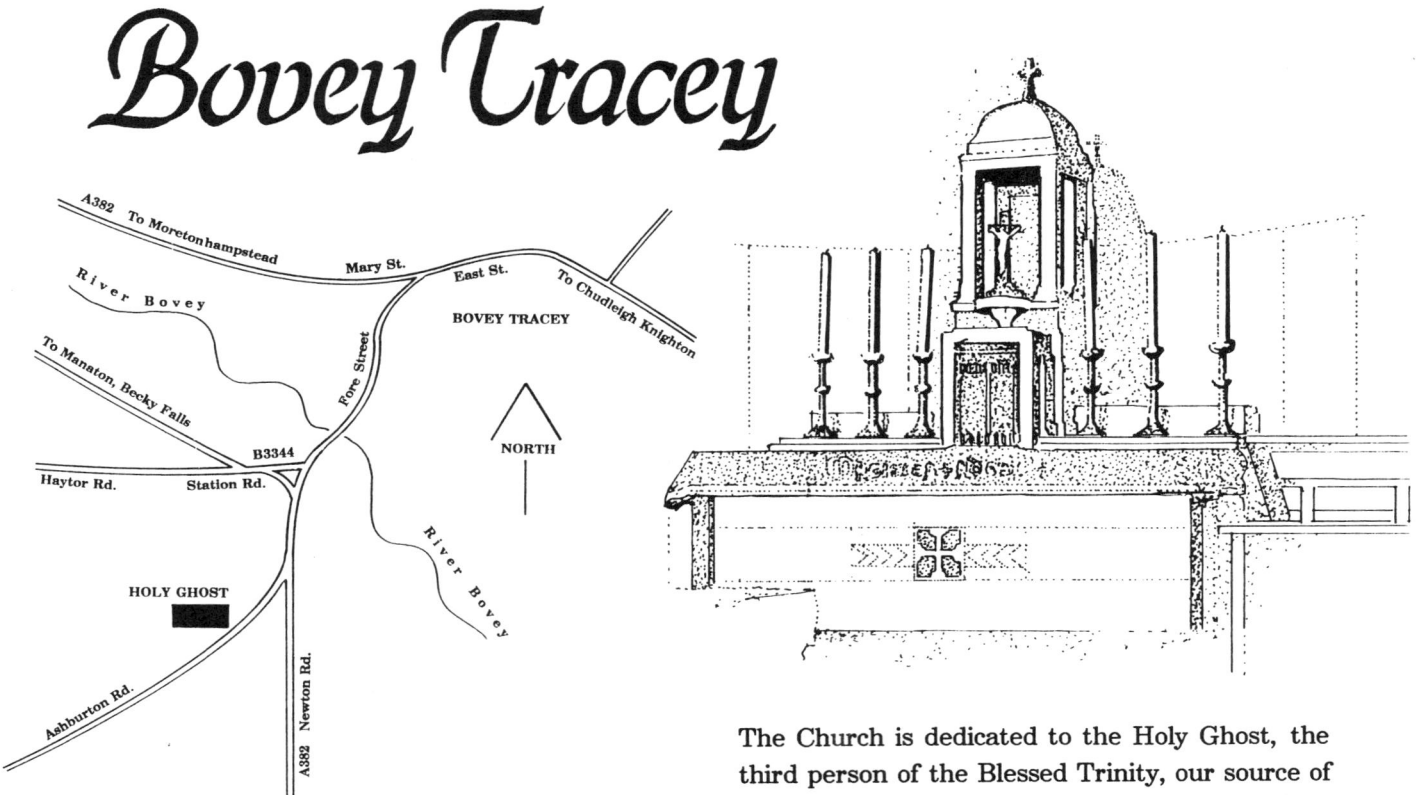

**Holy Ghost, Ashburton Road.**

From the A38 Plymouth-Exeter road take the turning for Bovey Tracey A382. Follow the road for two miles to the roundabout. (The first exit is marked Pottery Road, and the second exit is marked Town Centre and Moretonhampstead.) Take the third exit which is marked with a brown sign "Churches/Swimming Pool". Follow the road straight passing "The Church Army St. Mary's" on the left. As the road goes gently downhill take the first sharp left turn into Ashburton Road. The Church of the Holy Ghost is on the right set back from the pavement within its own garden. It is opposite the Parish Church of St. John. A large notice "Catholic Church" is apparent from the roadside. There is a car park within the church grounds, discreetly hidden behind hedging.

The Church is dedicated to the Holy Ghost, the third person of the Blessed Trinity, our source of consolation and guide through life. At the Last Supper, Jesus said to the Apostles: "I will ask the Father and He will give you another Advocate to dwell with you forever, the Spirit of truth whom the world cannot receive, because He will dwell with you, and be in you. (John 14:16-17) In the fourth century after Christ the Council of Constantinople defined the article of faith which we profess in the Creed at Mass: "We believe in the Holy Spirit, the Lord, the giver of life who proceeds from the Father and the Son. With the Father and the Son, he is worshipped and glorified. He has spoken through the Prophets."

# Holy Ghost

The building of this particular church, consecrated in 1936, came about through the devotion of two parishioners. It replaced a former tin hut. The building looks modern from outside. Once inside it has a feeling of tradition: an arched roof, a raised pulpit and one central aisle leading to the sanctuary. A simple crucifix set in a canopied shrine above the tabernacle is a reminder of the sacrifice of Calvary and the Real Presence here and now on the altar.

The Lady Chapel is located at the right of the sanctuary and contains both an unusual statue and a fine painting of the Holy Mother and Child. There is also a large plaque of the Last Supper scene here. The Stations of the Cross are carved in fine detail on the north and south walls. Some of the faces are grim, masklike, as if forcing back terrific emotion in the grip of torture, torment and death. Christ appears really stocky, in solid human form, yet at the twelfth Station his figure has visibly "sunken" into death, the breath of life "shrunk out". At the thirteenth Station the masks are gone. The face of Mary, Our Lady of Sorrows, in sorrow, but glorious also, the Mother beholding the "triumph" of the Cross!

Contact address of Priest:
The Presbytery, Ashburton Road,
Bovey Tracey, Devon. TQ13 9BY.
Telephone: (0626) 833432.

# Braunton

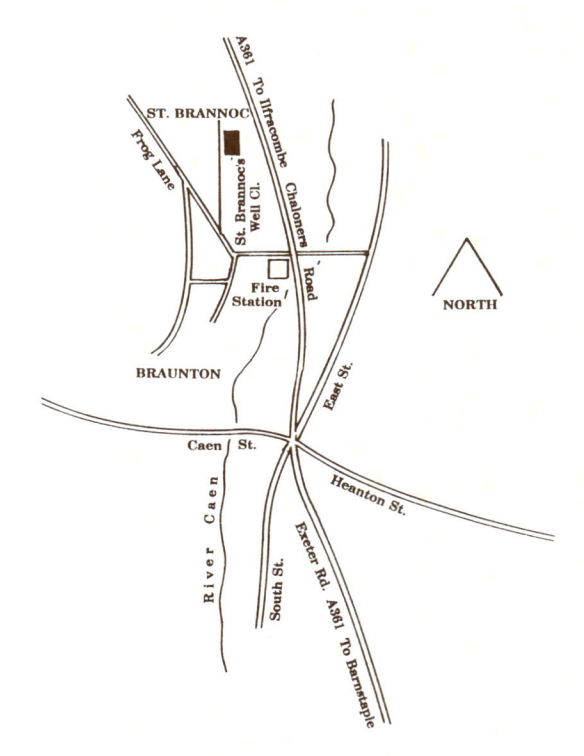

**St. Brannoc, Frog Lane.**

Travelling from Barnstaple take the Ilfracombe Road A361. Go through Braunton Village and continue to the crossroads. Take a left turn, then the second turning on the right. (St. Brannoc's Catholic Church is signposted from the main road near the Fire Station.) A long tree-lined pathway leads to this little stone church. Beside it is St. Brannoc's Well and a "Lourdes Grotto". A carved stone statue of St. Brannoc stands above the church porch. Braunton is on the Barnstaple/Ilfracombe bus route. Car parking is available near the church.

The patron of this parish is the Celtic (Goidal) Saint Brannoc, who lived during the sixth century. He was spiritual confidante and chaplain to the Goidal conqueror King Brychan of Brecknock. He married into the royal family, wedding Cymorth, the King's daughter. They had four children: three daughters Mwynem, Gwenllin and Gwenan and a son, Berwyn. In the course of time, St. Brannoc left the company of King Brychan, maybe Cymorth had died. He made a pilgrimage to Rome, to the Apostles' Tombs. On his way back he visited Brittany, tarrying a long while to preach the Gospel. Eventually he started back to Wales taking his tombstone with him, according to the custom of the Celtic saints. St. Brannoc apparently landed in the Taw Estuary (Braunton Burrows) and continued his missionary work there serving the needs of the people of Cornwall and North Devon. He died it seems on January 5th although the year is uncertain, some time between 557 A.D. and 570 A.D.

# St. Brannoc

St. Brannoc's is in a particularly beautiful setting. The Church has been built on the site of the ancient chapel of St. Brannoc, beside the Holy Well, in the grounds of Buckland Manor, the home of the Incledon Webber family whose generosity made the restoration possible. The foundation stone was laid on October 29th 1957 and the solemn inauguration occurred on 21st June 1958. Initially St. Brannoc's was a Chapel of Ease of the Parish of Barnstaple. Four years after the inauguration the benefactors kindly provided a presbytery and the Bishop appointed Father McAlinden as parish priest. The consecration of St. Brannoc's took place on 15th June 1978.

It "is said" that the Holy Well never freezes and has medicinal properties. Like the waters of the Jordan brought back from the Holy Land the waters of St. Brannoc's Holy Well have occasionally been used for the purposes of Baptism.

Of special interest in the church are the circular Stations of the Cross, the icons, the craftsman-made benches complete with Thompson "mouse" motif and the statues of St. Elizabeth of Hungary and St. Dympna (the patron saint of handicapped children) made out of Irish bog wood.

Contact address of Priest:
The Presbytery, Frog Lane,
Braunton, N. Devon. EX33 1BB.
Telephone: (0271) 812558.

# Bridport

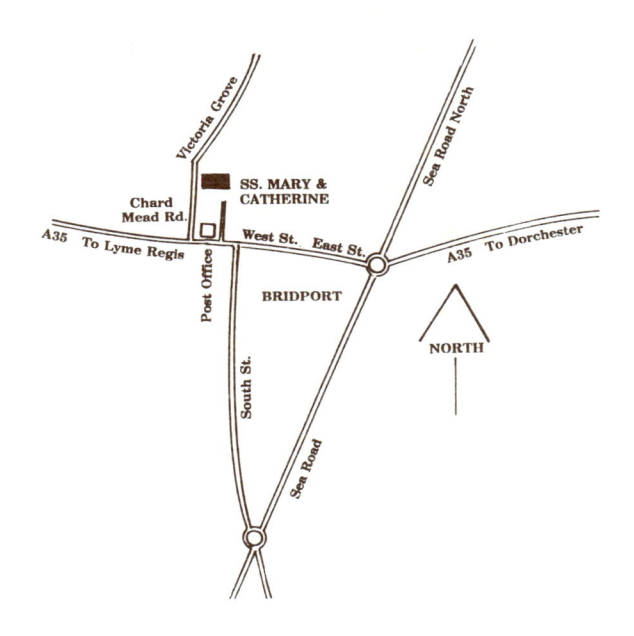

### SS. Mary & Catherine, Victoria Grove.

The A35, which connects Dorchester with Lyme Regis and Honiton, runs through Bridport town centre. From West Street, (A35), near the Post Office, turn off into Victoria Grove. The Catholic Church is located near the Baptist Church and the British Legion. It is an unusual modern building, in an elevated position, overlooking its own grounds and garden and set back from the road behind wrought iron gates. A notable external feature is the black cross, some 30 feet high. Car parking is available in Chard Mead Road.

The patronage of St. Mary & St. Catherine, that of the former church, built in 1846 has been retained. Catherine of Alexandria was one of the most celebrated saints in the Middle Ages, although, apparently, there is no mention of her in early martyrologies, no ancient pictorial record of her, and early Christian devotions did not include her. She is said to have lived some time in the fourth century. There are several well known legends. Catherine dedicated herself totally to God in her youth. She adamantly refused marriage with the pagan Emperor and endured persistant persecution for her belief. Philosphers and sages called in to dissuade her failed to alter her Christian ideal. Her martyrdom ensued: torture on a spiked wheel (hence the name "Catherine Wheel") followed by decapitation. In 1969 the Vatican removed the feast of the somewhat legendary Catherine from the liturgical calendar.

The Tuscan Saint of Italy, however, "Catherine of Siena", has long survived the scrutiny of the Church. This holy woman, a member of the Order of St. Dominic, sought sanctity from an early age. Her personal holiness and influence brought peace to some of the rifts in Medieval Italy and caused too some remarkable conversions. "Catherine of Siena" was also instrumental in restoring the Papacy, from Avignon, France, back to Rome. Her teachings were documented in letters and her "Dialogue". A biography of the saint, written by a senior member of the Dominican Order, aided the process of her canonization which took place in 1461. St. Catherine's feast is celebrated on 29th April each year.

# SS Mary and Catherine

"To the Glory of God and in honour of Saint Mary and Saint Catherine this Church was blessed and opened by the Right Reverend Cyril Edward Restieaux, Bishop of Plymouth, on Friday 12th May 1978."

The unusual interior, of brick and pine, is both warm and welcoming. The altar (a replica of a particular Irish design) and ambo, are manufactured from Italian calacatta marble. The century old stained glass windows of SS. Anthony of Padua and Michael the Archangel originated from the parish in Dorchester, the windows of SS. Mary and Catherine from the former church in Victoria Grove.

Contact address of Priest:
The Presbytery, Victoria Grove,
Bridport, Dorset. DT6 3AD.
Telephone: (0308) 22594

# Brixham

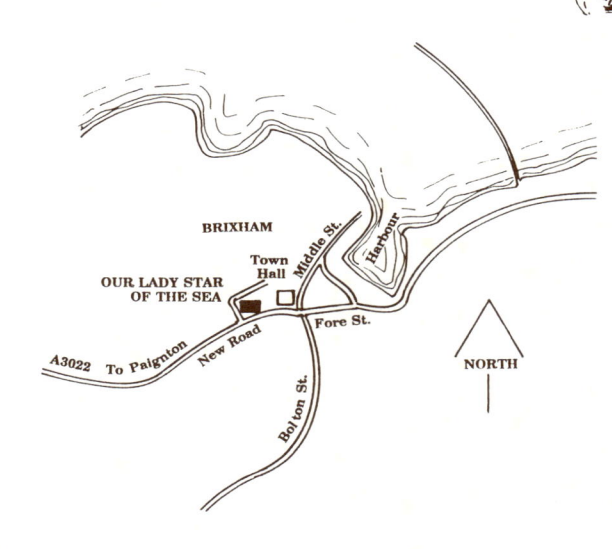

**Our Lady Star of the Sea,
New Road.**

From Paignton take the A3022 Brixham Road. Continue straight into New Road (A3022). Coming into the town the Church is clearly visible on the left, at the junction of New Road with Manor Road, before Bolton Cross traffic lights. Car parking is available on the roof of the Church!

The Church is dedicated to Our Lady Star of the Sea which is most apt as the town has involved itself for centuries with the sea. A rather lovely embroidered banner can be found beside the inside entrance to the Church, honouring "Stella Maris", Brixham. Inside at the shrine of Our Lady, the helper of seafarers and their families, there is a beautiful "Prayer with Candles"

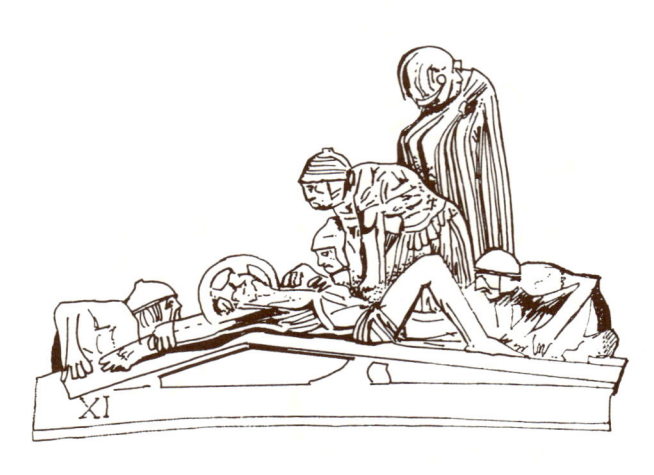

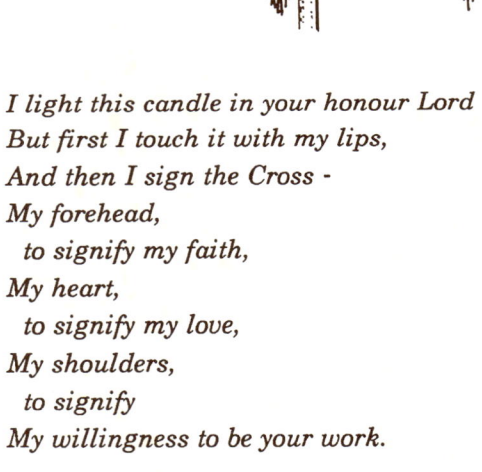

I light this candle in your honour Lord
But first I touch it with my lips,
And then I sign the Cross -
My forehead,
　to signify my faith,
My heart,
　to signify my love,
My shoulders,
　to signify
My willingness to be your work.

And then I fix it in its place
And light the wick;
And see in flame and wax
　the purity and fire of Love.

And in its light the light of faith
And mercy in its waxen tears.
And then I leave it there
To burn for me.
　　　　(John Southworth.)

# Our Lady Star of the Sea

The Church was built in 1966, opened in 1967 and consecrated on 8th March 1972. The consecration relics were those of St. Pope Pius X (1903-1914). The building is utterly modern, but conveys the "comfort" of a place to be in for devotion. The Church is actually found upstairs over the large hall. The pews are grouped in an arc around the Cornish granite altar with the Tabernacle still as a focal point behind, resting on an arched niche in the Sanctuary wall.

The Stations of the Cross, the work of a Dorset artist, are set on the balcony panels around the Church. The medium, of bronze fibre glass, emits an aura of clanging and clashing, of Christ in cold desolation. One can almost hear the banging in of the nails, at the beginning of the meditation, a foretaste of the cruel finale. Meticulous detail has created an extraordinary version of this old Lenten form of prayer, said to have been brought back from Jerusalem during the Crusades.

The Baptistry is in a recessed area at the back of the Church. It boasts a splendid stained glass window, an interpretation of the Baptism of Christ in the Jordan. More stained glass can be seen in the Blessed Sacrament Chapel depicting a glorious Rainbow of Peace with the Father, the Son and the Holy Spirit.

Contact address of Priest:
The Presbytery, 43, New Road,
Brixham, Devon. TQ5 8NB.
Telephone: (0803) 853406.

# Buckfast Abbey

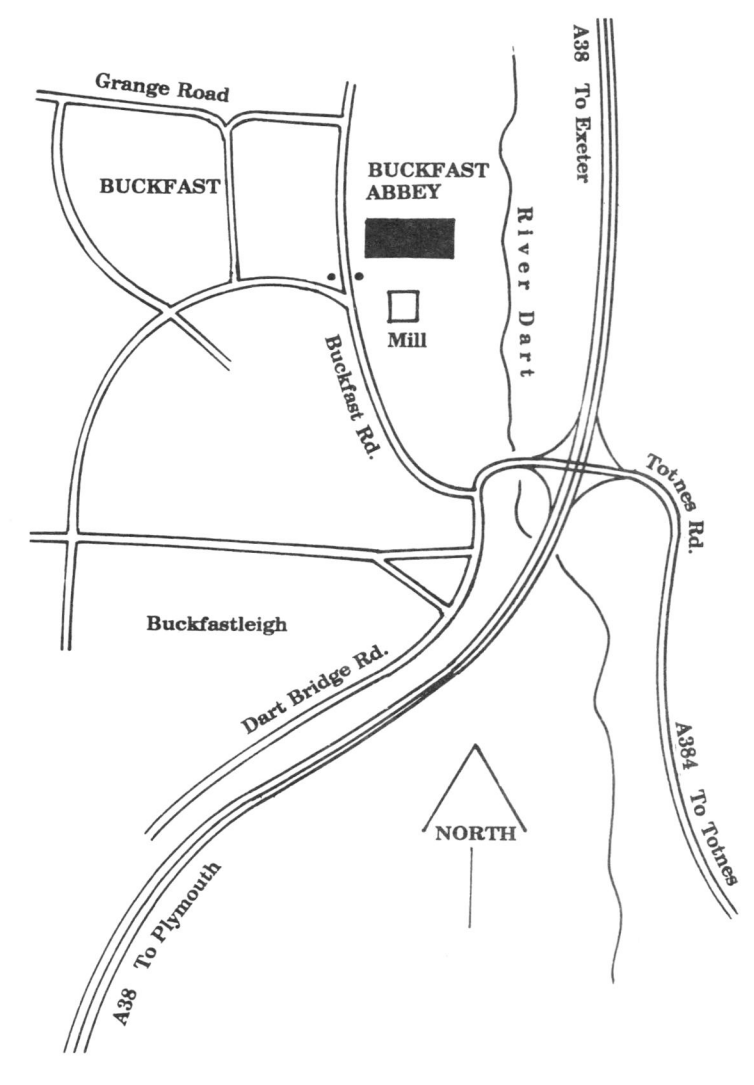

St. Mary's Abbey upholds a very ancient tradition by dedicating its monastic church to Our Lady. In 1884 fragments of a medieval statue were discovered by the monks of Buckfast. Sacrilegiously smashed during the reign of Edward VI, the pieces lay forgotten for centuries amongst the ruins of the former Cistercian Abbey. A large remnant retained its original colour and gilding, and from this fragment, based on the design of the ancient Abbey seal, the image of the Blessed Virgin and the Holy Child were restored. On May 24th 1903, the feast of Our Lady Help of Christians, the statue was joyfully blessed by Abbot Dom. Boniface Natter (the first Abbot since the Restoration of Buckfast). It can be seen in the fifteenth century style Chapel of Our Lady in the north transept of the Abbey Church.

From Plymouth follow the A38 east bypassing Ivybridge and South Brent; from Exeter follow the A38 south west bypassing Chudleigh Knighton, Newton Abbot and Ashburton; from Totnes follow the A385 through Dartington via A384 to Buckfast. The Abbey is well signposted. Ample car parking facilities are available at the Abbey. There is a local bus stop in Buckfast Road and a bus station in the village beside Victoria Park, off Plymouth Road. The nearest Main Line Stations are at Newton Abbot and Totnes.

# St Mary

The medieval Cistercian Abbey was formally dissolved by command of King Henry VIII on 25th February 1539. The original document of surrender, signed in the Abbey Chapter House on the feast of St. Matthias, can still be seen at The Public Record Office.

The Abbey buildings were then left abandoned for hundreds of years. The White Friars vanished like incense after prayer, leaving only a hint of holiness in the ruins of their monastery.

Across the Channel in France, in 1849, Jean Baptiste Muard, a venerable French priest, founded the Benedictine Abbey of La Pierre-qui-vire, near Avallon. But, unhappily, in 1880, due to the anti-religious policies of the French government, the monks were forced into exile. They fled to Dublin staying in a house lent to them by the Benedictines of Ramsgate. Two years later, the monks were alerted to a letter in "The Tablet" giving details of a property for sale in Devon, a former "Abbey" at Buckfast. They began earnest negotiations primarily for the lease of the vacant mansion and the ruins of the monastery in approximately 16 acres of ground.

On 28th October 1882, the feast of SS. Simon & Jude, the desolate Abbey was once more hallowed by the presence of Religious. Then began the tremendous work of restoration. The ambitious fervour of the foreign friars, all Frenchmen, except for Dom. Adam Hamilton, from Ramsgate, attracted the attention of many. A committee was set up, chaired by Lord Clifford of Chudleigh, to help bring to fruition the plans of the new religious foundation. On 25th March 1884, the feast of the Annunciation, a temporary monastic church was inaugurated.

In 1902 Buckfast became an independent Abbey foundation from that of La Pierre-qui-vire. It elected its first abbot. Sadly, though, Abbot Dom. Boniface Natter was drowned in a shipwreck on 4th August 1906 off the coast of Spain, near Cartagena. Another Buckfast monk survived the tragedy to return and tell the tale to his Benedictine brothers. It was this monk who was duly elected the second Abbot of Buckfast, Abbot Dom. Anscar Vonier. With great faith and determination he set about the task of organising the restoration.

Initially plans were made to build on the south side of the monastery buildings. Then one day, whilst working in the vegetable plot on the north side, one of the monks struck stone with his garden hoe. Excavations revealed the foundations of the medieval monastery. The idea of resurrecting the former Abbey Church on the same site became instantly closer to reality.

After the Conventual Mass on 5th January 1907 the very first stone of the building was carefully positioned by some of the monks, for it was they who would undertake the rebuilding of the Abbey just like the monks in the Middle Ages. Accordingly, following tradition, they commenced with the sanctuary and the east end. The master mason was Brother Peter who had received 18 months building tuition at the Abbey of En-calcat, in the south of France. He was the only one with any sort of building qualification.

God surely turned His countenance towards them. Critics sneered at the "bunch of amateurs", they had no money, only faith. One fell fifty feet off the scaffolding on to a pile of sand and walked away unharmed. They prayed and worked and ultimately the dream was fulfilled;

*Benedicamus Domino. Deo Gratias.*

The new Chapel of the Blessed Sacrament was dedicated in 1966.

There are excellent guide books always available at the Abbey, giving full details of the history of the building and its furnishings: the glorious stained glass, the "Golden Altar", the "Corona", the decorated Byzantine style fresco in the lantern tower, the cast bronze font, the replicas of thirteenth century altarpieces seen in the Stations of the Cross ...Here, indeed, a feast for the eye and refreshment for the soul.

*In a moment of personal peace*
  *- the aura of His Presence*
  *- the prayer of centuries*
  *- this very spot*
  *- God's House*
  *illuminabit te Christus!*
  *(Christ will give you light!)*

On 2nd July 1907, the feast of the Visitation of Our Lady, the foundation stone was laid by Bishop Graham of Plymouth. (It may be found in the south aisle of the Church.) On St. Michael's Day, 29th September 1910, fourteen bells were temporarily placed on top of the old Abbot's Tower. Not only their sound but their names were spiritually inspiring: George, Paul, Peter, Thomas of Canterbury, Gregory, Veronica, Boniface, Bernard, Raphael, Gabriel, Michael, Robert and Mary. (The "Hosanna" bell was added much later after the Consecration of the Abbey.)

In 1922 a section of building was ready for public worship, and after Vespers, on Wednesday 2nd August, this part of the Abbey Church was officially opened by Bishop Keily.

The solemn Consecration of St. Mary's Abbey Church, Buckfast, took place on 25th August 1932. For over thirty years, never more than six monks worked steadily at the task of rebuilding.

Contact address of Priest:
St. Mary's Abbey,
Buckfast, Devon. TQ11 OEE.
Telephone: (0364) 43301.

# Buckfastleigh

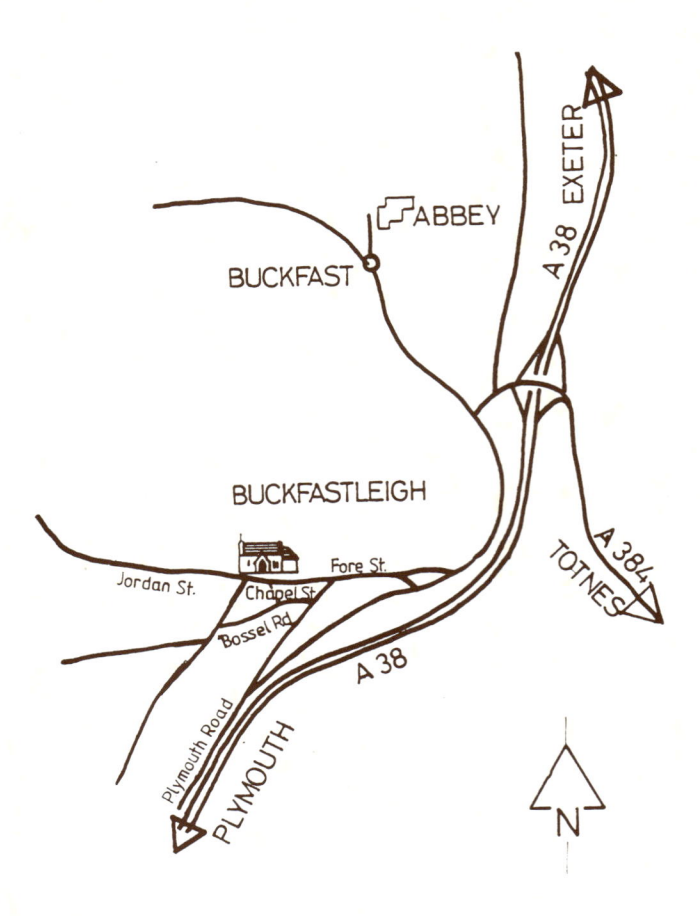

**St. Benedict, Chapel Street.**

Buckfastleigh is signposted off the A38 (Exeter to Plymouth). The church is easily found in Chapel Street directly opposite New Road. Next door to St. Benedict's is the Methodist Chapel. Adjacent to Chapel Street is Fore Street (the main shopping area) and Plymouth Road. There are several local buses travelling to and from Plymouth, Exeter, Totnes and Newton Abbot. Car parks are located in Chapel Street and Plymouth Road.

The Church is dedicated to St. Benedict, the founder of the Benedictine Order, to which Buckfast Abbey belongs.

St. Benedict was born of noble parents in the small town of Norcia in Umbria, Italy, in about 480 A.D. As a young student in Rome, he felt the call to strive for Christian perfection and went off to live as a hermit in a cave at Subiaco, about 80 km. east of Rome. After three years he was joined by other disciples and began monastic life.

In 529 Benedict moved to Monte Casino, a mountain top near one of the highways from Rome to Naples, where he established the great motherhouse of the Benedictine Order, for the reclamation and renewal of Europe. There he wrote his "Rule", which became the pattern of life in Western European monasteries during the early Middle Ages.

The fine carved relief of a monk above the water stoop inside the entrance door, and the beautiful cushion kneelers embroidered by the parish Tapestry Guild are worth seeing.

The Stations of the Cross are of particular note, being a combination of painting and applique work by a local artist, the Late Miss Hubbard. They are most unusual, in very rich detail, achieving great depth of perspective, and creating an atmosphere of the Divine: the essence of Love, faith, emotion, agony on the way to Calvary, all conveyed in 14 pictures, each only 22cm. square, within a plain wooden cruciform frame.

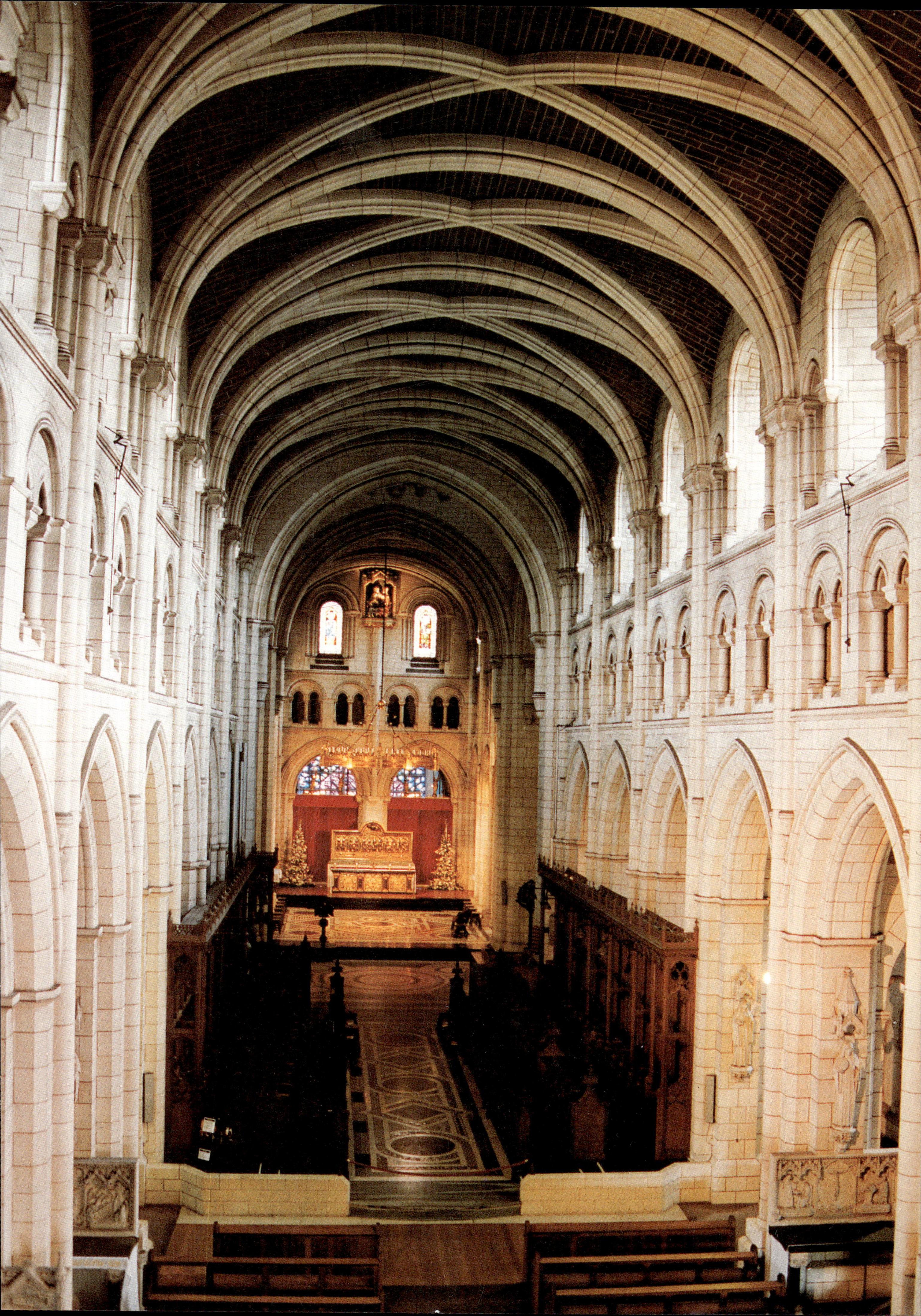

# St. Benedict

St. Benedict's Church was erected in 1939 to provide the people of Buckfastleigh with a place of worship of their own, separate from the Abbey. (Transport was not so readily available then as it is now.) It is built of local stone, in Romanesque style. A stone plaque with a latin inscription is set on the wall outside the Church. Above the porch there is a statue of St. Benedict holding his "Rule" and staff. For part of the year the porch is decorated with hanging baskets, and tubs of flowers flank the wall facing the street. Pointed, arched double entrance doors in oak, shipped from Canada during the 1939-45 War, bear a fine carving of St. John the Baptist.

St. Benedict's Church was consecrated by the Rt. Rev. John Barrett, Bishop of Plymouth, on 13th November 1946. Enclosed in the altar are relics of the Martyrs St. Boniface (our Diocesan patron) and St. Felicity.

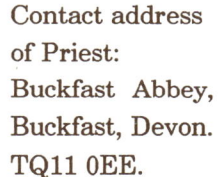

Contact address of Priest:
Buckfast Abbey,
Buckfast, Devon.
TQ11 0EE.

# Bude

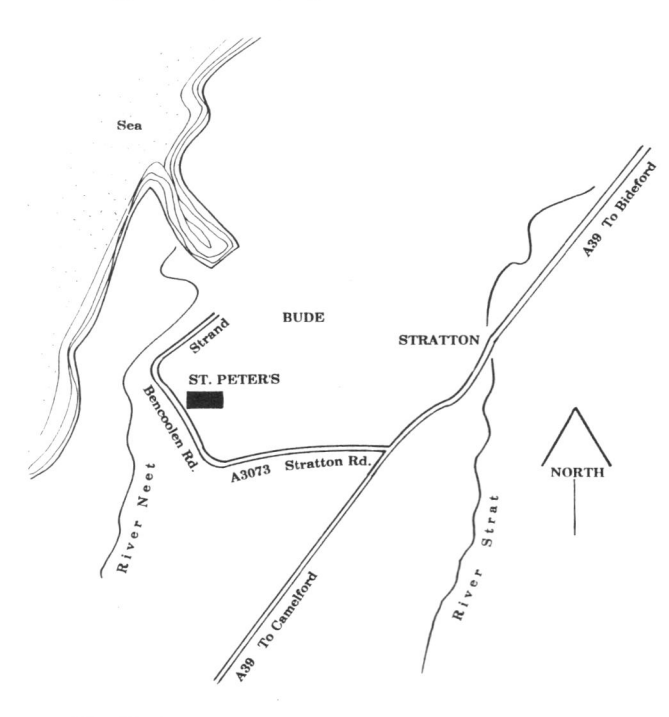

**St. Peter's, Bencoolen Road.**

Following the A39 Camelford/Bideford Road turn off on to the A3073 for Bude, Stratton Road, which leads into Bencoolen Road. St. Peter's Church, a red brick building in an elevated position, is found about half way down Bencoolen Road, on the right, opposite a garage. There is a glazed plaque, in blue, green and white, on the front of the Church, depicting the Holy Virgin and Child guarded by angels. Parking is available, up the drive, behind the Church.

The dedication is to St. Peter. Could Bude's rugged coastal Atlantic scene, the sand, the smell of the sea, the fresh breeze, give a hint of a link with the shores of Galilee, Bethsaida, the home of St. Peter? Our Lord called Peter "Kipha" an Aramaic word meaning "rock". Jesus said: "Upon this rock I will build my Church. I will give you the keys of the Kingdom of Heaven.." This universal saint has been invoked throughout Christianity as the patron of the Church and the Papacy, and, in more popular tradition, as the heavenly doorkeeper! St. Peter has often been the patron of monasteries such as Westminister, Glastonbury, Canterbury and Lindisfarne, and also Cathedrals such as Worcester and York. His feast day, together with that of St. Paul, is celebrated on June 29th each year.

# St. Peter

St. Peter's Church was built by the Augustinian Canons Regular of the Lateran (from Bodmin) in 1926. The Prior of Bodmin bought land for one hundred and twenty pounds. He then begged and borrowed the money for construction. It was a long and difficult struggle since the parish (part of Launceston till 1976) was so small.

Contact address of Priest:
St. Peter's Presbytery, Bencoolen Road, Bude, Cornwall. Ex23 8PJ.
Telephone: (0288) 353415.

# Budleigh Salterton

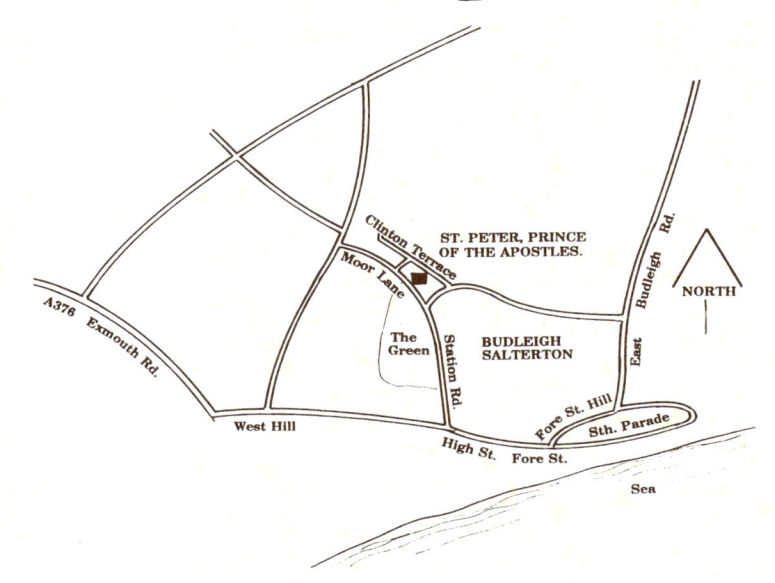

### St. Peter, Prince of the Apostles, Clinton Terrace.

From Exmouth follow the A376; from Newton Poppleford and Collaton Raleigh follow the A376 south to Budleigh Salterton. On the A376 Exmouth Road (from Exmouth) continue straight to West Hill. Turn at the traffic lights into Station Road. (Nat. West Bank on the corner and signpost East Budleigh, Collaton Raleigh, N. Poppleford A376"). The Public Library is on the right and District Council Offices on the left. Continue straight, passing "The Green". Turn left into Clinton Terrace. The Catholic Church is a small red brick building and its noticeboard is clearly visible from the road. A bus service operates to and from Exeter, Exmouth and Sidmouth. Car parking is possible in front of, and alongside the Church, in Clinton Terrace and immediately below "Normans" supermarket.

The Church is dedicated to St. Peter, Prince of the Apostles, the saint who was privileged to *really* know Christ, to be one of the greatest friends of the Son of God in Galilee. Jesus said He would make Peter into a "fisher of men", Peter would be the rock upon which He would build His Church. And so, in due time, the very "human" Peter launched himself into the role of leadership, a thorny path which led to his death in pagan Rome in 64 A.D. In that year the Emperor Nero attributed the burning of the City to the obscure sect of Christians. As a result many of them were arrested. Some of them were thrown to wild beasts, some burned alive and others, like Peter, were crucified. According to tradition, the Apostle Peter was crucified head downwards. Near the reputed site of his martyrdom is the renowned Basilica, St. Peter's, the largest church in Christendom! Situated far beneath the high altar in the Basilica, held in reverence, is Peter's tomb. The feast of St. Peter & St. Paul, a special holyday, is kept on 29th June.

The Parish of St. Peter Prince of the Apostles began with the first Mass being celebrated in a private house. As numbers increased the congregation moved to a Public Hall. Then a plot of ground in Clifton Terrace was donated and the Church was built, kindly paid for by a local benefactor. The consecration of the Church took place on 4th July 1938.

Special mention must be made of the Italian marble altar with its glorious painting of St. Peter amidst the angels and saints in heaven - a hint of Rome! Above the mural is the inscription "UBI PETRUS + IBI ECCLESIA

# St. Peter, Prince of Apostles

Contact address of Priest:
The Presbytery, 20, Clinton Terrace,
Budleigh Salterton, Devon. EX9 6RZ.
Telephone: (0395) 443339.

# Callington

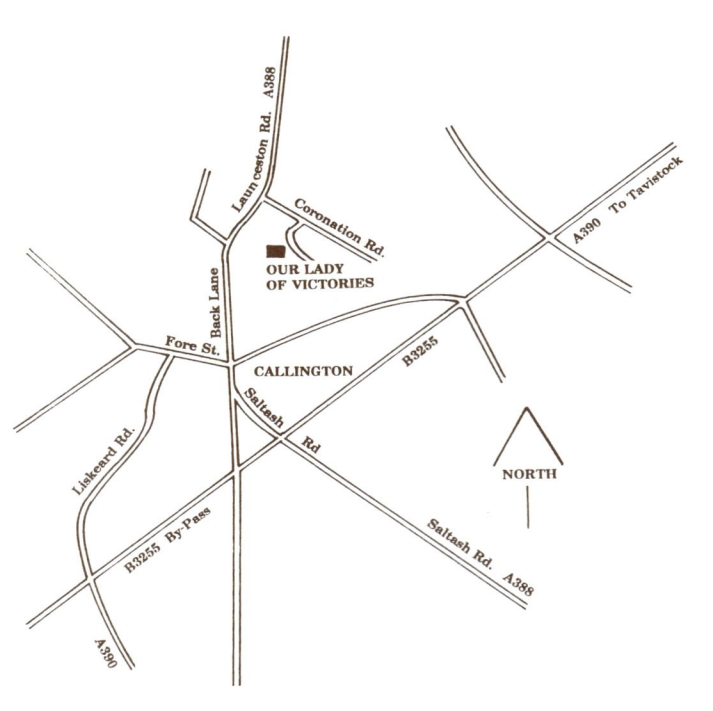

**Our Lady of Victories, Coronation Road.**

The Catholic Church is clearly signposted from Back Lane, Launceston Road and Coronation Road. Coming into Callington on the A388 Launceston Road turn left into Coronation Road at the first bend. The Church is about 50 yards down on the right. Parking is available at the roadside.

The Church is dedicated to Our Lady of Victories. The title honours Mary in a special way. Throughout the history of the Church Christian achievements and victories have been connected with the powerful help of the Blessed Lady. Devotion to Mary has enabled men and women to increase their religious fervour and to draw strength against evil in whatever form. Mary's intercession has led some to great conversions of faith and prompted others to seek the perfection of holiness.

# Our Lady of Victories

The original Catholic Church of Our Lady of Victories, a small green corrugated iron building, was erected in 1931 on a plot of high ground at the junction of Greenbank and Launceston Roads. During the Second World War the congregation was amplified by the additional attendance of Polish soldiers and Italian prisoners of war. In later years the Missioners of St. Francis de Sales took over and Callington became part of Tavistock parish.

The little church served as a Mass centre for local Catholics until 1954, when the local council decided to widen the road. This required the demolition of the little Catholic Church! However, the council provided a new site in Lower Coronation Street, and the second Church of Our Lady of Victories was opened in 1954 by Bishop Grimshaw.

As the Catholic population expanded, an extension was needed. The Missionaries of St. Francis de Sales left Tavistock in 1981, and Bishop Restieaux appealed to Buckfast Abbey to assist with the running of the Parish. Three years later, after major repairs and construction, the new extension was completed. On 2nd September 1984 the Blessed Sacrament was installed for the first time in this Church of Our Lady of Victories.

Contact address of Priest:
The Presbytery, 33, St. Stephen's Hill,
Launceston, Cornwall. PL15 8HP.
Telephone: (0566) 773166.

# Camborne

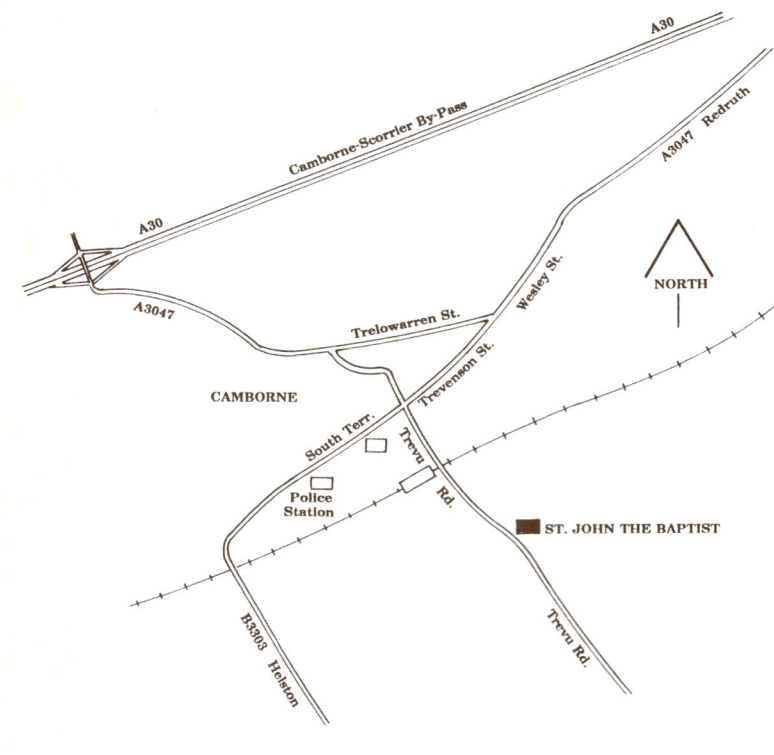

**St. John the Baptist, Trevu Road.**

The small Church of St. John the Baptist, noticeable by its high pitched roof, is near the railway station (main Paddington to Penzance line). From the town centre turn into Trevu Road and continue straight. The church is on the left about 100 yards up the hill past the station. St. John's Infant and Junior School is at the rear of the Church. Car parking is available beside the Church.

St. John the Baptist has always been one of the most popular saints. In the Middle Ages no less than 496 ancient churches were dedicated in his honour. In 841 A.D. the Battle of Fontenay was postponed because it was St. John's Day! This great saint, whose lifestyle resembled one of the Old Testament Prophets, living in the desert on wild honey and locusts, preaching repentance, "prepared the way for the Lord". His name so connected with the Messiah in life, centuries after his death, was linked again with the "path of the Lord": he was made the special patron of the Military order of the Knights Hospitallers whose main occupation was to guard the Holy Sepulchre at Jerusalem and protect pilgrims travelling to and from the Holy Land. His feast day is kept on June 24th.

# St. John the Baptist

Background details to the building of St. John's are quite interesting. In about 1845 Richard Pike, a Superintendent of the New West Cornwall Railway Company, a Quaker, married a Catholic, Elizabeth Lesher, whose family came from Alsace. His own family were of the "landed gentry" in Cork. He was also director of some of the tin mining companies in the area and when many of the Cornish miners left for foreign parts to mine for gold he brought in a large number of Irish labourers. The nearest Catholic Church was at Penzance (opened in 1843). Richard Pike was so impressed by the labourers who walked sixteen miles to Penzance for Mass, and especially his own maid, that he became a Catholic. In 1852 three priests came to Camborne and began a Mission in a store just north of the railway station in Trevu Road. A chapel was later assembled in a loft of Mr. Pike's coach house. In 1857 Mr. Charles Renolds, a barrister, offered a portion of his property as a site for a church. It was near the station. The foundation stone was laid on 24th June 1858. Bishop Vaughan solemnly blessed the new Church on May 26th 1859.

By the year 1863 the congregation stood at 1,400, but then the depression set in in the mines and numbers dwindled to a few hundred. Then, in the 1880's, Fr. Arthur McKay, brought over more labourers from Ireland to work in the mines and to boost his congregation. This was resented by the local people. In 1882, Richard Edwards, a local miner became involved in a skirmish with a gang of Irishmen on leaving the "Railway Inn". The two Irishmen who attacked Edwards were arrested, but the locals disagreed with the lightness of sentence given them by the court and set about the police escort, sparking off a general attack on anyone Irish. A mob set off to attack Irish homes at Brea and Dolcoath and later attacked St. John's Church, shattering windows, entering the Church and breaking up its statues. One hundred soldiers were brought from Plymouth, two hundred police from all over the County and the Riot Act was read. The mob dispersed quietly. A special collection was taken in the town to compensate for the damage caused: the present Lady statue was bought with some of this.

Contact address of Priest:
The Presbytery, 15, Trevu Road,
Camborne, Cornwall. TR14 7AE.
Telephone: (0209) 713143.

# Chagford

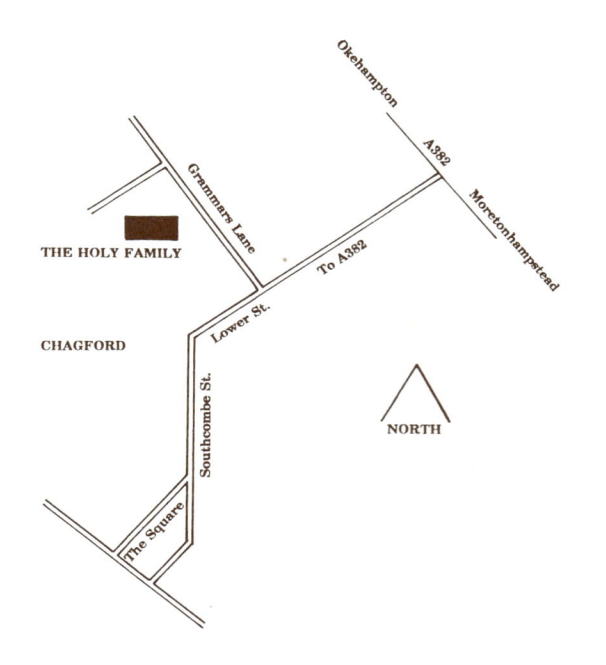

**The Holy Family, Valley View.**

From Okehampton or Exeter follow the A30 to Whiddon Down, then the A382 to the appropriate signpost. From Torquay follow the A380 then the A382 Newton Abbot, Moretonhampstead, Whiddon Down Road. The ancient stannary town of Chagford may be found signposted off the A382 between Whiddon Down (to the north) and Moretonhampstead (to the south east). The Church of The Holy Family is behind the Moor Park Hotel. From The Square in Chagford go down Southcombe Street. Continue straight into Lowe Street. Turn left into Grammars Lane. The Catholic Church is well signposted. It is situated in an elevated position overlooking the hills of Dartmoor. A bus service operates between Exeter and Chagford, Newton Abbot and Chagford. Car parking is available behind the Church.

The dedication is to The Holy Family. At the time of the Church's construction there were lots of families with small children in the parish and The Holy Family, of course, is the perfect model for any household. Jesus, Mary and Joseph lived in Nazareth, Our Lady's former home and the scene of The Annunciation. There they dwelt and worked and prayed together in some degree of poverty, in joy and sorrow, love and spiritual peace. They must at times have been refreshed by the tranquil splendour of the scenery around them, the hills of Lower Galilee. Their example inspires us all. The feast of The Holy Family is celebrated on the Sunday within the Octave of the Epiphany.

At one time Chagford was merely a Mass centre with Mass being said in the British Legion Hall. Then on 15th December 1957 the first bazaar was held to raise funds for a church. A modern building was designed by Robin McMillan Scott. The official opening took place in 1963.

Contact address of Priest:
The Presbytery, 95, Station Road,
Okehampton, Devon. EX20 1ED.
Telephone: (0837) 52229.

# The Holy Family

# Chideock

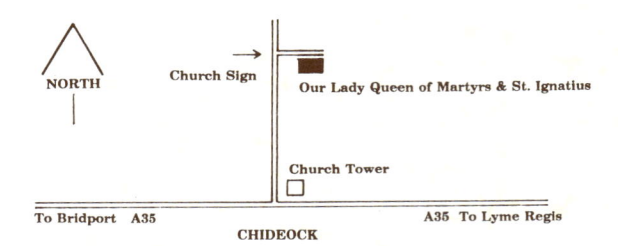

From the M5 exit at Taunton travel south on the A358 to Axminster, then on the A35 to Chideock. From Exeter use the A30 then A35 Honiton/Dorchester road. Turn off the A35 in the centre of Chideock, and follow the sign for "North Chideock" located beside the Anglican Church. About a half mile down, on the right, is another sign "Catholic Church". It points directly to a wrought iron gate, a pathway, and a little Romanesque Church. This shrine of the Dorset Martyrs lies in a glorious setting. It is enhanced visually and aromatically, by the richness of verdure, and, spiritually, by a healing aura of tranquility. There is a church car park nearby. It is also possible to park on the roadside outside the grounds.

Several of the English Martyrs were associated directly with the Parish of Chideock:

Venerable Father Thomas Pilchard, born in 1556 at Battle, Sussex, was ordained a priest at the English College at Rheims in 1583. He later became Chaplain to the Arundells at Chideock, but not for long. He was arrested, tried at Dorchester and cruelly martyred on 21st March 1587.

Blessed Father John Cornelius S.J. was born of Irish parents in Bodmin, Cornwall, in 1554. He was the nephew of the Lord of Kinalmeaky, Conor O' Mahoney of Castle Mahon in County Cork. A brilliant academic, he was expelled from

# Our Lady Queen of Martyrs and St. Ignatius

Exeter College, Oxford, by the Royal Commission, for Popery. He went off to the English College, Rome, and was ordained in 1583. He worked around London and the south before becoming a Chaplain at Chideock. He was betrayed on 14th April 1594 when the Castle was raided by two Justices of the Peace. Sir George Trenchard and Ralph Horsey. He was found in the "priest's hole", bound in chains, and led to Dorchester jail together with Blessed Thomas Bosgrave, a nephew of Lady Arundell, and two Irish servants, Blessed Terence Carey and Blessed Patrick Salmon. These four holy men were martyred on 4th July 1594.

Blessed Father Hugh Green was the last Chideock martyr. He was born in 1584, in London, of Protestant parents. A scholar of St. Peter's College, Cambridge, he later converted to Catholicism and trained for the priesthood at the English College at Douai. In the same year as his ordination, 1612, he took up an appointment as Chaplain at Chideock Castle. In 1642 he set out for the Continent, intending to comply, somewhat belatedly, with the law of exile for priests, but it was too late! He was recognised in Lyme Regis, arrested, sent off to Dorchester and subsequently martyred on 19th August 1642.

Chideock is one of the few villages in the Diocese where Holy Mass has been offered and the Sanctuary lamp kept alight from pre-Reformation times until now. Originally Mass was celebrated in the Parish church of St. Giles, then in Chideock Castle until its destruction by the Roundheads. Next, a farmhouse was used well hidden in North Chideock woodland, and owned by the Arundells. In the early nineteenth century, Humphrey Weld, the 6th son of Thomas Weld of Lulworth, built a chapel. The present Church was built in 1872 by Charles Weld. It is a grandiose amplification of the former chapel, completed in 1874 and solemnly opened by Bishop Vaughan on 15th March that year.

*"The Lord is in His Holy Temple - Let all the earth keep silence before Him" (Habacuc 11.20.)*
The inscription over the arched entrance to the Church is a fitting preface to the Shrine. It is not a place to visit for "just a minute", but set apart for prayer, the building holds a decorative bounty for reflection and meditation.

Of particular interest are the many portraits of the English Martyrs and eminent Catholics of the day painted by members of the Weld family. Venerable Father Thomas Pilchard, Blessed Father John Cornelius, Blessed Thomas Bosgrave, Blessed Terence Carey, Blessed Patrick Salmon and Blessed Father Hugh Green, SS. John Fisher and Thomas More and Sir John Arundell of Chideock who died in 1591 are included in the gallery.

The Church provides a connection between the first Christian martyrs and those in Reformation England. Enshrined under the High Altar is the body of St. Mercius a Roman martyr, once buried in the catacombs of St. Priscilla. A relic of Our Blessed Lady's Veil, brought from Chartres Cathedral, is also kept at the Shrine.

In the cloister long-room, entered from the Church, there is an exhibition of Chideock's village history and a display in honour of the martyrs.

Contact address of Priest:
St. John's Presbytery, Shortmoor,
Beaminster, Dorset. DT8 3EL.
Telephone: (0308) 862741.

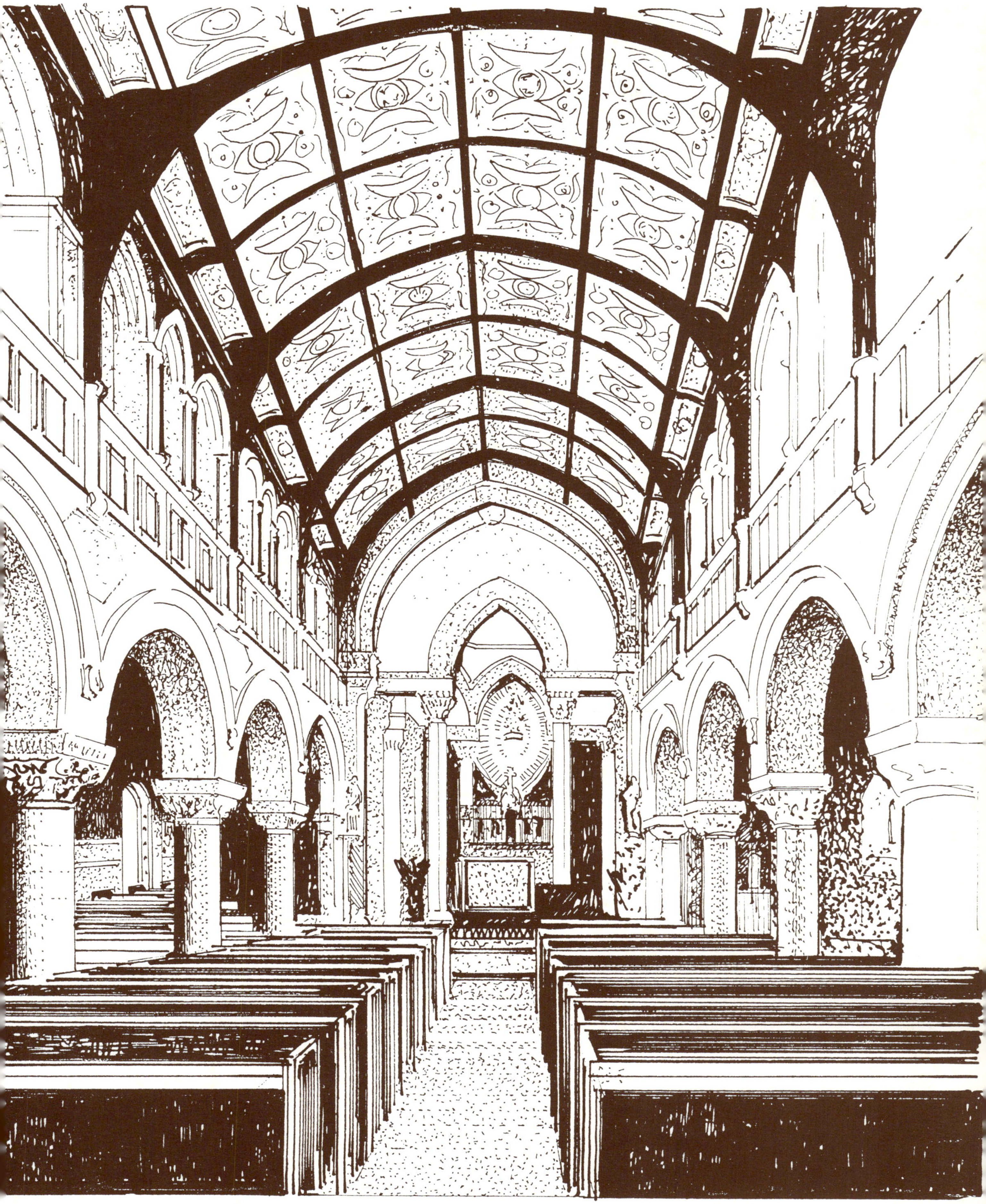

# Chulmleigh

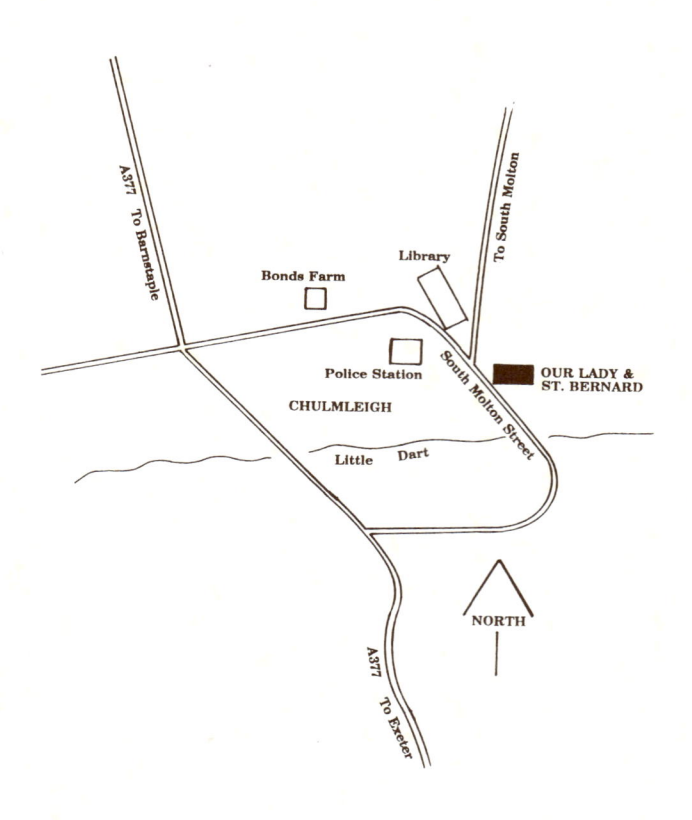

Our Lady & St. Bernard are the patrons of this parish. St. Bernard was born in 1090, the son of a leading noble family in Burgandy. At twenty two years of age he decided to become a Cistercian monk. He asked St. Stephan Harding to admit him into the monastery at Citeaux together with thirty other aspiring friends and relatives! After some years St. Bernard was elected Abbot of Clairvaux, a new religious foundation. Many other monasteries were founded from Clairvaux in France and throughout Europe. St. Bernard became involved in numerous ecclesiastical controversies in his lifetime. His name is linked with the Second Crusade. He preached passionately for the Christian cause in the Holy Land, but when disaster fell, St. Bernard became a scapegoat for blame. The Saint is remembered for his devotion to Our Lady and for his own mystical writings. He died in 1153 and was officially canonized in 1174. He was made a Doctor of the Church in 1830. His feast day is kept on 20th August.

**Our Lady & St. Bernard, South Molton Street.**

From Barnstaple follow the A377 south east; from Exeter follow the A377 north west. Turn off at "Colleton Mills" for Chulmleigh. The Church is situated at the northern end of the town. It is set back from the pavement behind decorative wrought iron gates and a small wall. Chulmleigh is on the Exeter to Barnstaple bus route. Cars may park beside the Church.

After the turn of the present century, it is recorded that the fifty or so parishioners in Chulmleigh and its surrounding area gathered together for Mass in the Town Hall. It was not ideal because of the oft lingering aroma, not of incense, but of tobacco!

At the beginning of 1955 a disused concrete army hut was bought. It was very carefully dismantled, piece by piece, re-erected on the chosen site in the midst of an apple orchard and then altered into a Church.

The building was solemnly blessed by His Lordship the Bishop in August 1955, the first church to be blessed by Bishop Restieaux in the Diocese.

Contact address of Priest:
The Presbytery, Higher Church Street,
Barnstaple, Devon. EX33 8JE.
Telephone: (0271) 43312.

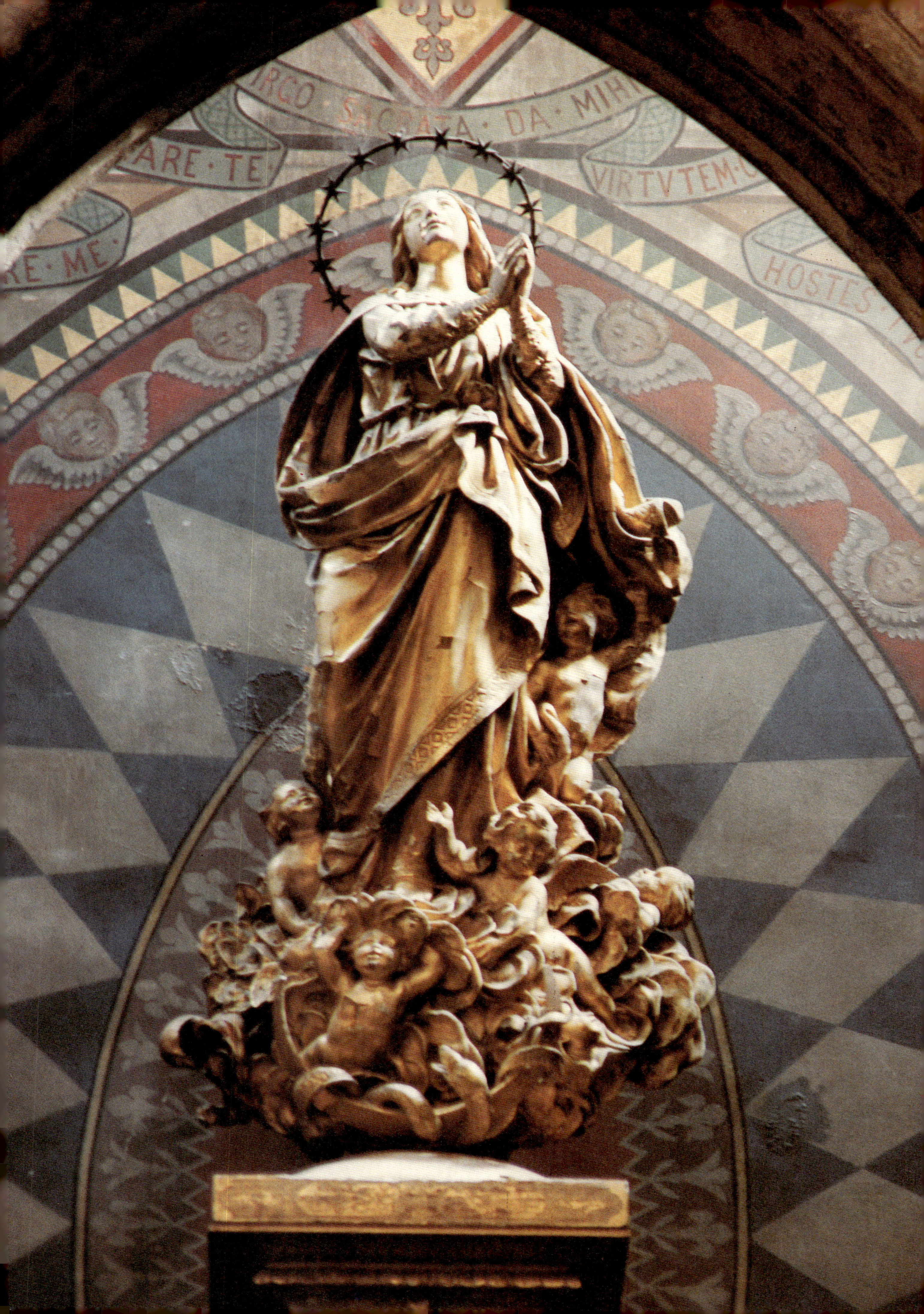
RGO SACRATA DA MIHI
ARE TE
VIRTVTEM
RE ME
HOSTES

# Our Lady and St. Bernard

# Combe Martin

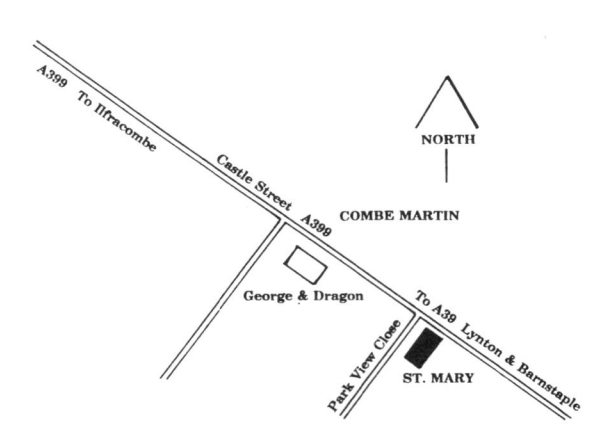

**St. Mary, Castle Street.**

Combe Martin is a large village on the north Devon coast. It is situated east of Ilfracombe on the A399. St. Mary's is in the centre of the village on the corner of the main street, Castle Street, and Park View Close. It is a modern church, a simple rectangular building with an attractive glazed entrance lobby which gives a view into the interior from outside.

Our Blessed Lady is the patron of this parish. There are many liturgical feasts which honour her throughout the year:

| | |
|---|---|
| 1 Jan. | Mary Mother of God |
| 11 Feb. | Our Lady of Lourdes |
| 25 Mar. | The Annunciation |
| 2nd Sun. aft. Pentecost | The Immaculate Heart of Mary |
| 31 May | The Visitation |
| 16 Jul. | Our Lady of Mount Carmel |
| 15 Aug. | The Assumption |
| 8 Sep. | Birthday of Our Lady |
| 15 Sep. | Our Lady of Sorrows |
| 7 Oct. | Our Lady of the Rosary |
| 21 Nov. | The Presentation of the Virgin Mary in the Temple in Jerusalem |
| 8 Dec. | The Immaculate Conception |

# St. Mary

*I thank you Lord for all I have, teach me to share with others in their need.*
*And should you choose to take away the gifts you gave, teach me to prize this greatest gift of all: the grace to gladly do your will and thank you still.*
*(From the Church noticeboard at St. Mary's September 1991.)*

Contact address of Priest:
The Presbytery, 45, Lee Road,
Lynton, Devon. EX35 6BX.
Telephone: (0598) 53255.

# Crediton

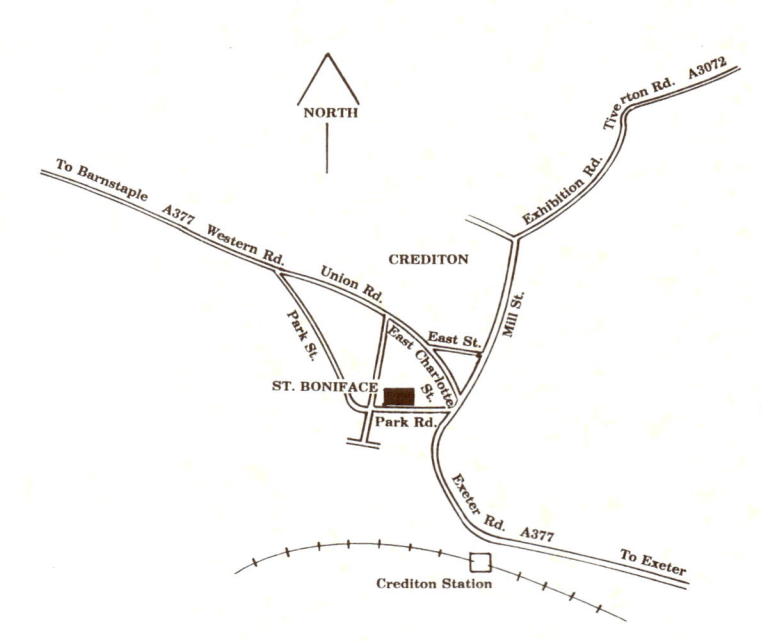

### St. Boniface, Park Road.

From Exeter follow the A377, Exeter to Barnstaple, north west for about seven miles, to Crediton. On entering the town take the first turning on the left at the brow of the hill into Park Road. St. Boniface's Church is about five hundred yards along on the right, recognisable by its thirty three foot white fibre glass spire. Cars may be parked by the side of the Church.

This is the National Shrine of St. Boniface, the greatest of all the Anglo-Saxon missionaries. He was born in Crediton about 675 A.D. and christened Wynfrith. Later named Boniface by Pope Gregory II (715-731). He was introduced to the Benedictine way of life at the age of seven. At thirty he was ordained a priest. In his early 40's he renounced the comparative serenity of English monasticism for the perils and insecurity of missionary life in barbarian Europe. During the next forty years this "Apostle of Germany" made many thousands of converts and established or restored dioceses and raised up monasteries. His missionary zeal laid the very foundation of the medieval German Church and it caused the reform of the Church in France and united Western Christendom under Papal authority. He was martyred by heathen Frisians whilst waiting to confer the Sacrament of Confirmation on a crowd of thousands at Pentecost. The brave eighty year old saint raised a holy book above his head, but the assasin's sword plunged savagely through to make its mark. After his death Holland also became part of Christian Europe. St. Boniface is acknowledged as Patron Saint of Germany and the Netherlands as well as Patron of our own Diocese of Plymouth. His feast day is celebrated on 5th June.

# St. Boniface

During the first World War Mass was said in Crediton Town Hall for a dozen parishioners and those troops convalescing at the Military Hospital.

After the War a Fr. T. Barney became parish priest of Exeter. He had great devotion to St. Boniface. He managed to rent and later purchase a former Methodist Chapel which had been previously sold in 1892 for use as a drill hall. Fr. Barney started to give due honour to the feast of St. Boniface: High Mass in the morning, an outdoor procession and sermon in the town in the evening, followed by Benediction and solemn veneration of the relic of St. Boniface.

In 1966 land was bought for a new Church and Shrine of St. Boniface and plans made. The foundation stone was solemnly laid by the Bishop of Plymouth on March 29th 1969. It was sent by the Bishop of Fulda (W. Germany) from the Ratgar Basilica, the splendid burial place of St. Boniface constructed at the beginning of the ninth century. The Vicar of Crediton also donated a stone from the pre-Reformation Church of the Holy Cross, to be incorporated into the new Church as a sign of the bond of unity, through "Boniface", our common Christian heritage. The Church and Shrine were blessed and opened by the Rt. Rev. Cyril Restieaux, Bishop of Plymouth, on 3rd October 1969.

Contact address of Priest:
The Presbytery, 25, South Street,
Exeter. Devon. EX1 1EB.
Telephone: (0392) 72815.

# Croyde

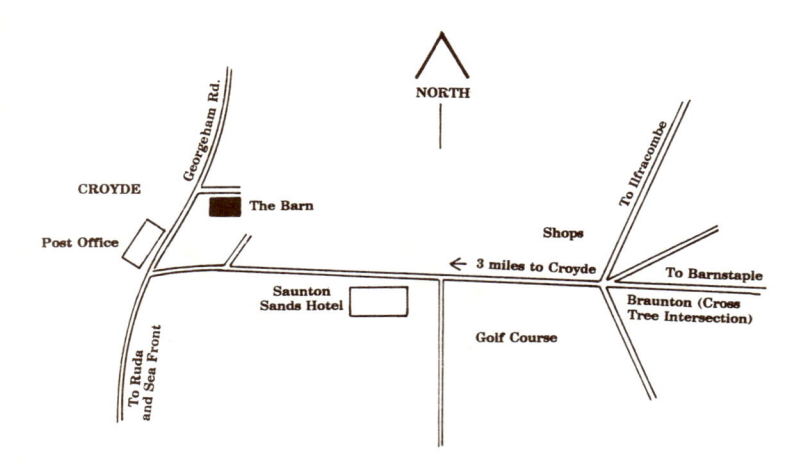

### THE BARN (Chapel)

From Barnstaple follow the A361 Braunton Road then B3231 Croyde Road. From Ilfracombe follow the B3231 south west. From Braunton follow the B3231 east to Croyde. Saunton Road leads into Croyde. Go through the main street. Look out for the Post Office. Take the Georgeham Road and then a right turn into "Watery Lane". Go over a little bridge. "The Barn" is right beside the bridge. There is no direct train service to Croyde but there is a train to Barnstaple and then buses are available from Barnstaple to Georgeham. Cars may be parked opposite "The Barn".

A Mass centre was started in Croyde Village in 1969 to provide for the increasing number of visitors coming to North Devon during the summer. "The Barn" was purchased in late 1970 from Col. Incledon-Webber. After planning permission had been obtained it was converted into a Chapel, the Stations of the Cross being kindly donated by the Nuns at Lakenham. The building was first opened as a Mass Centre in summer 1971. It seats roughly one hundred people and has a large overflow for the six weeks of the summer school holidays.

Contact address of Priest:
The Presbytery, Frog Lane,
Braunton, N. Devon. EX33 1BB.
Telephone: (0271) 812558.

# The Barn

# Cullompton

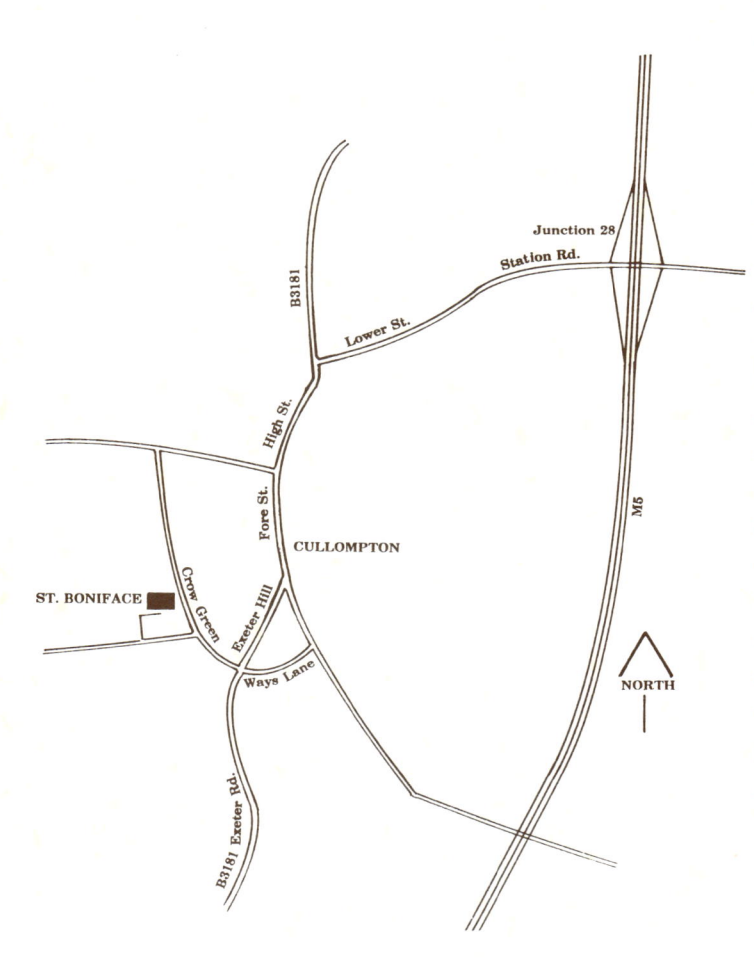

The dedication is to St. Boniface (Wynfrith) of Crediton who is also the Patron of the Plymouth Diocese. He was educated by the Benedictines, later became a priest and eventually a missionary, the Apostle of Germany. In 722 A.D. Pope Gregory II (715-731) consecrated him Bishop of Hessia and Thuringia. Hessia boasts the famous tale of how St. Boniface axed a huge oaktree consecrated to the god of thunder and when no harm befell him many of the pagan tribes converted. In 748 he was made Archbishop of Mainz and Primate of Germany. The Abbey of Fulda was very important to Boniface, it was under the immediate jurisdiction of the Holy See, and he deliberately spent some time there each year. His last journey to Frisia, the place of his first missionary ministry, was the site of his martyrdom. His body was returned to the Abbey at Fulda. This saint is greatly honoured in both Germany and Holland. We can be proud that he had his roots in Devon. His feast is kept on 5th June.

## St. Boniface, Shortlands.

Cullompton is well signposted off the M5 at Junction 28. Alternatively follow the A38 (B3181) from Exeter to Cullompton. Arriving at the town turn left through the market place. Ways Lane is on the left before Gateway Supermarket. Turn right down Crow Green, a very narrow street. The Church looks like a piece of Spanish architecture with its tiled roof, arched door and windows and campanile. A bus service operates from Exeter to Cullompton. Cars may be parked at the Church.

# St. Boniface

St. Boniface's Church was built in 1929 by a Spanish benefactor after the local convent had closed. People had formerly gone to the convent for Mass or to St. John's, Tiverton.

Contact address of Priest:
The Presbytery, Shortlands,
Cullompton, Devon. EX15 1EW.
Telephone: (0884) 32253.

# Dartmouth

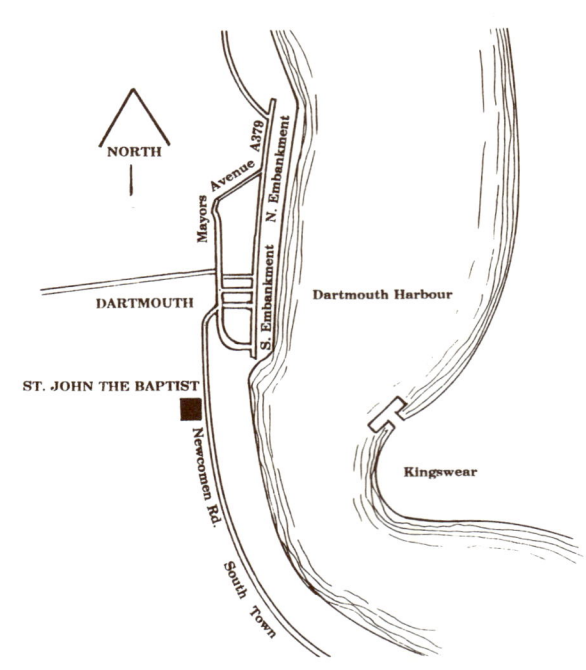

### St. John the Baptist, Newcomen Rd.

Locating the Catholic Church is not as difficult as parking a car in Dartmouth. Cars can be left beside the water and elsewhere on dotted lines (waiting limit 2 hours). The centre of Dartmouth is most easily explored and enjoyed as a pedestrian. From the promenade, with boats to the left and gardens to the right, one route through the narrow streets passes Mayors Avenue and straight on to turn right at Tippers Quay, with a telephone box on the corner, down Coles Court into Lower Street, and up the hill by road or steps into Newcomen Road. The grey stone Church and presbytery are part of a terrace of buildings crowding on to the footpath with houses to either side.

The dedication is to St. John the Baptist, possibly because it was a Fr. Jean Baptiste who was in charge of building the Church. St. John the Baptist was related to Christ through his mother, Elizabeth. She was the Blessed Virgin's cousin. The Gospels reveal certain details about this saint who "prepared the way of the Lord". His birth (foretold by the archangel, Gabriel, to a disbelieving father, Zachary) took place when Elizabeth was quite old. He was given the name John meaning "Jahweh has shown mercy". In adulthood St. John gathered many disciples together teaching them a life of prayer and fasting. With great missionary zeal, he exhorted the people to repent and prepare for the coming of the Messiah. John baptized many in the River Jordan, including Jesus whom he realised was the Messiah. After openly rebuking King Herod Antipas for an incestuous marriage with Herodias, he was arrested and imprisoned in the mountain fortress of Machaerus. St. John was beheaded to appease the whim of the dancer Salome, Herodias' daughter. His death occurred about one year before Our Lord's. His feast is celebrated on 24th June.

# St. John the Baptist

In 1782 Bishop Charles Walmesley sent a priest to Dartmouth to found a small mission in Lower Street. He was called the Rev. Charles Timings. He not only served the small population of Catholics in Dartmouth, but also ministered to those over a very wide area including Plymouth, the South Hams, and Totnes, where he lived. In 1784 Fr. Timings began recording Baptisms in a Parish Register. A French priest, the Abbe P.G. Le Verrier, from Normandy, took over the Mission in 1794, but in 1796 Fr. Timings returned once more to Dartmouth. He stayed there with his assistant until 1801 when he became chaplain to the Cary Family at Folleton House, Totnes.

In 1805 Fr. Le Verrier transferred to Teignmouth. Fr. W. Davis moved into Dartmouth, but poverty and ill-health were strongly against him. He died in 1814. The Mission had practically expired also! A Fr. Alexander Simon seems to have ministered to Dartmouth Catholics until 1820, although he did not live at the fishing port himself. By 1821 the Bishop had closed the Dartmouth Mission. Some years later a Catholic convert, formerly an Anglican priest of Dittisham, the Rev. Lord Henry Kerr donated one thousand pounds for the sole purpose of building a Catholic Church in Dartmouth town. Fr. Jean Baptiste Laborie Rey took over the project. This present Church of St. John the Baptist, Dartmouth, was solemnly blessed and opened by His Lordship Bishop William Vaughan in 1869.

Contact address of Priest:
The Priest's House, 20, Newcomen Road, Dartmouth, Devon. TQ6 9BN.
Telephone: (0803) 832860.

# Dawlish

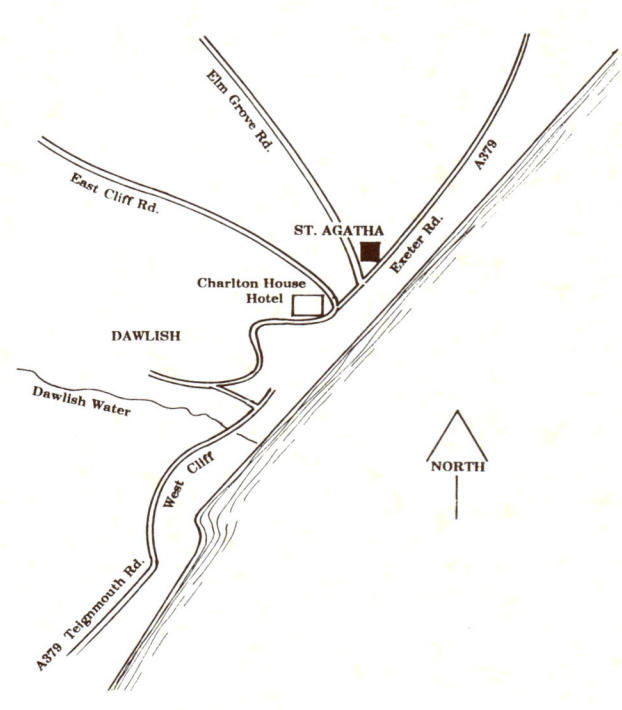

**St. Agatha, Exeter Road.**

From Teignmouth take the A379 to Dawlish. Continue following the coast on to the Exeter Road. Go past the Charlton House Hotel and East Cliff Road. St. Agatha's Church and Presbytery are dignified red sandstone buildings, in a prominent position, on the corner of Exeter Road and Elm Grove Road. Car parking is available, but masked by the Church buildings: the entrance is found off Elm Grove Road.

The dedication is to St. Agatha. She was one of the renowned virgin martyrs of the ancient church, but few details of her life have survived. Palermo and Catania in Sicily both claim to have been her place of birth. Early devotion to St. Agatha is verified by her being included in the Martyrology of St. Jerome and also in the Roman Canon of the Mass. During the sixth century two churches in Rome adopted her patronage. The fifth/sixth century Basilica of St. Apollinare Nuovo in Ravenna also honours St. Agatha, where she is depicted in a mosaic frieze, as one in a procession of female saints moving towards Christ and the Blessed Virgin, to offer her martyr's crown. St. Agatha met her death in Catania, possibly during the persecution of Decius. She was canonized by Pope Gregory I (590-604 A.D.). A chapel in Catania Cathedral is dedicated to her. St. Agatha's feast day is celebrated on 5th February.

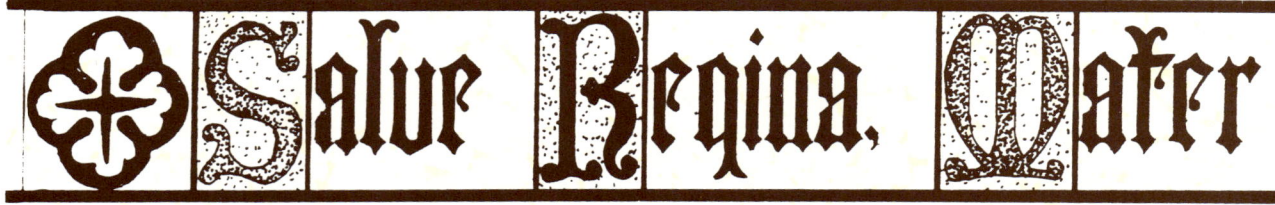

Salve Regina, Mater

# St. Agatha

The site for this Church was purchased in November 1906. The foundation stone was laid on June 5th 1907, the feast of St. Boniface. The first Mass was celebrated on 18th February 1909 with a congregation of forty people.

The interior of the Church is of particular interest for its richness of stone and variety of marble. The High Altar and Lady Altar are of alabaster. The Statue of Our Lady, Shrine of St. Agatha, and the Stations of the Cross are carved out of Seaton stone. There is also a calligraphic frieze relating the words of the ancient prayer, the Salve Regina.

misericordiæ; V

Contact address of Priest:
The Presbytery, 27, Exeter Road, Dawlish, Devon. EX7 0BU.
Telephone: (0626) 863279.

# Dorchester

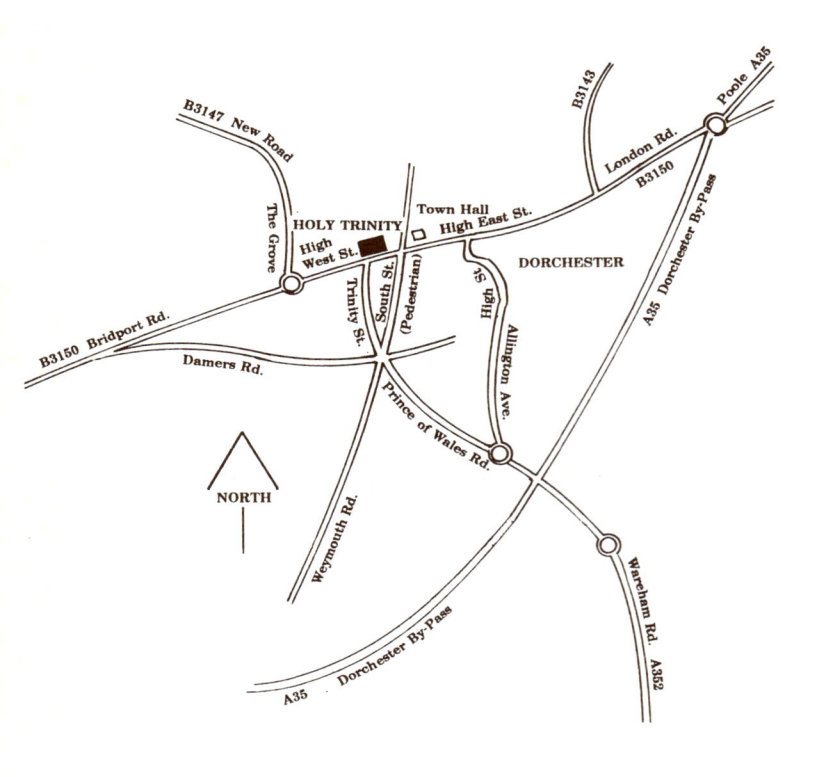

**Holy Trinity, High West Street.**

Dorchester is situated off the A35 Bridport /Poole Road, the A37 from Yeovil, A354 from Weymouth. A352 from Wareham. Holy Trinity is located in the centre of the town on the High Street going east to west just past the Museum and Anglican Parish Church. Parking is available in the town, but not on the road outside the Church.

Holy Trinity is a parish existing from medieval times. The very title acknowledges the doctrine of the Triune God: the Father, the Son, the Holy Spirit. A church honouring the Trinity has been on this site for nine centuries or more, the dedication recorded in the Domesday Book. There is a screen inside the present Church, a wooden register, which lists the names of the Parish Priests and Vicars since 1302.

When the former Catholic Church of Our Lady Queen of Martyrs & St. Michael became too cramped, an opportunity arose to negotiate the purchase of a redundant Anglican Church, built in 1876, Holy Trinity. Through the generosity of the Church of England, the Diocese of Salisbury, the transaction proved successful and in due course Her Majesty the Queen initialled the final document. The inaugural Mass for the Catholic Church of Holy Trinity took place on 28th May 1976. Many of the internal features of the former Anglican Church were kindly left in situ: the carved reredos from Oberammergau, the font and the alabaster pulpit. Other items were brought from the old Catholic Church: the onyx marble altar, the Stations of the Cross, the Crucifix and some of the Statues.

# Holy Trinity

An unusual tale may be told too about the old Catholic building. It was once situated seventeen miles away at Wareham, a monastic church, built in 1890 for the Congregation of the Passion. When the Community departed from the county in 1906 their little church was carefully dismantled, each stone numbered and then transported by horse and cart to High West Street, Dorchester, where it was reassembled as the Church of Our Lady Queen of Martyrs & St. Michael. The title honoured the Dorchester martyrs of the Reformation: Fr. John Cornelius, Fr. Hugh Green, Thomas Bosgrave, John Carey and Patrick Salmon (beatified in 1929), also Fr. Thomas Pilchard and William Pike (beatified in 1987).

Contact address of Priest:
The Presbytery, 20, Princes Street,
Dorchester, Dorset. DT1 1TP.
Telephone: (0305) 262486.

# Exeter

**Blessed Sacrament, Fore Street, Heavitree.**

Exeter can be confusing for the first time visitor to the city. As the R.D.& E. Hospitals are well signposted it is not too difficult to find the Catholic Church from either of them. From the bus and coach station roundabout take the exit into Heavitree Road. Go past St. Luke's College on the right and the R.D.& E. Hospital (Heavitree) on the left. Continue straight on into Fore Street (B3183). The Catholic Church is on the left. It is just past Church Terrace on the right and before Homefield Road on the left. From the R.D.& E. Hospital (Wonford) go down Barrack Road. Turn right at Magdalen Road or Heavitree Road into Fore Street, as above. Parking facilities are available.

The Church of the Blessed Sacrament is an imposing building in cherry red brick, enriched with white, set back from the road in a garden setting. It has an eighty foot brick tower at the West end and a copper domed, semi-circular, red brick sanctuary, surrounded by ten white pillars at the East.

High above the portico is a golden mosaic monstrance defining the dedication of the Church to The Blessed Sacrament. A group of statues represents the believers on earth. Malachias, from the Old Testament, is portrayed with arms outstretched, proclaiming the prophecy "from sunrise to sunset .. in every place there is sacrifice". St. John the Baptist stands in the middle, between the Old Testament and the New; he is pointing to the monstrance, to the Lamb of God. St. Andrew, from the New Testament is bent on one knee, adoring. On the other side of the portico is another group of statuary representing the heavenly choirs: there are two angels, one with a thurible of incense, the other kneeling in adoration before The Blessed Sacrament.

The Sacred Host is reserved in the tabernacle of every Catholic Church. The celebration of the Blessed Eucharist occurs every day at Mass. A special holy day in honour of The Blessed Sacrament is "Corpus Christi" kept on the Thursday after Trinity Sunday each year.

VI

Veronica Wipes the Face of Jesus.

# Blessed Sacrament

The interior of this Church follows the form of a classic basilica, with the atmosphere of tranquility which comes from a space of diffused light and rounded arches, framing the view in perspective to focus on the tabernacle. An international variety of marble is represented: Convent Siena marble, Pedrara onyx, Vert Numidie, Belgian black, Swedish green, Pierstraccia, two varieties of red Moroccan onyx, black and gold, Breche violette, Vert des Alpes and tiles in Roman travertine.

The Church of the Blessed Sacrament was formally blessed on Saturday 28th May 1932 by the Rt. Rev. John Barrett, D.D. Bishop of Plymouth. Then on Sunday 29th May (within the Octave of Corpus Christi) Solemn Pontifical Mass was celebrated by His Lordship the Bishop and later in the afternoon there was an outdoor procession of the most Blessed Sacrament and Benediction.

Contact address of Priest:
The Presbytery, 29, Fore Street,
Heavitree, Exeter, Devon. EX1 2QJ.
Telephone: (0392) 72596.

# Exeter

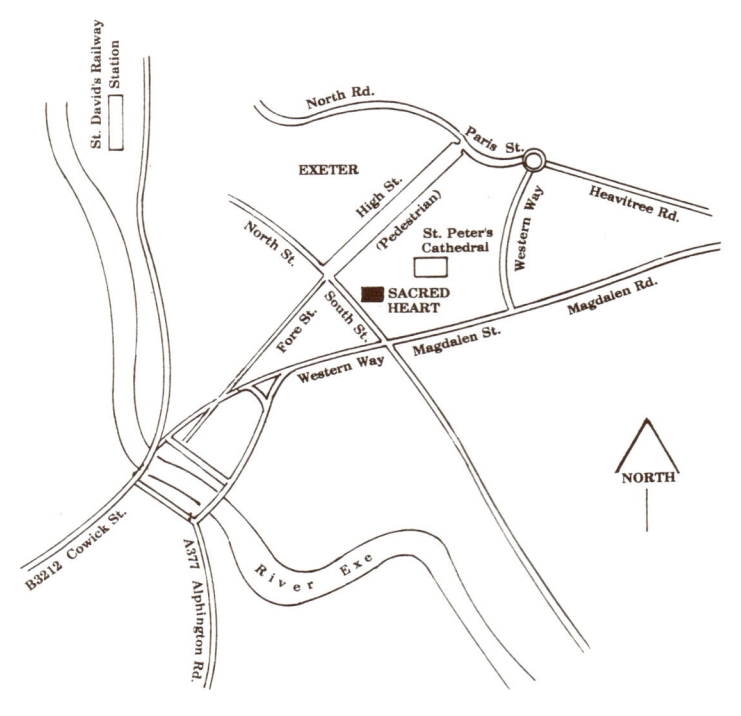

**Sacred Heart, South Street.**

Exeter is well signposted from all surrounding routes: A30 from Okehampton, A38 from Plymouth, A377 from Barnstaple, B3212 from Moretonhampstead, A396 from Tiverton, B3181 from Cullompton, A30 from Honiton, and from the M5 motorway.

The Church of the Sacred Heart is close to Exeter Cathedral in the City centre. It is situated in the lower end of South Street. Landmarks include the "White Hart Hotel" and the Baptist Church. There is no Church car park. Parking is possible in South Street on Sundays and in the neighbouring side roads, but this facility can be unpredictable. The local car parks are signposted. Exeter has its own British Rail Station. A blue or silver minibus service operates in the city.

Near the Sanctuary is a Shrine to the Sacred Heart to whom the Church is dedicated. The universal church has kept a feast in honour of The Sacred Heart since 1856. The feast is celebrated on the Friday after the second Sunday after Pentecost.

# Sacred Heart

During James II's reign, a "Mass house" was opened in Exeter, but in 1688 this was flattened to the ground. After 1745 Mass was said in an upper back room of King John's Tavern, in South Street. From Christmas 1775 part of "St. Nicholas" mansion was rented and a large upper chamber transformed into a Chapel. Later, the premises were purchased and a proper chapel built. On Epiphany Sunday 1792, the first Mass was offered in the new chapel, in the Mint, close to the remains of the pre-Reformation priory of St. Nicholas.

The present Church of the Sacred Heart is built on the site of the famous Bear Tavern, the former town house of the Abbots of Tavistock, which was leased out as an inn. The foundation stone for the Church was laid by Bishop Vaughan, (2nd Bishop of Plymouth) in 1883. The solemn opening took place on November 18th 1884; on the feast of the Dedication of the Basilicas of SS. Peter & Paul with the Rt. Rev. Bishop of Clifton officiating, in the presence of Archbishop Errington, the Bishop of Plymouth and the Bishop of Newport and Menevia.

Stepping off the city street into the Church is almost like entering a Cathedral. Everything is large scale, the interior spacious, comfortable, old, hallowed by prayer. Of notable interest is the stained glass, particularly the windows of the Sacred Heart and St. Margaret Mary. There is a vast amount of carved stone work to enjoy, a gloriously decorative high altar reredos, Lady altar and St. Joseph altar. There seem to be carvings of saints everywhere including the pulpit and the dark wood of the organ is embellished with carved angels and trumpets.

The Stations of the Cross are typical nineteenth century paintings, powerful in their own way, nothing abstract. They are painted on zinc and came from Munich, donated to the Church in 1886.

Towards the Sanctuary is a painted mural of James Turbeville, the last Catholic Bishop of Exeter, 1570.

In Saxon times the seventh century Abbey of St. Mary & St. Peter in Exeter fostered the education and vocation of Wynfrith of Crediton, later known as Boniface.

Along the north aisle may be found a large stained glass window depicting St. Boniface. Beneath the window is an elaborately carved altar dedicated to the Early English Saints showing:

ST. WILLIBALD (d.786/7 A.D.) the brother of St. Winnibald and St. Walburga. At the request of St. Boniface, Pope Gregory III (731-741) sent Willibald to do missionary work in Germany;

ST. BURCHARD (d.754 A.D.) who came from Wessex. He offered his services to Boniface in Germany;

ST. SIDWELL who was born at Exeter. From early times a devotion to her has existed at Exeter;

ST. RICHARD (d.720 A.D.) He was the father of St. Willibald, St. Winnibald and St. Walburga;

ST. GREGORY III (d. 741 A.D.) a sage of Sacred Scriptures who knew the psalms by heart. This Pope gave full support to Boniface's missionary work in Germany;

ST. WILLIBRORD (658-739) who was a missionary in Frisia. At one stage he was joined by Boniface;

ST. LULLUS (Lull) (710-86 A.D.) who became Archbishop of Mainz, was born in Wessex. He followed his cousin Boniface into the mission field in Germany.

ST. WALBURGA (d.779 A.D.) sister of St. Winnibald and St. Willibald, also helped Boniface with his missionary apostolate. She became Abbess of Heidenheim.

# Sacred Heart

Contact address of Priest:
The Presbytery, 25, South Street,
Exeter, Devon. EX1 1EB.
Telephone: (0392) 72815.

# Exeter

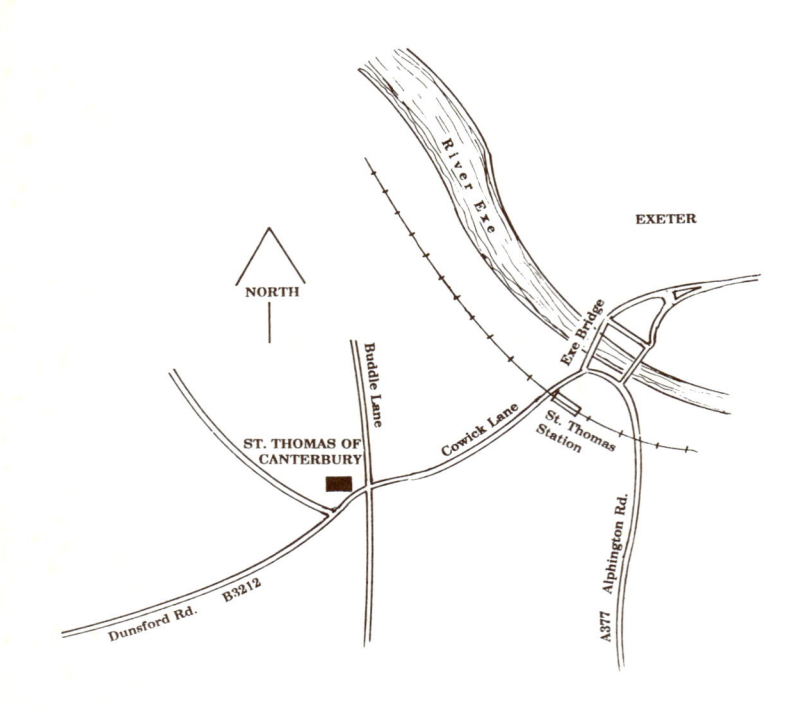

**St. Thomas of Canterbury, Dunsford Rd.**

From Exe Bridge take the Cowick Street turning (B3212) passing Sainsbury's on the left. Go straight up the hill into Dunsford Road. The grey stone Catholic Church is on the right, set back a little from the pavement. It is next door to "John Stocker Middle School" and just before the sign "B3212 Moretonhampstead 12". Cars have to park at the roadside as there is no church car park. Red and yellow minibuses operate in the area. The church is a fair walk from St. Thomas Railway Station.

The dedication is to St. Thomas of Canterbury. The saint was born in 1118 A.D. in London, the son of a rich merchant from Normandy. He studied Law and was ordained deacon. When King Henry II (great-grandson of William the Conqueror) ascended the English throne he appointed Thomas as his Chancellor. Thus a successful career seemed assured. But, in 1162 the King decided to nominate Thomas for the position of Archbishop of Canterbury, and he was duly elected by the monks of Canterbury. From that very moment his lifestyle altered to fit the spiritual calling of an archbishop: it was a life of fasting, prayer, vigils and penance. He began to oppose the King on matters of taxation, and law, and the Church. Their friendship became strained, and Thomas went into exile in France for six years, befriended by the French King. Pope Alexander III (1159-1181) was asked to help to intervene to solve the dispute between the Monarch and Archbishop. In 1170 Thomas returned to England. Within a month four barons carried out the assassination which rid King Henry of "the turbulent priest". Thomas was martyred in his own Cathedral at Canterbury. He died a saintly death, and many miracles occurred thereafter at his tomb. He was canonized in 1173 only three years after his demise. His shrine became a place of special pilgrimage. The feast of Thomas of Canterbury (Thomas a Beckett) is kept on 29th December.

Contact address of Priest:
The Presbytery, 25, South Street
Exeter, Devon EX1 1EB.
Telephone: (0392) 72815.

# St Thomas of Canterbury

# Exeter

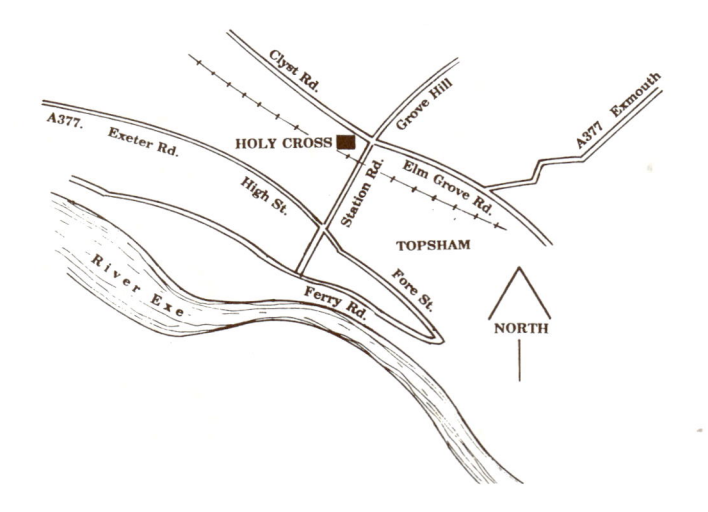

**Holy Cross Station Road, Topsham.**

From Exeter take the Exmouth road A376. Topsham is signposted 1 mile. The A377 Exeter Road leads into High Street. Turn left into Station Road, and continue to the end, to the junction with Clyst Road and Elmgrove Road. Opposite Topsham railway station, the red brick Church and tower of Holy Cross can be seen set back from the pavement in its own walled garden. There is a frequent minibus service from a bus stop right outside the Church. Trains run half hourly from the Station. There is limited parking available near the Church and in adjacent roads.

The feast of The Exaltation of the Holy Cross is kept on 14th September. Christ's Crucifixion occurred outside Jerusalem but near the city wall and next to a public highway. Nearby there was a garden and a tomb. In 135 A.D. the Emperor Hadrian decided to put a stop to the veneration of Mount Calvary by the militant Early Christians. He built a great terrace and pagan temple over the sacred spot and beside it he made a forum, a market place. In 326 A.D. St. Helena made a pilgrimage to the Holy Land determined to discover the Holy sites. Bishop Mecarius of Jerusalem was able to tell her that Calvary lay underneath the pagan shrine. Helena persuaded her son, Constantine the Great, to find Golgotha and he ordered the area to be excavated. Fortunately, the Romans had covered Calvary with mounds of earth without destroying it. So, was revealed the place of Crucifixion and an empty tomb. In a cistern in the rock were found Jesus' Cross and two others together with Pilate's inscription. The verification of these holy sites has been confirmed by archaeologists and revered by Roman Catholic, Oriental Orthodox Christians and others worldwide.

For each church in the Diocese there is a story of determination, often stubborness, and always good humour. In the case of Topsham Church the struggle is recorded in an account, written by hand by Fr. Cahill who was clearly a priest who liked to make things happen.

Fr. Barney of the Sacred Heart Church, Exeter, purchased an ex-Wesleyan Chapel as a Church for Topsham, but the Bishop disliked the surroundings and so in 1932, when Topsham became part of Heavitree parish, the old Chapel was closed down. A dozen Topsham Catholics are recorded as having to go by taxi to The Blessed Sacrament, Heavitree, on Sundays.

In 1932 the energetic Fr. Cahill returned from 10 years in Australia and a further 32 making things happen in New Zealand, *"in the face of strong opposition, especially from the Poles at Carterton - very difficult work"*. Failing health compelled him to seek a change of climate. The climate of Topsham appears to have been conducive.

In 1934 the Topsham Church site and property were purchased from Heywood Bros. of Exeter with six hundred pounds of Fr. Cahill's money for the property, and one thousand from the Bishop for the house. Fr. Cahill noted that a benefactor *"later took over the house from the Bishop, at one thousand pounds, and later still, she made a present of the house to Bishop Barrett. And thus the Bishop acquired the Topsham church property without having to pay anything for it."*

# Holy Cross

Fr. Cahill was still short of building funds, but determined to see a Catholic Church in Topsham. He had become acquainted with a Mr. Wilfred Mangan of Preston, a well-known church architect, and, with the Bishop's approval asked him to design a small church. In due course the plans were finished and tenders advertised, but the Bishop would not let the project go ahead without sufficient funding.

Despite the generosity of benefactors, Fr. Cahill was short of eight hundred pounds for a new church. The Bishop could only offer two hundred, and a benefactor one hundred.

*"To collect the remaining five hundred pounds was impossible. There, then, was the impasse, with no hope of a church for many years - to say nothing of No. 2 War and its shortages. Father Cahill then and there asked himself the question: could he possibly give that five hundred pounds and thereby start the building - could he spare it as against the needs of old age. He decided to give the five hundred pounds to God who had helped him to work for it."*

The Bishop then agreed to allow the project to go ahead. No time was lost!

*"The next day Fr. Cahill signed the Contract with Turl Bros.- 2 promising young builders of Topsham..(who)..under the expert advice and direction of the Architect did a fine job of work."*

Further good work from kind benefactors allowed the Church to be funded in full.

*"and The Church of the Holy Cross was dedicated by Bishop Barrett on the Feast of the Exaltation of the Holy Cross Sept. 14. 1936, practically free of debt. Arthur Heard who used to serve Mass at Topsham and had been away for some years, on his return, seeing the new church said "It is a miracle." It was, indeed, a miracle of God's Providential help. Thanks be to God. Amen."*

Contact address of Priest:
The Presbytery, Station Road,
Topsham, Exeter, Devon. EX33 OEE.
Telephone:(0392) 873898.

# Exmouth

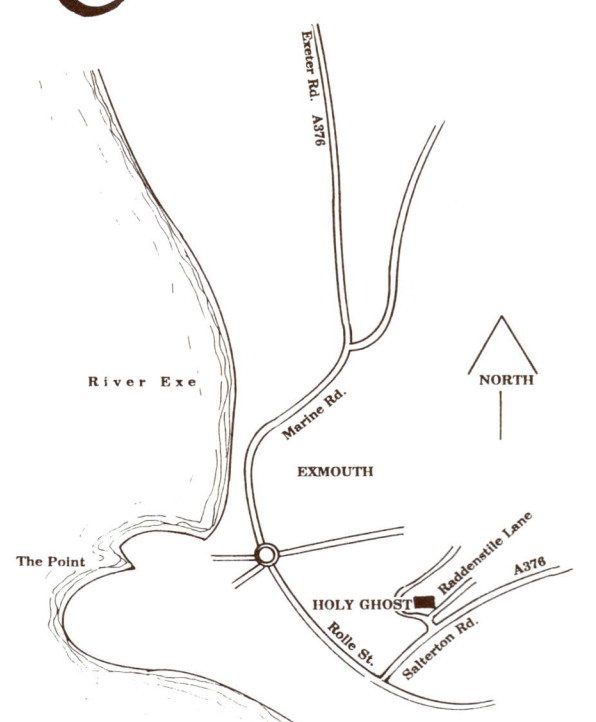

SPIRITUS SANCTUS SUPERVENIET IN TE
The Church is dedicated to the Holy Ghost, the Spirit of God, the Spirit of Love, the Spirit of wisdom, of truth, source of all goodness. He is our guide, our strength, our consolation. The Holy Ghost is our greatest patron, for He is God Himself.

**Holy Ghost, Raddenstile Lane.**

From Exeter take the A376 south to Exmouth. From Lyme Regis take the A3052 west, then A376. From Honiton take the A30 west then B3180 south. From the direction of Budleigh Salterton via the A376, at the mini roundabout take a right turn into Raddenstile Lane. If you miss the turning, keep going left, and approach from the other end of Raddenstile Lane. The Church of the Holy Ghost is an impressive stone building with a pitched roof and tall tower. There is a fine carved tympanum above the main entrance depicting the Annunciation scene, the presence of the Holy Spirit.

# Holy Ghost

Inside this large gothic style church there is a magnificent carved altar reredos with an array of saints: St. Thomas the Apostle, St. Mary Magdalene, St. David of Wales, St. Bernard, St. Elizabeth of Hungary, and St. John the Evangelist. The English patron, St. George, is depicted in one of the stained glass windows, together with St. Edward.

The Stations of the cross are memorable through their imagery: the awful gruesome truth that Christ shed all His blood for us.

From the first station the artist shows Jesus dripping blood from His temple down His neck. When the eighth station is reached, the artist shows Our Saviour having turned His face, blood from His thorn-crowned head spilling down the other side of His face. At the third fall there is "Jesus Forsaken". At the tenth station blood streams down His face on to His half stripped, punished body. At the eleventh station it pours from His hand nailed to the Cross, then from the other sacred wounds. Soon "it is finished".

Contact address of Priest:
the Presbytery, Raddenstile Lane,
Exmouth, Devon. EX8 2JH.
Telephone: (0395) 263384.

# Falmouth

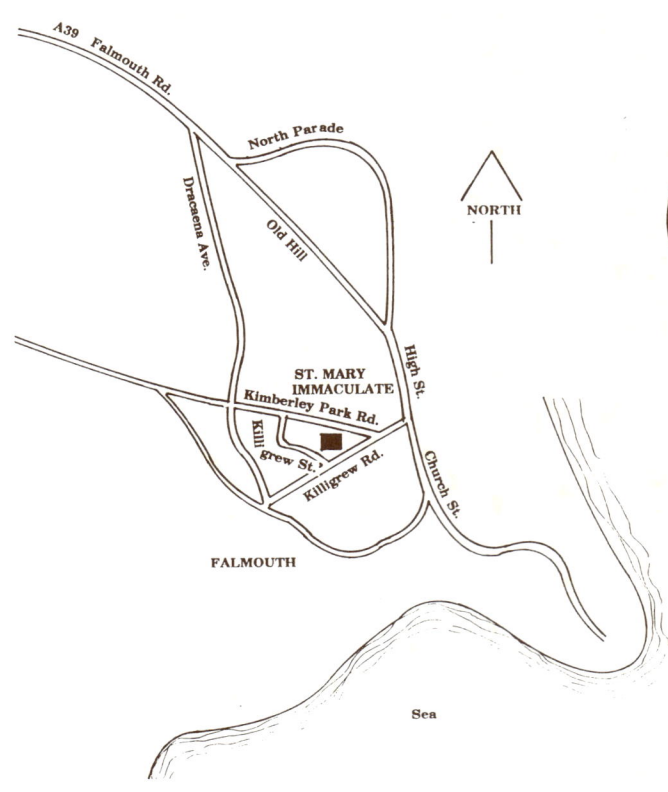

**St. Mary Immaculate, Killigrew Street.**

From Penryn (A39) follow the main road into Falmouth. Go straight over the first roundabout along Dracaena Avenue (B3290). Continue straight on, passing three sets of traffic lights, to a small roundabout. Turn left into Killigrew Street. The Catholic Church is easily recognised, a traditional building, situated halfway down on the left hand side. There is car parking for a limited number of cars to the rear of the Church.

Ancient Christian belief, beginning with the writings of the Church Fathers, soon after the death of St. John, clearly acknowledged Mary's Immaculate Conception. In the Eastern Church the feast was kept from the seventh century, in the West from the ninth. At the Lourdes apparition of 1858 Our Lady said: "I am the Immaculate Conception".

*Queen, conceived without original sin,
pray for us. (Litany of Loreto).*

The first Catholic Church in Falmouth after the Reformation was a hut sited near the present Customs House. It was put up at the beginning of the nineteenth century by French fishermen who needed a place for private prayer when they visited the port. The hut was destroyed by fire, but nevertheless, rebuilt. In 1818 a French emigre priest, Father De La Gresille, moved the Church to Well Lane, becuse the original ground was required by the Government. Another site was subsequently found on Greenbank. Five hundred pounds was collected and donations also came from the French Royal Family of Napoleon III. The foundation stone of the new church was dedicated to "Our Immaculate Lady". The Church, accommodating one hundred and fifty people, was solemnly opened on 24th October 1821.

# St. Mary Immaculate

In due course the congregation outgrew the little church. Negotiations began with Lord Kimberley, who agreed to sell a plot of land on the moor above the Market Place. Three months later the land was purchased and the Church immediately started according to plans made by Mr. Joseph Hansom (of Hansom Cab fame). The new Church of St. Mary Immaculate, constructed mainly of granite and Portland stone was solemnly opened on 26th August 1869 by Bishop Vaughan of Plymouth, and Bishop Ullathorne of Birmingham. The Grotto of Our Lady of Lourdes was added in 1929. The granite pulpit erected in 1939 was the first memorial in the country to the late Pope Pius XI (1922-1939). The Church narrowly escaped total destruction during an air-raid in 1941 when it sustained severe damage to the roof and windows. The Church of St. Mary Immaculate was consecrated on 8th September 1948 by Bishop Grimshaw of Plymouth.

Contact address of Priest:
The Presbytery, Killigrew street,
Falmouth, Cornwall. TR11 3PR.
Telephone: (0326) 312763.

# Germoe

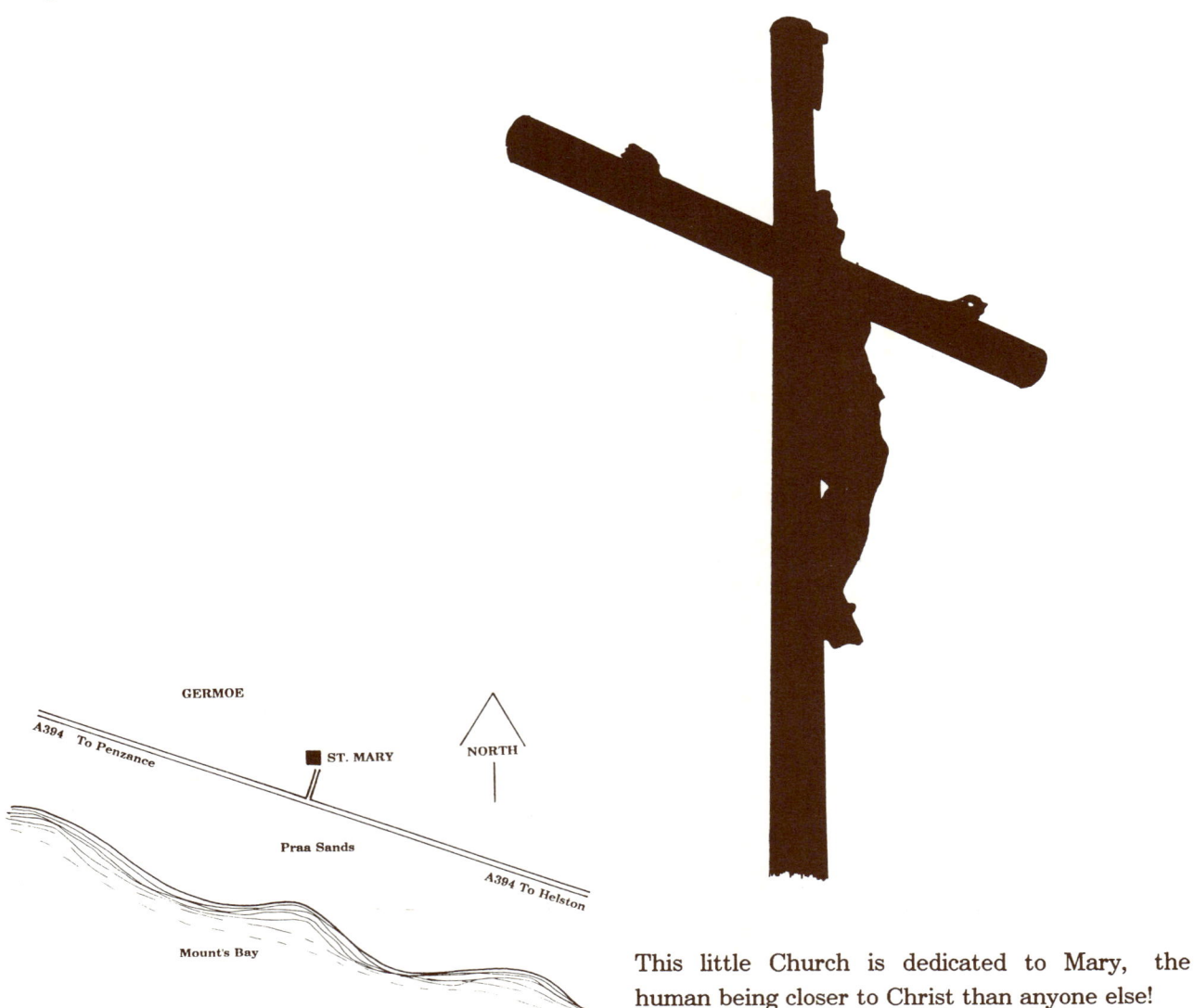

This little Church is dedicated to Mary, the human being closer to Christ than anyone else!

### St. Mary, Praa Sands.

St. Mary's, a large wooden sided hut with pitched roof and porch entrance is located at the top of a field off the main Penzance to Helston Road (A394), about six miles from Helston, opposite the Praa Sands Golf Course. There is a tarmacadam drive up from the road, and parking space is available in the field.

In 1961 Father A.P. Byrne, C.R.L. had the opportunity to purchase a private Chapel on the main road at Praa Sands. (It is thought that the building was first used for Sunday Mass in 1925, by permission of the owner who, apparently, lived in one or more railway carriages next door). The Chapel had originally been opened and blessed by Bishop Barrett in 1935, and later abandoned. During the period of disuse, Mass was celebrated at "Seaforth" a house on the main road at Praa Sands, and thereafter Mass was said at Tregembo Manor, Relubbus.

Dominating the road and entrance to St. Mary's is the large wayside Crucifix, blessed by Bishop Barrett when he opened the chapel. The lifesize figure of Christ is carved out of teakwood.

# St. Mary

Contact address of Priest:
The Presbytery, St. Michael's Hospital,
4, Trelissick Road, Hayle, Cornwall. TR27 4JA.
Telephone: (0736) 753123.

# Gillingham

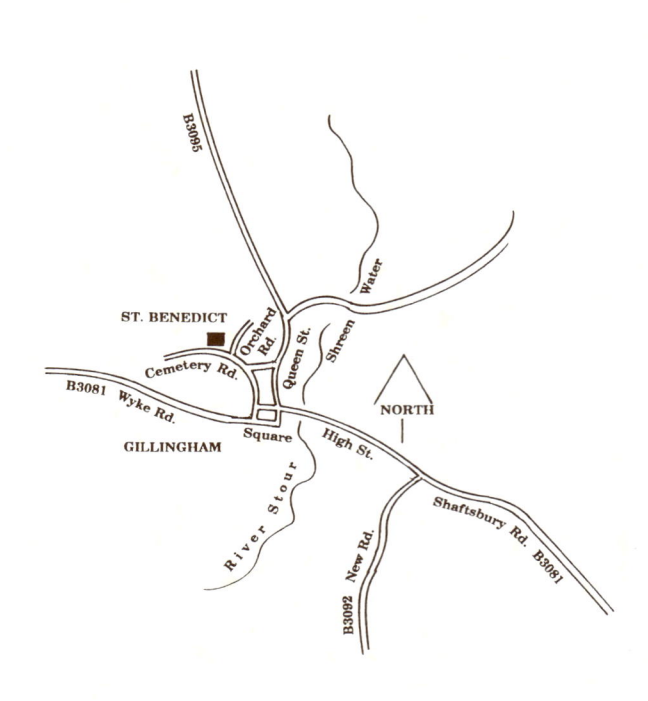

St. Benedict (480-547 A.D.) was declared the Patron of Europe by Pope Paul VI (1963-1978) as recognition of the Benedictine involvement in Christian Europe. His influence, particularly through his Rule, written so long ago at Monte Cassino, crosses the centuries and, also, religious divisions. When we honour St. Benedict we honour a saint of the "Undivided Church"! His feast is celebrated on 11th July each year.

Going back through the centuries to the times of persecution, property confiscation and crippling fines for being a "papist", Gillingham can boast of two brave and faithful families, the Dirdos and Gildons. Back in the twentieth century, in 1907, another loyal family, called Freame, descendents of the eminent Husseys of Nash Court, Marnhull, made it possible to begin the Catholic Church building in Gillingham.

With reference to Nash Court, it may be interesting to note that it had a brief change of lifestyle in the latter part of the eighteenth century. English Benedictine Sisters, who had fled the horrors of the French Revolution, found a temporary refuge at the Manor House. They left in 1807 and eventually settled in Staffordshire. Another Benedictine, a Father Edward Hussey, one of the grandsons of George Hussey of Nash Court, worked in Marnhull in his later years. The original manuscript of the Register of Baptisms which he started in 1772 is one of the oldest surviving Catholic registers in England today. Maybe the presence of the Benedictines at Nash Court, the Husseys, the link with the Freame family, provided enough reason to choose St. Benedict as the patron of Gillingham parish.

**St. Benedict, Rolls Bridge.**

The parish of Gillingham in North Dorset is well served with roads: the B3081 Shaftsbury/Leigh Common, the B3092 East Stour/Milton on Stour and several other minor routes. From High Street in the centre of Gillingham go down Queen Street, then left into Turner's Lane towards Cemetery Road. There is a sign indicating the presence of a Catholic Church. St. Benedict's, a modern light brick building situated in its own small garden, is adjacent to the cemetery. There is a Calvary outside in the hedge. It bears the following inscription:
*" Pray for our sailors and soldiers now serving and for the souls of those who have given their lives for their country and for us R.I.P. "*

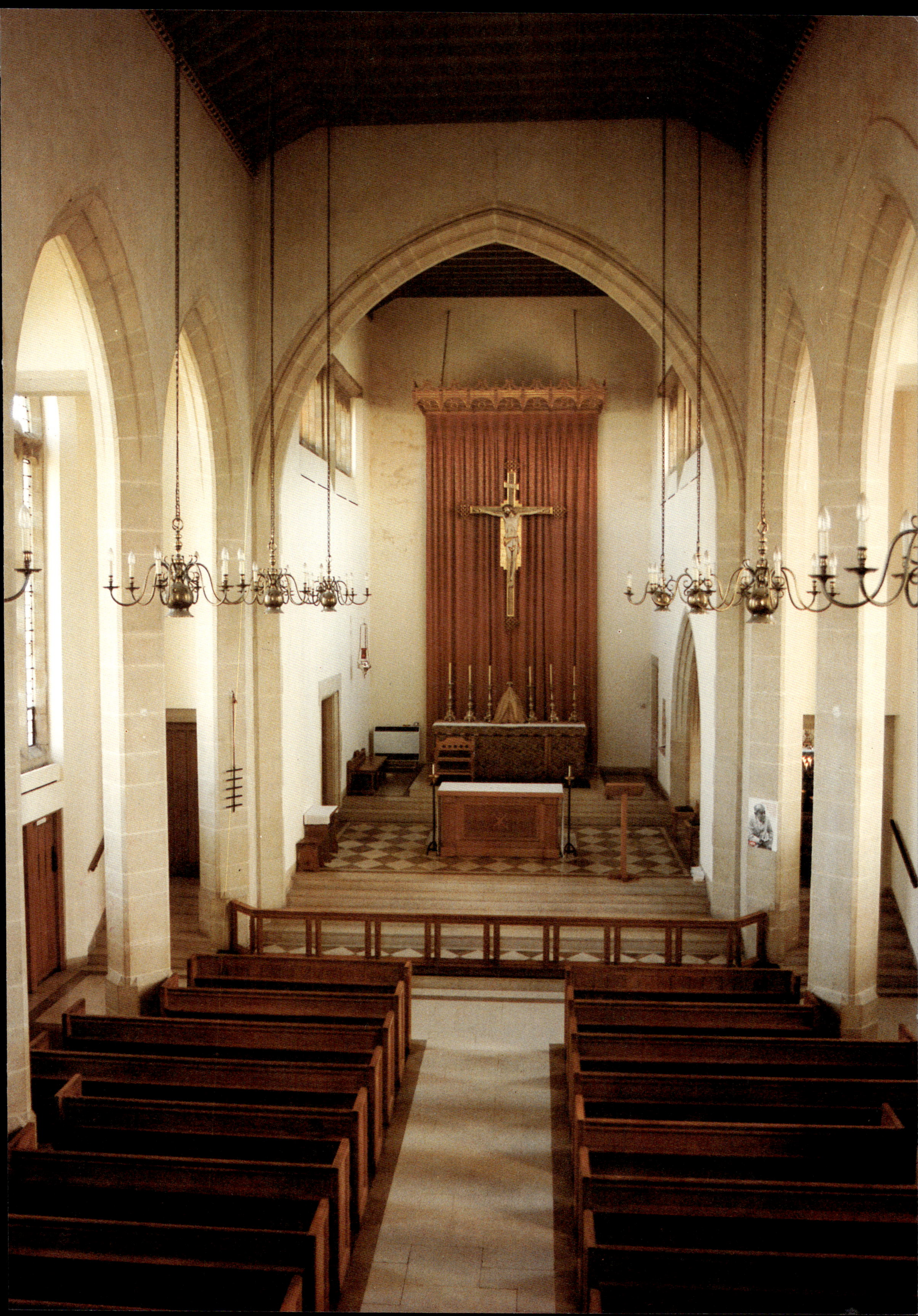

# St Benedict

Contact address of Priest:
The Presbytery, Old Mill Lane, Marnhull,
Sturminster Newton, Dorset. DT10 1JX.
Telephone: (0258) 820388.

# Gunnislake

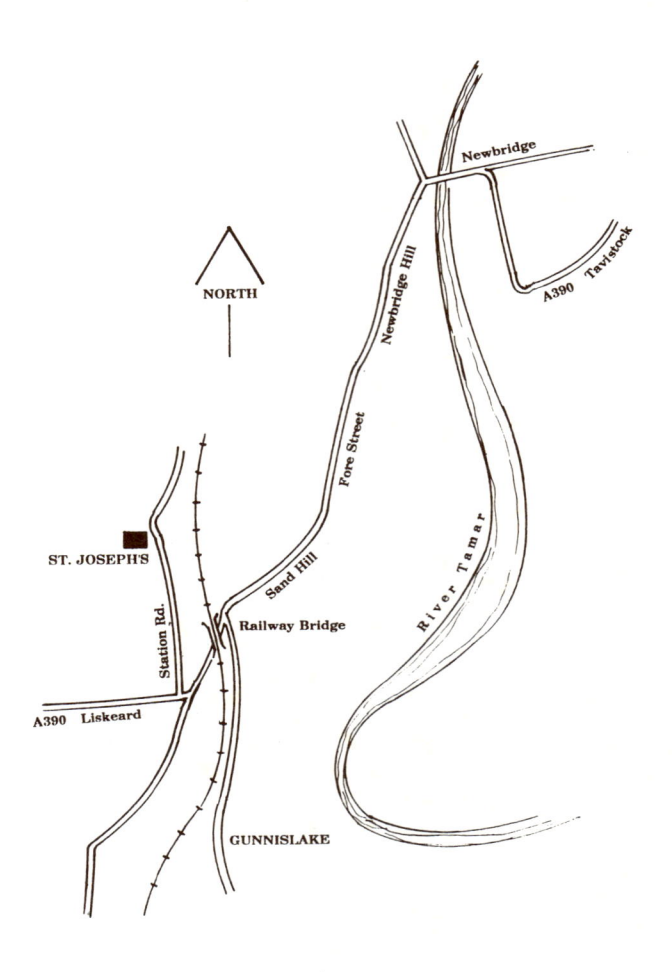

**St. Joseph's, Station Road.**

From Tavistock or Liskeard follow the A390 into Gunnislake. Travelling uphill with the railway bridge overhead turn into Station Road: the turn is on a sharp bend opposite a garage. There is a sign "Catholic Church" about a quarter of a mile down the road. The driveway is on the left. Car parking is available. The Church building is unusual. It is a triangular glass structure, designed by a musician, a former conductor of the Catholic Plymouth Choral Society.

The Church is dedicated to St. Joseph whose patronage has helped many towards the realms of sanctity. The great Spanish saint, Teresa of Avila, chose St. Joseph as the patron of her reformed Order of Carmelites. In 1689 the Carmelite Sisters were given the privilege of keeping a feast in honour of St. Joseph. On December 8th 1870 Pope Pius IX (1846-1978) proclaimed St. Joseph the patron saint of the Universal Church.

St. Joseph's Church, Gunnislake, was solemnly blessed by Bishop Restieaux on September 18th 1977.

# St Joseph

Contact address of Priest:
The Presbytery, Callington Road,
Tavistock, Devon. PL19 8EH.
Telephone: (0822) 612645.

# Hartland

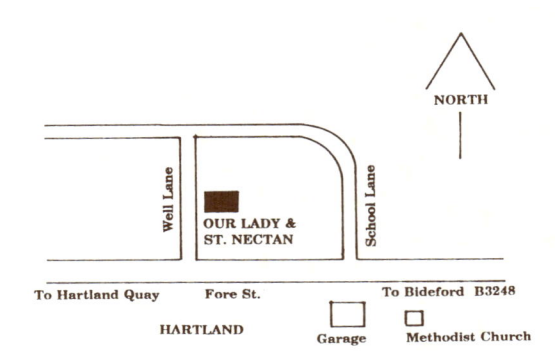

**Our Lady & St. Nectan, Well Lane.**

The area is well signposted. From Bideford follow the A39 west towards Clovelly and Hartland, from Bude follow the A39 north. Turn off the A39 on to the B3248, for Hartland, the road leads directly into the main street, Fore Street. Turn down Well Lane. The Church is situated behind Lloyds Bank. Car parking is available in the main square and at the Church in dry weather.

The dedication is to Our Lady & St. Nectan, a sixth century hermit. According to ancient manuscripts Nectan was the son of a Welsh prince, the eldest and most honourable of the family of Brychan. He became a monk then left South Wales for North Devon and settled in the Hartland area. St. Nectan lived a life of prayerful solitude in a remote wooded valley of great beauty. One day he helped a swineherd to recover some lost pigs and was rewarded with a gift - two cows! Unfortunately they were promptly stolen. St. Nectan located the robbers, forgave them and tried to convert them, but his words were ignored. The thieves beheaded him. Considerable devotion to St. Nectan developed in the West Country. The medieval parish church at Stoke, outside Hartland, honoured his patronage. Stoke also had an Abbey of Augustinian Canons which prospered until the Reformation when it became a private mansion. There are several feast days in honour of St. Nectan including 17th June and 14th February.

In 1959 Hartland was put on the list of possible Mass Centres to be visited by the Diocesan Missioner, Father Sean Mason, M.S.F.S. The first Mission Mass took place on the feast of The Holy Family in 1960 in a Catholic household. Later on other families enjoyed the privilege of providing a venue for Mass. Eventually it was decided to hire the Womens' Institute Hall each Sunday. In 1961 Father Mason set up a Church Building Committee which became immediately involved in raising funds. When sufficient money had been collected a plot of land was purchased in the town centre, in Well Lane. On 3rd December 1964 the Church of Our Lady & St. Nectan was solemnly blessed and opened by the Rt. Rev. Cyril Restieaux, Bishop of Plymouth.

Contact address of Priest:
The Presbytery, North Road,
Bideford, Devon. EX39 2NW.
Telephone: (0237) 472519.

# Our Lady and St. Nectan

# Hayle

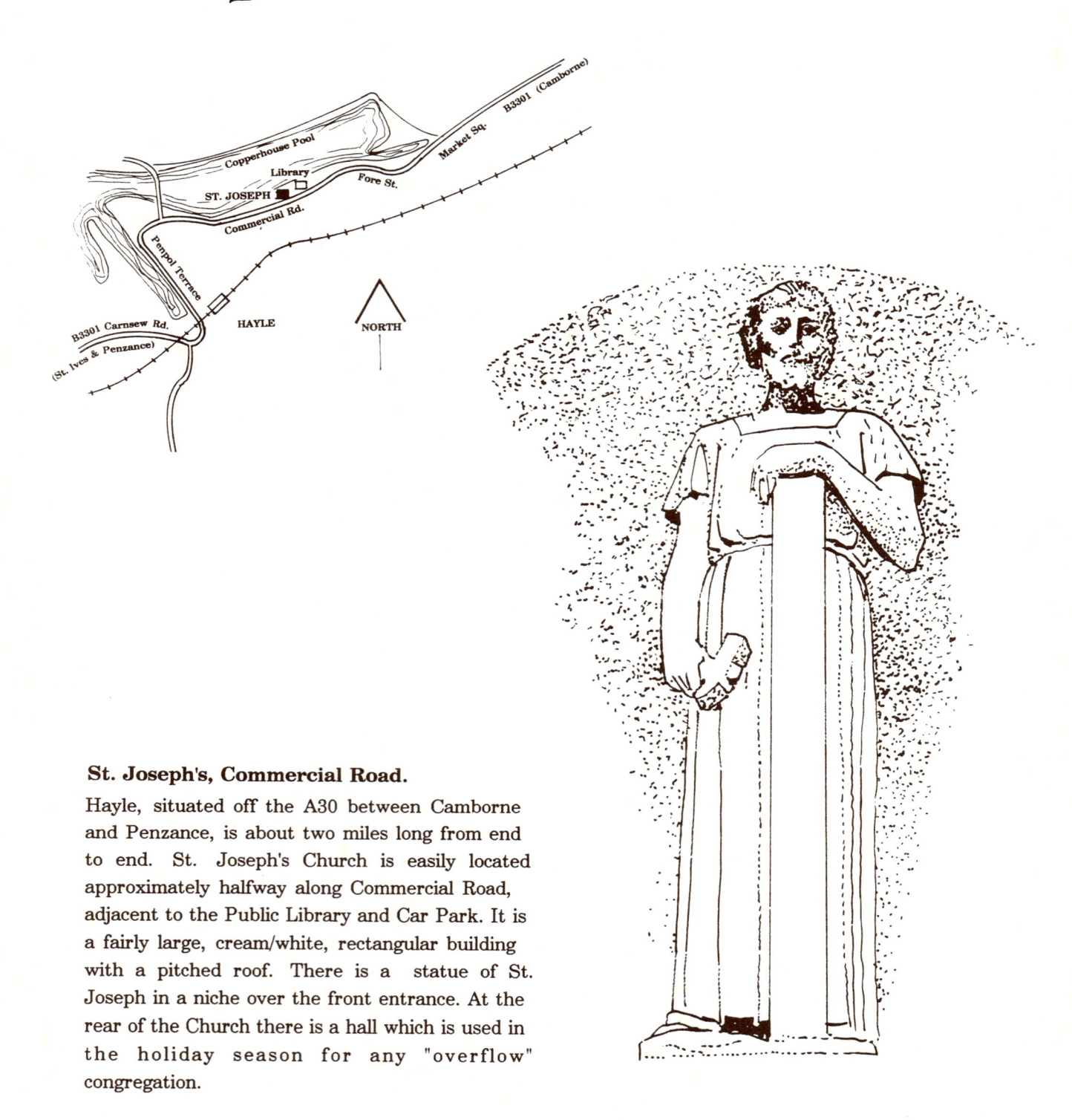

### St. Joseph's, Commercial Road.

Hayle, situated off the A30 between Camborne and Penzance, is about two miles long from end to end. St. Joseph's Church is easily located approximately halfway along Commercial Road, adjacent to the Public Library and Car Park. It is a fairly large, cream/white, rectangular building with a pitched roof. There is a statue of St. Joseph in a niche over the front entrance. At the rear of the Church there is a hall which is used in the holiday season for any "overflow" congregation.

The Church is dedicated to St. Joseph the Worker whose special feast, instituted by Pope Pius XII (1939-1958) in 1955, is celebrated on May 1st each year.

# St. Joseph

Hayle was already an established parish in the 1920's linked with the public hospital supported by a religious community. It also had connections with Perranuthnoe, eight miles away, on the southern coast of Cornwall. Former parishioners of Hayle bought a large house called Acton Castle and turned what was an old coach house or barn into a small chapel dedicated to St. Ciaran. It was served by the priest from Hayle, and, occasionally, by a visitor, the Abbot of Douai.

In 1901 a Miss Ellis, who lived with her mentally handicapped sister at the Convent in The Downs, kindly sent donations to the Bodmin Mission which prevented its closure. A year later one of the Canons Regular from Bodmin was sent as chaplain to The Daughters of the Cross Convent, Hayle. He began also to serve the tiny local Catholic population with the Sisters' Chapel in The Downs functioning as a "Parish" Church.

On 29th September 1926 Bishop Keily blessed the foundation stone of the present St. Michael's Hospital Chapel and it became officially the Parish Church, although it was not licensed for weddings.

The present Church building was erected about one hundred years ago as a Baptist Chapel. After being derelict for some time, on 11th October 1958, it was registered as a Place of Worship for Roman Catholics. A licence for weddings was also obtained. On 12th October 1958 St. Joseph's was formally blessed and opened as the Catholic Parish Church of Hayle.

Contact address of Priest:
The Presbytery, St. Michael's Hospital,
Trelissick Road, Hayle, Cornwall. TR27 4JA.
Telephone: (0736) 753123.

# Helston

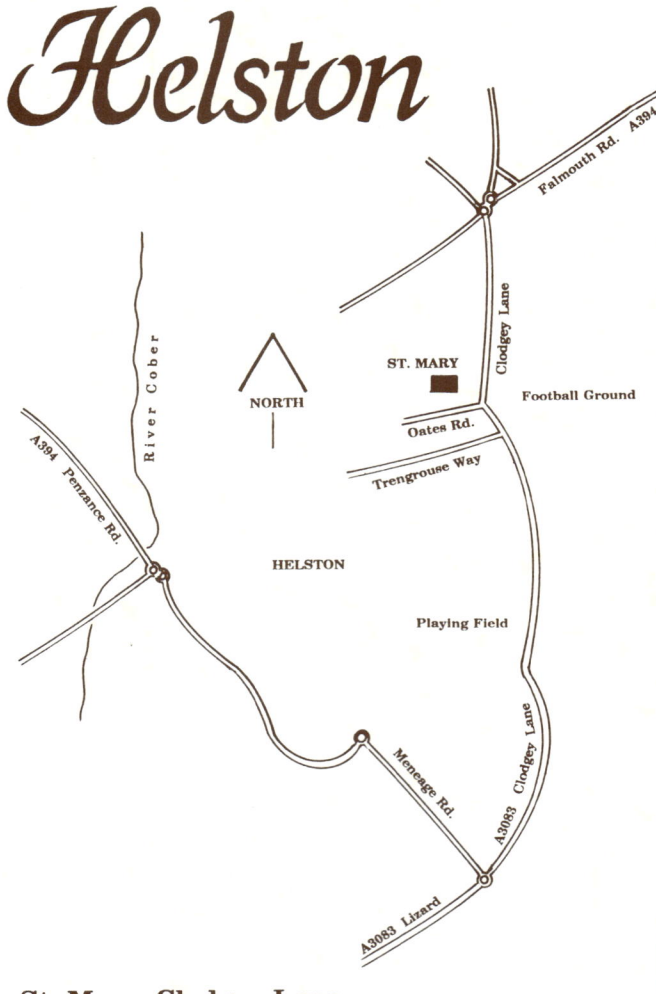

**St. Mary, Clodgey Lane.**

St. Mary's Church is very easy to find. Arriving in Helston, from Redruth or Falmouth, follow the road to the Lizard, that is "Clodgey Lane". The Church is on the right hand side of Clodgey Lane, going towards the Lizard, on top of the hill, opposite the Church of the Latter Day Saints. It is a large modern building with a pitched roof. Car parking is available at the front and rear of the Church.

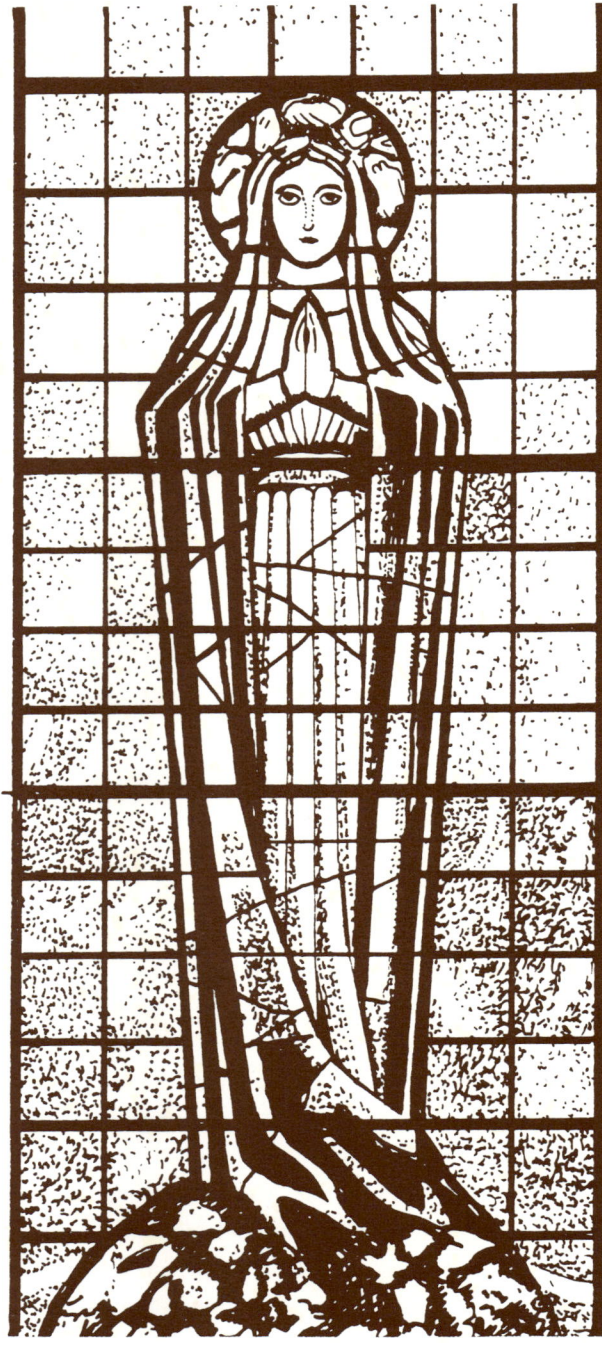

Helston Parish honours Mary with its dedication: honouring Mary it honours God her Creator. All generations indeed call her blessed amongst all women. Her life leads us to Christ and, as always, through the centuries, her patronage as the Holy Mother of God intercedes for us with the Almighty.

# St. Mary

In the 1920's a Mass centre was opened at Helston and for several years Mass was offered each Sunday in various hotels and halls in the town. When the Royal Navy, Fleet Air Arm, came to the district it became important to find a site for a permanent Mass centre. In 1953 a plot of land of three quarters of an acre was acquired for a church building in the development area of the town. The first Mass was celebrated at its opening on Easter Sunday 1955.

The new Church of St. Mary, built by Fr. Joseph Richardson, was opened by Bishop Cyril Restieaux on August 2nd 1967.

Contact address of Priest:
The Presbytery, Clodgey Lane,
Helston, Cornwall. TR13 8PJ.
Telephone: (0326) 572378.

# Hemyock

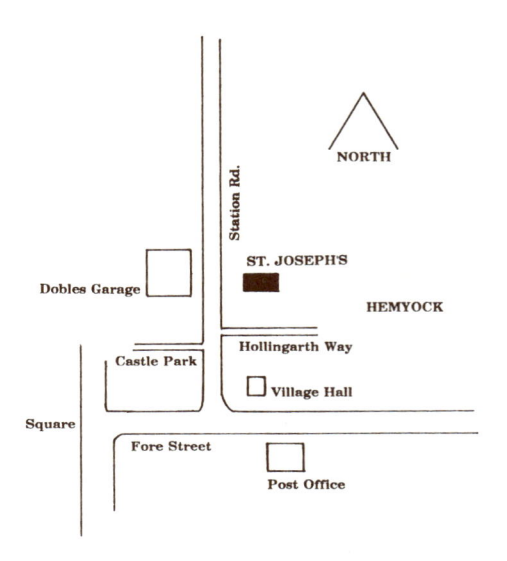

**St. Joseph's, Station Road.**

From the M5 north of Exeter, south west of Taunton, turn off at junction 27 for Uffculme B3391 then Culmstock. Turn off the B3391 at Culmstock on to the country road for Hemyock. The Church of St. Joseph is a small prefabricated Chapel situated halfway down Station Road opposite Dobles Garage. It is set back off the pavement in a small garden. A simple wooden cross can be seen at each end of the roof and above the entrance porch. Car parking is possible outside the Church grounds. A bus service operates from Hemyock to Wellington and Taunton. Trains run from Tiverton Parkway or Honiton.

The Church is dedicated to St. Joseph, the foster father of Our Blessed Lord, the husband of Our Blessed Lady. Although St. Joseph is mentioned in the Gospel early on in Jesus' life he is not referred to after the "Finding in the Temple". It seems probable that he did not live to see Christ begin His public ministry. There is no record of his death. Devotion to the saint has existed in the East since the fourth century. In the seventeenth century Pope Gregory XV (1621-1623) made St. Joseph's feast a "Holiday of Obligation", everyone had to go to Mass (not an obligatory day now). Early in the eighteenth century Pope Clement XI (1700-1721) wrote a new Office for St. Joseph's day. In the nineteenth century during the Vatican Council (1869-1870) some three hundred prelates asked Pope Pius IX (1846-1878) to declare St. Joseph Patron of the Universal Church. In 1962 Pope John XXIII (1958-1963) included St. Joseph in the Canon of the Mass. St. Joseph's feast is celebrated on 19th March and 1st May.

The Church of St. Joseph was built in 1940 by a benefactress who lived in the adjoining bungalow. Hemyock has never had a resident priest. Fr. Boucher was the first priest to serve the area.

# St. Joseph

Contact address of Priest:
The Presbytery, Shortlands,
Cullompton, Devon. EX15 1EW.
Telephone: (0884) 32253.

# Holsworthy

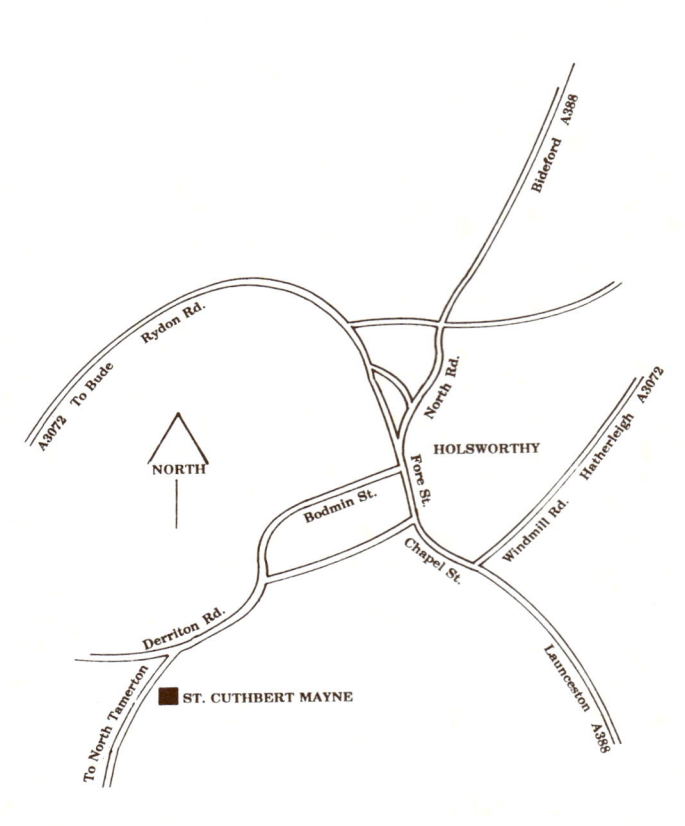

**St. Cuthbert Mayne, Derriton.**

Holsworthy is located off the A388 Launceston/Bideford, or A3072 Hatherleigh/Bude Roads. Once in Holsworthy, follow directions for North Tamerton. St. Cuthbert Mayne's Chapel is about one mile outside Holsworthy. There is a garage (Derriton Garage) on the left. The Chapel is roughly half a mile further on from there. Parking is available outside the Chapel.

Out of the forty Devonshire martyrs, St. Cuthbert Mayne was one of the two canonized by Pope Paul VI (1963-1978) in 1970. The other was St. Richard Reynolds, a Bridgettine monk, who was executed at Tyburn in 1535. St. Cuthbert was born at Youlston, near Barnstaple, N. Devon. At Shirwell, the square font can still be seen in the old Parish Church where he was baptized. After studying at Barnstaple Grammar School he went on to Oxford University where he took a degree in Arts. He became a Catholic and then sought ordination at the English Seminary in Douai in 1573. He was ordained in 1575 and became a Bachelor of Theology in 1576. Soon after Holy Orders he commenced a daring mission pastoral work in his own native part of England. He joined the household of Francis Tregian at Golden Manor, Tregony, seven miles from Truro, Cornwall. To disguise his priesthood he acted as a steward. His missionary work lasted almost two years before he was captured, together with sixteen members of the family, and locked up in the underground dungeon of Launceston Castle. He was condemned to death. Then one November day he suffered the dreadful execution, being hanged, drawn and quartered, and his head cut off and set on a pike as an awful warning to others. He was the first seminary priest to be martyred for the faith in Reformation England. A contemporary portrait of St. Cuthbert Mayne exists in the Ashmoleon Museum, Oxford. A relic of his skull remains in Cornwall, in the care of Lanherne Carmel.

# St. Cuthbert Mayne's Chapel

Contact address of Priest:
The Presbytery, 33, St. Stephen's Hill,
Launceston, Cornwall. PL15 8HP.
Telephone: (0566) 773166.

# Honiton

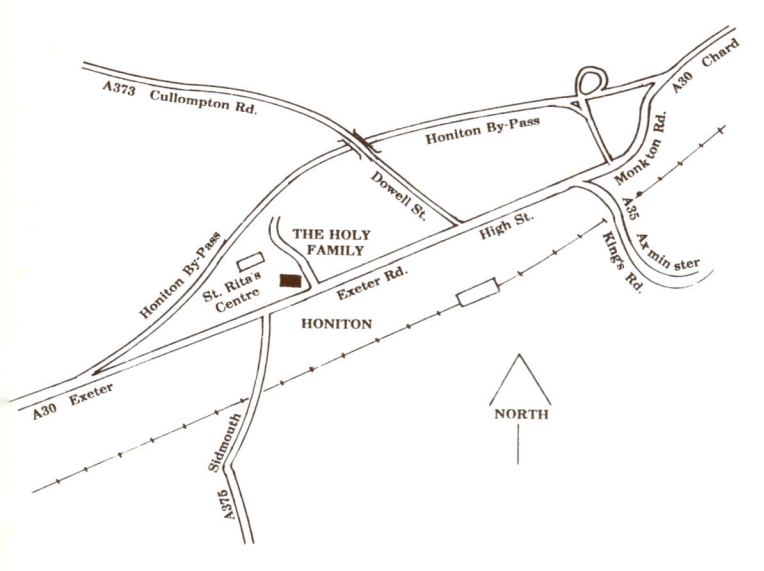

**The Holy Family, Exeter Road.**

From Exeter follow the A30, from Axminster the A35, from Cullompton the A373, from Sidmouth/Sidford the A375 into Honiton. The Church of The Holy Family is located off Exeter Road at the turning for Ottery Moor Lane, adjacent to St. Rita's Centre.

On December 6th 1819 the Hon. Colin Lindsay was born at Muncaster Castle. (He was the 4th son of James, 24th Earl of Crawford and 7th Earl of Balcarres of Scotland and the Hon. Maria Margaret Pennington, only child and heiress of John 1st Earl of Muncaster). He married Lady Francis Howard (daughter of William 4th Earl of Wicklow). In 1862 they went to live in Brighton and Mr. Lindsay started writing a book concerning the 39 Articles of the Anglican Church. In the process he decided to become a Catholic like his wife who had converted two months previously. He was received into the Church by Cardinal Newman at the Oratory, Birmingham.

110

# The Holy Family

The family returned to their home at "Deer Park", Buckerell, near Honiton in 1877 and there they founded the first Catholic mission in the area. They were fortunate enough to have a domestic Chapel with a resident chaplain. Mass was said for the first time at "Deer Park" on August 3rd 1877. A year later, another part of the house (once a private brewery) was converted into a Chapel. The first Mass there took place on September 1st 1878. Between 1880 and 1882 there was no resident priest at the "Mission". Then, from 1882 to 1886 a Rev. Canon Mitchell came from Taunton for weekend Mass. After that Bishop Vaughan asked the Canons Regular of the Lateran from Marnhull (Dorset) to look after "The Holy Family" at Deer Park at the weekends. When the C.R.L. moved from Marnhull to Spetisbury they carried on their care of the Mission.

The Hon. Colin Lindsay died in 1892 followed by his wife in the summer of 1897. The Chapel remained open until Christmas. During that time two sisters of the late Duke of Norfolk, Ladies Mary and Margaret Howard discovered a disused "Iron Church" at Herons Ghyll, Uckfield, Sussex. They kindly donated this to the Honiton Mission. Not far away from the Railway Station some land was acquired on Church Hill. The "Iron Church" was carefully transported from Sussex and re-erected, except for one bay, on this new site. The Church furnishings and altar were transferred from Deer Park and stained glass windows were added. The first Mass in the "Iron Church" was celebrated on February 10th 1898. (During the removals the Blessed Sacrament was reserved in a room on the top floor of Manor House, High Street, the home of Mrs La Batre.)

112

SANCTUS + SANCTUS + SANCTUS

# The Holy Family

In 1914 "Broomhills" was bought by Mr. & Mrs Leonard Lindsay (4th son of the late Hon. Colin Lindsay). They made a chapel in their home and were privileged to have the Blessed Sacrament reserved there. Mass was celebrated on Sundays in the "Iron Church" and on weekends at "Broomhills". A Belgian priest, Father Julius Van Heede, a cousin of Canon Ketele at Lyme, was asked by Bishop Keily to serve the Honiton Mission and also look after the Belgian refugees (World War I). Father Van Heede resided at "Broomhills" until 1919.

From 1920-1927, except for a few intervals, monks from Buckfast Abbey served the Mission. They also served a Chapel in a Catholic Convalescent Home at Ottery St. Mary (founded by the Misses Cottrell and Cortiff). Dom. Petrock Dangel said the first Mass there.

In 1931 the Lindsays retired to London and their Honiton property was handed over to Bishop Barrett for the use of a Religious Community. It came into the care of the Augustinian Recollect Fathers from St. Austin's Priory, Ivybridge and Father Mariano Ortiz travelled from there at weekends to Honiton. Easter 1934 the Fathers took up residence at "Broomhills" (St. Rita's College). They built a temporary chapel on to the College, blessed by Provost Burns on March 24th 1935. The "Iron Church" on Church Hill now fell into disuse. It was sold for storage purposes, and dismantled in 1961.

The Augustinian Recollect Fathers fulfilled their obligation to build a permanent Diocesan Church. On April 15th 1937 Bishop Barrett laid the foundation stone. Only seven months later, on November 21st he came again for the solemn ceremonial blessing of the new Church. The consecration took place on 11th September 1969.

The feast of The Holy Family is celebrated on the Sunday in the Octave of Christmas.

Contact address of Priest:
St. Rita's Centre, Ottery Moor Lane,
Honiton, Devon. EX14 8AP.
Telephone: (0404) 42601.

# Ilfracombe

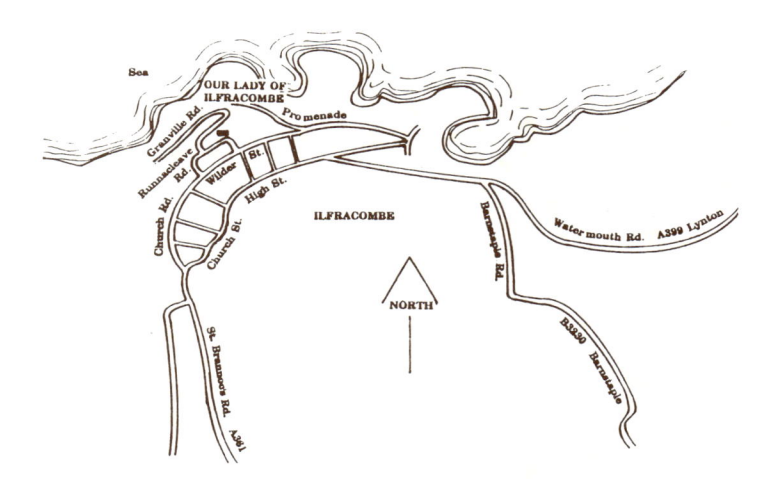

Our Lady is the patron of this parish so favourably situated on the North Devon coast. The title "Star of the Sea" or Stella Maris is a customary dedication for any town with a marine connection: fishing, sailing, shipping or trading ... Many fishing communities throughout Europe have dedicated their churches to Our Lady Star of the Sea. Here also, in this part of Devon, the Blessed Virgin's intercession is recognised and sought under a specific invocation, "Our Lady of Ilfracombe".

**Our Lady of Ilfracombe, Star of the Sea, Runnacleave Road.**

From Lynton follow the A39 then A399 from Combe Martin. From Barnstaple/Braunton follow the A361 into Ilfracombe. Coming into the town from Barnstaple turn left at the first traffic light, then left at the second set of lights. The stone Church of Our Lady is easily recognised. It has a red tiled roof and a stone "campanile" with a statue of Our Lady of Ilfracombe. Car parking is available at the Church only for Mass or devotional attendance.

The nave of the Church was built by a Fr. Bromley in 1874. Two side aisles were added in 1929. The interior contains some heavily embellished wood carvings - the work of a local craftsman. In the Sanctuary there is an ornately carved wooden reredos and separate altar depicting St. Edward, St. Swithin, St. Hugo, Our Lady of Ilfracombe, St. Boniface, St. Thomas & St. Alban. Another finely carved reredos can be seen in the Blessed Sacrament Chapel, also a most unusual silver, nautical sanctuary lamp.

# Our Lady of Ilfracombe Star of the Sea

The altar on which the first Mass was offered in Ilfracombe after the Reformation is located in the Sacred Heart Chapel. Around the Church there is a prolific and rich display of memorial windows, amongst the unusual representations are those of St. Philip, St. Alexander and St. Rosalia.

The old pulpit has been resited and carefully remodelled into an altar honouring St. Joseph. A former rood screen is now the Shrine of the Holy Cross and beside it there is a picture of the tabernacle from the Parish of Herxheim (Our Lady Assumed), Ilfracombe's twin town in Germany. Their tabernacle was constructed in 1520, in late Gothic style.

*Lord keep us happy in the faith of our forefathers and in our belief in the Real Presence (Church of Our Lady of Ilfracombe.)*

Contact address of Priest:
The Presbytery, Runnacleave Road,
Ilfracombe, Devon. EX34 8AQ.
Telephone: (0271) 863563.

# Ipplepen

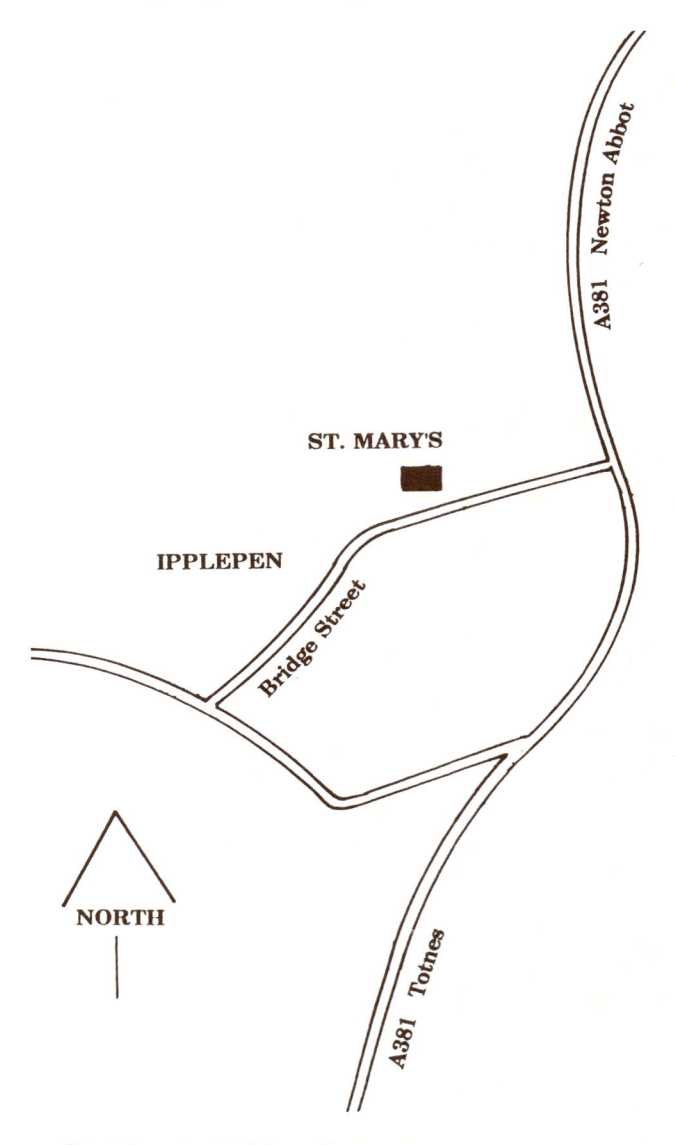

**St. Mary's, Bridge Street.**

From the Totnes/Newton Abbot Road A381, going towards Newton Abbot, turn left into Foredown Road which becomes Bridge Street. The Catholic Church of St. Mary is one hundred yards past the Methodist Church, opposite a garage. It is located off the street in a lawned garden with trees and shrubs, a pleasant setting within the centre of Ipplepen Village. There are parking facilities within the Church grounds.

The dedication is to St. Mary - our Blessed Lady. There is a very beautiful ancient prayer "Salve Regina", an antiphon which is said or sung after the Office of Lauds and Compline. It is one of the earliest antiphons to St. Mary. It was put in the Roman Breviary by Pope Pius V (1566-1572). This prayer is thought to have been composed by Hermannus Contractus, an eleventh century Benedictine monk. The final part of the antiphon is possibly the wording of St. Bernard: "O Clemens, O Pia, O Dulcis Virgo Maria" (O Clement, O Loving, O Sweet Virgin Mary).

This Church has tiled cedar wood walls and a grey slate roof with a cross on top. The windows contain obscure glass. St. Mary's Church, Ipplepen, was solemnly blessed and opened by His Lordship Bishop Cyril Restieaux on 8th May 1974.

# St. Mary

Contact address of Priest:
The Presbytery, 61, Fore Street,
Totnes, Devon. TQ9 5NJ.
Telephone: (0803) 862126.

# Ivybridge

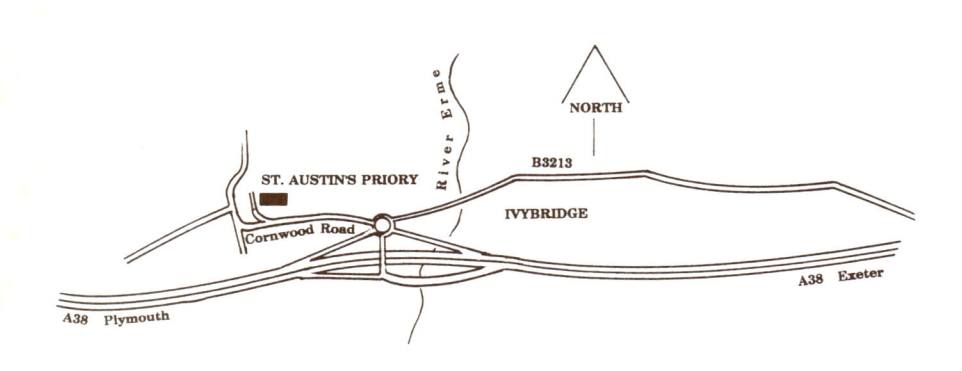

**St. Austin's Priory, Cadleigh.**

From the A38 Exeter/Plymouth Road turn off for Ivybridge. Follow the sign for "R.C. Church" and " Leisure Drive". Turn left into Cornwood Road going past the Police Station and Dame Hannah Rogers School for the Disabled. Continue until there is another "Leisure Drive" sign on the left and there turn left. Follow the country road until the notice "St Austin's Priory Catholic Parish Church" is visible on the right. There is a car park at the Priory.

Contact address of Priest:
St. Austin's Priory, Cadleigh,
Ivybridge, Devon. PL21 9HW.
Telephone: (0752) 892606.

The Church is dedicated to Austin (Augustine) of Hippo, one of the greatest names in the history of the Christian Church. Augustine was born at Tagaste (Algeria) in 354 A.D., the son of a pagan father and a Christian mother. He was brought up in the Christian faith, but not baptized. He studied rhetoric and philosophy at Carthage University and, when qualified, he taught in Rome and Milan. Austin totally rejected Christ and led an immoral life for fifteen years. Then he came under the influence of St. Ambrose, Bishop of Milan. After a long personal struggle, described in his "Confessions", one of the world's most notable autobiographies, he was converted and baptized. (The life long prayers of his mother, St. Monica, answered.) He returned to North Africa. In 391 he was ordained and four years later made Bishop of Hippo. He died in 430. As a theologian and philosopher he is outstanding among the Church Fathers. Apparently honoured as patron of theologians and printers.

# St. Austin's Priory

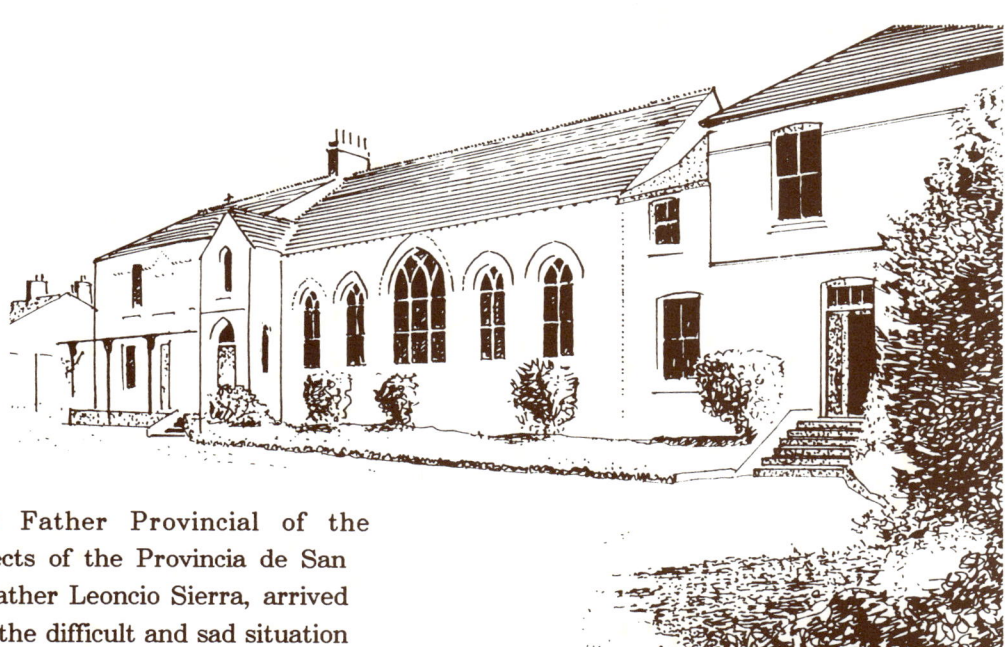

In January 1932 Father Provincial of the Augustinian Recollects of the Provincia de San Nicolas in Spain, Father Leoncio Sierra, arrived in England. Due to the difficult and sad situation in Spain he needed to find a safe retreat for his priests and seminarians. This was also a chance to make the first religious foundation of the Order of Augustinian Recollect Priests in England. So, near the little town of Ivybridge he discovered exactly what he needed, a large religious house, a convent that was up for sale. With the blessing and approval of the Bishop of Plymouth, the Rt. Rev. John Barrett, he purchased "Cadleigh Convent". It now became a monastery. On September 14th 1932 the Daily Mirror recorded the arrival of twenty-three Spanish monks at St. Austin's Priory situated on the perimeter of Dartmoor. The Recollects came from Spain, the United States and Trinidad. By the end of 1932 there was a Community of some thirty Augustinian Recollects. The Priory became a successful Novitiate and Study House. Most of the staff and students came from Spain. The Priory Chapel also continued then, as it does today, to act as the Parish Church for the local Catholic Community.

The Augustinian Recollect Order can trace its distant origins back to the early fifth century to St. Augustine of Hippo. The Recollects became a separate Order from a renewal movement within the original Spanish Augustinian Order in the sixteenth century.

St. Austin's is set in a beautiful garden, away from the busy town, a place set apart to pray.

The Priory is a large white building with the Parish Church as its central feature. It was originally "Cadleigh House" bought by the Sisters of the Sacred Hearts of Jesus & Mary in 1910. The Sisters were a French congregation founded by Marie Therese Auffray in 1821. Evicted from their convent at St. Quay in Brittany they sought refuge in Cornwall making their home at Sclerder in 1904. In 1910 the Sisters decided to move on to larger premises. They converted "Cadleigh House" into a convent founding a school and also building a large Chapel which was opened in 1913. As there was no Catholic Church in the vicinity the Chapel was also used as a Parish Church, the French chaplain serving the "Parish".

# Kingsbridge

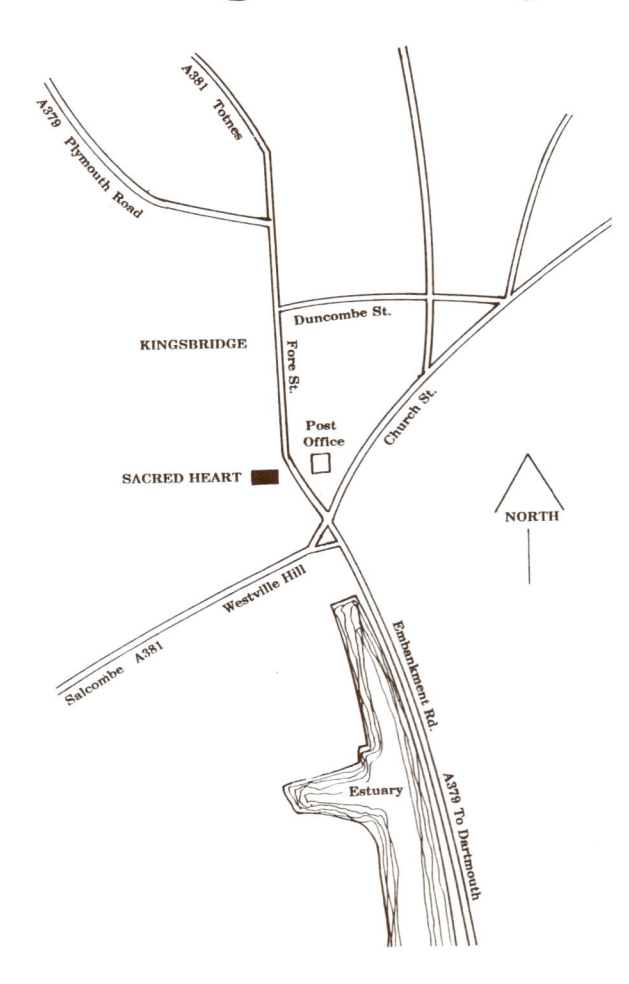

**Sacred Heart, Fore Street.**

From the A38 Exeter/Plymouth Road turn off at the sign for Ermington and then follow signs for Modbury. Continue along the A379 for Kingsbridge. An alternative route is to turn off the A38 earlier at Buckfast and follow the A381 through Totnes, Harbertonford, Halwell to Kingsbridge. The Church is easily found in the centre of the town, a small white building adjacent to the Midland Bank, halfway up the main shopping street (Fore Street). There are large car parks above and below the shopping area.

The Church is dedicated to the Sacred Heart and Our Lady of Compassion. The Sacred Heart of Jesus: a living symbol of His Incarnation, His Passion and the Institution of the Holy Eucharist. In art, the Sacred Heart is represented as wounded to remind us of the fact that God's great love for us is unrequited, ignored, or despised by so great a part of mankind. Devotion to the Sacred Heart of Jesus can be traced back to the eleventh century. St. Mechtilde and St. Gertrude are two of the early saints renowned for such a devotion. Initially prayers or praises in honour of the Sacred Heart were said or sung in private. The devotion gradually became better known and loved among the laity after Our Lord's revelations to the Visitation nuns, St. Margaret Mary Alacoque at Paray le Monial (1673-5) and Ven. Anne Madeleine Remuzat at Marseilles (1713). Pope Leo XIII (1878-1903) consecrated all mankind to the Sacred Heart in 1899. The feast of the Sacred Heart was established in 1856, it is celebrated on the Friday after the second Sunday after Pentecost.

The Church at Kingsbridge was built originally as a Quaker Hall. It was acquired 1902/3 by the Monks of Woodbarton at a time when the Catholics of the neighbourhood numbered only six or seven. Later, in the 1960's the building was extended over the old Quaker cemetery. The Home Office allowed the extension to be carried over the burial ground as long as the graves (at least a hundred years old) were not disturbed. Seventeen gravestones are preserved at the rear of the Church and at least seventeen Quaker graves lie underneath the building itself.

# Sacred Heart

Contact address of Priest:
The Presbytery, 19, Foss Road,
Kinsbridge, Devon. TQ7 1NG.
Telephone: (0548) 852670.

121

# Kingskersvvell

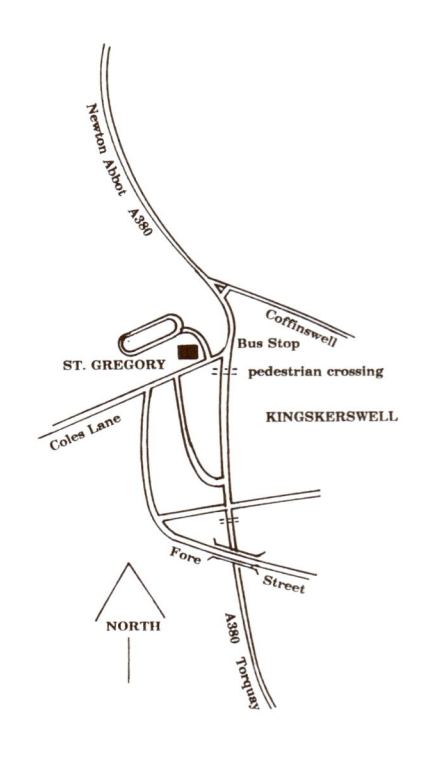

**St. Gregory, Coles Lane.**

Follow the A380 Newton Abbot/Torquay Road. From Newton Abbot, turn right at the sign "Kingskerswell" and then first right again. From Torquay take the third turning left after the road bridge over the A380. Coles Lane leads into the village of Kingskerswell. St. Gregory's red brick Church with its tiled roof and tall tower is easily identified, situated on the corner of Coles Lane and The Roundhay. Buses from Torquay/Newton Abbot stop in Priory Avenue. Car parking is available in the Church grounds.

The dedication is to St. Gregory, the patron saint of singers, scholars and teachers. He was one of the most eminent writers and leaders of the Church in the Middle Ages. He was born about 540 A.D., the son of a wealthy Roman senator. At the age of thirty three, having been deeply involved in affairs of state, the world and its problems, he renounced it all and became a Benedictine monk. However, he was not left to the anonymous sanctity of seclusion. Pope Benedict I (575-579 A.D.) made him one of the seven deacons of Rome, then Pope Pelagius II (579-590 A.D.) conferred on him the role of ambassador in Byzantium. Eventually he returned to become Abbot of the monastery of St. Andrew, once his own home, on the Coelian Hill, Rome. Gregory is remembered particularly for his interest in church liturgy. "Gregorian" chant became the plain chant music of the church. St. Gregory was the first monk to become Pope (590-604 A.D.). One of his renowned papal initiatives was the mission he gave to St. Augustine and some forty fellow monks, the conversion of the Anglo-Saxons in 596 A.D.. Gregory was so revered that he was canonized soon after his death on March 10th, 604 A.D. His feast day is kept on March 12th.

The foundation stone for St. Gregory's was laid on April 9th 1961 by His Lordship Bishop Restieaux. The Church was solemnly blessed and opened later in the year on November 9th 1961. St. Gregory's was sadly destroyed by fire (arson) on May 13th 1976. Almost immediately, however, restoration work began and Mass was celebrated for the first time in the restored Church on Sunday July 24th 1977.

# St Gregory

Contact address of Priest:
The Presbytery, 96, Queen Street,
Newton Abbot, Devon. TQ12 2ET.
Telephone: (0626) 65231.

# Kingsteignton

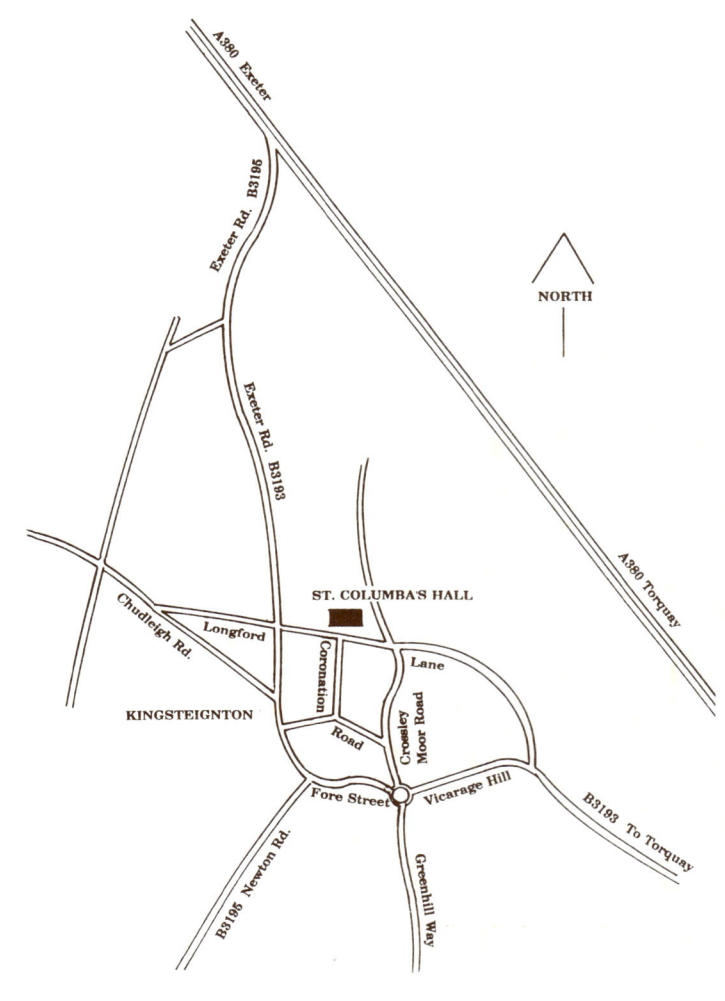

**St. Columba's Hall, Longford Lane.**

From Newton Abbot follow signs for Teignmouth/Exeter A380. From Newton Road B3195 leading into Kingsteignton turn right into Clifford Street (or Fore Street), then left into Crossley Moor Road and again left into Longford Lane. St. Columba's Hall is on the right, directly opposite Coronation Road and the Royal British Legion. It is a red brick building with a pan-tiled roof, set in a large site, a grassy field, well back from the road behind a large wrought iron farm gate. There is a bus service, 77, from the town centre. Car parking is available on site.

The patron of the Hall is St. Columba, poet, statesman, and saintly scholar of his day. The reason for his patronage is that a great deal of the work on the Hall was done voluntarily by members of the Knights of St. Columba. The saint was born in about 521 A.D. at Gartan, County Donegal, of Irish royal descent. St. Columba entered monastic life and was ordained in 546 A.D. In 549 he set off with a band of monks for south west Scotland. Authorities vary as to the absolute reason for his departure. Was it to preach the Gospel, to aid his countrymen overseas or a penance? He founded a monastery on Iona which, for a long time, was the centre of Christian civilisation in the north. St. Columba died one day in 597 A.D. just before Matins prayers. His feast is kept on 9th June.

St. Columba's Hall was opened in 1953 to serve the needs of the Catholics in Kingsteignton. The land was donated by the then Lord Clifford of Chudleigh. There is enough ground to build a church and presbytery if this becomes necessary. In the past few years the hall has been re-ordered to include a sealed off sanctuary area so that it can be used for other functions.

# St. Columba's Hall

Contact address of Priest:
The Presbytery, 96, Queen Street,
Newton Abbot, Devon. TQ12 2ET.
Telephone: (0626) 65231.

# Lanherne

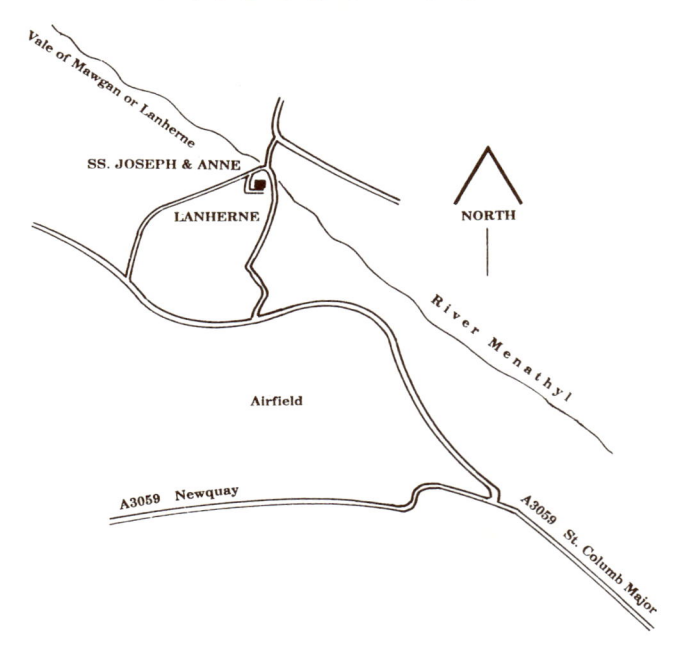

**SS Joseph & Anne, St. Mawgan.**

From the A39 Wadebridge/Truro Road take the A3059 for Newquay, then a right turn for St. Mawgan (RAF St. Mawgan nearby). The Church is part of Lanherne Carmel. The building, an ancient Manor House, is situated behind the C.of.E. Parish Church in St. Mawgan. After finding the Parish Church keep turning left, following the Enclosure Wall. This will lead to the Convent. There are signs indicating the way to the Chapel. Car parking is available at the Convent. There is also pedestrian access from the village: going up the hill from the public house, on the right, a gateway and path lead to the Convent.

The Carmelite Convent was dedicated to St. Joseph and St. Anne when it was first founded in Antwerp on 1st May 1619. Devotion to St. Joseph has existed at Carmel for centuries. Carmelite breviaries from 1480 onwards mention a special feast in his honour. The great St. Teresa dedicated the mother-house of her reformed convents at Avila to St. Joseph. However, very little is known about him, what is is contained in a few passages of the Gospel according to St. Matthew and St. Luke. Nevertheless, St. Joseph's intercession is world renowned, and two feast days are kept on March 19th and May 1st.

St. Anne was the mother of Our Blessed Lady. Although historical details of her life are completely unknown, the veneration of St. Anne can be traced back to the fourth century in the East, and the eighth in the West. In 1584 St. Anne's Day was promulgated for the Universal Church. Her patronage is still popular in Brittany and in Canada. Her feast day is celebrated with that of her husband, St. Joachim, on 26th July.

The Manor House of Lanherne was mentioned in the great survey of Manors, the Domesday Book, in 1085. It became the property of the Arundells, as a dowry gift, when Lady Alice married Sir Remphrey Arundell of Treby and Trembleth in 1231. Saint Cuthbert Mayne, the first of the Douai seminary priests martyred in the English Reformation, said Mass at Lanherne during the years 1576-1577. In 1594 Lord and Lady Arundell of Wardour gave Lanherne to a group of English Carmelite nuns fleeing from the horrors of the French Revolution. The Manor needed some repair and alteration for the Sisters. It is reported that shortly after their arrival the good ladies explored a tunnel leading from the House. They discovered it was occupied. Smugglers! The fearless ruffians fled at the sight and sound of the heavenly apparition of holy nuns in calm candlelight procession!

The Chapel of Lanherne serves as the Parish Church. It is very small, built in the style of Louis XIV, with some highly decorative features including the Bathstone altar with carved medallions depicting the Agony in the Garden, the Crucifixion and the Last Supper. Of particular interest is the Arundell sanctuary lamp. Tradition claims that it has not been extinguished since pre-Reformation days.

Lanherne is the oldest Carmel in England. Its Chapel, especially for the solitary visitor, is very much a place in which to be still, to drink in inner silence of mind and soul, and, within the beauty of silence, to find Christ.

# SS Joseph and Anne

Life's one reality,
Lord,
Is your love:
And through Carmel
You have willed
That it shine forth to men

May other hearts
Burn with this flame -
To sacrifice all for your love.

And strenghthen those
Who are already consecrated,
That from their solitude
The suffering world
may receive
The healing
Prayer
And joy
Of the Gospel.
  (Porch noticeboard at Lanherne.)

Contact address of Priest:
Lanherne Carmel, St. Mawgan-in-Pydar,
Nr. Newquay, Cornwall. TR8 4ER.
Telephone: (0637) 860205.

# Launceston

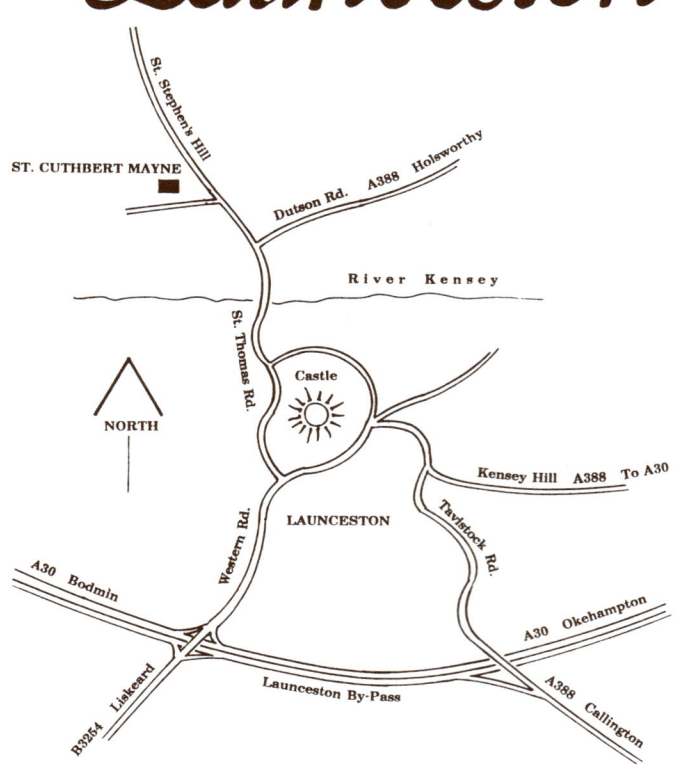

Every June Launceston is host to "The Launceston Pilgrimage", a pilgrimage in honour of St. Cuthbert Mayne martyred for the "Old Faith" in Launceston Market Square over four hundred years ago. The saint was born in 1544 at Youlston near Barnstaple, North Devon, baptized in St. Peter's Church, Shirwell on 20th March 1544. He probably attended Barnstaple Grammar School, later studied at St. John's College, Oxford where he also served as Anglican Chaplain. He had Catholic friends both at University and abroad. In due course Cuthbert Mayne converted to the "Old Faith". He entered the English Seminary at Douai in 1573 and was ordained in 1575. He volunteered immediately for the treacherous English Mission to serve "in the West Country". His priesthood lasted only two years. In 1577 Cuthbert Mayne was arrested by the Sheriff of Cornwall, Richard Grenville.

**St. Cuthbert Mayne, St. Stephen's Hill.**

The Church, containing the National Shrine of St. Cuthbert Mayne, is situated off St. Stephen's Hill, overlooking the town. Once in Launceston follow the A388 Holsworthy/B3254 Bude Road to the roundabout. Go straight on up St. Stephen's Hill. A prominent landmark is the entrance to St. Joseph's just before St. Cuthbert's Close. The Byzantine style Catholic Church is about 100 yards past St. Cuthbert's Close, on the left going up the hill. There is a driveway and limited parking is available at the site. Launceston is on the Western National bus route from Plymouth.

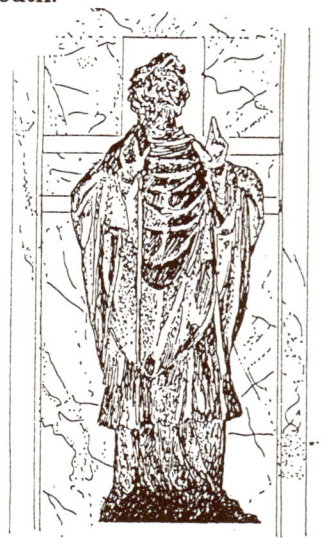

He spent three months in Launceston Castle jail awaiting trial, then was condemned and executed according to the prevailing custom on 30th November 1577. His head, set up on a pike, was reverently rescued by a brave member of the Lanherne Arundell family. Today the oldest Carmel in England, Lanherne has the privilege of posssessing a part of the martyr's skull.

Shrine of St Cuthbert Mayne

# St Cuthbert Mayne

The mission at Launceston was established in 1886 at Kensey Villa, by a convert Anglican clergyman, Fr. Charles Langdon. A year later a temporary Church was erected adjacent to the original mission (the presbytery). A permanent Church, designed by Fr. Langdon's brother and dedicated to the English martyrs, was constructed and opened in 1911. Ten years later the first pilgrimage in honour of Blessed Cuthbert Mayne was organised by the parish priest, Fr. Richard McElroy. He also set about providing a fitting shrine for the Launceston martyr in the Chapel which Fr. Langdon had built, but not furnished. An altar was installed and consecrated in the shrine in 1922. Eleven years afterwards a Lady Chapel was added on the other side of the building. In September 1935 Bishop Barrett consecrated the Church, dedicating it to St. John Fisher and St. Thomas More and the Blessed English Martyrs. During World War II the pilgrimages ceased. Various eminent church dignatories have visited the Shrine through the years, their names proudly stated on the record at the rear of the Church. In 1970 Pope Paul VI (1963-1978) canonized Blessed Cuthbert Mayne. The Church was renamed Saint Cuthbert Mayne in 1977

*St. Cuthbert Mayne you were the first of the Seminary Priests to suffer imprisonment and death in witness to the truth of the Catholic Faith.*

*Intercede for all priests that following in your footsteps they may be faithful preachers of the Word and ministers of the Sacraments.*

*Pray that others may be called by God to serve Him in the priesthood and may imitate your example in responding generously to that call.*

*Pray for all our people and obtain for them the grace to believe firmly and live sincerely the faith for which you died. Amen.*

(Prayer on the prie dieu at the Shrine of St. Cuthbert Mayne.)

Of particular interest at the Shrine is the relic of the saint's skull and the "Inspeximus", issued by the Crown to Sir George Carey in 1581, giving details of the capital charge against Cuthbert Mayne. The latter provides evidence that the saint suffered martyrdom solely because of his religion.

Contact address of Priest:
The Presbytery, 33, St. Stephen's Hill, Launceston, Cornwall. PL15 8HP.
Telephone: (0566) 773166.

# Liskeard

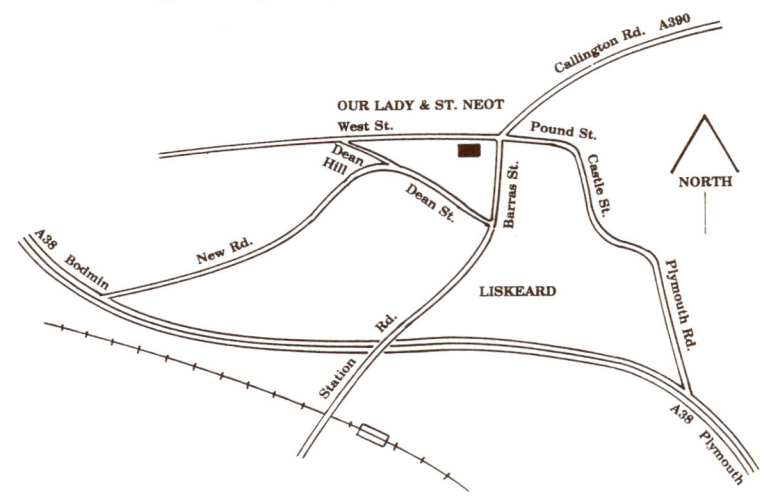

**Our Lady & St. Neot, West Street.**

Liskeard is well placed for access off the A38 Plymouth/Bodmin, A390 Tavistock/St.Austell, or B3254 Launceston/Looe Roads. The Church of Our Lady & St. Neot, a traditional stone building adjacent to the pavement, is located in West Street, opposite the Public Hall, in the centre of the town. Next to the Church is Westbourne Car Park, the main car park for the town (free parking on Sundays and weekday evenings). Liskeard is on the London to Penzance British Rail route.

The dedication to Our Lady & St. Neot is most appropriate. Devotion to Our Lady of Liskeard or Liscarret has probably existed for over a thousand years. (Liskarret, the Celtic name for Liskeard, also Liskerrett, or Lyscerruyt, incidentally, means "town with a castle".) St. Neot was born in the parish about 820 A.D. He was a relative and advisor to King Alfred whom he prompted to found Oxford University. Early chroniclers claim that he became a monk of Glastonbury Abbey, later a hermit near Bodmin Moor where he founded a small monastery. He died about 883 A.D. His feast is celebrated on 31st July.

The Church of Our Lady & St. Neot was the first in the Diocese to be built following the 1829 Catholic Emancipation Act. A helpful coincidence occurred around that time: the conversion to the Catholic Faith of Sir Harry Trelawny of Trelawne (between Polperro and Looe) and the commencement of a mission

# Our Lady and St. Neot

there. The Trelawny's French chaplain, Fr. Oleron, purchased a house in Redcow Lane (now West Street) in 1830 and this became the original foundation, sufficing as a place of worship and a school. When Fr. Oleron departed Liskeard was served by visiting priests. Eventually the Misses Trelawny handed over Sclerder Farm, Looe, to the Franciscan Order and one of the monks came to Liskeard each Sunday to say Mass.

In 1863, due to the influx of Irish miners, the Catholic population needed a larger Church. The present building adjoins the original which now acts as a small hall and overflow seating area. the design and specification of the 1863 Church were by Mr. Joseph Hansom. The first regular parish priest was Fr. George Poole of Torquay who, in later years, would reminisce on his having been forced to travel to Bodmin on horseback in order to conduct a second Mass. In the 1860's two hundred Irish miners would come to Liskeard to attend Sunday Mass.

Bishop Cyril Restieaux consecrated the Catholic Church in Liskeard, together with its new granite altar, on 17th September 1983. Enclosed in the altar are the relics of Saint Gerard Majella, also Saint Polycarp, Bishop and Martyr, there is also the seal of his Eminence Cardinal Ugo Poletti, Vicar General of His Holiness for the City of Rome.

Contact address of Priest:
The Presbytery, 2, West Street,
Liskeard, Cornwall. PL14 6BW.
Telephone: (0579) 43392.

# Looe

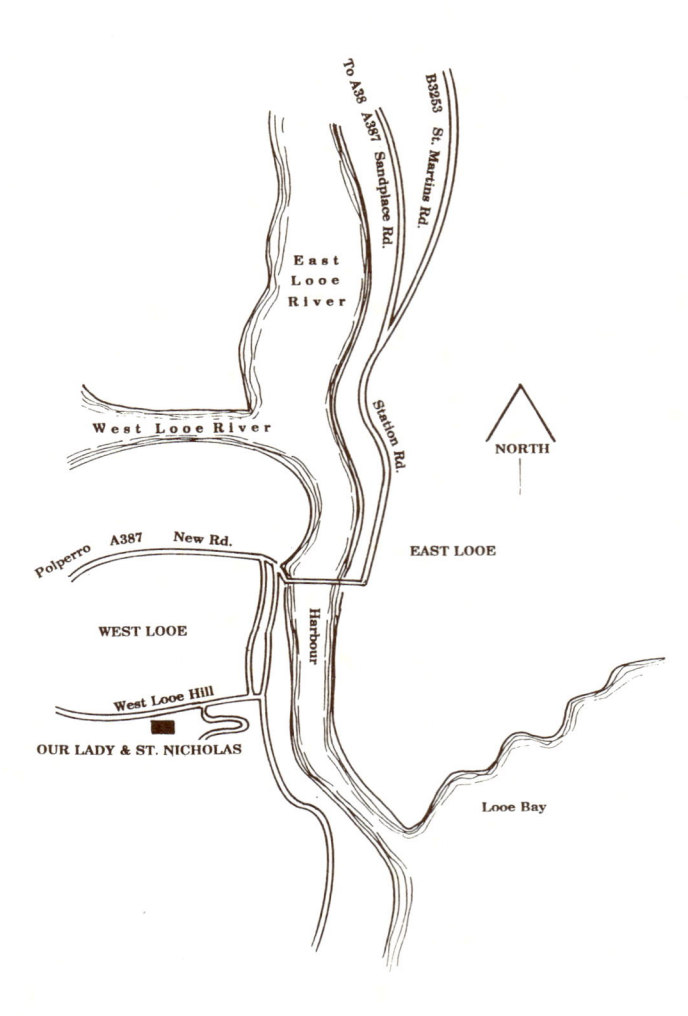

**Our Lady & St. Nicholas, West Looe Hill.**

Looe, being a popular Cornish resort, is fairly well fed with roads: A387 or B3253 from the east and B3359 from the west. The Catholic Church is situated on a steep incline, West Looe Hill, a short distance up from the quay and the Fire Station.

The Church is dedicated to Our Lady and St. Nicholas the names of two older, local ecclesiastical buildings: the thirteenth century Chapel of St. Mary near the town beach, East Looe, and the former Medieval Chapel of St. Nicholas on the quay, West Looe.

St. Nicholas, the fourth century Bishop of Myra in south western Turkey, is one of the most universally admired saints. Early artistic impressions of him include an eighth century fresco in Santa Maria Antiqua, Rome, a tenth century mosaic in Santa Sophia, Istanbul, a twelfth century mosaic in St. Mark's, Venice and stained glass versions in Chartres and Tours Cathedrals in France. In 1087 A.D. relics from St. Nicholas' Shrine at Myra were taken to Bari in southern Italy. The cult of "Nicholas" rapidly spread from east to west. Barely any historical facts about the saint's life exist, but many legends have survived the centuries. Traditional tales tell of miracles, a love for children and charity for the poor: he saved three sailors from drowning off the Turkish coast, he brought back to life three boys after they had been murdered by a butcher, he provided marriage doweries for three daughters of an impoverished nobleman to save them from worse than destitution...It is said the Myra Christians kept alive the memory of their beloved Bishop by leaving a surprise gift for a child on the night before his anniversary. Based on St. Nicholas' patronage of children "Santa Claus" emerged - now a prominent figure in the Festive Season, variations occurring according to cult and custom! The feast of St. Nicholas, patron of fishermen and sailors, is recorded on 6th December in the liturgical calendar.

# Our Lady and St. Nicholas

Contact address of Priest:
The Presbytery, Sclerder,
Looe, Cornwall. PL13 2JD.
Telephone: (0503) 72627.

# Lyme Regis

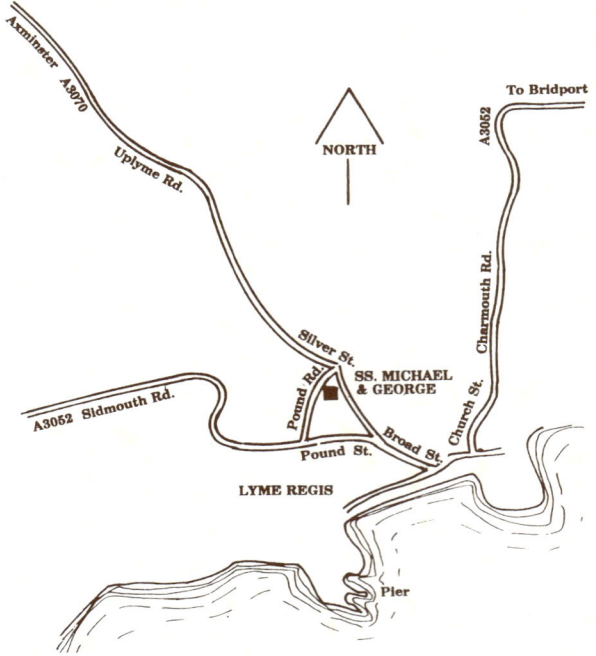

### SS. Michael & George, Silver Street.

The A3052 going east (from Clyst St. Mary, Sidford and Colyford) and the A3070 going south (from Raymonds Hill and Uplyme) lead into Lyme Regis. The A35 lies about a mile away north east of the town. From the centre, from the museum, go up Broad Street. As the road forks bear right into Silver Street. A noticeable landmark is the Baptist Church on the right corner. Continue on past the library. The Church of SS. Michael & George is further up on the left side immediately opposite "Nags Head Inn". The building is set well back from the road. Large shallow steps lead up to the path.

There is an interesting probable reason for the dedication. In 1284 King Edward I gave the town its Royal Charter. It became Lyme Regis (Kings Lyme). It then had its own official seal made depicting SS. George & Michael the Archangel. Devotion to St. George has surely existed since the fourth century made more apparent by the discovery of an ancient inscription (367 A.D.) referring to his cult in the Holy Land east of the Sea of Galilee. Pope Benedict XIV (1740-1758) officially proclaimed George as patron of England. His feast is kept on 23rd April each year. St. Michael, the Archangel, has been the special patron of the people of God, a guardian for the Chosen Race, in the Old Testament, and invoked as a healer by the Early Christians. St. Eutropius, disciple of St. John Chrysostom, declared the Archangel the special guardian of the Blessed Sacrament. The feast of St. Michael is celebrated with SS. Gabriel and Raphael, Archangels, on 29th September.

The present Church site was purchased in February 1835 and the building, designed by E. Goodridge (of Bath), started almost immediately. On 23rd April 1835 the foundation stone was laid, but not long after work ceased due to lack of funds. It recommenced in February 1836. The first Mass was celebrated

# SS Michael and George

(privately) on 27th August 1837. In 1838 a Father William Vaughan (later Bishop of Plymouth) started to build a presbytery, designed by Welby Pugin. He also built a school and purchased more land for the Church. The Rt. Rev. Bishop Baggs, Vicar Apostolic for the Western District, consecrated the High Altar on 22nd October 1844. The Altar contains relics of St. Francis Xavier and the Gorkum Martyrs (priests martyred in the Netherlands in 1572). As time went on the Church neared completion. The Lady Chapel dates from 1851 as also the Stations of the Cross. Between 1863 and 1866 the exterior of the Church was finished together with the spire and the pinnacles. Sometime between 1881 and 1919 stained glass windows of the Immaculate Conception and the patrons SS. Michael & George were placed above the High Altar. The original spire, damaged by storm, had to be removed. A new spire and belfry were erected in 1936.

Contact address of Priest:
The Presbytery, Lyme Road,
Axminster, Devon. EX13 5BE.
Telephone: (0297) 32135.

# Lympstone

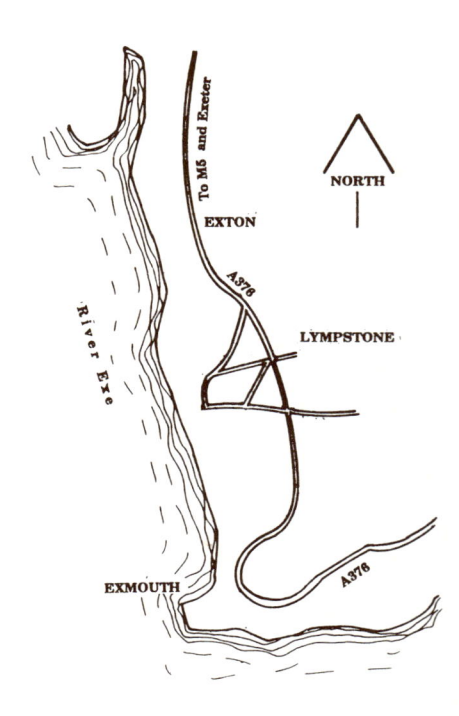

**St. Boniface, Longmeadow Road.**

From the M5, Exeter, junction 30, follow the A376 south. From Exmouth follow the A376 north for Lympstone. St. Boniface's is located in the village in Longmeadow Road. It is a pleasant little country Church, with a red tiled, pitched roof, set in its own garden. It was built in 1955. There is a carved stone statue of the patron, St. Boniface, above the entrance porch.

St. Boniface was baptized "Wynfrith", meaning joy and peace. In later years Pope Gregory II (715-731) gave him another name "Boniface", meaning one who does good. Wynfrith had met the Pope in Rome where he had gone to seek spiritual and material support for his missionary work in Frisia - the most feared domain of northern barbarians, peopled by tribes who spoke a language similar to his own, Anglo-Saxon. Wynfrith dared also to hope to reform Christianity in the mighty kingdom of the Franks (what is today much of modern France, Belgium and Southern Germany). What seemed an impossible task grew into a reality. This great Devonian not only changed the lives of a nation(s) but most definitely altered the course of the history of Europe. In doing so he readily gave away his Faith, in the end his life, most surely now in the joy of God. The feast of St. Boniface is on June 5th in the liturgical calendar.

# St. Boniface.

Contact address of Priest:
The Presbytery, Raddenstile Lane,
Exmouth, Devon. EX8 2JH.
Telephone: (0395) 263384.

# Lynton

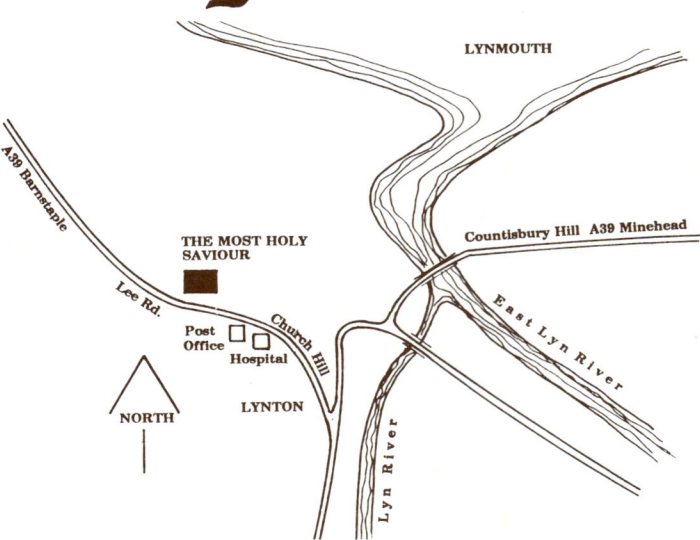

**The Most Holy Saviour, Lee Road.**

Leave the M5 at junction 25, Taunton, and follow the A358 north west; from Barnstaple follow the A39 north; from South Molton follow the B3226 then the A39; from Ilfracombe follow the A399 then the A39 east into Lynton.

The Church of The Most Holy Saviour is near the Post Office and Hospital. Family Choice Food Store is also close by as a landmark. The Church has a rendered facade, grey tiled, pitched roof and campanile. The building is attached to the Poor Clare Convent. There is an inscription above the round window on the Church front "Christo Salvatore". Lynton is served by County Bus Route 3 from Barnstaple. A local authority car park is situated in Lynton Village, and limited parking space is available at the roadside.

The Church is dedicated to the Most Holy Saviour and is privileged to contain fragments of the Rock of Calvary and of the Holy Sepulchre.

A convert Anglican clergyman, a Mgr H.V. Lean, wanted to establish a convent and church in his birthplace of Lynton. Fortunately Bishop Charles Graham had already given permission for an exiled group of Poor Clares to make a foundation in the Diocese. In 1904 Mgr. Lean was put in touch with a group of Poor Clare nuns, from Rennes (France), who were staying with the Franciscan Sisters in Woodchester, Gloucestershire. Mgr. Lean settled the nuns in a house in Lynmouth while he built a convent and chapel for them in Lynton. Construction work was completed and the buildings dedicated in 1910. The Church was later extended and consecrated as a Parish Church on 8th September 1931.

# The Most Holy Saviour

The building was designed by the architect Leonard Stokes and the style is "free" or "Italian" Byzantine. There is an eighteenth century marble altar from the disused Church of SS. Simon & Jude in Rome, also an Italian statue of the Blessed Virgin Mary which dates from the eighteenth or even possibly seventeenth century. Above the statue is the inscription:

*"Nihil ergo nunc damnationis est eis qui sunt in Christo Jesu qui non secundem carnem ambulant Deus erat in Christo mundum reconcilians sibi quem cum non videritis diligitis in quem quoque non videntes creditis."*

Beneath the High Altar there is an urn containing the remains of four martyrs. At the consecration ceremony Bishop Barrett inserted in the sepulchre, in the mensa, the relics of SS. Vicentius and Felicitas, and the decorpore relics of the Martyr Blessed John Southworth.

From the rather anonymous exterior one would not know the "hidden gem" within this place. What a rich variety of churches, indeed, exist in our Diocese.

The Poor Clare Convent is the reason for there being a priest resident in Lynton. The Poor Clares are the only Contemplative Catholic Franciscans in the Diocese.

Contact address of Priest:
The Presbytery, 45, Lee Road,
Lynton, Devon. EX35 6BX.
Telephone: (0598) 53255.

# Marnhull

**Our Lady, Old Mill Lane.**

Although Marnhull is firmly marked on the map it can take quite a while to find! It is signposted off the A30 at East Stour. Go through Stour Provost. Keep straight on. Look for a sign on the right pointing to the *R.C.Church,* Great Down Lane. Keep straight on. Look again for a sign on the left, pointing to the right, *"Catholic Church & School"*, Old Mill Lane. The Church of Our Lady is here. The search is certainly worthwhile.

This Church of Our Lady was opened on July 3rd 1832, the feast of St. Leo I, Pope (682-683 A.D.) and Confessor. It was located beside the priest's cottage, the latter originally built by a Fr. Thomas Cornworth, who arrived in Marnhull in 1725. Fr. Cornworth purchased land in Old Mill Lane and then proceeded to build a cottage with a large upstairs back room, which he converted into a Catholic Chapel for a congregation of thirty. A school was also started in 1832 for local Catholic children, situated at the end of Old Mill Lane.

This little country Church, dedicated to Our Lady is set, it seems, in splendid secrecy and seclusion in the Dorset countryside. What a marvellous place for prayer. *"Hail Mary"*.......
On a hot summer's day the sun's beams burst forth in glorious felicitous array enhancing the vision of a patch of English heaven. Horses graze in a nearby paddock and bees, in virtuous vibrato, hum into a hallowed aura of peace....."*Hail Mary! Full of grace....*"

# Our Lady

Marnhull Parish has witnessed a number of changes through the years. In 1884 the church was enlarged by the Canons Regular of the Lateran then serving the Parish. They found it necessary to extend the sanctuary in order to accomodate their Choir. They also built the Priory of St. Joseph adjacent. In 1902 the Priory was taken over by a religious order of nuns the "Filles de Jesus" and then, later on, by Cistercians, Trappistine Sisters, an Enclosed Order,

Brief mention must be made of Nash Court, the Manor House of Marnhull. In 1651 it was bought by George Hussey, a Catholic Squire from Blandford St. Mary, actually a descendant of Hubert Huse, a Knight of William the Conqueror. The Hussey family did much to promote the Faith and to protect the priesthood in the area throughout all the difficulties of the Reformation and beyond.

In 1992 the Priory no longer exists. There is just St. Mary's School and the Church of Our Lady.

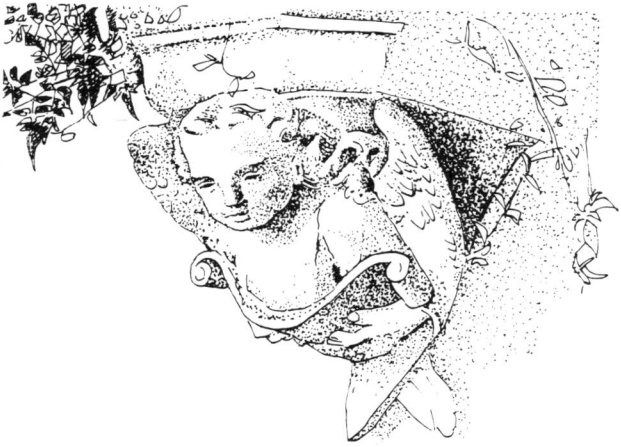

The six tapestries on the reredos are of particular note, showing the Diocesan saints (Blessed John Slade, St. Walburga, St. Aldhelm, St. Boniface, St. Edward and Blessed John Cornelius). These were made by a local artist and parishioners. They furnish a link with the old "Marnhull Orphrey" dating from the thirteenth century.

Contact address of Priest:
The Presbytery, Old Mill Lane,
Sturminster Newton, Dorset. Dt10 1JX.
Telephone: (0258) 820388.

# Mawnan Smith

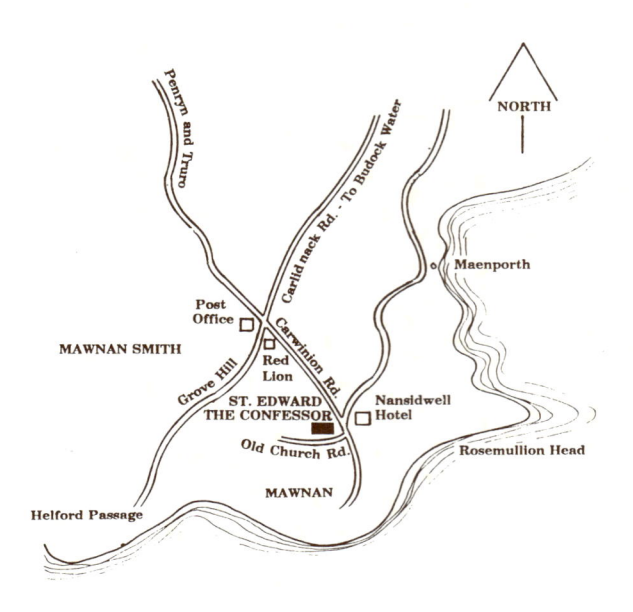

**St. Edward the Confessor, Old Church Road.**
From Falmouth follow the Coastal Road for six miles to Mawnan Smith. If travelling inland, follow the Helston Constantine Road. Entering Mawnan Smith near the Red Lion Inn and the Post Office, take the left fork into Carwinion Road and then a right turn into Old Church Road. St. Edward's, a small, modern Church with a pitched roof, is located on the right.

St. Edward the Confessor was born about 1003 A.D., the son of King Ethelred the Unready. He was educated at Ely Monastery, then lived in exile with his uncle the Duke of Normandy. After the death of the "English" Monarch, the Scandinavian Cnut, in 1042, Edward was acclaimed rightful King of England. At the age of 40, through his own example of prayer and charity, he had acquired a reputation for holiness. During his 24 year reign he made every effort to strengthen relationships between the Old English Church and the Papacy, sending bishops to Leo IX's Councils in 1049-50, and, eleven years later, receiving papal legates. It was widely rumoured that Edward experienced visions and had the power of healing: scrufulous sores disappeared at the touch of his majestic ring. He died in 1066 and was buried in Westminster Abbey. His canonization was sought in 1138, but Pope Innocent II (1130-1143) postponed any pronouncement urging the monks at Westminster to obtain more details. Eventually, in 1161, the "Good King" was canonized. The "idol of the common people" became a Saint! The feast of St. Edward the Confessor is celebrated on 13th October.

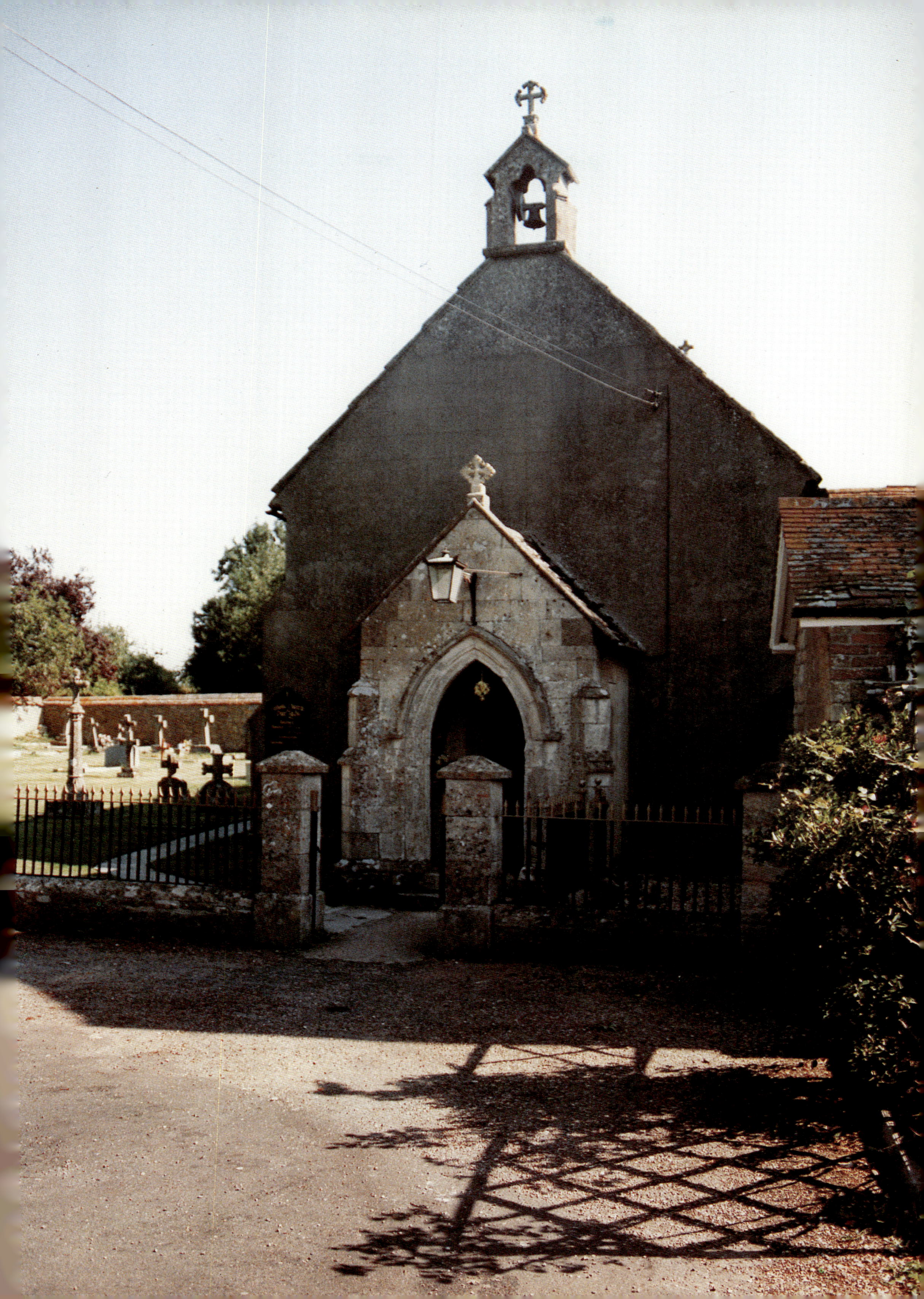

# St. Edward

In July 1952 Mawnan Catholics asked the Bishop to send them a priest to say Sunday Mass in the village Memorial Hall. He complied with their request on the condition that the congregation was never less than twenty! The number was often difficult to sustain, but within a decade, attendance at Mass had risen, sometimes to 120 residents and visitors.

In July 1962 Canon Adrian Chapple came to Falmouth from Bournemouth and was offered land for a church by a Mrs Pilgrim of Nansidwell, the gift being in memory of her husband, Edward. Parishioners and visitors combined to raise funds for a building and furnishings, including a fine stained glass window of St. Edward the Confessor which stands thirty feet above the porch. The Church was completed on 8th December 1964. The solemn opening and blessing, by Bishop Cyril Restieaux, took place on 19th December 1964 followed by a votive Mass of St. Edward. The Vicar of Mawnan, Pike Hill's Methodist Minister, clergy from Bodmin Abbey and Sisters from Tremough Convent were present at the initial celebration.

St. Edward's is ideal for parishioners living in a large rural situation, also for holiday makers visiting the Helford River Coastal area.

Contact address of Priest:
The Presbytery, Killigrew Street,
Falmouth, Cornwall. TR11 3PR.
Telephone: (0326) 312763.

# Modbury

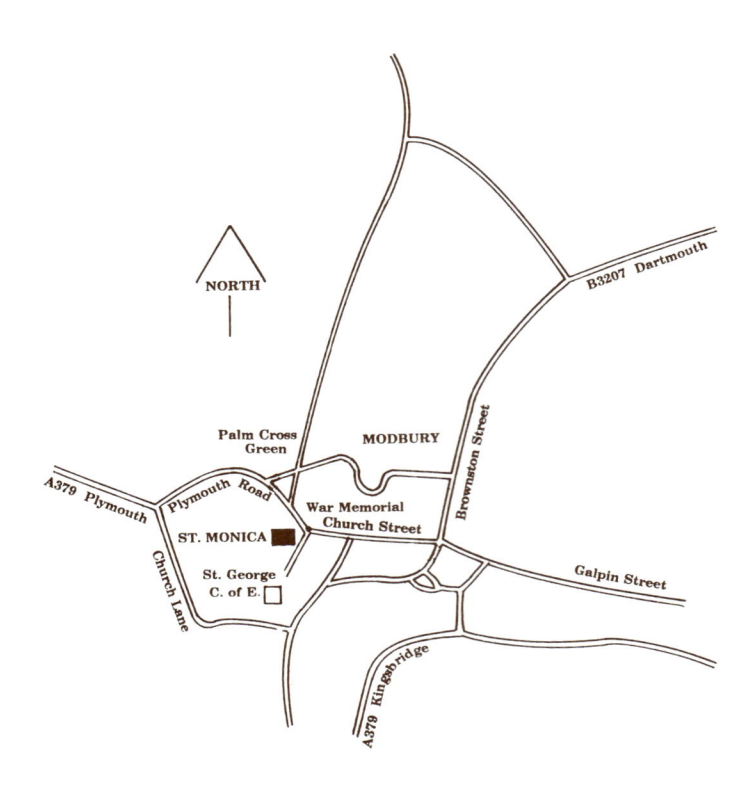

**St. Monica, Palm Cross Green.**

From the A38 Exeter/Plymouth Road turn off at the sign for Ermington. From Ermington follow signs for Modbury. On entering Modbury continue along Plymouth Road (A379) past Church Lane, on the right, and Palm Cross Green, on the left. Before the hill dips down into Modbury Village turn right at the War Memorial into Church Walk. The little driveway to St. Monica's is on the right of the War Memorial. (Beyond, to the left, can be seen St. George's Parish Church.) There is a private car park for parishioners outside St. Monica's.

The chapel is dedicated to St. Monica, the mother of St. Augustine. She was born in 332 A.D. and at the age of twenty married a pagan official, Patricius, in Tagaste (Algeria), North Africa. He was a dissolute husband and a man of violent temper, but through Monica's prayers, patience and good example he became a convert a year before he died. Their three children were Augustine, Navigius and Perpetus. Monica spent most of her life praying for the conversion of the eldest son, Augustine. When he was young she enrolled him as a catechumen, but she had to wait all her life for him to actually embrace the Faith. She suffered greatly awaiting his acceptance of Christ, arguing with him, then turning to prayer, fasting and vigils. Her constancy was eventually rewarded. Augustine was baptized in 387 A.D. together they set off for Carthage, but Monica died on the way at Ostia, the port of Rome, aged 54 years. Her feast day is celebrated on 27th August.

# St. Monica

The Church of St. Monica was built thirty years ago on the grounds of a former French Priory, which had met its fate like many others at the Dissolution. St. Monica's was built for the benefit of the handful of Catholic families in the area. In the first half of the fifteenth century there had been a Prior of Modbury. It was, therefore, quite an historic occasion when, on 23rd December 1962 the Rt. Rev. Cyril Edward Restieaux, Bishop of Plymouth, blessed and opened the new Church and presided at the first Mass said by the Prior of Ivybridge.

Contact address of Priest:
St. Austin's Priory, Cadleigh,
Ivybridge, Devon. PL21 9HW.
Telephone: (0752) 892606.

# Mullion

**St. Michael the Archangel, Meavers Road.**

From Helston take the road to the Lizard. Turn right into Mullion. The Church looks like a little white castle or fort off Meaver Road on the right. There is a large sign outside. Car parking is available beside the Church.

The dedication is to St. Michael the Archangel, for the following reason. In March 1925 the Bishop of Plymouth, the Rt. Rev. John Keily, wrote to congratulate the parish on the progress of its Church building. He asked for "the title". The parish initially requested St. Peter or St. Melor, a Cornish saint, as patron. However, these were both rejected. The Bishop suggested instead "Our Lady Star of the Sea" or the "Archangel Michael". The parishioners elected for "St. Michael the Archangel" which the Bishop affirmed on March 20th 1925.

"Michael", a Hebrew name, means "who is like to God?" In the Old Testament St. Michael is depicted as the special guardian of Israel. In the New Testament, the Apocalypse, St. Michael and angelic host defend heaven against the evil of the dragon, Satan. In Pre-Vatican II liturgy there was a prayer said after Mass invoking the intercession of St. Michael:

*Holy Michael Archangel defend us in the day of battle. Be our safeguard against the wickedness and snares of the devil....*

The feast of St. Michael is kept on 29th September.

# St. Michael the Archangel

The most southernly part of Cornwall comprising Helston and the Lizard Peninsula had no church until the 1920's. In fact, it wasn't until 1925 that a tiny Church was built on private ground, owned by a parishioner, at Mullion. Prior to the laying of the foundation stone, in January 1925 Mass was celebrated at Kenabos, the home of Miss M. Balfour, adjacent to the site of the present Church. Father Dobbeliers, from Belgium, was the priest in charge of the widespread parish of Mullion, the Lizard and Ruan Minor. On June 25th 1924 a tent 20'x12' was erected on the spot where the Church now stands and Mass was said at 8.30.a.m. every Sunday for the next three months. On September 25th 1924 the tent was moved closer to the bungalow. Unhappily, it was destroyed by fire on October 1st 1924, the result of a chimney spark from next door. After that Mass was said at Kenabos, and the Blessed Sacrament kept there until the new building was ready.

On April 5th 1925 St. Michael's Church was opened, solemnly blessed, and the first Mass was celebrated. Ten years later an extra wing was added to the Church, it included the Lady Chapel and little tower. A further extension, the Sacred Heart Chapel, was added in the 1950's.

In 1991 this cherished little church offers the pilgrim a glimpse of something different, be it a touch of character or an aura of the past. Much of the Church furniture was purchased in Belgium in 1924 so the interior has a "continental" flavour particularly emphasised by the paintings from the St. Croix Studio, Bruges.

Contact address of Priest:
The Presbytery, Clodgey Lane,
Helston, Cornwall. TR13 8PJ.
Telephone: (0326) 572378.

# Newquay

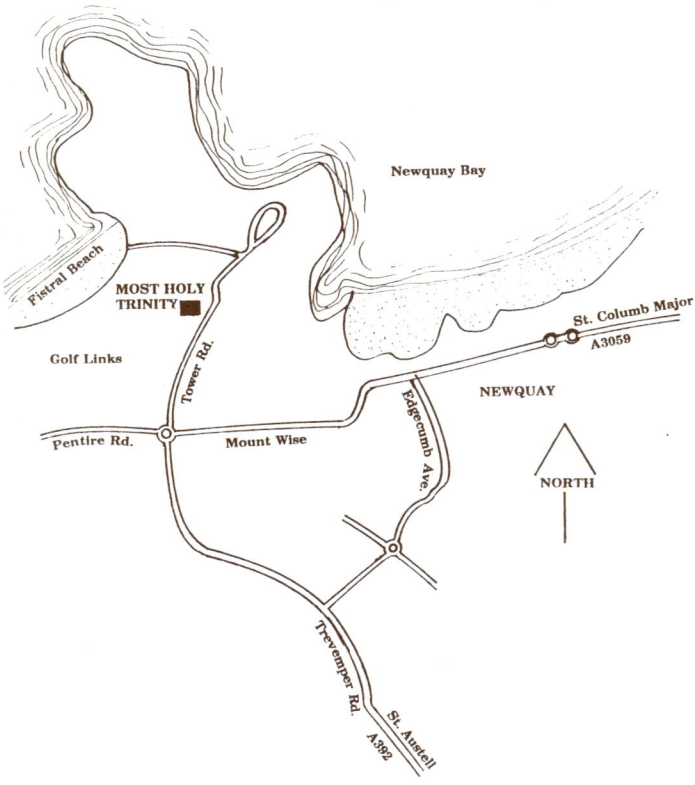

**Most Holy Trinity, Tower Road.**

From the A38 or A39 follow the signs for Newquay. Follow directions for Town centre and then Fistral Beach. The Church is easily located on the main road to Fistral Beach next to the Golf Course. A large car park is attached to the Church site.

The dedication is to the Most Holy Trinity: the title an act of faith, a reverence for the Divine Mystery of Three Persons in One God, the Father, the Son and the Holy Spirit. The reality of the Trinity is stated in the Gospel description of the Baptism of Christ in the Jordan: when the heavens opened and the Spirit of God descended in a visible form like a dove upon Jesus and a voice from heaven was heard declaring "This is my beloved Son..." Life is full of mysteries so why be surprised that the inner life of God, the Most Holy Trinity, is the deepest of all mysteries! Within the Church liturgy nearly every act of worship is performed in their name: the sign of the Cross and the Doxology are ancient prayers in honour of the Father, Son and Holy Spirit. Trinity Sunday is celebrated on the first Sunday after Pentecost each year.

There is a record of Mass being celebrated at Newquay, occasionally, in 1897, in a private chapel of "The Tower" (now the Golf Club), a house owned by Lady Molesworth, widow of Sir Paul Molesworth. Great efforts were made to organise a weekly Mass. In 1902 the Canons Regular from Bodmin agreed to send a priest every Sunday. In 1903 Lady Molesworth donated part of her estate for a Church and Miss Ellis of Hayle donated five hundred pounds for the building. With great joy on Trinity Sunday 1903 the Catholic Church of the Most Holy Trinity was opened. In 1918 Newquay was made a Parish. The Lady Chapel was built in 1935 and the Parish Hall in 1938. In 1981 the Church was extended by the provision of a narthex. Although for sometime the Parish continued to be served by the Bodmin Fathers, in 1985 it was transferred to the Diocese of Plymouth. The induction of the First Diocesan Priest in Newquay by His Lordship Bishop Christopher Budd took place in January 1988.

An interesting note from pre-Reformation Newquay: in the year 1439, Bishop Lacey of Exeter granted an indulgence to those involved in the construction, repair and maintenance of the harbour!

# Most Holy Trinity

Contact address of Priest:
The Presbytery, Tower Road,
Newquay, Cornwall. TR7 1LS.
Telephone: (0637) 872359.

# Newton Abbot

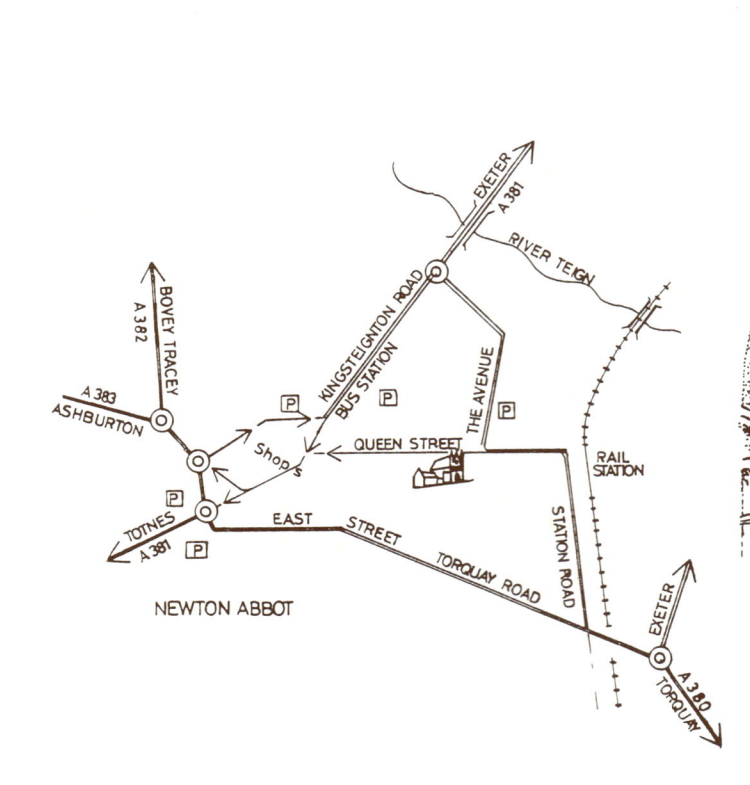

**St. Joseph's, 96 Queen Street.**

Newton Abbot is signposted off the A38 Exeter to Plymouth and the A380 Exeter to Torquay Roads. The Church is situated in Queen Street near the War Memorial, and next to Queen Street Post Office. There are local as well as long distance coaches, and a main line railway station serving the area. Parking is available in Osborne Street Car Park off The Avenue.

The church is dedicated to St. Joseph, the patron saint of carpenters, all working people, and all who desire a holy death. Information is sparse about him. A few details are found in the Gospels of St. Matthew and St. Luke. Joseph, a descendant of David, was specially chosen by God to be the earthly father of Jesus, the Son of God. He earned his living as a carpenter. Angelic visions in his sleep prompted him to protect the Holy Family by fleeing with them to Egypt to avoid Herod's murderous plotting. Later, they returned safely to settle in Nazareth. After the Finding in the Temple, St. Joseph is not referred to again in the Scriptures. His feast day is celebrated on 19th March.

The exterior of the Church is traditional, with the west gable facing the road. Below the stone cross, in a niche, there is a sculpted stone statue of the patron, St. Joseph. Over the west door there is a fine coloured mosaic, illustrating the words from St. Matthew's Gospel *"Rise up, take the child and his mother, and return to the land of Israel"*.

# St. Joseph's

Early in the nineteenth century devout Catholics in Newton Abbot had to travel to Ugbrooke or Tor Abbey for Mass. In 1861 Augustinian nuns arrived from Spettisbury in Dorset and allowed them the use of their Chapel. In 1867 Newton Catholics used a temporary chapel in a rented house in Higher St. Paul's Road. Then in the summer of 1868, the Earl of Devon sold a plot of ground to the Parish, and building began in earnest. St. Joseph's Church was first opened in June 1870, with some work still to be completed.

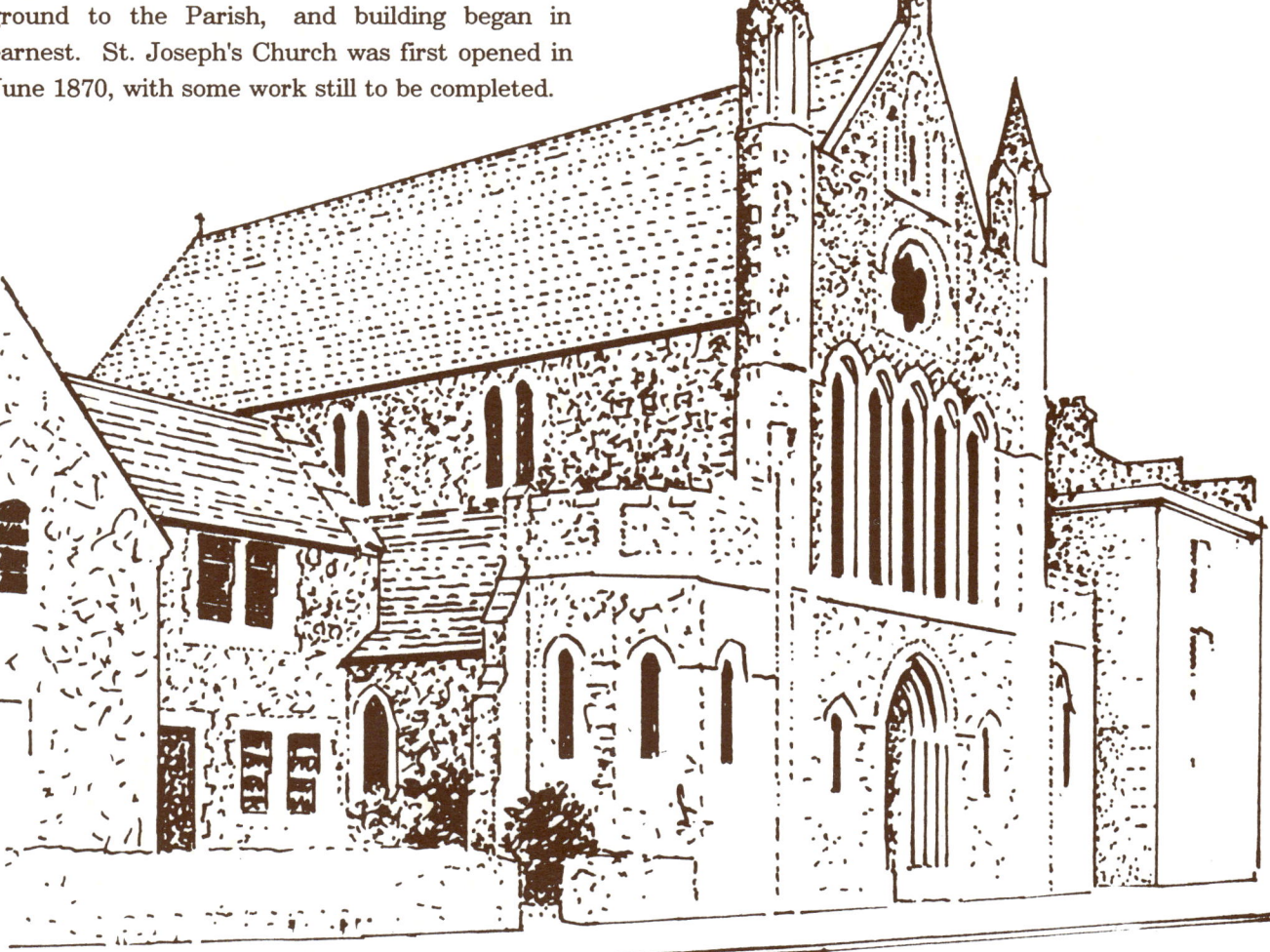

A post Vatican II re-ordering of the interior of the Church took place in 1981. There is a combination of old and new. The new tabernacle, set on the right of the Sanctuary, is cast in bronze. In an alcove on the north wall there is a modern carving in wood of the Holy Family. The older, finely detailed oil paintings of the Way of the Cross, with a large oaken Calvary as the Twelfth Station, are all relocated on the south wall.

Contact address of Priest:
The Presbytery, 96, Queen Street,
Newton Abbot: (TQ12 2ET).
Telephone: (0626) 65231

# Okehampton

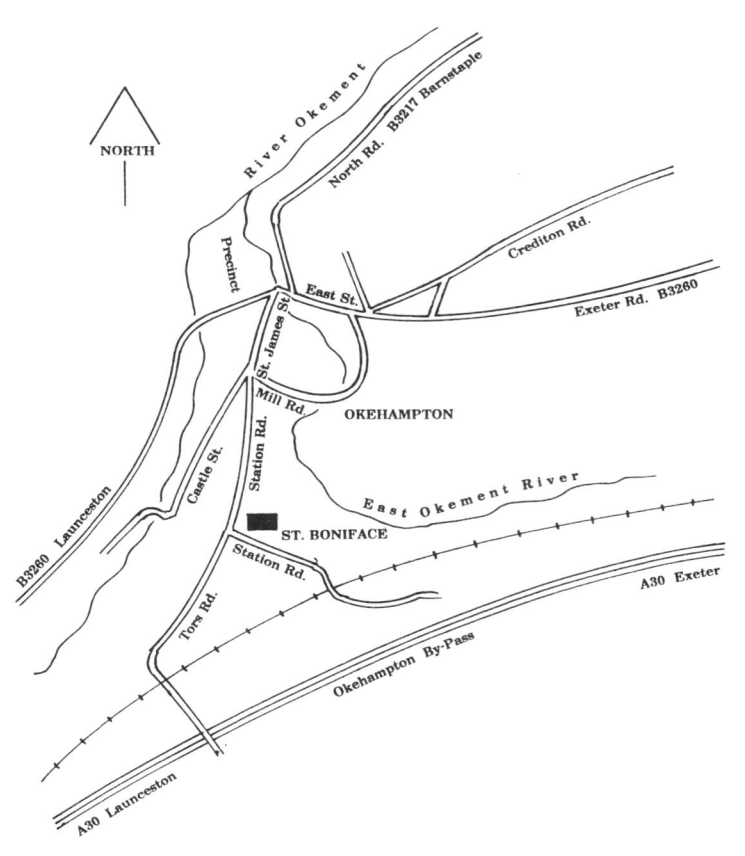

**St. Boniface, Station Road.**

From Exeter follow the A30 west; from Launceston follow the A30 east; from Plymouth /Tavistock follow the A386 north; from Bideford follow the A386 south; from Bovey Tracey follow the A382 to Okehampton. At the traffic lights follow the sign for the Golf Links. Go past the Police Station and take the second turning on the right into Station Road. The Catholic Church is about six hundred yards up Station Road, on the left, just before the fork in the road. Okehampton is on the bus route from Exeter. Car parking facilities are available at the Church.

The dedication is to St. Boniface who was born at Crediton only 18 miles from Okehampton. The saint did not forget his birthplace. When Aedhilherd, King of Wessex founded and endowed a monastery in Crediton in 749 A.D. it was attributed to the influence of St. Boniface. His significant role in the eighth century, however, was his missionary work with St. Willibrord and other selfless pioneers in Germany. The names of some of his companions have come down to us and include Lull of Malmesbury, who became his successor, Wigbert and Burchard, Eoban, his companion in martyrdom, and Sturm, who was the Abbot of Fulda where St. Boniface spent some time each year training his monks. Courageous women also joined the missionary force dedicated to the conversion of the savage northern tribes. Amongst these brave souls were Lioba, Abbess of Tauberbischofsheim (Boniface's cousin); Tecla, Abbess of Kitzingen-on-main and St. Walburga, Abbess of Heidenheim, sister of St. Willibald (who was a monk sent out to the German Mission by Pope Gregory III (731-741). The "Apostle of Germany" is buried at his monastery of Fulda. Many German churches possess his relics. The oldest surviving painting of the saint is a tenth century Fulda Sacramentary. Artists of the sixteenth, seventeenth and eighteenth centuries showed Boniface with his mitre and staff. In the same way, the saint is portrayed on the St. Boniface Banner in this Church in Okehampton. The feast of St. Boniface is celebrated on 5th June.

# St. Boniface

The first Catholic Church in Okehampton, after the Reformation, was opened in 1906. It was made of corrugated iron. The present Presbytery and Church was formerly a school. Built of granite, the exterior resembles a large house rather than a church, by coincidence a solid reminder that every church is a house, the house of God!

Contact address of Priest:
The Presbytery, 95, Station Road,
Okehampton, Devon. EX20 IED.
Telephone: (0837) 52229.

# Ottery St Mary

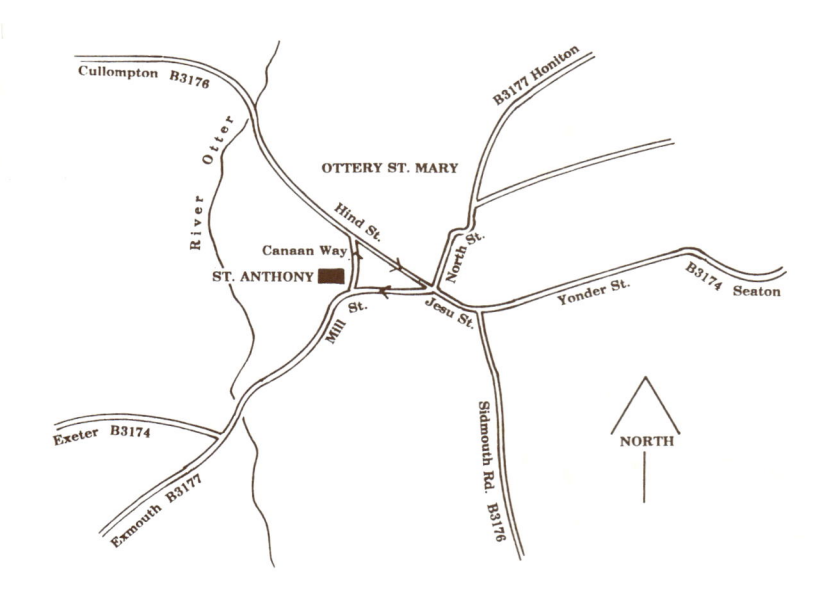

**St. Anthony, Mill Street.**

From the A30 Exeter/Honiton follow the B3176 south; from Sidmouth follow the B3175/6 north; from Seaton the B3174; from Exmouth the B3180/77 to Ottery St. Mary. The red brick Church of St. Anthony is on a corner of the junction of Canaan Way and Mill Street. It is set back from the pavement with a patio style garden alongside it in Canaan Way. The Church is on the 380 bus route from Exeter. There is a public car park in Canaan Way which is signposted, about 20 yards further down from the Church.

The dedication is to St. Anthony of Padua who was born in 1195 in Lisbon, Portugal. He joined the Canons Regular of St. Augustine when quite young. Then, being increasingly interested in missionary life and the Moroccan martyrs, he received permission to join the Franciscan Order with the intention of serving God in Africa. Due to ill health he had to return to Europe to pursue a role of sanctity. There he discovered and developed his gift for preaching. He died when only 36 years old. His holiness was so well acclaimed that he was canonized a year later in 1232 by Pope Gregory IX (1227-1241). St. Anthony's feast day is kept on 13th June.

# St. Anthony

When the Augustinian Recollect Fathers took up residence at "Broomhills" (St. Rita's College) in Honiton in 1934 they also took charge of Ottery St. Mary. Fr. Mariano Ortiz, their Superior, inspired with determination and enthusiasm for the area, organised the Church of St. Anthony to be built out of some old stables. His Lordship the Rt. Rev. John Barrett gave his solemn blessing to the Church on June 16th 1935.

Contact address of Priest:
St. Rita's College Centre, Ottery Moor Lane, Honiton, Devon. EX14 8AP.
Telephone: (0404) 42601.

# Padstow

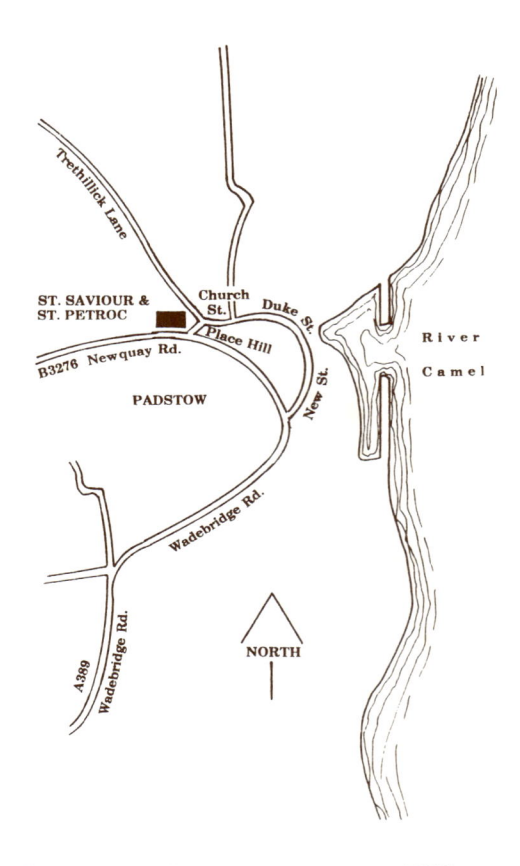

**St. Saviour & St. Petroc, Place Hill.**

From Wadebridge A389 or from Newquay B3276 follow directions for Padstow. Turn at the sign for Fentenluna. Look out for the first lane on the left beyond which it becomes one way. The Catholic Church enjoys an elevated position on Place Hill opposite the large wall of Prideaux Place.

St. Saviour is a particularly appropriate dedication for it is the dedication of the Papal Cathedral, the Lateran, the namesake of the Canons Regular who came from Bodmin and served Padstow for so many years. St. Saviour is the title too of a long defunct pre-Reformation chapel in the town. The patronage of St. Petroc is also quite apt. The saint founded a monastic church in Padstow late in the sixth century. King Alfred the Great (849-901 A.D.) inaugurated an historical record of contemporary events "The Anglo Saxon Chronicle". It was this formal document which mentioned the name Petroc's Stowe meaning the church or monastery of St. Petroc.

# St. Saviour and St. Petroc

For about fifty years Padstow Catholics worshipped in a humble wooden ediface. Then in 1962 John Prideaux Brune kindly donated a plot of land for a new Church near the site of the ancient Celtic monastery of St. Petroc. His Lordship Bishop Cyril Restieaux gave his solemn blessing to this new Church on 1st June 1975.

Contact address of Priest:
Treban, Trevanion Road,
Wadebridge, Cornwall. PL27 2PA.
Telephone: (0208) 812429.

# Paignton

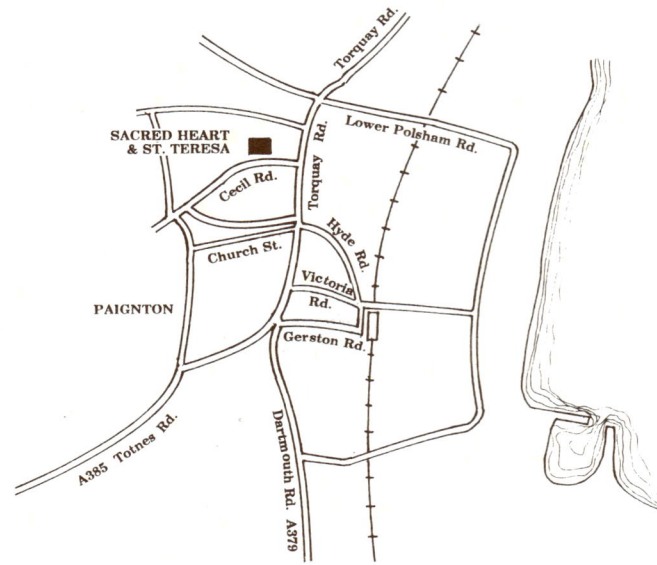

**Sacred Heart & St. Teresa, Cecil Road.**

The red brick Church of the Sacred Heart & St. Teresa is easily discovered. From Paignton town centre, take the Torquay Road, A379. Go past the Post Office on the right. Pass through one set of traffic lights. Pass through another set of traffic lights and turn left immediately into Cecil Road. Coming the other way, from Torquay, take the right turn off Torquay Road at the "milk bottle" (dummy on wall) opposite Victoria Park. The Church is on the right. There is a fire station opposite the Church. The Torquay bus stop is at the end of the road. A car park is available at the Church, just follow the large white painted arrow to find a space.

The Church is dedicated to the Sacred Heart & St. Teresa. The previous Church was also consecrated to the Sacred Heart. Devotion to the Sacred Heart of Jesus can be traced back to the 11th century. St. Mechtilde and St. Gertrude are two early saints renowned for such a devotion. Initially prayers or praises in honour of the Sacred Heart were said or sung in private. This altered in the seventeenth century when St. John Eudes composed an Office and Mass for his Order of Jesus and Mary. The feast of the Sacred Heart is kept on the Friday after the second Sunday after Pentecost.

Fr. Conran, Parish Priest between 1926-1932, put an advert in the Catholic newspapers asking for help in building the first shrine to St. Teresa in the West Country. St. Teresa (1873-97) was christened Marie Francoise Therese Martine, the last of nine children of a devout French family at Alencon. At the age of fifteen she entered the Carmelite Convent at Lisieux. Her "Little Way of Perfection" revealed in her world renowned autobiography "The Story of a Soul" has been a source of inspiration for countless ordinary people. Her feast day is October 1st.

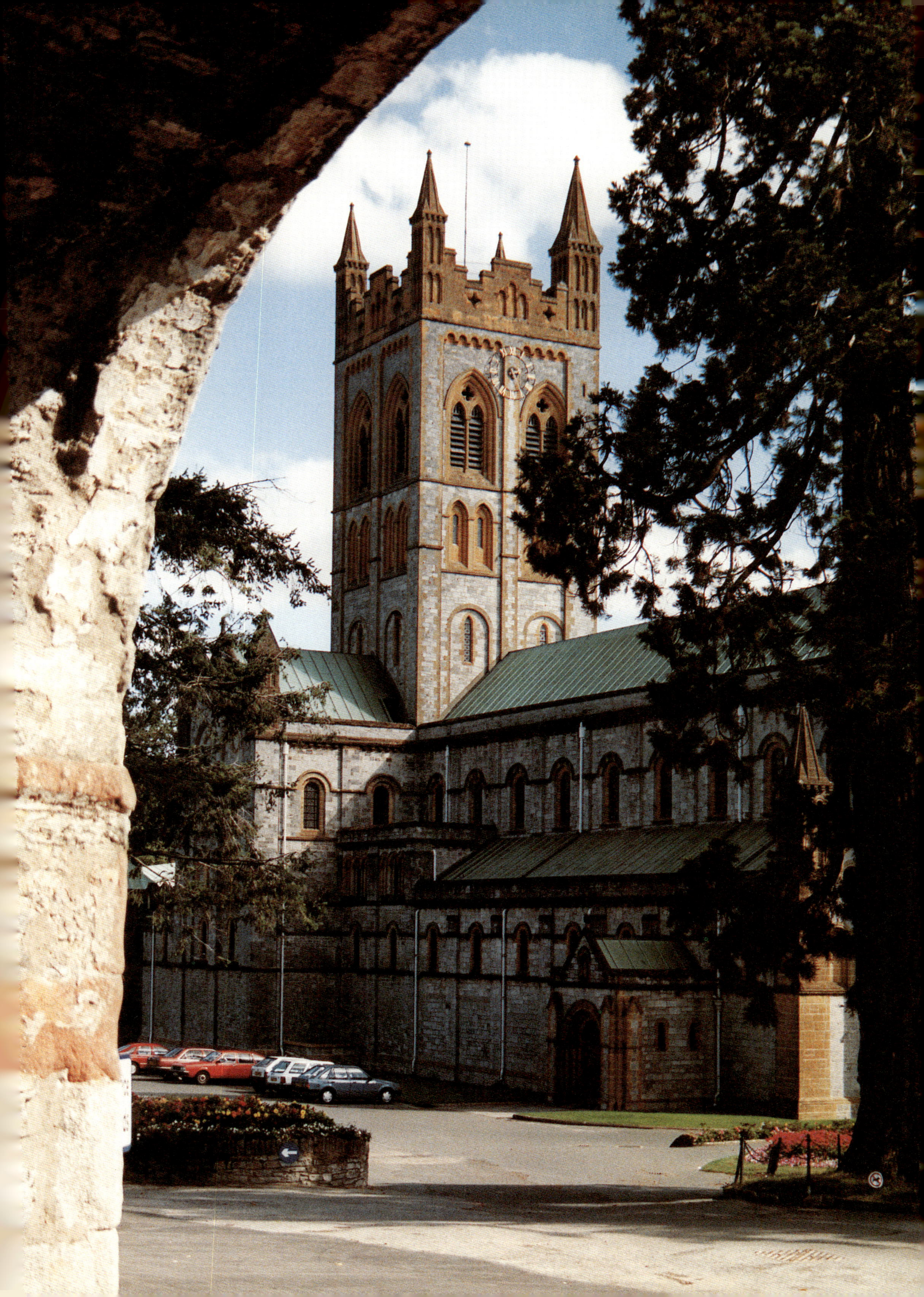

# Sacred Heart and St. Teresa

From 1660 the Chapel at Torre Abbey, owned by the Cary Family, provided the facility for Mass for Paignton Catholics. Then in 1881 the Marists built their Monastery and French Gothic style Church on St. Mary's Hill. In 1898 a temporary Parish Church was opened in Colley End Road. It was replaced by the present Church of the Sacred Heart & St. Teresa, opened on 30th July 1931 by the Bishop, the Rt. Rev. John Barrett. Particular features of this busy seaside Church include the beautiful mosaics of the Sacred Heart, Our Lady and St. Teresa above the entrance, the brick arches inside which separate the side aisles, creating the effect of a monastic cloister, and the hand carved Stations of the Cross from the Austrian Tyrol in memory of Fr. Patrick Meagher S.M.

# Sacred Heart and St. Teresa

There is also a shrine in honour of St. Peter Chanel at the west end of the north aisle of the Church. St. Peter Chanel was a Marist missionary, who, on Christmas Eve 1836 set sail from Le Havre in a small schooner. He was accompanied by a Bishop and six other Marist missionary priests and brothers all intending to preach the Faith in the Western Pacific. However, on Christmas Day, they were forced to seek shelter in Torbay from a violent storm. After a treacherous voyage lasting six months, the missionaries reached Valparaiso and from there went on to Western Oceania. Father Chanel and a brother went to live on a tiny island called Futuna. It contained about one thousand inhabitants, little more than cannibals. There they strove to live and preach the Gospel.

Father Chanel toiled for three and a half years, in spite of fever, tropical heat and storms, seclusion and failure. On April 24th 1841 he was clubbed to death and became the first martyr of the Pacific. In his lifetime he baptized a mere few, but two years after his death the entire island sought baptism! Father Chanel, Marist, was canonized by His Holiness Pope Pius XII (1939-1958) in the Marian year June 12th 1954.

*O God, who endowed St. Peter Chanel, Thy Martyr, with marvellous meekness, ardent charity and invincible courage to preach the Gospel: Grant we beseech Thee, that following in his footsteps, we may cherish until death, the faith we profess. Amen.*
*(Prayer at the Shrine.)*

Contact address of Priest:
The Presbytery, 24, Cecil Road,
Paignton, Devon. TQ3 2SH.
Telephone: (0803) 557518.

# Penzance

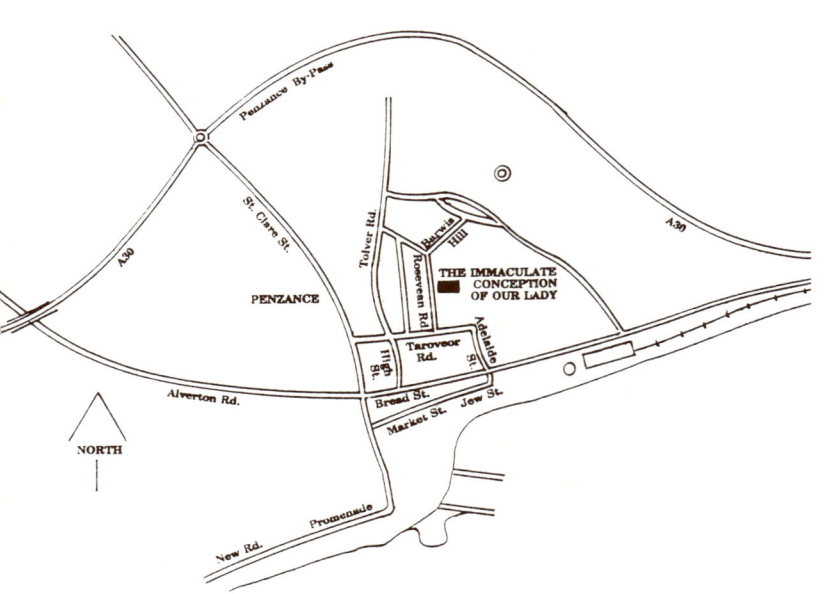

### The Immaculate Conception of Our Lady, Rosevean Road.

The A30 Okehampton, Launceston, Bodmin, Camborne route leads to Penzance then continues to Lands End. Being a popular holiday resort, both bus and train services are available. The Catholic Church is an extremely imposing, tremendous ediface adjacent to the pavement in Rosevean Road, the latter situated between Taroveor Road and Barwis Hill. The building is magnificently constructed out of large blocks of granite. A niche above the entrance contains a beautiful stone carving of Our Blessed Lady, a look of compassion and sweet maternal love on her countenance. There is no car park at the church only street parking whenever possible. Public car parks are about five minutes walk away.

This Church of Our Lady was officially opened on 26th October 1843. At that time there were very few known Catholics in the area. The dedication was probably influenced by the fact that the Immaculate Conception of Our Lady was to be defined and promulgated in 1854, by Pope Pius IX (1846-1878). It may be of some interest to know that in 1497 the University of Paris and, apparently, subsequently many other seats of learning demanded of their students an oath to defend and uphold the Immaculate Conception of Mary. After 1839 the Litany of Loreto added the prayerful invocation *"Queen conceived without original sin, pray for us."* In 1858 at the Grotto in Lourdes, S. France, Our Lady told St. Bernadette: "I am the Immaculate Conception". The patronal feast day of this Church is 8th December.

# The Immaculate Conception of Our Lady

The dignified, grandiose, lofty interior of this Cornish Church is worth a glimpse and a prayer. A new east window was fitted over the High Altar, Easter 1991, constructed in the workshops of Mr. Roy Mead of Falmouth. The new window, providing double glazing against the existing, is built up from a composite of textured water glasses from America and from various Cathedral glasses.

The Parish Priest of Penzance is also responsible for the *Mission on the Isles of Scilly*. There is a small Church of Our Lady Star of the Sea and a priest's flat on *St. Mary's*. Clergy who wish to have a holiday and say Mass for the Catholic population there are most welcome.

Contact address of Priest:
The Presbytery, Rosevean Road,
Penzance, Cornwall. TR18 2DX.
Telephone: (0736) 62619.

# Perranporth

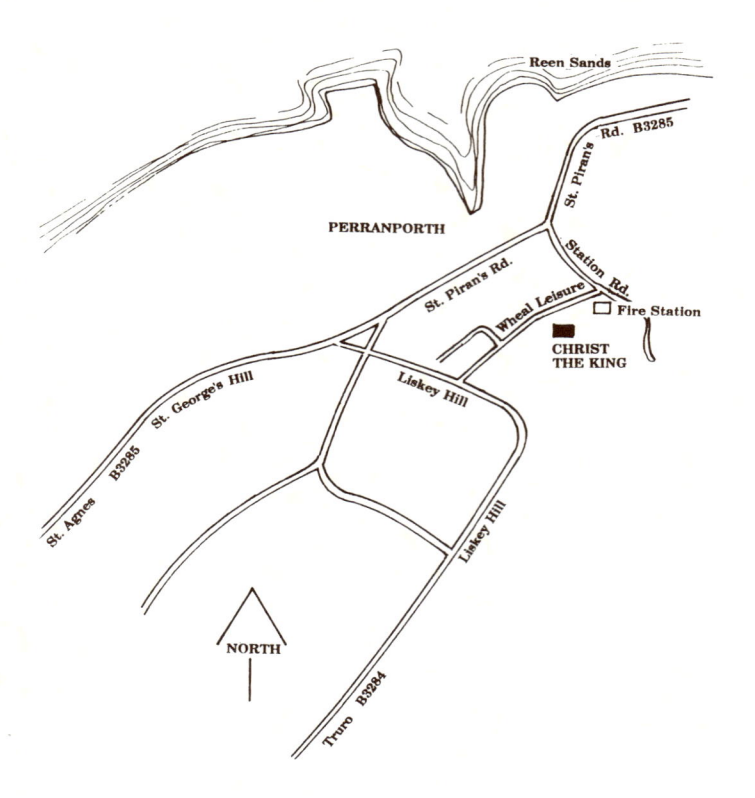

**Christ the King, Wheal Leisure Road.**

From Bodmin follow A30 south, then B3285 to Perranporth. From Truro follow B3284 to Perranporth. The Catholic Church is adjacent to the Fire Station, opposite the doctor's surgery, in Wheal Leisure Road. The latter runs parallel with the main street, St. Piran's Road. Limited parking is available but there is a large municipal car park next to the Church.

As Truro Parish already had a dedication to St. Piran - the saint of Perranporth - it was decided to dedicate the tiny Church in Perranporth to Christ the King.

At the end of the Holy Year 1925, Pope Pius XI (1922-1939) instituted the Feast of Christ the King for the last Sunday in October, close to the end of the liturgical year.

# Christ the King

Fr. John Jeffrey, C.R.L., much loved parish priest of Truro built this little timber clad Church in 1931 on land donated by Lord Falmouth. It is fairly typical of chapels built in smaller towns in Cornwall during the century to bring the Church to the people. The few Catholics in Perranporth worked hard to raise funds for the building. It contains some stained glass work from Buckfast Abbey.

Contact address of Priest:
The Presbytery, Wheal Leisure Road,
Perranporth, Cornwall. TR6 0EZ.
Telephone: (0872) 573162.

# Plymouth Cathedral

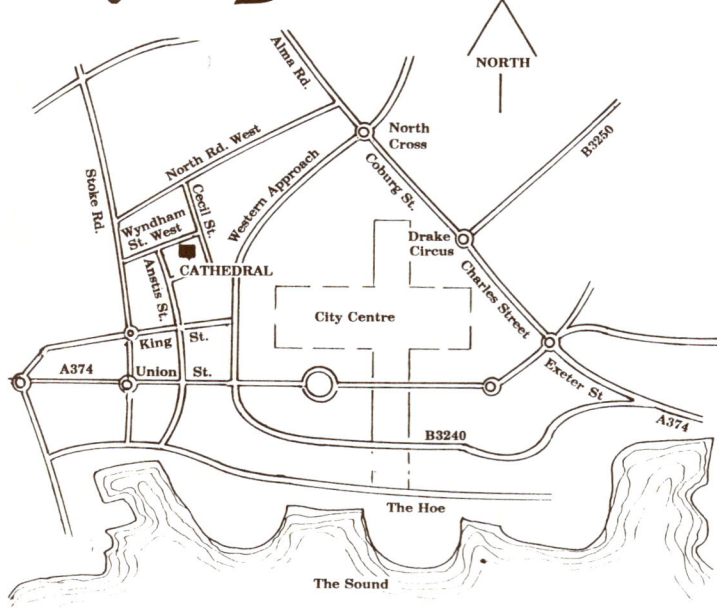

The Cathedral is at the corner of Wyndham Street West and Cecil Street, between the main North Road West and the A388 Western Approach. From Union Street in the City centre turn right into Octagon Street leading into Anstis Street. Then turn right into Wyndham Street. A clear landmark for the Cathedral is the tall spire on the tower over the North Porch, two hundred and five feet in height. The Railway Station is within walking distance of the Cathedral. There are several local buses. Cars may be parked in the Car Park at the corner of Anstis Street and Wyndham Street West, also in the Western Approach Public Car Park.

The Cathedral is dedicated to Our Lady and also to St. Boniface, Bishop and Martyr, Patron of the Plymouth Diocese.

St. Boniface was born in Crediton near Exeter about 675 A.D. He was christened Wynfrith. At the age of seven he entered the Benedictine Monastery in Exeter. After some time he went to Nursling, a larger monastery between Winchester and Southampton and at thirty he was ordained a priest. About ten years later he left the peace and tranquility of Nursling and set out to convert barbarian Europe. He joined St. Willibrord in Frisia. When he made his first journey to Rome Pope Gregory II (715-731) latinized his name to Boniface. He became the greatest of all Anglo-Saxon missionaries, the great Apostle of Germany, Bishop of Central Europe, Papal Legate and Archbishop of Mainz. He was martyred on the banks of the River Borne near Dokkum whilst waiting to administer Confirmation, aged 80+. His feast day is celebrated on 5th June.

169

When the main door is locked entry is through the south door via a walled garden. This leaves the austere atmosphere of ashlar stone, the milieu of houses and the city street, the paraphernalia of the secular firmly outside. The "garden" door leads into the Chapel of the Blessed Sacrament with its intricately carved alabaster altar, decorative canopy, ornate wrought iron screen and thoughtful crucifix: a stately shrine for the Holy Eucharist.

There is much to involve the eye and soul in this "Mother Church" of the Diocese. The slender columns and pointed arches, the very high clerestorey windows, emit a quality of transparency and peace. Over the Chancel the painted ceiling panels are worth noting. There are many beautiful stained glass windows for perusal, depicting a multitude of popular saints, including St. Francis of Assisi, St. Joseph, St. John the Baptist, St. Edward the Confessor, St. Brigid, St. Oliver Plunkett, St. George and St. Patrick.

The west wall of the nave encloses a most dignified epic in stained glass: the "Boniface Window", illustrating fifteen scenes from a daring saintly life! Stations of the Cross, on the walls of the north and south aisles were carved by Joseph Cribb of Ditchling (1958) out of stone from the quarries at Beer. The same quarries supplied stone for Exeter Cathedral centuries ago. Music enthusiasts will find the Cathedral organ interesting. It was built by Elliott in 1799 originally for the Church in St. Martin-in-the-Fields and used by the famous composer Handel.

The Lady Chapel, in the Sanctuary, behind the High Altar, also contains magnificent stained glass and there is a very fine carved reredos beneath Mary's statue. The stained windows portray the fifteen Mysteries of the Rosary: the whole history of salvation from the announcement of Christ's birth to Mary to the ineffable joy of heaven united with Him. The glorious blue tones of glass, "Mary's colour", predominate and enhance the chapel with its calm appeal to meditate and pray.

# St. Mary and St. Boniface.

The Cathedral was designed by Charles and Joseph Hansom (of Hansom Cab fame). it was opened on 25th March, "Lady Day", 1858. Remarkably that was the very same day that St. Bernadette, in Lourdes, heard the Lady say, "I am the Immaculate Conception". The Cathedral is dedicated to Our Lady under that title. The Cathedral building was founded by Bishop William Vaughan. He was the nephew of Cardinal Thomas Weld of Lulworth (Dorset) and the uncle of Cardinal Herbert Vaughan, the founder of Westminster Cathedral.

Contact address of Priest:
Cathedral House, 45, Cecil Street,
Plymouth, Devon. PL1 5HW.
Telephone: (0752) 662537.

# Plymouth

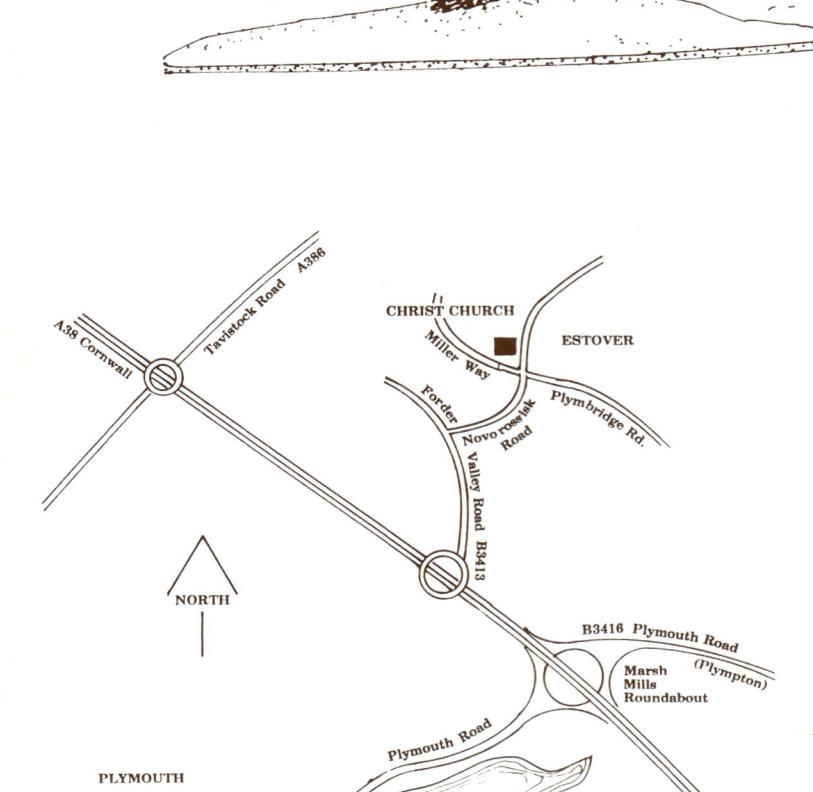

**Christ Church, Estover.**

Christ Church is situated on top of a hill, off Novorossisk Road B3432. From Tavistock Road A386 turn on to the Plymbridge Road B3432. Take a right turn into Novorossisk Road. From Marsh Mills Roundabout follow the Forder Valley Road B3413 for Estover. Take a right turn into Novorossisk Road. There is a large sign "Estover Shopping Centre". Turn down by the sign into Miller Way. The Church is a square shaped brick building and forms part of a complex which includes the Asda Supermarket, shops and the Elm Community Centre. There are ample car parking facilities.

The Church is dedicated to Christ. People, rich or poor, healthy or sick, saint or sinner, are gathered together in unity with the Father, the Son and the Holy Spirit. They believe in Christ and follow Him. Hierarchy and members live joined together around Christ according to His words: *"Where two or three are gathered together in my name, there am I in the midst of them".*

# Christ Church

Christ Church was built in 1980 as an Ecumenical Church to cover the areas of Estover, Thornbury, Leigham and Mainstone. It was an exciting step forward in religious co-operation in this part of Plymouth having been organised by the local Catholic, Anglican, Methodist and Baptist Authorities. There is an underground font for Baptism by immersion. The dedication service was one in which not only the building but also the people dedicated themselves to the service of Almighty God.

The Dedication of Christ Church, Estover took place on September 7th 1980. The following Religious Leaders were involved in the ceremony: the Rt. Rev. Cyril Restieaux, Catholic Bishop of Plymouth, the Rt. Rev. Eric Mercer, Anglican Bishop of Exeter, the Rev. Amos Cresswell, Chairman of the Plymouth and Exeter District of the Methodist Church and the Rev. Ronald Cowley, Superintendent of the Western Area of the Baptist Union of Great Britain and Northern Ireland.

In the Blessed Sacrament Chapel there is a large stained glass window designed and made by the Benedictine monks of Buckfast Abbey:

*The theme of the design is "Christian Unity"*
*"That they may be one as I and the Father are one" (St. John)*
*The strands of the woven pattern suggest the different denominations being knit together in the purpose - the worship of God. All the lines of the design lead up to the Alpha and Omega, the symbol of Divinity, the beginning and the end of all Christian Worship.*

Contact address of Priest:
St. Peter's Presbytery, Tavistock Road, Crownhill, Plymouth. PL5 3AX.
Telephone: (0752) 701660.

# Plymouth

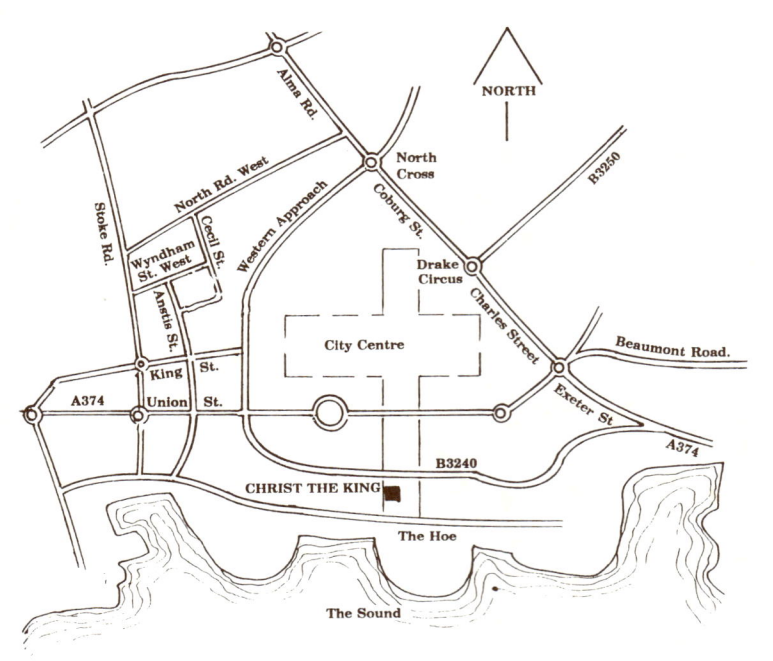

**Christ the King, Armada Way.**

The pedestrianisation of the City Centre has given the Church a very prominent location on the north/south pedestrian route linking North Cross and the Railway Station in the north, with the Hoe in the South, across the shopping centre. Barclays Bank is directly opposite the Church, and another landmark is the Holiday Inn. Within close proximity are Notte Street, Windsor Place and Citadel Street. The Church can be reached easily from several of the city centre car parks, and shorter term parking is allowed in adjacent streets.

The Church is dedicated to Christ the King. Christ is our anointed King who overcame suffering and death and so brought us out of darkness into His Kingdom:

*"As King he claims dominion over all creation, that he may present to you, his Almighty Father, an eternal; and universal kingdom of holiness and grace, a kingdom of justice, love and peace...".*

(From the preface of the Mass for the Feast of Christ the King, the last Sunday of the liturgical year.)

Christ the King was built 1962/63 as an auxiliary church to the Cathedral for the benefit of all Plymouth parishes. It was solemnly opened on 19th September 1962.

As it is so conveniently near the city centre it gives many people the opportunity to "drop in and quietly pray". There is usually a Mass or Holy Communion every weekday at noon.

The dedication plaque in the porch records that the Church was a gift to the Diocese from Mr. and Mrs. Rye. It is also interesting to note that Sir Giles Gilbert Scott was commissioned to design the building towards the end of a long and prolific career as an architect. In 1988 "Christ the King" became the Catholic Chaplaincy to students studying in the City of Plymouth.

# Christ the King

From Armada Way, the external view is of a red brick building with a conspicuous square tower. The interior is simple, but dramatically awesome, a development of the Gothic tradition. A huge canopied crucifix overhangs the high altar. From inside the entrance the eye is drawn compulsively along the nave to the sanctuary, to the tabernacle, to Christ the King! The Lady Chapel contains a beautiful modern triptych of the Nativity:

*"Puer natus est nobis - et Filius Datus est nobis."*
*(A child is born to us and a Son is given to us.)*

Contact address of Priest:
The Presbytery, Armada Way,
Plymouth, Devon. PL1 2EN.
Telephone: (0752) 266523.
and 232261.

# Plymouth

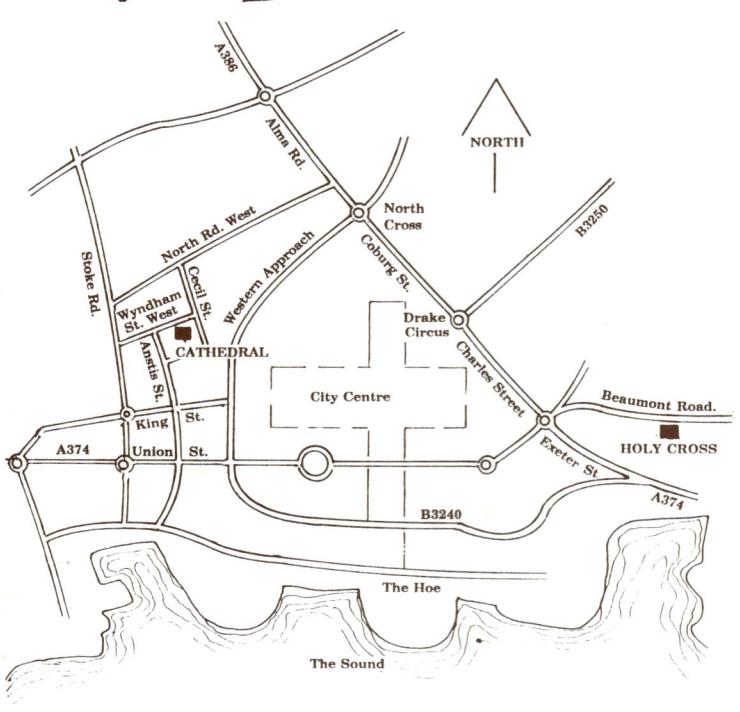

### Holy Cross, Beaumont Road.

To find Holy Cross, follow the signs for the City Centre to Charles Cross roundabout (marked by the ruins of the bombed church, kept as a war memorial) At the roundabout, take the exit at Ebrington Street, which leads into Beaumont Road. The Catholic Church is on the right, about 200 yards from the roundabout. It is within six minutes walk of Bretonside Bus Station.

The Church is dedicated to the Holy Cross. When Our Saviour was condemned to death, He was taken to the courtyard of the Praetorium where three crosses awaited prisoners, and crucifixion. Lovingly, Jesus took up the one prepared for Him. Bent beneath its load, He walked to Calvary, to the site of our redemption. From quite early in Christian history, a special feast day was created to celebrate the finding of the Holy Cross. In 326 A.D. St. Helena, mother of the Emperor Constantine organised excavations which resulted in the discovery of the Cross, together with Pilate's inscriptions. Part of this sacred wood is now preserved in the Basilica of the Holy Cross in Rome. By the Holy Cross, Jesus redeemed the world. By the Holy Cross He revealed His total love for us. When we carry the Cross, we are so very close to Him. The feast of the Triumph of the Cross is kept on 14th September.

This Church, in east Plymouth, was opened and blessed by Bishop Vaughan on December 20th 1881. Originally, it had been situated in Teignmouth, dedicated to Our Lady & St. Charles Borromeo, and built in 1845 on land belonging to the South Devon Railway Company. A tunnel ran under part of the site. Eventually the railway authority decided to make alterations to the track, forming a cutting in

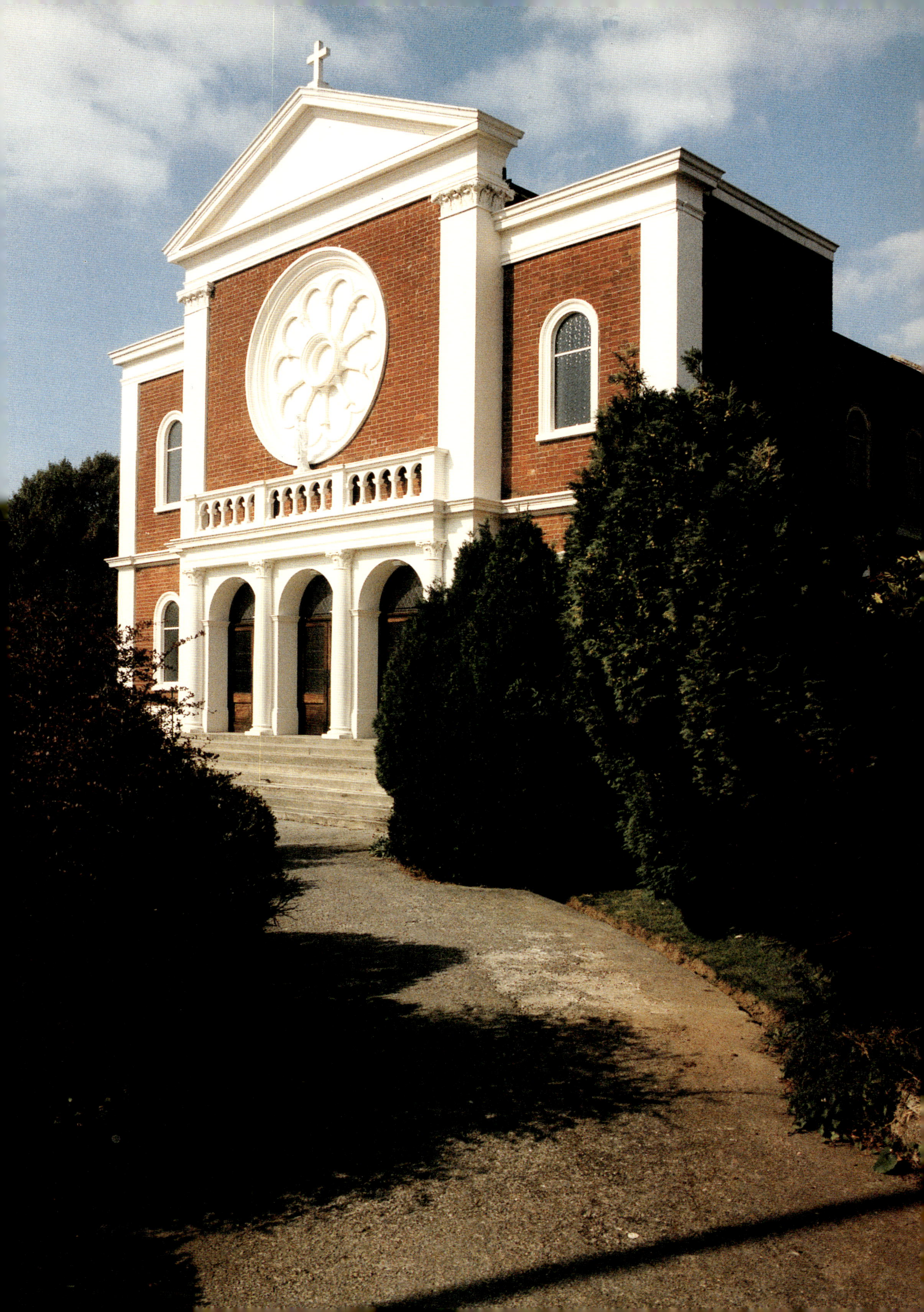

# Holy Cross

place of the tunnel. The Church had to be demolished, but was not lost. It was carefully dismantled, transported, and rebuilt in "Tothill Lane" adjacent to the (then) Friary Road Railway Station - now "Beaumont Road", next door to Friary Court. The Church was renamed Holy Cross. It is thought to have been reconstructed on part of the grounds of a pre-Reformation Carmelite Friary, one that had existed for 200 years before its dissolution by King Henry VIII in 1539. The present Church serves one of the city's oldest parishes, the first parish in the Diocese to provide a Bishop for the Diocese. (Bishop Keily).

Contact address of Priest:
The Presbytery, 2 Beaumont Road,
Plymouth, Devon. PL4 9BE.
Telephone: (0752) 662603.

# Plymouth

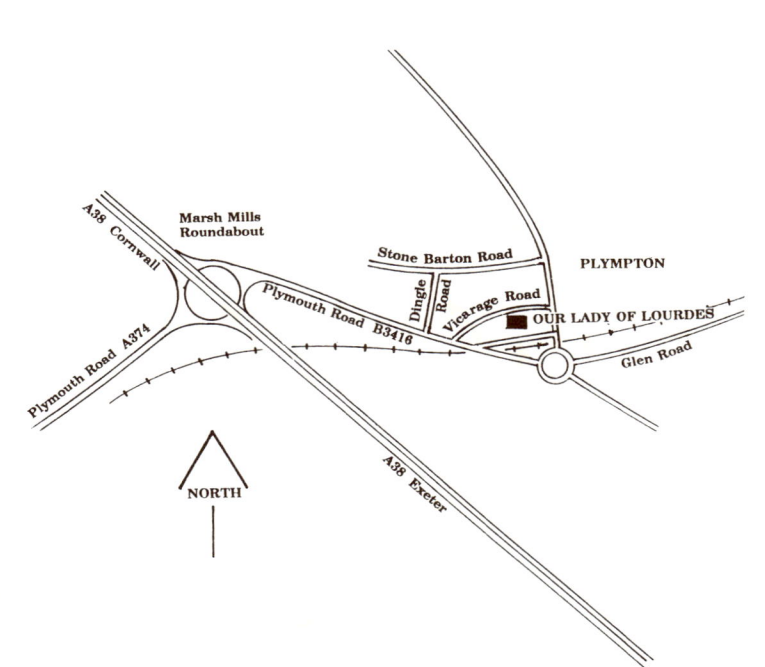

### Our Lady of Lourdes, Vicarage Road. Plympton

Plympton is clearly signposted off the A38 East of Plymouth. From the Marsh Mills roundabout below the A38 fly-over, take the B3416, Plymouth Road to Plympton. Continue past Woodford Avenue, Larkham Lane and Dingle Road on the left. Then take a left turn into Vicarage Road. The Church is a long, low building, almost like a long, large house, marked by a small cross on the gable of the roof. It is opposite Oakfield Road. There is a Lourdes Grotto outside the Church, and above it the inscription: "Hail Holy Queen Mother of Mercy".

A low wall encloses the garden. Buses to Plymouth stop at the end of Vicarage Road. Car parking is available in the streets near the church.

The Church is dedicated to Our Lady of Lourdes, built as a memorial to Bishop Keily, Bishop of Plymouth for seventeen years, who had great devotion to Our Lady of Lourdes.

In 1858, in the Grotto of Massabielle, near Lourdes, in the south of France, the Holy Virgin appeared eighteen times to fourteen year old, asthmatic, Marie Bernadette Soubirous. (St. Bernadette) Ever since then physical and spiritual healing has occurred there. Miracles are countless! Lourdes has been transformed into one of the most popular pilgrimage centres in the world; a place for penance, for prayer, solace for the sick and disabled, for everyone a time, a place, to be with God. The feast of Our Lady of Lourdes is celebrated on 11th February.

# Our Lady of Lourdes

Plympton was once a small corner of Holy Cross Parish. Then it became the site for Bishop Keily's Memorial Church. Building work started in 1931 and was completed in 1932. When all the debts were cleared it was consecrated by Bishop Barrett on 25th September 1935.

The dedication is appropriate. The local C. of E. parish is also dedicated to St. Mary the Virgin. In the pre-Reformation Church there are carved figures in niches beneath a tomb, five monks saying the rosary and "St. Mary and the Holy Child". Nearby is the remnant of a shrine to Our Lady of Plymbridge. In 1455 Pope Nicholas V (1447-1455) granted special indulgences to the priests because of the enormous crowds visiting the shrine.

Contact address of Priest:
The Presbytery, 17, Vicarage Road,
Plympton, Plymouth. PL7 4JX.
Telephone: (0752) 336137

# Plymouth

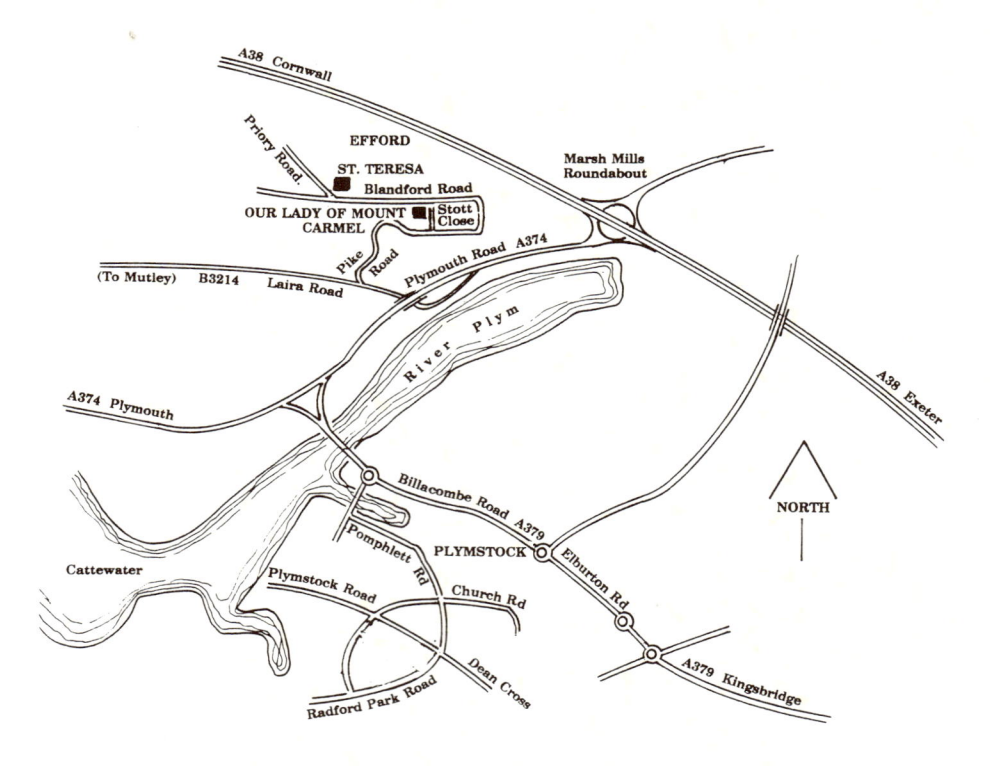

**Our Lady of Mount Carmel,
Pike Road, Efford.**

At the main approach to Plymouth from the East, from the A38 at Marsh Mills roundabout, follow the A374 towards the City along the embankment, and take the nearside lane signposted for Mutley. After going through the underpass, continue for about a hundred yards and turn into Pike Road. Near the top, turn left into Stott Close, where the Parish Church of Our Lady of Mount Carmel is clearly visible. Car parking for about five cars is avaliable outside the monastry. Parishioners generally park beside the kerb in Stott Close. Plymouth Railway Station is roughly three miles away, similarly Bretonside Coach Station.

Mount Carmel, overlooking the plains of Galilee, not too distant from Nazareth, is appropriately under the protection of the Blessed Virgin. Under Mount Carmel there is a cave called "the school of the prophets". According to tradition it was the home of the Old Testament Prophets Elijah and Elisha. During the period of the Crusades, Christian hermits settled in caves on the holy mountain, but in the thirteenth century they had to flee to Europe to avoid being massacred by Saracens. Under the guidance of St. Simon Stock the hermits of Carmel changed to a community life and became known as "Carmelites". The feast of Our Lady of Mount Carmel is on 16th July.

# Our Lady of Mount Carmel

This Parish Church was once the Chapel of Carmelite Sisters who moved away after World War II. The Bishop invited the Redemptorist Fathers to take over the parish in 1964. The Church is very simple, homely and devotional. If one looks very carefully one can see the outline of the Carmelite Grill in the wall, to the right of the altar. The Carmelite Sisters chose the dedications "Our Lady of Mount Carmel" for this Church, and "Teresa of Avila", after the great Carmelite saint, for the nearby building in Blandford Road.

Contact address of Priest:
The Monastery, Pike Road,
Efford, Plymouth, Devon. PL3 6HH.
Telephone: (0752) 667433.

# Plymouth

**Our Most Holy Redeemer,
Ocean Street, Keyham.**

From the A38 "The Parkway/ Tavistock Road/ Outland Road" roundabout, take the A38 exit for Outland Road. Continue straight, going past Plymouth Argyle Football Ground on the left. Turn right into Wolseley Road A388, then take the left turn into Saltash Road. Turn immediately left again into Ocean Street. The Church of Our Most Holy Redeemer, a large stone building with a red, tiled, pitched roof, is further down on the right.

(Coming from Cornwall, from the Tamar Bridge, turn left into Pemros Road A388 leading into Wolseley Road. Then turn right into Saltash Road, and left into Ocean Street.)

The Church is dedicated to Our Most Holy Redeemer, who offered Himself as a victim of reparation and of love: humbled, obedient to death, even death on a cross. Christ said *"I am the Way and the Truth and the life"*, Salvation is offered to all mankind through Christ. Humanity is redeemed by His total sacrifice. The Church opens its doors to saint and sinner alike. No-one is excluded. Here is a place, set apart, for us to raise our hearts and minds to the Most Holy Redeemer.

# Our Most Holy Redeemer

This Church was opened in 1902,
and consecrated on 10th April 1957.

*"Father
Pour Out Your Spirit
Upon the people of this parish
And grant us
A new vision of your glory
A new experience of your power
A new faithfulness to your Word
And a new consecration to your service
That your love may grow among us
And your kingdom come
Through Christ Our Lord. Amen."
(Parish Prayer - Church Noticeboard.)*

Contact address of Priest:
The Presbytery, Raglan Road,
Devonport, Plymouth, Devon. PL1 4NQ.
Telephone: (0752) 562976.

# Plymouth

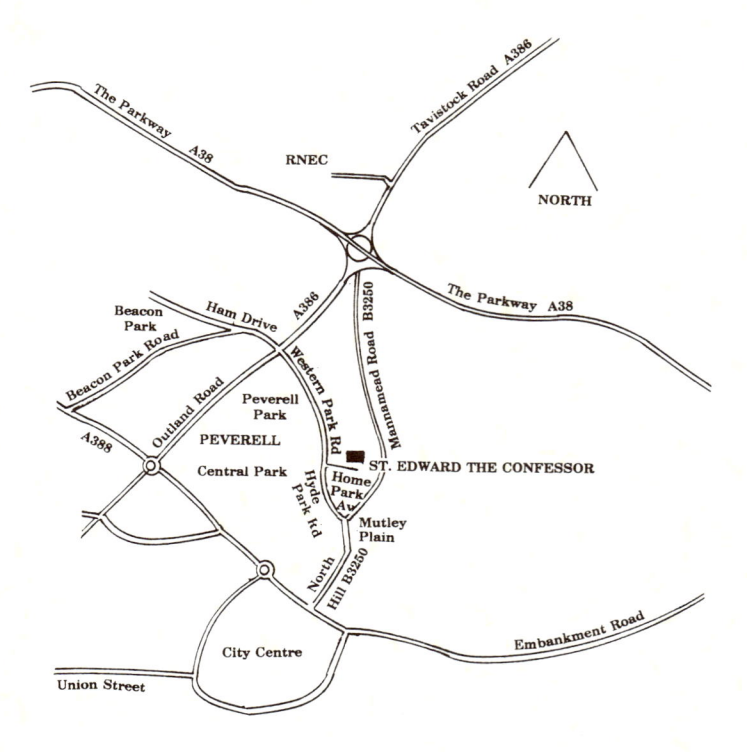

**St. Edward the Confessor, Home Park Avenue.**

The Church is near Mutley Plain shoppping area. Take Hyde Park Road from Mutley leading into Western Park Road. Turn right into Home Park Avenue. The Church of St. Edward the Confessor is built directly behind the pavement. An attractive name plate makes it easy to identify. The Railway Station is 15 minutes walk away. There is no special car park, but parking is allowed in the road outside the Church.

The Church is dedicated to Edward, the Confessor, a very popular saint in the Middle Ages, and once thought of as patron of England. In 1042, when he became King, Edward was already renowned for his works of holiness, his devotion to prayer, and his works of mercy. Combining the Mercian, the West Saxon and Danish laws into one, he made every effort to govern according to Christian principles. His abolition of the "Danegelt" tax, earned him the title "Good King Edward."

During his reign, he strengthened the bond between the Papacy and the Church of England and he sought to restore long-abandoned monasteries. Westminster Abbey, the place of coronation and burial of English Royalty, was grandly restored by Edward. When he died in 1066 he was buried in the Abbey, and his relics are still enshrined there. The feast of St. Edward the Confessor is celebrated on 13th October.

# St. Edward the Confessor

The original Church, built in 1907, is now the Blessed Sacrament Chapel. The main part of the Church was constructed in 1935. The solemn Consecration took place on 6th June 1949.

Contact address of Priest:
The Presbytery, Home Park Avenue,
Peverell, Plymouth, Devon. PL3 4PG
Telephone: (0752) 665406.

# Plymouth

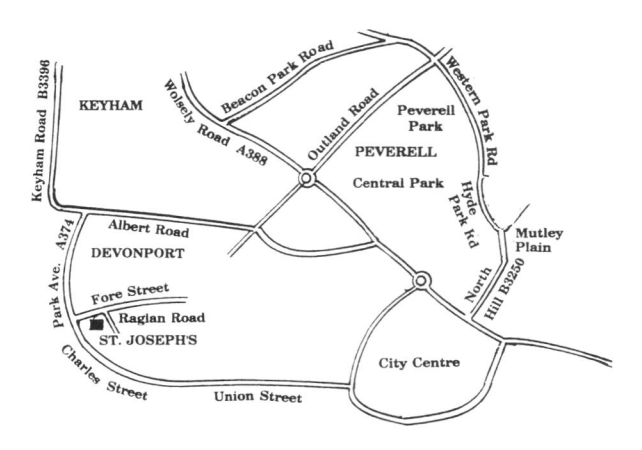

**St. Joseph's, Raglan Road. Devonport.**

Follow signs for Devonport (B3396) then A374. From Plymouth centre, proceed down Union Street and turn right into King's Road, passing the College of Further Education on the right. Continue into Fore Street, then turn left into Raglan Road. The Church building is easily recognised by its high pointed roof line. It includes a presbytery and meeting hall. There is a lychgate at the entrance to St. Joseph's. Car parking is available at the Church. A bus service operates from Royal Parade (Plymouth centre) to Devonport.

Although the date of his death, and the location of his tomb both remain a mystery, devotion to St. Joseph has existed from early in Christian history. In the fourth century the Eastern Coptic Church celebrated a feast in his honour. Many saints, including Bridget of Sweden, Bernard of Siena, Theresa of Avila, and Ignatius of Loyola, advocated devotion to St. Joseph. In 1870 Pope Pius IX (1846-1878) declared him Patron of the Universal Church. His feast is celebrated on 19th March and 1st May.

# St. Joseph's

St. Joseph's began as a parish in the Autumn of 1793 when an Irish Franciscan, Fr. Flynn, the first resident priest in the area since the Reformation, celebrated Mass in a stable loft in Devonport. Fr. Flynn hired the loft from the owner of the George Inn in Fore Street. During his years in the parish, Fr. Flynn's duties included giving the last rights to two Catholic marines who were hanged on Plymouth Hoe in 1797. In 1803 a French exile priest Abbe Jean Louis Guilbert took over the Devonport ministry. On 20th December 1807 he celebrated the first Mass in the Chapel of St. Mary & St. John. In 1838 this Chapel became Plymouth's first Cathedral. The Cathedral Clergy served Devonport until the new Church of St. Michael & St. Joseph was blessed by the Bishop on 19th December 1861.

The parish continued to grow with great speed due to the increasing numbers of Irish immigrants escaping the aftermath of the Irish Potatoe Famine, and seeking employment in the Armed Services or Devonport Dockyard.

During the Second World War, sadly most of the houses in Mutton Cove were devastated in the bombing of Plymouth. In 1964, when an old boy of the Parish, Fr. Charles Foley became Parish Priest, he faced a small congregation (due to post war rehousing restrictions) and a large dilapidated church. With determination and courage he acquired land in the midst of his "flock", and in time a Catholic school was built. On 15th May 1984, the old St. Joseph's was sold.

On 19th March 1985, the feast of St. Joseph, Bishop Restieux laid the foundationof a new "St. Joseph's", in Raglan Road, adjacent to the original site of the "chapel in the stable". The solemn dedication occurred on 10th November 1985.

The Church building has a clear identity due to its outline of steeply pitched roofs. The use of the sixty degree angle is extended inside the building in the shapes of the pine boarding and the modern stained glass windows. The Church retains a permanent memorial to the first Church at Mutton Cove. All the stained glass windows, holy water stoops, and some of the stonework of windows have been incorporated into the Narthex. At the time of its installation in the old St. Joseph's, the window representing St. Cuthbert Mayne was the only one of its kind in the Diocese. The circular window depicting St. Cyril was formerly in All Saints Church, Plymouth, and was given by the Anglican Community. The altar crucifix and the Stations of the Cross were donated by nuns from a convent that was closing. The Stations of the Cross, which have been restored, date from the late 1700s.

Contact address of Priest:
The Presbytery, Raglan Road,
Devonport, Plymouth, Devon. PL1 4NQ.
Telephone: (0752) 562976.

# Plymouth

**St. Margaret Mary,
Quarry Park Road. Plymstock.**

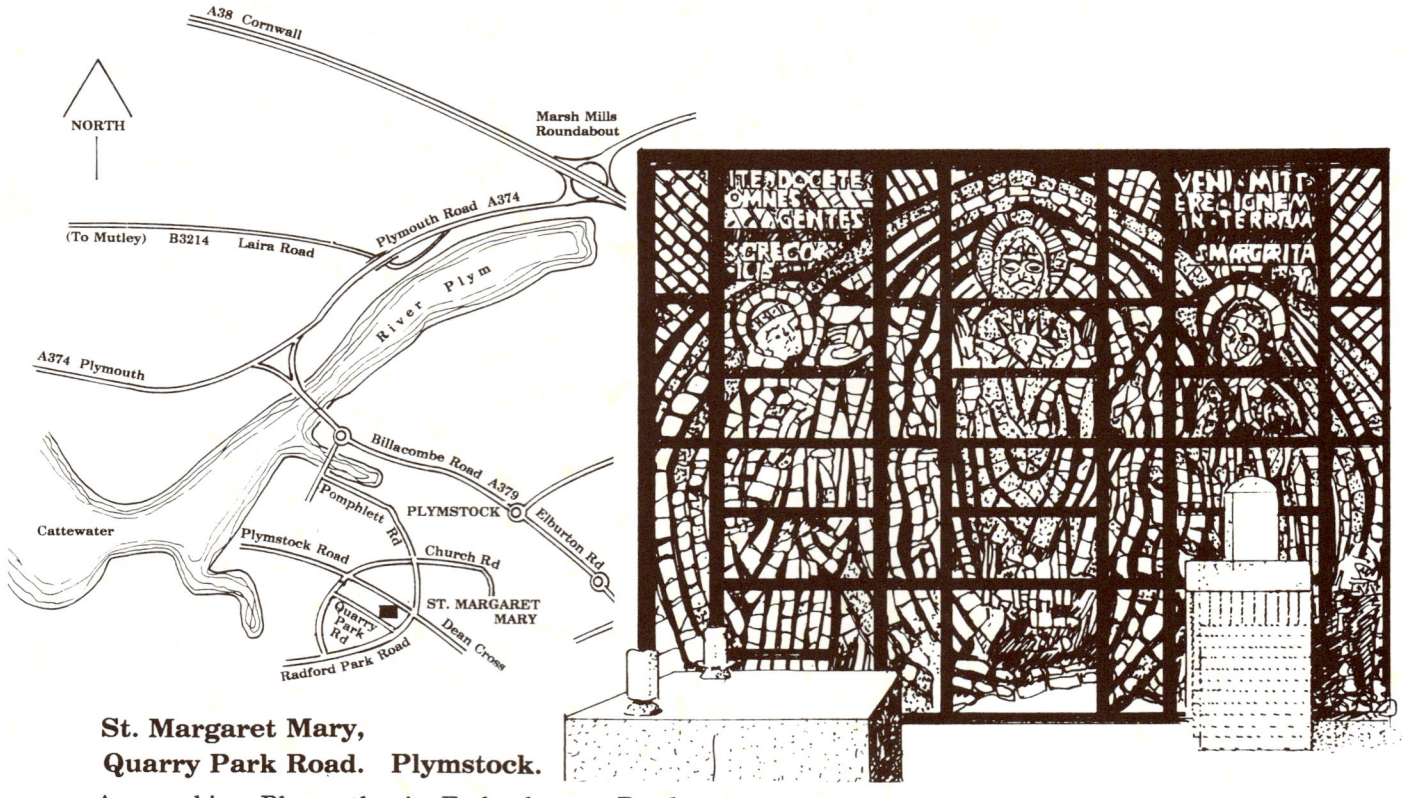

Approaching Plymouth via Embankment Road A374, follow signs for Plymstock A379, then Laira Bridge Road into Pomphlett Road. At the cross roads with traffic lights, turn right into Dean Cross Road. Continue to the next cross roads and go straight across into Park Road. Turn right into Quarry Park Road. There is a sign "Catholic Church" on the left at the corner of Quarry Park Road. St. Margaret Mary's is on the right.

The Church is dedicated to St. Margaret Mary Alacoque, a seventeenth century French nun, who spread devotion to the Sacred Heart of Jesus. Margaret Mary was born in 1647 in Janots, Burgandy, in the reign of the worldly Louis XIV. She was the fifth child of a notary. In 1671, at the age of twenty four, she entered the novitiate of the Visitation Convent at Paray le Monial. A few years later she was privileged to receive visions of Christ. Our Lord asked her to encourage devotion to His Sacred Heart, a devotion already introduced in the Middle Ages by the Benedictine Saints Mechtilde and Gertrude. Margaret Mary was, nevertheless, doubted and criticised by her Religious Community. She was supported only by Blessed Claude de la Columbiere, her Jesuit confessor. Eventually, however, devotion to the Sacred Heart was officially approved. St. Margaret Mary is remembered in the Church Calendar on 16th October each year.

# St. Margaret Mary

Plymstock and the surrounding district was at one time part of the Holy Cross Parish in Plymouth. In 1931 Mass was celebrated for the first time since the Reformation in a local Catholic household. In 1933 a small church was built, dedicated to St. Gregory, and served from Holy Cross. In 1947 Plymstock became a parish in its own right, with its own resident priest. As the congregation grew, the need for larger accommodation became more pressing. In 1961, the present Church was built adjacent to the old building, linked to it at the northern end by a low wing. The Church was solemnly blessed and opened by Bishop Restieaux on 26th March 1961. The consecration took place on 16th October 1981, the patronal feast day.

There is a gloriously rich window in the west wall of this Church, from the stained glass workshop of Buckfast Abbey. It depicts St. Margaret Mary, the Sacred Heart & St. Gregory. Another stained glass window, forming a screen between the Baptistry and the rear part of the Church, came from behind the High Altar in the old Church (originally from St. Theresa's in Ebrington Street, Plymouth).

Contact address of Priest:
The Presbytery, 20, Radford Park Road,
Plymstock, Plymouth. PL9 9DW.
Telephone: (0752) 401281.

# Plymouth

### St. Paul, Pemros Road, St. Budeaux.

The Church is found on the west side of Plymouth on roads leading to Cornwall. An obvious landmark is the Tamar Bridge at the other end of Pemros Road from the Church. Driving from the City Centre, A388 Wolseley Road leads into Pemros Road. Another route can be via The Parkway A38 to Tamar Bridge Road, with a left turn into Pemros Road A388. Small roads near the Church include Barne Lane, Saltburn Road and Victoria Road which leads to Crownhill (B3413). Local transport is possible on the Saltash Hoppa bus. Car parking is available at the rear of the Church and school in Barne Lane (on the right of the Church as you face it).

The Church is dedicated to St. Paul, the great convert and "Apostle of the Gentiles", tireless missionary, patron saint of saddlers and tentmakers, the latter his own self supporting trade. St. Paul was born at Tarsus, between 5 and 10 A.D., of strict Jewish parents who were Roman citizens. He did not know Christ personally, but received a special call from Him when on the road to Damascus on his way to persecute Christians. The Acts of the Apostles relate his presence and involvement in St. Stephen's martyrdom, give details of his conversion and his various missionary journeys. His letters to the Early Church have as great a relevance for us today. The feast of St. Peter & St. Paul is kept on 29th June. The feast of the Conversion of St. Paul is celebrated on 25th January.

# St Paul

The Church of St. Paul is sited in a mature garden. It has accommodation for 160 seated, and has a pleasing, homely and prayerful atmosphere. It was built in 1933, a miniature St. Paul's Outside the Walls in Rome! It was the first of five churches built in the Diocese by the Misses Robinson, when the city was beginning to expand, and erected on the site of a rugby pitch. It is now in the centre of a densely populated area, but still retains its village atmosphere.

Above the entrance, a white wheel panel refers to the majesty of God: Wisdom, Justice, Goodness, Holiness, Infinity, Power, Immensity, Immutability, Eternity. Inside this very "Roman" Church it is worth finding the tympanum above the Confessional, a magnificently modelled plaster relief panel portraying Christ, with his apostles, teaching the Sacrament of Reconciliation. The Stations of the Cross, represented in tableaux style, and the gentle Madonna, were carved by Stufflesser, Ortisei, N. Italy.

Contact address of Priest:
The Presbytery, 66, Pemros Road,
St. Budeaux, Plymouth, Devon. PL5 1NE.
Telephone: (0752) 361161.

# Plymouth

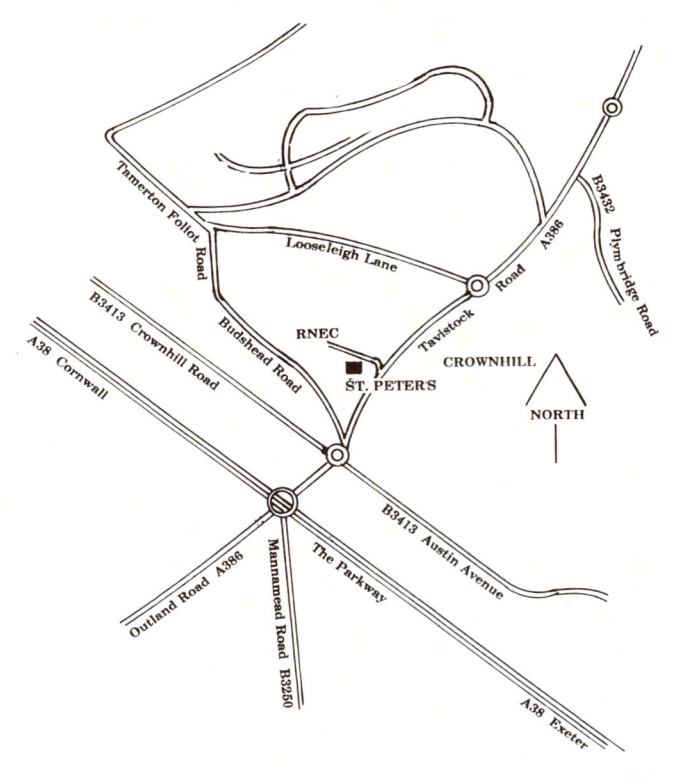

**St. Peter's, Crownhill.**

The A38 from Exeter, Devon, and the A38 from Cornwall meet at Manadon Roundabout in Plymouth. From there take Tavistock Road A386 towards Tavistock. Continue for about a quarter of a mile. On the left hand side there is a slip road with a sharp left turn signposted RNEC (Royal Naval Engineering College), Manadon. There is also a "Catholic Church" sign. For St. Peter's, take the first entrance on the left. It is adjacent to St. Boniface's College and opposite playing fields and swings. Car parking is available in the Church grounds. There are buses at fairly frequent intervals.

The Church is dedicated to St. Peter, the apostle specially chosen to become "fisher of men", leader of Christ's Church on earth, the first Pope. Born at Bethsaida on the shores of the Sea of Galilee, in due course he married, and went to live in Capernaum. He became a disciple of John the Baptist, and later a follower of Christ. Our Lord called him "Peter", the rock upon which He would build His Church. After the Resurrection he was one of the first to whom Our Lord appeared reaffirming Peter's supremacy over His flock. At Pentecost Peter assumed the role of leader. He preached over the election of the apostle Matthias to replace Judas Iscariot, received the first Jewish converts and later the first pagan converts into the Church. Peter was the first apostle to perform a miracle, and at the inaugural Church Council he spoke the decisive word. He suffered martyrdom, crucifixion upside down, in Rome in 64 A.D.

ANNO·PAOS·LAFRENS·HENRICV·SCHILLER·EX·VOTO

# St. Peter

This Parish was originally served from St. Edward's Peverell. Before that, the soldiers and the small Catholic population of civilians of Crownhill attended Mass in the Barracks. Thanks to generous benefactors, including the Misses Robinson, the new "Military Church of St. Peter" was built at Crownhill. It was blessed by Bishop Barrett on December 19th 1937.

After the war many new houses were built in and around Crownhill. The Catholic community expanded, and in 1948 Archbishop Grimshaw established the area as a separate parish. Twenty one years later the present Church of St. Peter was built, the foundation stone laid by Bishop Restieaux on August 2nd 1969. The Church was consecrated on the feast of St. Peter & St. Paul 29th June 1987.

Contact address of Priest:
St. Peter's Presbytery, Tavistock Road,
Crownhill, Plymouth. PL3 5LR.
Telephone: (0752) 701660.

# Plymouth

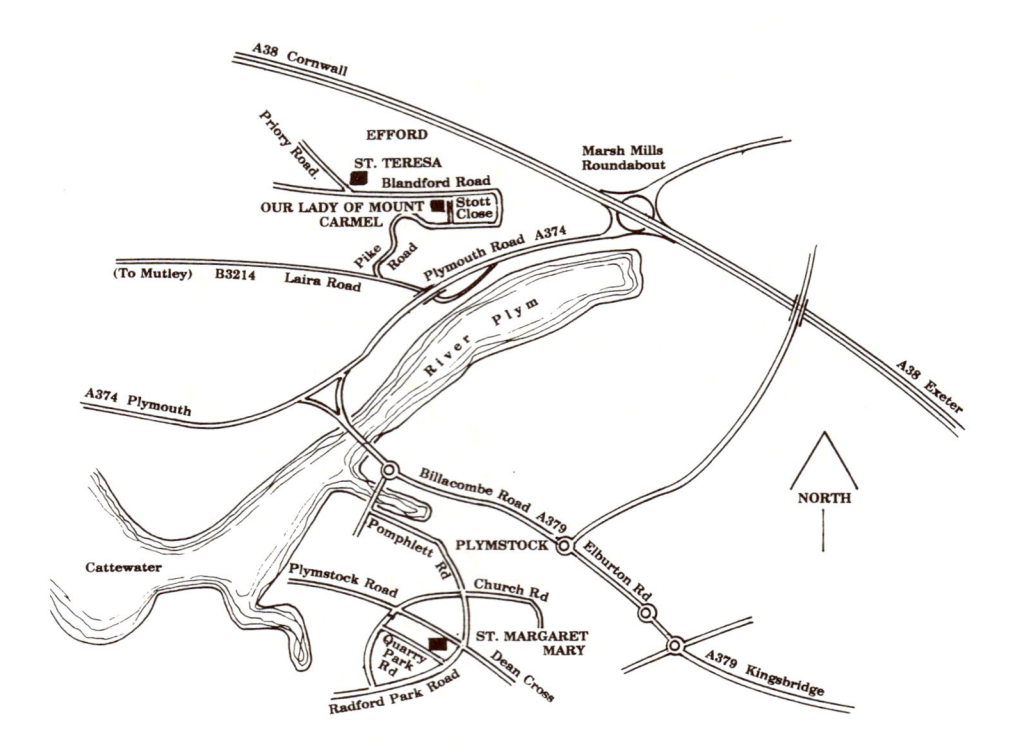

**St. Teresa, Blandford Road.**

From Marsh Mills roundabout on the A38, take the A374 towards the City along the embankment. Move into the Mutley traffic lane. Go under the underpass and and along the road for about 100 yards. Turn left into Pike Road which will lead into Blandford Road. Continue down hill passing Dartmeet Avenue on the right. The red brick exterior of St. Teresa's with its unusual spire is clearly visible on the right. It is opposite a bus stop.

This little Church is dedicated to St. Teresa, the foundress of the reformed religious order of (Discalced) Carmelites. The saint was born of aristocratic parents, in 1515, in Avila, Old Castile, fifty miles north west of Madrid. At the age of eighteen, during a period of convalescence, Teresa read the letters of St. Jerome and decided to join a Carmelite convent. She suffered from ill health most of her life, but was not deterred from improving the sanctity of religious life in Carmelite monasteries. St. Teresa left us a legacy on prayer with her life story, "The Way of Perfection" and "The Interior Castle". Her feast day is October 15th.

# St Teresa

Contact address of Priest:
The Monastery, Pike Road, Efford,
Plymouth, Devon. PL13 6HH.
Telephone: (0752) 667433.

# Plymouth

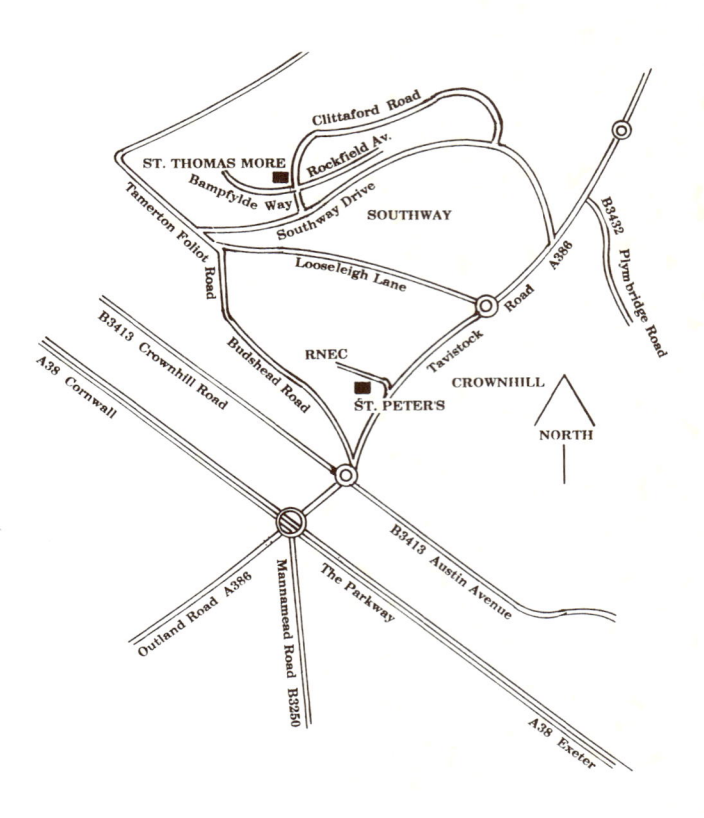

**St. Thomas More,
Bampfylde Way, Southway.**

From Tavistock Road A386 (the section close to Plymouth Airport) turn into Southway Drive, a left turn if driving out of Plymouth. Continue along Southway until you find Clitteford Road. Turn right. (Clitteford Road can be encountered twice as it forms a loop off Southway Drive). Bampfylde Way is a turning off Clitteford Road. The Church of St. Thomas More is adjacent to the local Infant/Junior School. It is situated on the 40/41 Bus route. Car parking is available outside the Church and there is also a small area within the Church grounds for parking.

The Church is dedicated to St. Thomas More who was born in 1478. His father, Sir John More, was a barrister and judge. Thomas studied law at Oxford and then at Lincoln's Inn. He entered the bar and, later, Parliament. He was a deeply religious young man. At the age of 27 he married, but sadly his loving wife, Jane Colt, died only six years later, leaving him with four small children. He remarried another good woman, a widow, Alice Middleton. In public life he was a member of King Henry VIII's Privy Council and then, following the downfall of Cardinal Wolseley, Lord Chancellor of England. His success did not demean his spirituality. He was "the King's good servant, but God's first". His allegiance to "God first" brought him fifteen month's imprisonment in the Tower for refusing to take the Royal Oath of Succession. He was beheaded on Tower Hill on 6th July 1535, only two weeks after the execution of his good friend John Fisher. The feast day of SS Thomas More & John Fisher is kept on 22nd June.

In 1524 St. Thomas More moved to Chelsea where he allowed his celebrated family to be painted by Hans Holbein. There is a reproduction of the painting in the Church.

# St. Thomas More

At one time, travellers from Plymouth would enjoy open country and farm land on the western side of the main road into Yelverton. By the early 1960's the scene had changed to one of factories and hundreds of houses - the Southway Estate. Fr. McSweeney started a Mass centre in a farmhouse. Then the local county primary school was used for Sunday Mass. A continued steady influx of Catholics into Southway required a Church. In January 1963 a site already reserved for church building was purchased from Plymouth Corporation. Construction began on 27th May 1963. Bishop Restieaux laid the foundation stone:

>*Ad Majorem Dei Gloriam*
>   *et*
>*In honorem Sancti Thomae More*
>   *Cancellarii Angliae*
>*Martyris pro fide Catholica*
>   *Hunc Lapidem Posuit*
>*Cyrillus Episcopus Plymutensis*
>   *die XXIV Julii MCMLXIII*
>   (24th July 1963)

The Church was completed in 1964. It is a light brown brick building with white stone facings and a single sloping roof. High clerestory windows extend the whole length of the southern wall projecting plenty of light into the Church. The High Altar is made from Portland stone. Statues of Our Lady and St. Joseph, the Stations of the Cross and the Altar Cross were hand carved in wood at Oberammergau in Bavaria. The side chapel is separated from the main Church by a glass screen and houses the Blessed Sacrament.

Contact address of Priest:
The Presbytery, Bamyfylde Way,
Southway, Plymouth, Devon. PL6 6SP.
Telephone: (0752) 778269.

# Plymouth

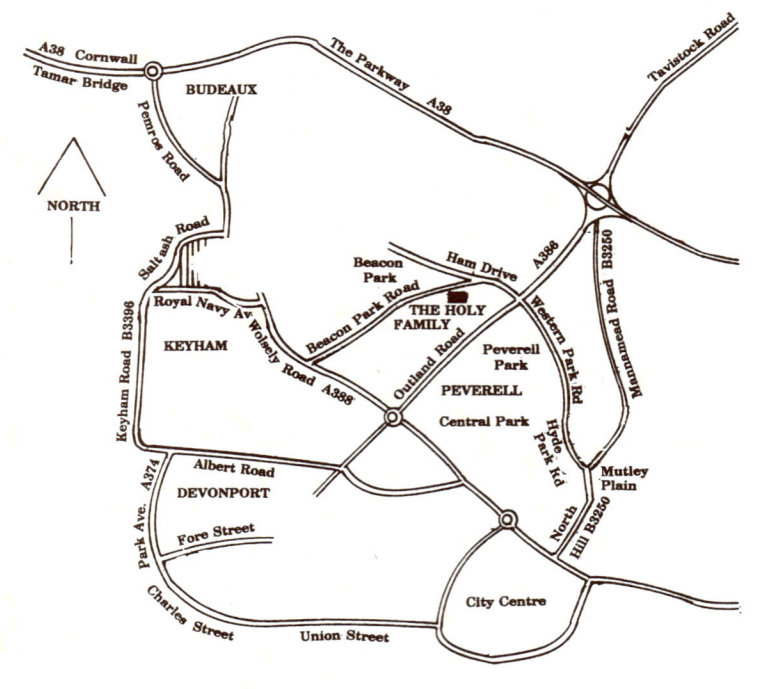

### The Holy Family, Beacon Park Road.

The Church is easily found on a corner site near the Plymouth Albion Rugby Ground, on Beacon Park Road. The Parklway (A38) leads into Outland Road (A386) which runs practically parallel with Beacon Park Road. Small roads near the Church include Lyndhurst Road, Montpellier Road, and Westeria Terrace. There are several local buses from the city centre (4, 17, 33, & 34) Ample street parking is available.

The Church is dedicated to the Holy Family of Nazareth, Jesus, Mary and Joseph, the model for all Christian families. In 1893, Pope Leo XIII (1878-1903) instituted a special holy day in honour of the Holy Family, and Pope Benedict XV (1914-1922) extended it to the Universal Church in 1921. The Feast of the Holy Family is celebrated on the Sunday in the Octave of Christmas.

# The Holy Family

The Assembly Hall at St. Boniface's College was used from 1939 until 1955 when the present Church of the Holy Family was built. It is an unpretentious building, set in its own low walled garden, amidst attractive trees. There is a large blue cross inset above the entrance porch.

The interior consists of a single, simple space. At the south end, the portals curve round to form an apse behind the canopied altar. A humble crucifix hangs above the tabernacle. The Lady Chapel continues the theme of simplicity with a solitary white statue of Our Lady holding a rosary.

The Stations of the Cross are modern, carved in detail, the faces portraying the tremendous experience of the journey to Golgotha. The Baptistry, behind wrought iron railings at the back of the Church has an interesting, modern, octagonal font, embellished with appropriate motifs in tile mosaic. Outside the Baptistry there is a plaque to commemorate the Ursuline sisters from Quimperle, Brittany, who ran a school on the adjoining site of Beaconsfield, 1907-1930.

Contact address of Priest:
The Presbytery, Westeria Terrace,
Beacon Park, Plymouth, Devon. PL2 3LR.
Telephone: (0752) 772181.

# Poole

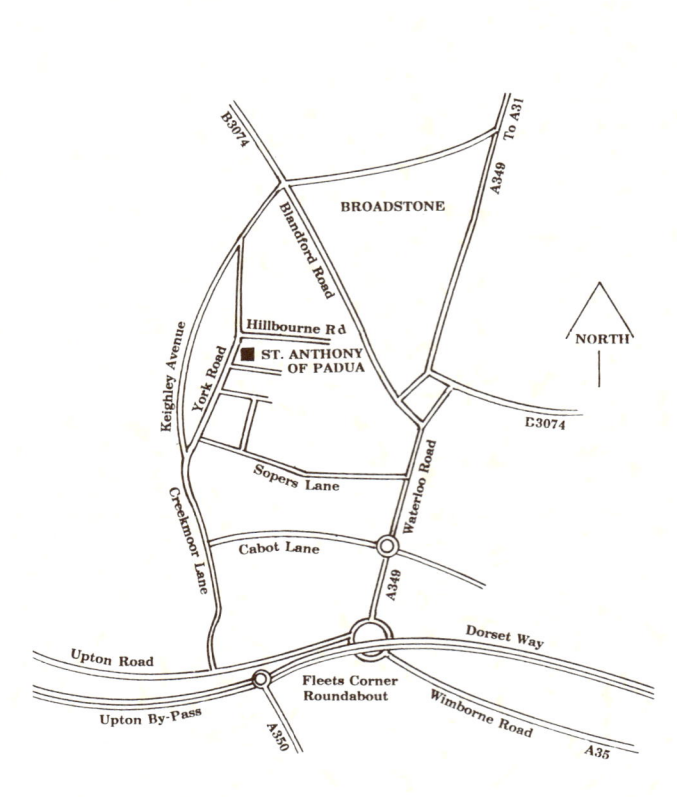

**St. Anthony of Padua,
York Road, Broadstone.**

From the centre of Poole take the main Wimborne Road A349. It becomes A35. At Fleets Corner Roundabout take the third exit along Waterloo Road, again A349. Pass Hemworthy Engineering. Turn left into Sopers Lane. Turn right at the end into York Road. A quarter of a mile ahead, on the right, is St. Anthony's, situated on the corner of Hillbourne Road at its junction with York Road. It is a modern red brick building set back in its own grounds. A carved stone statue of St. Anthony of Padua is set in a niche on the facade. Car parking is available in the immediate vicinity of the church and off the road.

The dedication honours St. Anthony of Padua. He was born in 1195 in Lisbon, the son of a noble Portuguese family who christened him Ferdinand Bouillon. In his youth, realising his religious vocation, he joined the Canons Regular of St. Augustine. A burning zeal for martyrdom, fuelled by the sight of the Franciscan martyrs retrieved from Morocco, led him to join the Franciscan friars, in 1220. However, his missionary activity was soon curtailed, when, due to illness he had to return to Europe. The Order sent him to a small monastery, Sao Paolo, near Forli. He concealed his intellect, through humility, but his gift for oratory soon received recognition. He was moved to positions of greater responsibility, teaching Theology, first of all at Bologna. His last days were spent at Padua, wholly employed in preaching. He died in 1231 and was canonized in 1232. This well-loved saint, renowned for his powerful intercession, particularly in the recovery of lost objects, is remembered in the liturgical calendar on 13th June, his feast day.

# St. Anthony of Padua

The site was chosen for the Church to serve the strong Catholic population in the adjacent Waterloo Estate. The building was opened by Bishop Cyril Restieaux in 1959.

Contact address of Priest:
The Presbytery, 135, York Road,
Broadstone, Poole, Dorset. BH18 8ER.
Telephone: (0202) 693336.

# Poole

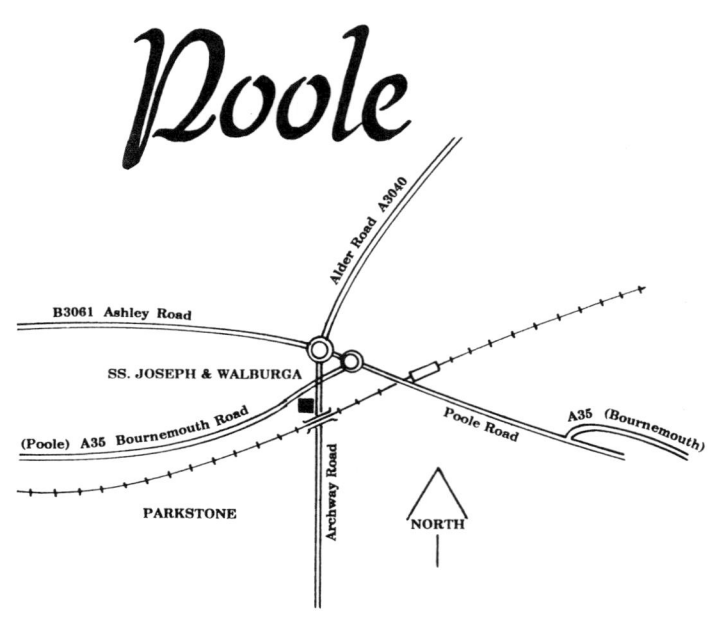

### SS. Joseph & Walburga, Archway Road, Parkstone.

From Bournemouth follow A35 towards Branksome Railway Station. Carry on about 200 yards to the roundabout. Take the first exit towards the town centre. The Church is 100 yards further on the left. From Poole, follow A35 signs for Bournemouth. The Church is on the right between Bournemouth Road and Archway Road, about 100 yards before the Ashley Road/Poole roundabouts. The Church is obvious, once located ! Its pitched roof has an adjacent bell tower, some 75 feet high, supporting a large cross, 24 feet high. The building is in an area of considerable vehicular traffic, but set back, off the busy road. There are ample parking facilities.

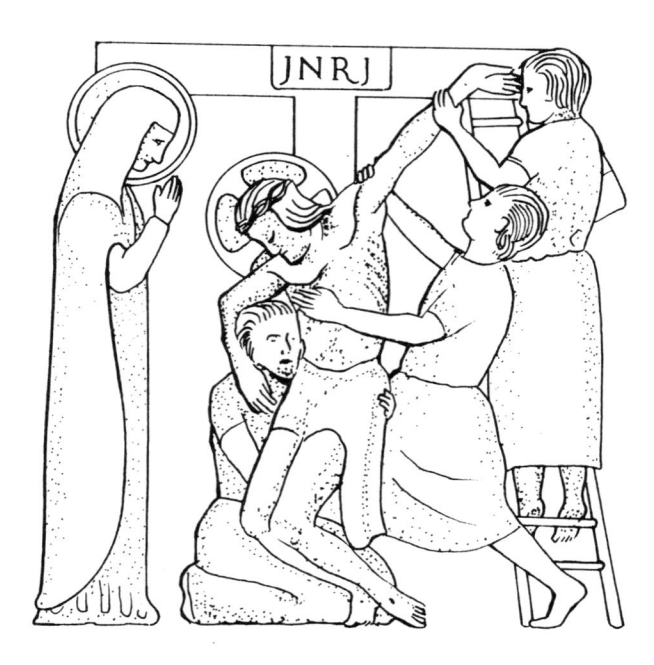

St. Walburga was born in 710 A.D. Her mother, Winna, was the sister of St. Boniface, the Apostle of Germany. Royal blood flowed in Walburga's veins through her father, Prince Richard, and grandfather King Hlothere of Kent. When she was twelve, she was sent to Wimborne Benedictine Convent. At that time her father and brothers, Willibald and Winnibald, set off on a pilgrimage to the Holy Land. Many years later, in 748 A.D. St. Walburga left England with over thirty members of her Community, to do missionary work in Germany. This was in response to requests from her uncle, Archbishop Boniface, and Bishop Burkhard of Wurzburg. Eventually, St. Walburga became Abbess of the double monastery at Heidenheim, in Bavaria, a position which she held until the end of her holy life in 799 A.D. The cave where she was buried became a place of pilgrimage after a curious phenomenon occurred there. A miraculous healing oil extruded from her tomb, and numerous miracles were connected with her intercession. St. Walburga's feast day is celebrated on 25th February.

# St. Joseph and St. Walburga

In 1896 a small Church of St. Joseph was built off Archway Road. It catered for one hundred and fifty people with a presbytery for three clerics. In 1958 the parish expanded to a population of one thousand Catholics. A new building was a priority. The parish priest, Fr. Joseph Lombardi, asked a Catholic architect, Mr. Lamprell-Jarrett to design a new building within the same site. (This was pre-Vatican II). Work began in August 1958. In November the parish priest died suddenly, and the building project was taken over by Fr. Francis Gallagher. On Sunday evening, 30th April 1961, the foundation stone was blessed by the Rt. Rev. Bishop Cyril Restieaux. On 20th February 1962 the first Mass was celebrated.

The Church has a modern, light brick exterior, which conceals an interior impressive in its statement of faith. In the main part, there is an enormous crucifix of Christ the King, High Priest. Large stone sculptures on the balcony panels reverently record the Passion of Christ. In the side chapels, glorious stained glass enhances the atmosphere of prayer. In one there is a fine woodcarving of the Holy Mother & Child, the work of Tom Praetor, and, on the side wall a highly decorative traditional tryptych. In the other chapel, rays of coloured light radiate from a focal centre that is the Blessed Sacrament.

Contact address of Priest:
The Presbytery, 1a, Archway Road,
Parkstone, Poole, Dorset. BH14 9AZ.
Telephone: (0202) 746539.

# Poole

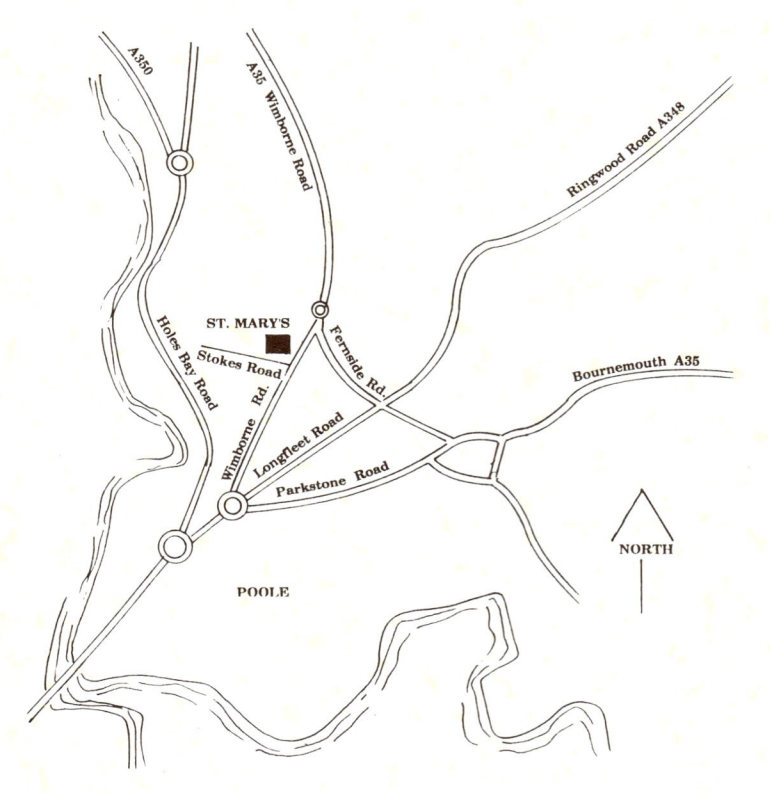

**St. Mary's, Wimborne Road, Poole.**

The A350 south from Blandford Forum, A35 south from Wimborne, A35 west from Bournemouth, A349 south from Oakley, and A348 south from Ringwood, all lead to Poole. St. Mary's is located on the main Wimborne Road, on the left hand side as you leave Poole centre. A sign points to the church, an octagonal building set well back from the road, down a drive between houses. There is a large car park which fills rapidly for Sunday Masses. Poole has a bus and railway station, the latter some 15 minutes walk away.

The dedication honours Mary, who, "overshadowed by the power of the Most High" became the dwelling place of God.

# St. Mary

Early in the nineteenth century a Catholic mission started in Poole. Abbe Pierre Lanquetint, a French emigre priest, rented a farmhouse at Longfleet off Wimborne Road and said Mass there. In 1820 another French priest, Abbe Jean Coupe, purchased some land and built a little house and chapel. Thereafter several different priests served in the Mission.

In 1837, as an Act of Thanksgiving for the healing of his daughter, a parishioner, Mr. Tichbourne Doughty, of Upton House, started to build a Church in honour of Our Lady and St. Philomena, in West Quay Road. In 1839, the building was solemnly blessed and opened. In 1850, the Vicar General of the Diocese, Canon Wollet, bought more land. A school was built, later a presbytery.

In 1973, due to insufficient accommodation and a poor condition, as well as the industrial development of West Quay, the Church buildings were demolished. They were replaced by a new Church, sited once more in Wimborne Road, not far from Abbe Lanquetint's original Mass Centre.

St. Mary's was solemnly blessed and opened by the Rt. Rev. Cyril Restieaux, Bishop of Plymouth, on 25th February 1973. Several relics of the former bulding are to be found: the enormous crucifix in the sanctuary and, outside in the entrance foyer, a treasured piece of moulding from ten arches which supported the side aisles; also two superb stained glass windows, one of St. John the Evangelist, the other of the Blessed Virgin.

Contact address of Priest:
The Presbytery, 211a Wimborne Road,
Poole, Dorset. BH15 2EG.
Telephone: (0202) 675412

# Poole

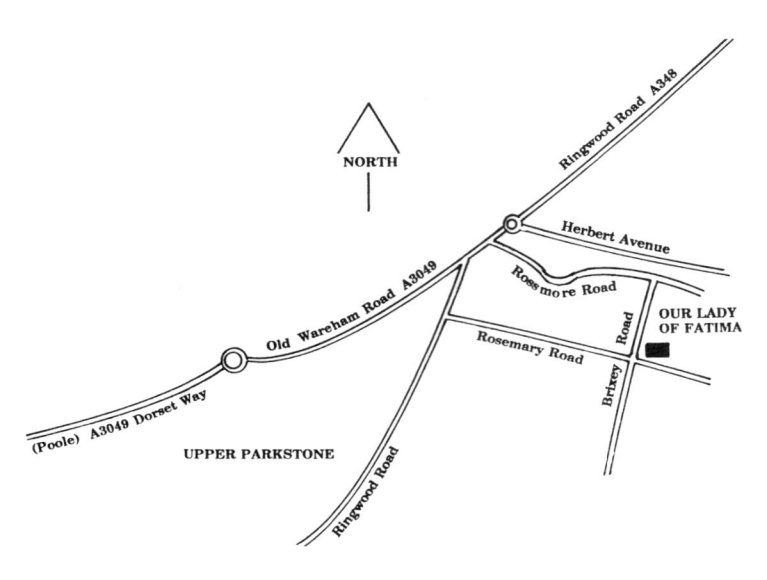

**Our Lady of Fatima,
Brixey Road, Upper Parkstone.**

The Church is signposted off a busy main road, Ringwood Road, A348. Going south from West Howe on the Ringwood Road towards Poole centre, go past the Waterworks and then the Hospital. Continue straight past Herbert Avenue and Rossmore Road. Then take a left turn into Rosemary Road. At the crossroads turn left into Brixey Road. The Church of Our Lady of Fatima is located on the right.

The dedication honours Our Lady, and recalls the apparitions at Fatima, a small town in the middle of Portugal, during the third year of the first World War. On 13th May 1917, three children, Lucia (aged 10), Francisco (aged 9) and Jacinta (aged 7) were playing at the Cova da Iria. They suddenly beheld a vision, the Mother of God, surrounded by light. On the thirteenth day, in subsequent months, Our Lady reappeared. She asked for prayer for sinners, and penance. She requested that the Rosary be said often and devoutly for the peace of the world and with an additional prayer at the end of each decade:
*"My Jesus, forgive us our sins, save us from
the fires of hell, lead all souls to heaven,
especially those in most need of Your mercy."*
On October 13th, the day of the final apparition, in pouring rain, seventy thousand people, from every sphere of life and degree of spirituality, packed the Cova da Iria. They were rewarded with the sight of an extraordinary and terrifying phenomenon, that of solar rotation and coloured lights. The children learned the identity of the visionary Lady: "I am the Lady of the Holy Rosary". The first tiny shrine and then the first little chapel at the Cova were destroyed during a display of anticlerical anger. But, it was not long before even the hardened soldiers were reciting the Rosary! Francisco died on 4th April 1919, the day after his First Holy Communion. Jacinta died not long after. Lucia survived to endure the trauma of investigation, ridicule, recognition. She became a lay sister with the Dorothean nuns near Porto four years after the Apparitions. Later she entered Carmel at Coimbra. The feast of Our Lady of the Rosary is celebrated on 7th October.

# Our Lady of Fatima

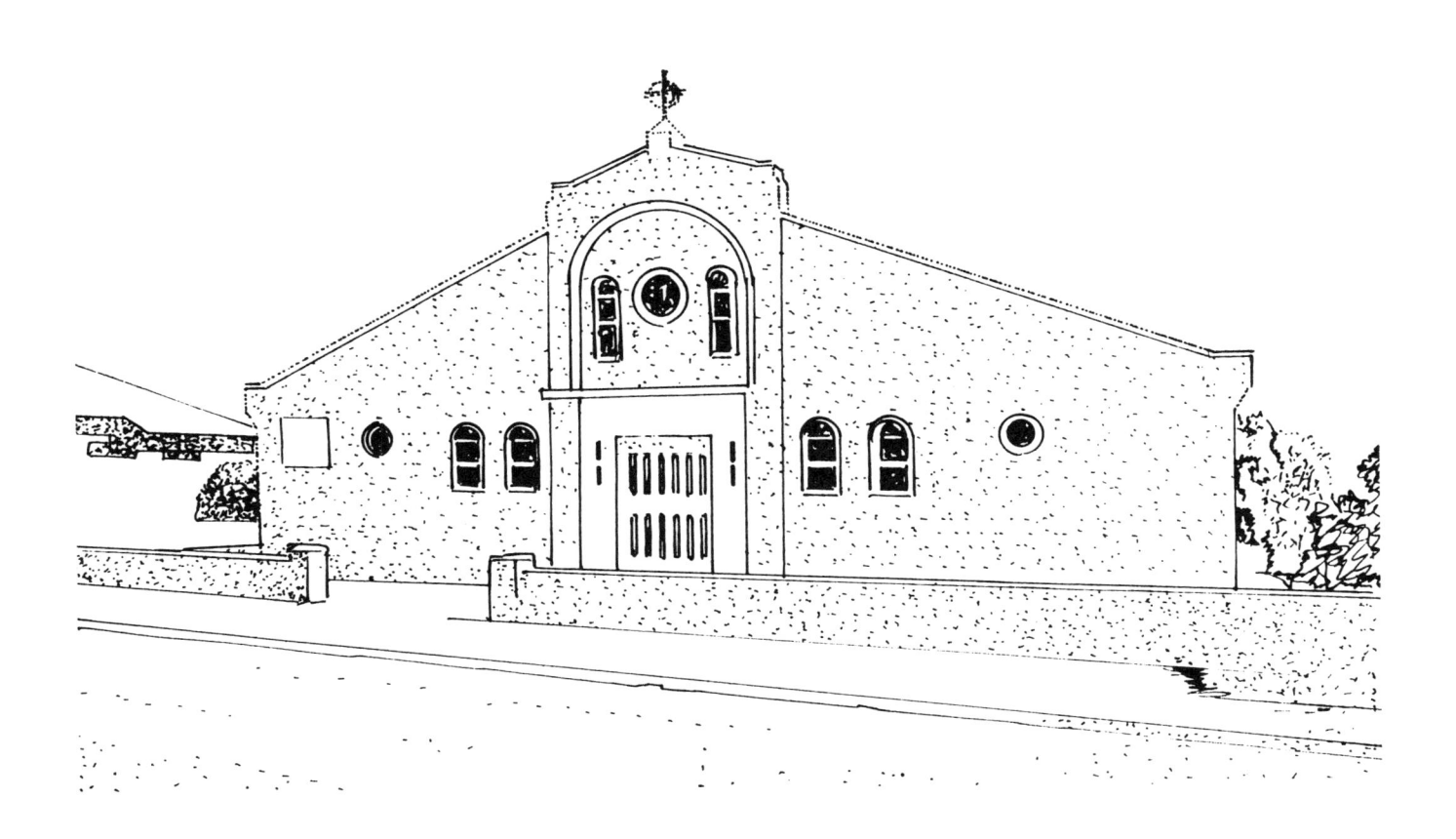

The Church of Our Lady of Fatima was opened in 1950 by Bishop Grimshaw.

Contact address of Priest:
The Presbytery, 35, Brixey Road,
Upper Parkstone, Poole, Dorset. BH12 3PB.
Telephone: (0202) 748166.

# Portland

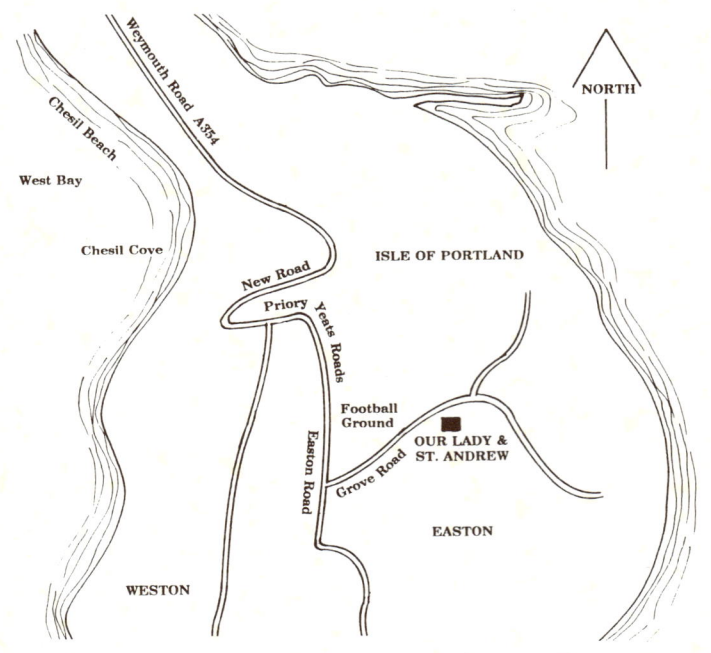

**Our Lady & St. Andrew, Grove Road.**

From Weymouth follow the A354 south to the Isle of Portland. Follow signs for Fortuneswell. Notice the sign to Grove. Go up past the "Portland Heights Hotel". The Catholic Church is signposted from the main road. It is situated about 100 yards past the football pitch in Grove Road, right on to the pavement and directly adjacent to other property. It is built of light coloured stone with a pitched roof and decorated stone cross. There is a statue of Our Lady in a niche between the windows of the facade. A noticeboard is prominent. Landmarks a few yards further up the road include a telephone box and "The Clifton Hotel". Car parking is possible at the roadside.

The dedication honours Our Lady and St. Andrew, the Apostle. St. Andrew was one of the first disciples of Christ. His home was the city of Capernaum, a busy centre for manufacturing and trade, and an important fishing port, on the north west shores of the Sea of Galilee. Like his brother, Simon Peter, Andrew was a fisherman. One day, whilst working at the nets, Our Lord called, "Come follow Me, I will make you a fisher of men." There are more references to the apostle in the Gospel. At the Feeding of the Five Thousand it is Andrew who says to Jesus, "There is a boy here who has five barley loaves and two fishes, but what is that among so many?" On another occasion, near the Paschal Feast, certain Gentiles (Greeks) wishing to speak to Jesus ask Philip to introduce them. Philip consults Andrew and then they both go to ask the Lord. St. Andrew's feast day, in universal existence from the sixth century, is celebrated on 30th November.

# Our Lady and St. Andrew

This Church, small and unpretentious, built in 1868, is hallowed by over a century of prayer. "Apud Dominum Est Misericordia".

Contact address of Priest:
The Presbytery, 47, Grove Road,
Portland, Dorset. DT5 1DA.
Telephone: (0305) 820492.

# Preston

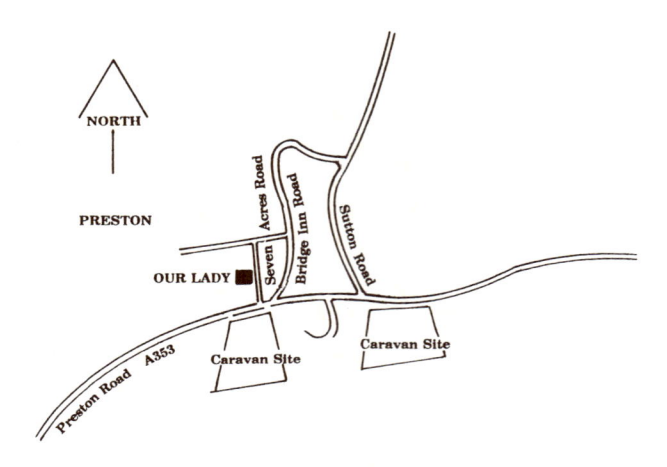

**Our Lady, Seven Acres Road.**

From St. John's Church at the bottom of Dorchester Road, Weymouth, go initially along the Sea Front, the A353 (Preston Road) signposted to Wareham. Continue for about two and a half miles. The Catholic Church is signposted. Turn left into Seven Acres Road. The Church is situated approximately one hundred and fifty yards down on the left. The Church of Our Lady is a large rectangular building of timber construction with weatherboard cladding. The windows are plain, the gable roof felted. The most noticeable external visual feature is an unusual white plaster sculpture of angels on the front end wall beside the entrance door. A bus route serves the end of Seven Acres Road. Car parking is available in the Church grounds.

The dedication honours Our Lady. Her powerful intercession helps everyone to creep closer to Christ. One of the most ancient forms of devotion to her has been the Hail Mary in use from the seventh century, as a fragmentary salutation; from the fifteenth century, in full. During the twelfth century there was a devotion called the Crown of the Virgin - it consisted of 63 Hail Mary prayers. A century later the Rosary was devised, it is thought, by St. Dominic. Another Marian tradition, dating from the fourteenth century, has been the Angelus: morning, noon and night prayer accompanied by the sound of the Church bell.

# Our Lady

This Church was built in 1967 to serve the local parishioners and the summer holidaymakers from nearby vacation camps.

Contact address of Priest:
The Presbytery, 38, Dorchester Road, Weymouth, Dorset. DT4 7JZ.
Telephone: (0305) 786886.

# Redruth

**The Assumption, West End.**

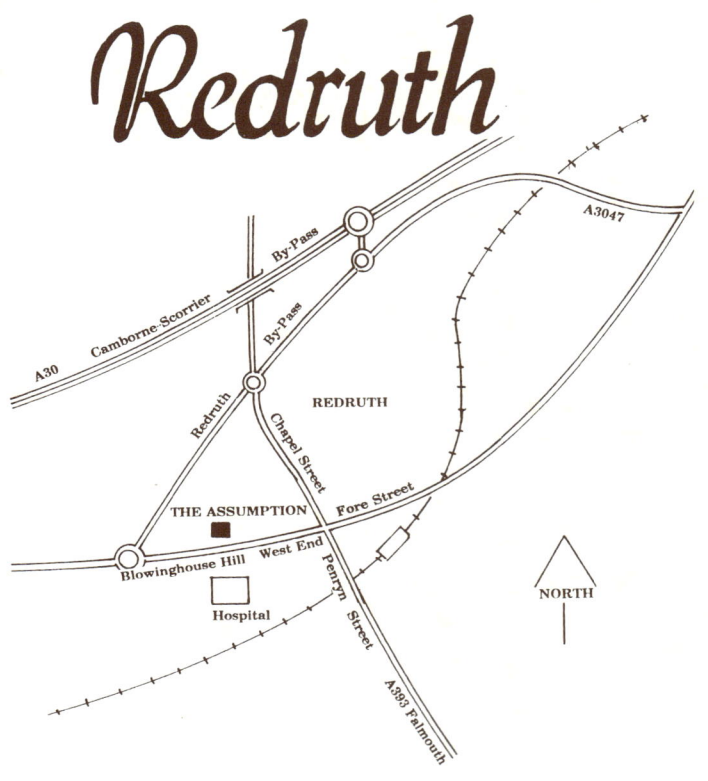

Follow the A30 from Penzance or Bodmin to Redruth. From Falmouth follow the A39 then A393 or B3298. The Church of The Assumption, a small modern building in its own little garden, next to the Convent of the Sisters of St. Joseph of Annecy, is located off the main road, West End, opposite Camborne/Redruth Hospital. Look out for a telephone and a post box on the pavement outside the Church precinct, and the municipal car park nearby. Parking at the Church is limited to the small space within the grounds. Street parking is possible after 6.00.p.m. but again very limited. A bus service between Redruth and Camborne is available and Redruth has a Railway Station (Western Region) Penzance/Paddington Main Line.

The dedication is to The Assumption of the Blessed Virgin Mary, an infallible teaching of the Church in 1950; an age old belief that Mary was taken into heaven body and soul at the end of her earthly life. History cannot tell us when or where the Blessed Virgin died. There are several theories: possibly Jerusalem was the site of Mary's passing, or maybe Ephesus, from the tradition that Mary accompanied St. John there. We believe that Mary went to God in a special way, that the body from which Jesus, the Son of God, had taken his human body should not undergo corruption. Our Lady's principal feast in the liturgical calendar, The Assumption, is on 15th August.

# The Assumption

The little Church originated from the Catholic parish of Camborne in 1936.

Contact address of Priest:
The Presbytery, 15, Trevu Road, Camborne, Cornwall. TR14 7AE.
Telephone: (0209) 713143.

# St. Agnes

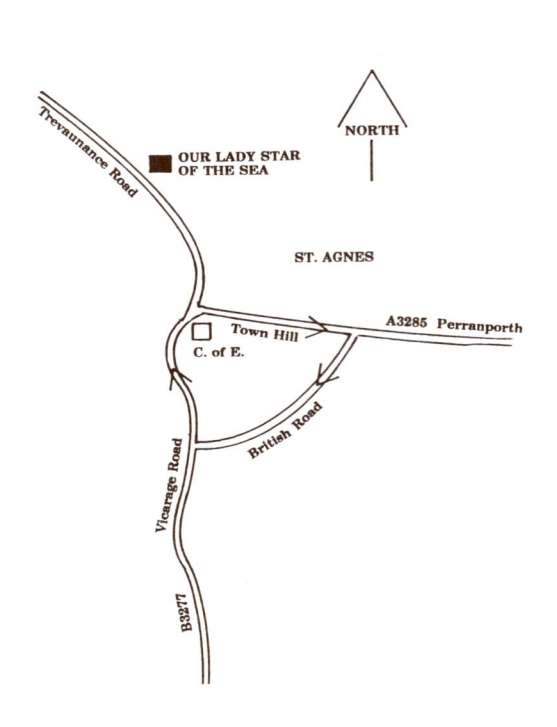

**Our Lady Star of the Sea, Trevellas Road.**

From the A30 take the B3277 to St. Agnes. From Perranporth follow the B3285. The road into the town has a clockwise one way loop. With the Parish Church (C.of E.) on the right, (a landmark because of its prominent spire), take the Trevaunance Road immediately opposite, up the hill. The Catholic Church is about 150 yards along on the right, a small modern building with a shallow pitched roof. There is a niche above the porch containing a white statue of Our Lady. Parking is available within the grounds. A local bus connects St. Agnes with Truro and Redruth.

The Church is dedicated to Our Lady Star of the Sea - a most fitting patronage as the building overlooks the Cove.

# Our Lady Star of the Sea

The Parish developed from a Mass Centre started in the time of the Irish immigrants in the mid nineteenth century. Between wars people had to walk to the nearest Mass centre at Perranporth! The present Church was built in June 1958 as a Chapel of Ease to Redruth Parish. Previously Mass had been held in the Womens' Institute room in St. Agnes village.

Contact address of Priest:
The Presbytery, Wheal Leisure Road,
Perranporth, Cornwall. TR6 0EZ.
Telephone: (0872) 573162.

# St. Austell

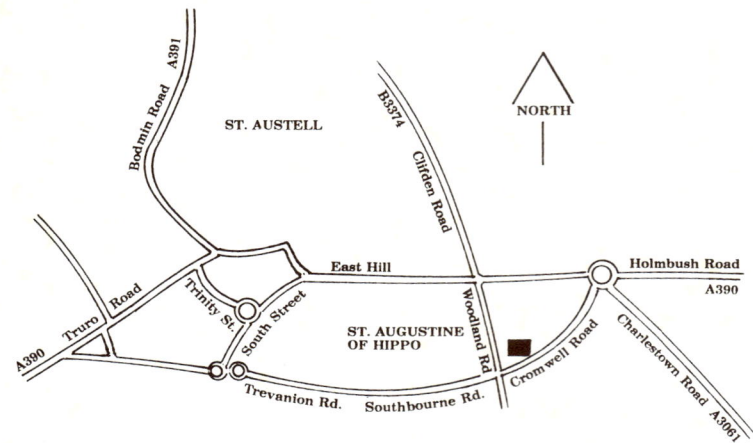

**St. Augustine of Hippo, Woodland Road.**

St. Augustine's Church is located at the junction of the A390 Cromwell Road and Woodland Road, opposite Asda Supermarket. Car parking is available within the grounds.

St. Augustine of Hippo was born in Algeria (Tagaste) in 354 A.D. Although his mother was St. Monica he did not convert to Christianity until the age of thirty three. From then on he spent his life in search of sanctity. Monasticism followed conversion, then ordination to the priesthood. At the age of forty two, he was made Bishop of Hippo. He was a great theologian and philosopher; one of the great Fathers of the Church. His writings include the famour "Confessions" and "The City of God". He died of a fever at the age of seventy six, during a Vandal attack on Hippo. His feast is celebrated on 28th August.

# St. Augustine of Hippo

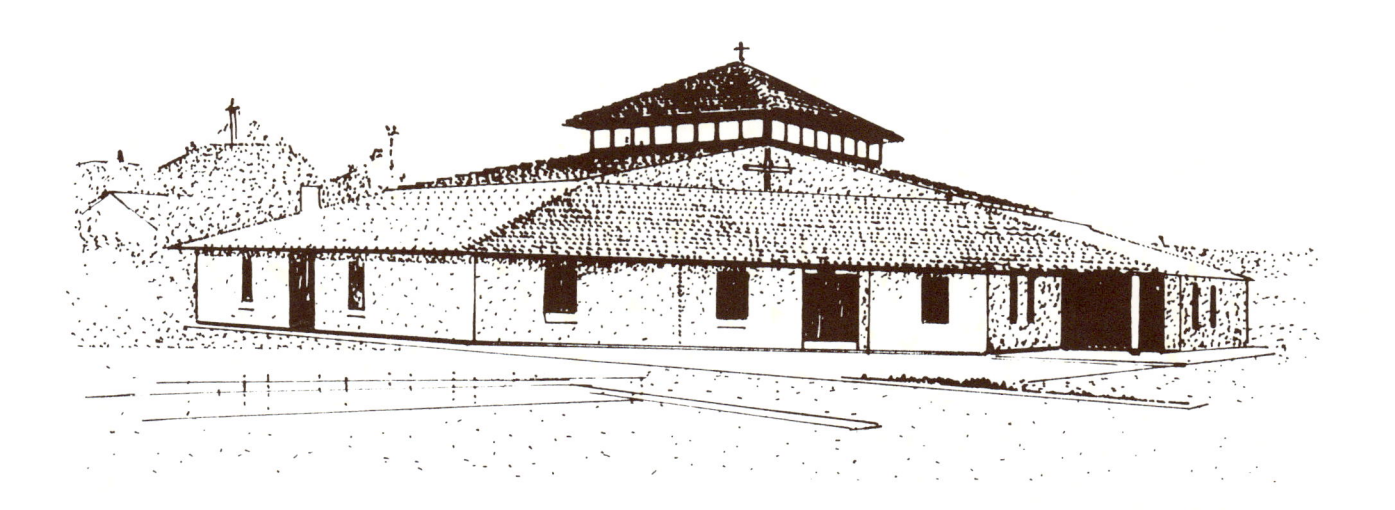

There is a record of the Bishop of St. Pol de Leon, Brittany, finding shelter in a Catholic house in St. Austell in May 1802. He had escaped from the French Revolution, and spent 72 hours in an open boat before drifting into Penzance harbour!

Catholic directories from 1857 mention Mass being said here at intervals by clergy travelling from Bodmin or Plymouth, Sclerder or Lanherne, Liskeard, Camborne or Par. The history of the Parish possibly dates from 1911 when a Sunday Mass centre was inaugurated in East Hill, St. Austell, above a painter and decorator's workshop. In 1913 the Prior of Bodmin asked the Catholic Missionary Society to come to Cornwall. Their visit prompted the establishment of a permanent Chapel in St. Austell. The Dowager Lady Bute donated one hundred pounds for the cost of the site in Ranelagh Road. Twenty four years later, on 25th March, 1937, a large site was purchased on the St. Austell By-Pass. This was due to the help of a non-catholic, Mrs Cobbold Sawle, the generosity of Mr. Julian Leacock of Wadhurst and Porthpean, the sale of the Ranelagh Road property and the fruit of years of hard saving. The Church was built that year and solemnly opened by Bishop Barrett on 8th September.

The Parish of St. Augustine had its first resident priest, in fact, its first parish priest (from Bodmin) on 30th October 1960. Thirty years later, 6th May 1990, saw the dedication of a new Church of St. Augustine of Hippo on the same hallowed spot in Woodland Road. The ceremony was blessed with the presence of the Rt. Rev. Christopher Budd, Bishop of Plymouth, and His Excellency Archbishop Luigi Barbarito, Apostolic Pro Nuncio to Great Britain who brought a letter from His Holiness Pope John Paul II for the occasion.

There are some rather special items of modern art work to be seen within the Church interior: sculpture by David John and stained glass by Marc Angus. The plaque in the Lady Chapel depicts The Holy Family with St. Anne, portrayed in the background are the local clay tips. The wooden crucifix before the altar shows Christ with St. Augustine and St. Monica at the foot of the Cross. On the reverse is carved the Lamb of Sacrifice. There is a deep font for Baptism by full immersion. (In Early Christian times, at the adult baptism ceremony on Easter night, the catechumens were "plunged" three times!) The bronze sculpture above the font illustrates St. John baptizing the Lord in the Jordan.

# St. Augustine of Hippo

**6. VERONICA WIPES THE FACE OF JESUS**

The Stations of the Cross, painted by a parishioner, Pamela Platt, in 1966, were brought from the old Church, thus adding a personal link with the past. Their individual style promotes yet another thought on the Passion of Christ Our Lord. A relic of St. Augustine (formally in the possession of the Benedictine Nuns of Teignmouth) and a relic of St. Cuthbert Mayne (from Lanherne Carmel) are contained within the altar of the Church here in St. Austell.

Contact address of Priest:
The Presbytery, Woodland Road,
St. Austell, Cornwall. PL25 4RA.
Telephone: (0726) 73838.

# St. Ives

### Sacred Heart & St. Ia, Tregenna Hill.

Enter St. Ives from the A3074 off the A30 Camborne/Penzance Road, the B3311 from Penzance or the B3306 from St. Just. The Church of the Sacred Heart & St. Ia, built of Cornish granite in Early English style, is set on the hill in a busy position. It is obviously Catholic, not only proved by the sign outside, but also proudly revealed by the wall plaque commemorating the four hundredth anniversary of the Western Rising 1549-1949, when John Payne the Mayor (Portreeve) of St. Ives and fellow townsmen fought and died for their Faith. The memorial plaque, of bronze set on polished granite, shows Christ on the Cross, the Church near the sea, a martyr on a gibbet, St. Ia the patron, and a priest celebrating Mass. There is a stone seat beneath the plaque offering an opportunity for rest or contemplation. Opposite the Church is a telephone kiosk and the sign "Tregenna Hill". A large car park is located by St. Ives Railway Station and another one, clearly signposted, is approached from the top of Tregenna Hill, to the left. For rail travellers, the London to Penzance train stops at St. Erth Station with a connecting train to St. Ives.

The Church is dedicated to the Sacred Heart of Jesus and the patroness and name saint of St. Ives, St. Ia. A legendary biography of St. Ia was mislaid or spoilt in the Reformation, but a few details exist. St. Ia was apparently, one of a group of Irish missionaries who came to Cornwall about 460 A.D. The saint found herself separated from her companions, but after praying she spotted a coracle, (some legends tell of an enormous leaf), which carried her safely to the port of Hayle. She built an oratory in St. Ives, now the site of the present Parish Church. St. Ia worked hard to foster the Christian faith in this part of Cornwall. She was martyred with several other missionaries on the orders of Theodoric, a local chieftain who had a castle in Hayle. Her relics were placed in the oratory which she had founded. During the fifteenth century a new Parish Church was built and her relics were laid there. St. Ia's feast is recorded in the liturgical calendar on 3rd February. The following Sunday a special Mass and procession are held in her honour in the Catholic Church here and then the whole town celebrates a public holiday "Feast Monday".

# Sacred Heart and St. Ia

During the eighteenth and nineteenth centuries St. Ives seemed to have completely broken with the Faith which it had formerly cherished. Foreign visitors, Breton fishermen, Irish workers, shipwrecked sailors had to go as far as Penzance for Mass. In 1901 a site in Street-an-Pol, once used as a shop and warehouse, was bought by a rich Catholic convert who then presented it to the Canons Regular of the Lateran for a new "Mission". The first Mass was celebrated on 16th February 1902 with only a very few people present. As time went on Mass attendance increased and it became necessary to find a more suitable location at the top of Skidden Hill facing Tregenna Hill. The new Church was blessed on 21st September 1908 by Bishop Charles Graham and solemnly opened with the celebration of Pontifical High Mass on 24th September 1908.

The Church has fulfilled an artistic role, past and present, in this renowned part of Cornwall. The memorial plaque, already mentioned, was made by a Benedictine monk, Fr. Charles Norris of Buckfast Abbey. Other artists' work can be seen in the interior. The wooden statue of St. Ia was carved by a parishioner, Faust Lang of Oberammergau, from a thick section of Austrian Oak found floating in St. Ives Bay. Near the statue are seventeen painted panels, in the style of El Greco, depicting Our Lord with the Twelve Apostles and four Latin Doctors of the Church: St. Ambrose of Milan, St. Augustine of Hippo, Pope St. Gregory the Great and St. Jerome. The panels were a gift of the late Mr. & Mrs Philip Hill for the Consecration of the Church on 8th May 1946.

*"When you come into this church remember
that Our Lord Jesus Christ is here.
He is present and to be adored in the
Blessed Sacrament.
Kneel down and worship Him.
Give thanks for your blessings.
Bring to Him your needs.
Remember all in distress, sorrow, pain.
Pray that the dead may rest in peace.
And do not forget those who minister
and worship here."*

Contact address of Priest:
The Presbytery, Tregenna Hill,
St. Ives, Cornwall. TR26 1SE.
Telephone: (0736) 796412.

# St. Mawes

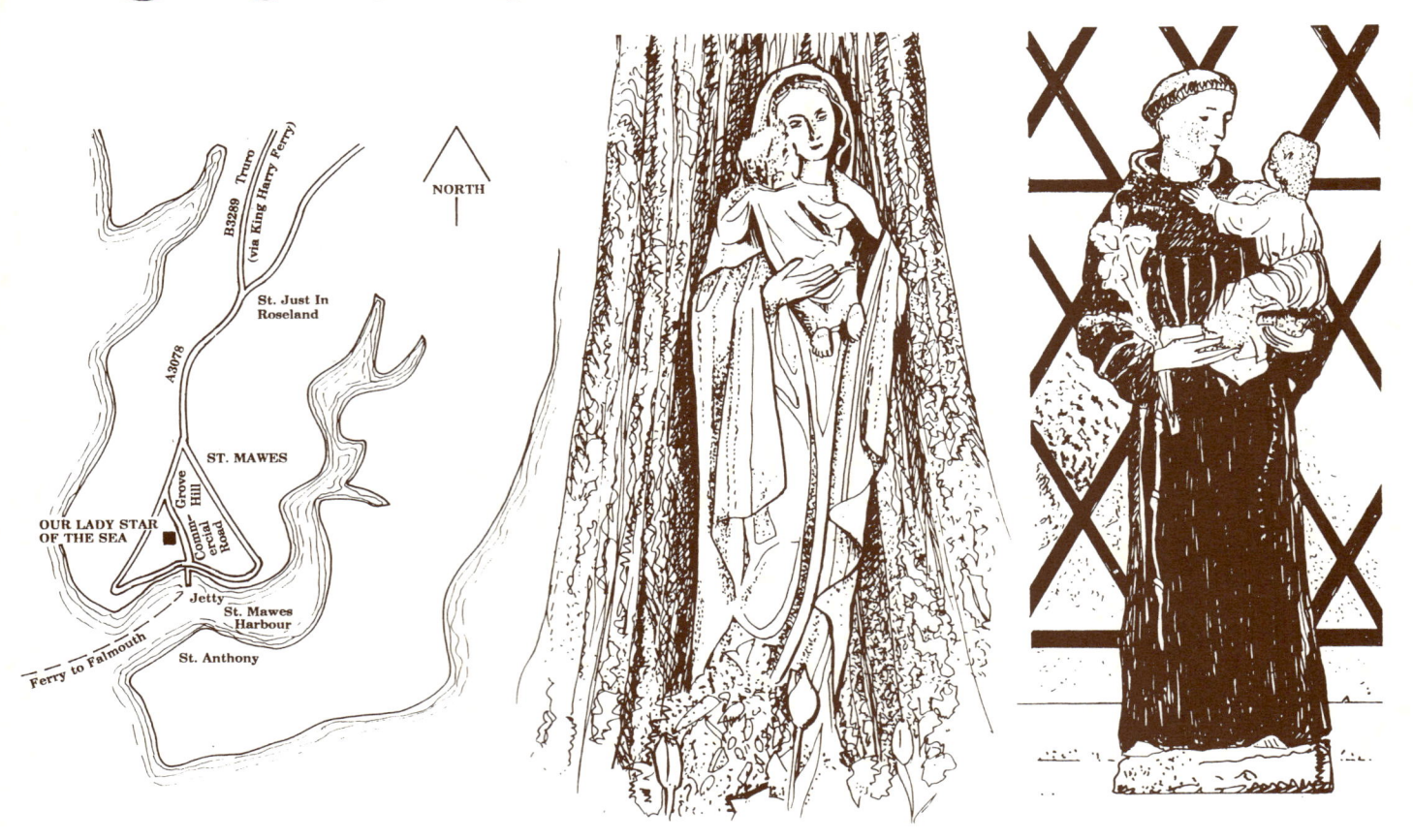

### Our Lady Star of the Sea
### & St. Anthony of Padua,    Grove Hill.

From St. Austell take the A390 south west, turn left on to the B3287 then the A3078 to St. Mawes. From Truro go south on the A39, turn left on to the B3289 then follow the A3078 to St. Mawes. Nearly opposite the stone jetty is Commercial Road and a sign indicating the proximity of the Catholic Church. There is a steep climb up to Grove Hill to the Church of Our Lady Star of the Sea & St. Anthony of Padua, situated on the left, built of stone, with decorative curved detail on its gable and celtic cross.

The dedication is twofold: the patronage topical, honouring Our Lady Star of the Sea and also St. Anthony, the saint popularly invoked by those in danger of shipwreck and renowned for his intercession in the recovery of lost things. St. Anthony's feast day is kept on 13th June.

*"We welcome you to this beautiful*
*House of God.*
*Stay, rest and pray a while*
*and give thanks for life*
*and all its blessings."*

The Foundation stone for this Church was laid on May 6th 1875 by the Bible Christians. They held their first service on Christmas Day in the same year. Between 1929 and 1932 they decided to reunite with the Methodist Community and they moved to the Methodist Chapel. In 1937 a group of St. Mawes' Catholics got together and raised enough funds, seven hundred and fifty pounds, to buy this Church. After some restoration and an extension the building was ready for use.

# Our Lady of the Sea and St. Anthony

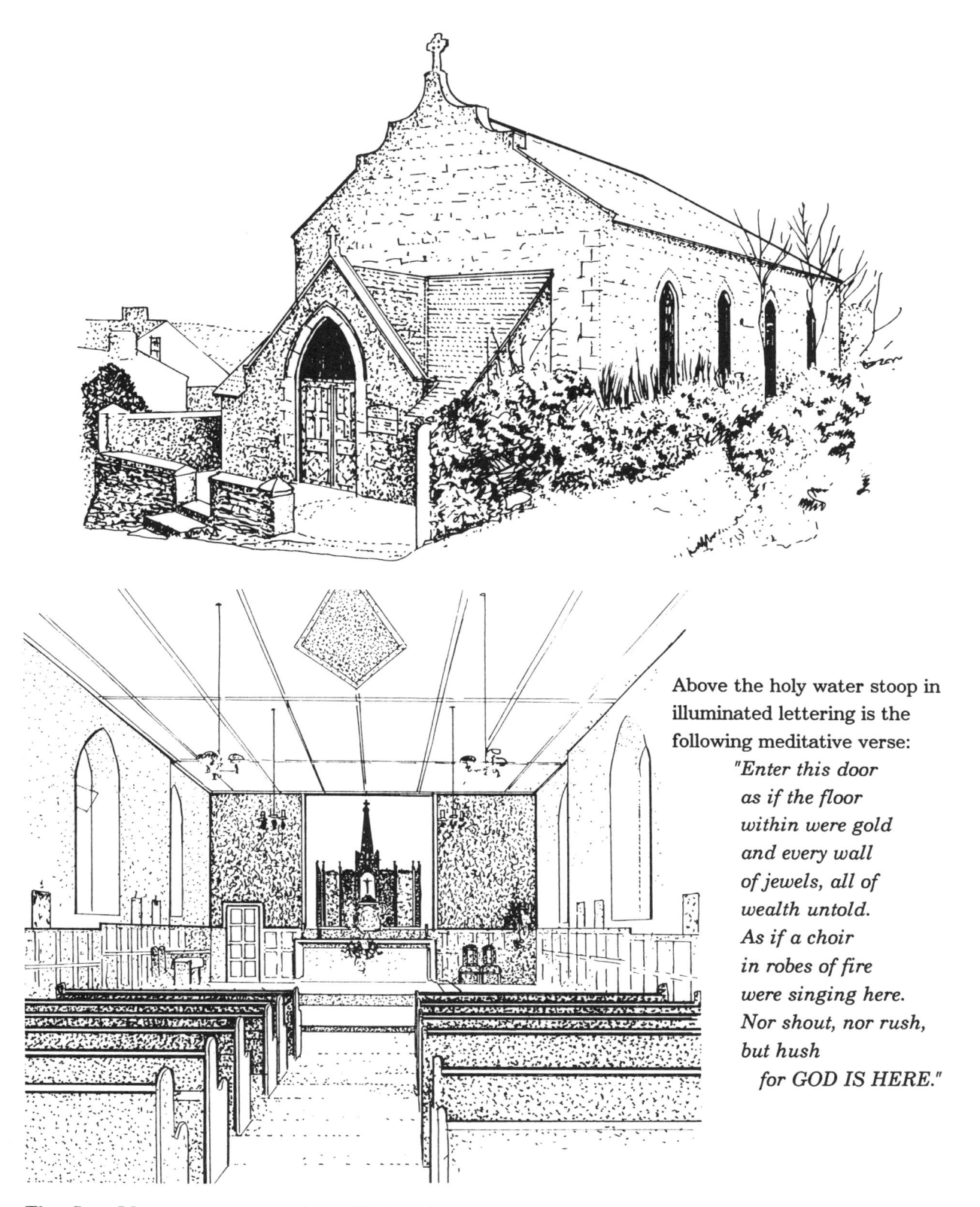

Above the holy water stoop in illuminated lettering is the following meditative verse:

> "Enter this door
> as if the floor
> within were gold
> and every wall
> of jewels, all of
> wealth untold.
> As if a choir
> in robes of fire
> were singing here.
> Nor shout, nor rush,
> but hush
>    for GOD IS HERE."

The first Mass was celebrated in 1938 and the parish was served then from Falmouth. A presbytery was added eight years later. It was not until 1956 that St. Mawes had its own resident Catholic priest.

Contact address of Priest:
The Presbytery, St. Austell Street,
Truro, Cornwall. TR1 1SE.
Telephone: (0872) 72291.

# Salcombe

Salcombe is a seaside town, hence the dedication to Our Lady Star of the Sea. "Stella Maris", Star of the Sea, Mother of God and of us all. This particular Marian title is invoked by seafarers and their families worldwide:

*Our Lady, Star of the Sea    Pray for us*
*Our Lady, Mother of Families    Pray for us*
*Our Lady, Mother of Sorrow    Pray for us*
*Our Lady, Mother of Justice    Pray for us*
*Our Lady, Mother of the Lonely    Pray for us*
*Our Lady, Mother of Joy    Pray for us*
*Our Lady, Mother of Hope    Pray for us*
*Our Lady, Blesssed among all women  Pray for us*
*Our Lady, Mother of God    Pray for us*
*Our Lady, Help of Christians    Pray for us*
*(Short Litany to Our Lady Star of the Sea)*
*(Apostleship of the Sea)*

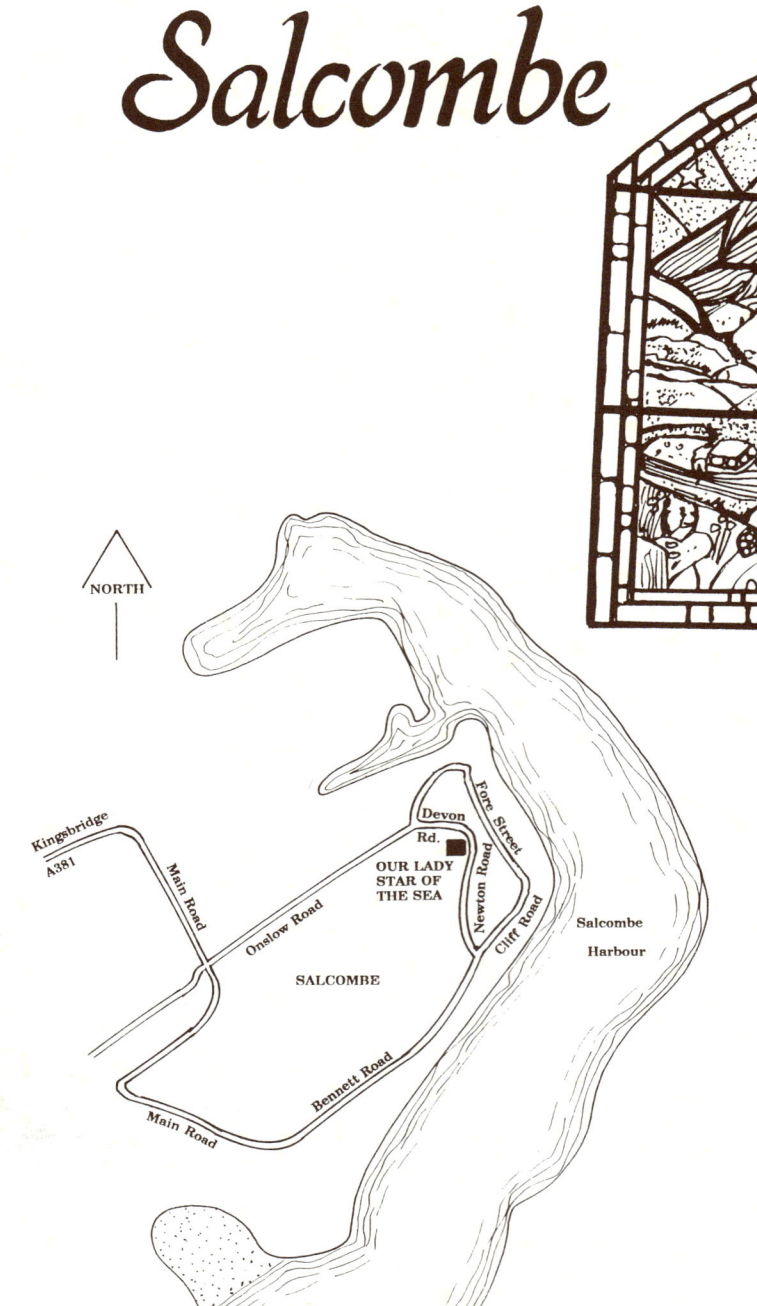

**Our Lady Star of the Sea, Devon Road.**

Salcombe is well signposted from Kingsbridge on the A381, a six mile drive. On entering Salcombe initially follow the signs for the town centre, but before reaching there, notice the road starting to go down hill, Devon Road. The Church is situated about three quarters of the way down on the left hand side. It is a red brick building, set back from the pavement, in its own small plot. There is a notice board well visible from the road. A tiny car park is available for Parishioners' use in front of the Church, but note that the space is limited and parking can be very difficult in the summer holiday season. There is a bus service from Kingsbridge.

TOTA PULCHRA ES MARIA

# Our Lady Star of the Sea

The Church was built about 1960. Before that Catholics joined a good family nearby for Sunday Mass in their Chapel converted from a stable. The present building is small, seating approximately one hundred. There are few adornments, but mention must be made of the unusual stained glass windows honouring Mary, Star of the Sea, blessed by Bishop Budd in Autumn 1988. The windows are on the north and south walls of the sanctuary. There is more stained glass at the west end of the Church.

Contact address of Priest:
The Presbytery, 19, Foss Road,
Kingsbridge, Devon. TQ7 1NG.
Telephone: (0548) 852670.

# Saltash

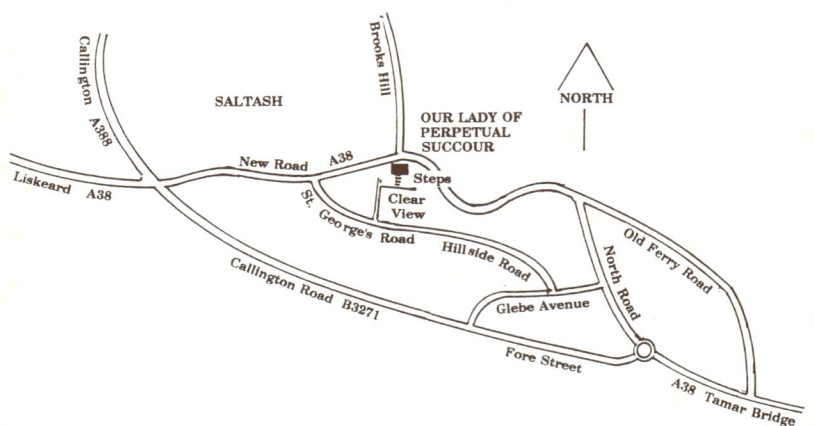

**Our Lady of Perpetual Succour, Newton Road.**

From Plymouth follow the A38 west over the Tamar bridge into Cornwall; from Liskeard follow the A38 east; from Launceston/Callington follow the A388 south to Saltash. The Church of Our Lady of Perpetual Succour is situated off New Road. Its bold, distinctive, white shape with a large black wrought iron cross on top can be seen from a distance. Car parking is available in front of the Church building. From Hillside Road there is a small wrought iron gate with a sign "Catholic Church" and beyond it steps lead down to the Church.

The patron of this Parish is the Blessed Virgin and a copy of the thirteenth century Byzantine picture of Our Lady of Perpetual Succour adorns the Marian altar. (The original is in the Redemptorist Church of St. Alphonsus in Rome.) There is quite a story to the original painting which was initially housed in a Church in Crete. In the fifteenth century it was stolen by a merchant and transported to Rome ending up in St. Matthew's Church in the Hermitage of St. Augustine where it remained for three hundred years. When Napoleon ordered his troops into Rome in 1798, many churches (including St. Matthew's) were demolished and used to strengthen defences. The picture of Our Lady of Perpetual Succour was safely concealed by the monks, but not forgotten. It was later placed with the Redemptorists whose Novena, in honour of Our Lady, under this invocation is perpetual and said from east to west!

# Our Lady of Perpetual Succour

On 1st May 1884 French Franciscans came to open a novitiate in Saltash. Their new church was called "Our Lady of the Angels". The Catholic Parish of Saltash had begun. In 1896, the Franciscans left the area and returned the Mission to the Bishop who purchased the property. At the beginning of the twentieth century a Fr. Morford was the Parish Priest. He was a talented musician, a former pupil of the renowned Abbe Franz Liszt. When he departed in 1916, the Sisters of Charity of St. Vincent de Paul arrived. They intended to use the buildings at Port View as a country house for St. Teresa's Orphanage in Plymouth. At this particular time the parish was served from St. Joseph's in Devonport, until a Fr. Northcote became Parish Priest in 1919 and bought himself a house in North Road. Two years later the Sisters of the Good Shepherd settled in Saltash and founded St. Ann's Convent. On 4th November 1935 Bishop Barrett laid the foundation stone for the present Church of Our Lady of Perpetual Succour, attached to the Convent. The Church was opened in 1935. When the Sisters left Saltash in October 1959 they kindly sold the Church, part of the Convent for a presbytery, and a portion of land to the Diocese.

Contact address of Priest:
The Presbytery, 291, New Road,
Saltash, Cornwall. PL12 6HQ.
Telephone: (0752) 843622.

# Sclerder Abbey

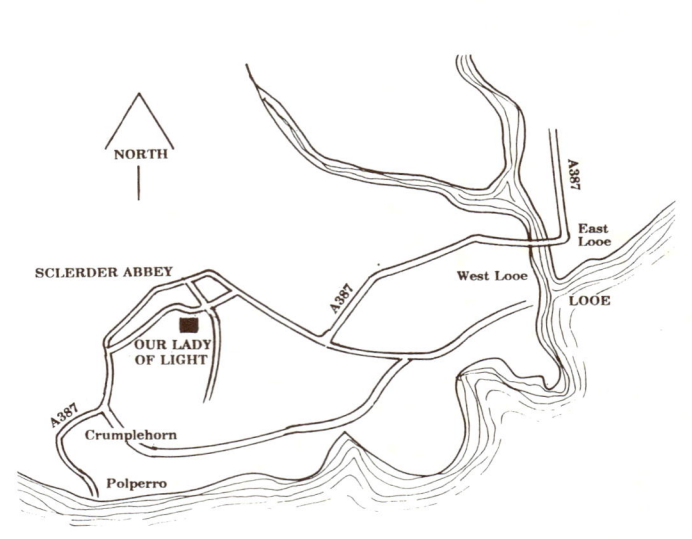

**Our Lady of Light, Nr. Looe.**

From Plymouth follow the A38 over the Tamar Bridge into Cornwall. Continue along the A38 for about 8 miles. Then follow the A374. Turn right on to the A387, Looe is signposted. Follow signs for West Looe then signs for Polperro. On the road to Polperro go past West Wayland Farm on the left, telephone kiosk outside. Continue straight. Follow the road as it curves then immediately notice the sign for Talland and turn left down the lane. There are also signs for Newton Farm and Porthallow Farm and another sign "Catholic Church". Go down the lane. Turn right. There is a notice "Carmelite Monastery - Sclerder Abbey". The entrance to the Church of Our Lady of Light is through a little gate at the far end of the Abbey. It is possible that the design of the building originated from some of Pugin's sketches. It is built of local slate stone and some Portland stone. There is a car park behind gates.

The dedication is linked with the word Sclerder and a certain connection between Brittany and Cornwall, for the old Breton word for light is Sclerder, and is used in the title of the Shrine of "Our Lady of Light" near St. Pol de Leon. (Incidentally, during the French Revolution Cornish smugglers rescued the Bishop of St. Pol de Leon, so there may have been an association throughout the centuries.)

# Our Lady of Light

The inaugural Mass and Vespers took place on 6th October 1843. Father Marc Oleron, of Rennes, was the first cleric in charge of Sclerder. During his ministry the patron of the Church was St. Charles Borromeo possibly because Father Marc was an Oblate of St. Charles. In the middle of the nineteenth century Sclerder was served from other parishes and in due time it was decided to invite a Religious Order to Sclerder to sustain its Catholicism. From 1851-1852 some French Sisters, Dames de la Retraite, from Lannion in Brittany lived at Sclerder. When they left the place became an abode for priests needing a rest. According to the Records, in 1856, the title for the Mission was the "Church of St. Mary apud Sclerder". A year later, however, the dedication was formally altered to "Our Lady of Light".

From 1858-1864 a Community of Franciscan Recollect Fathers (from Belgium) lived at Sclerder. Their departure made room for a first Carmelite foundation (from Lanherne). The sisters stayed for seven years and then moved on. For over thirty years there was an absence of Religious. Then from 1904-1910 Sisters of the Sacred Hearts of Jesus and Mary, French refugees, from a Convent at St. Quay in Brittany, came to live at the Abbey. From 1914-1920 a different French Community took up residence, Poor Clares, from Rennes. They were succeeded in 1922 by Poor Clares from Bullingham, Hereford, who remained for nearly sixty years. On 30th May 1981, a second foundation of Carmelites, from Quidenham, Norfolk, came to Sclerder. It was the feast of Our Lady of Light!

# Our Lady of Light

Contact address of Priest:
The Presbytery, Sclerder,
Looe, Cornwall. PL13 2JD.
Telephone: (0503) 72627.

# Seaton

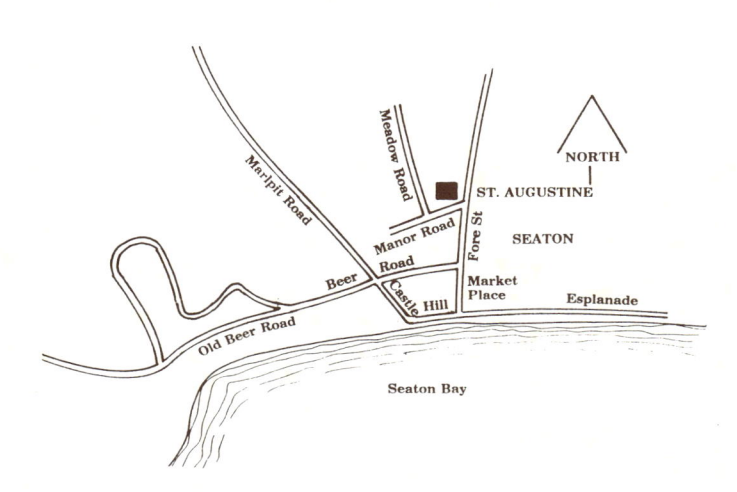

**St. Augustine, Manor Road.**

From Exeter (twenty three miles) or from Lyme Regis A3052 turn at the Water Tower into Seaton Down Road. At the road junction (1 mile) turn right and then first left into Manor Road. The red brick Church of St. Augustine is located on the left at the bottom of Manor Road. There is restricted parking in the streets adjoining the Church. The nearest car park is approximately a quarter of a mile distant, in the town. The nearest Railway Station is seven miles away at Axminster.

The dedication is to St. Augustine, Bishop of Hippo, in N. Africa, who lived 354-430 A.D. Soon after his conversion at the age of thirty three, he founded a hermit community at Tagaste (Algeria). From that hermitage evolved many other monasteries. By the Middle Ages the Rule of St. Augustine was being followed by religious orders in several countries. In 1256 Pope Augustine IV (1254-1261) made these communities unite under the Order of Hermits of St. Augustine. In 1588 after the religious turmoil in parts of Europe, caused by the Reformation, there was a return to a more austere observance which was particularly successful in Spain. In due course, the "Recollection" permeated throughout Europe. In 1912, Pope St. Pius X acknowledged the Recollect Communities as a separate Religious Order. In 1612 the Recollects, with Fr. Thomas Semple, began a Mission in Scotland. There was no community in England until 1931 when, as a consequence of the anti-clerical atmosphere in Spain, the Order first sought refuge on English soil at Ivybridge, followed by Honiton. The feast of St. Augustine is kept on 28th August.

# St. Augustine

In 1910 Catholicism began to re-emerge in Seaton with a succession of Priests coming to live in the district. They included a Fr. Patrick O'Toole, a retired priest. He said Mass at "The Breakers" and also, it is reported, at what is now York Villa, New Road, Beer. Many Catholics fled the horrors of Europe at War in 1914. Quite a large number of Belgians came to live in and around Seaton. One of the Catholic refugees was a Father Jules Van Heede. He came first of all to stay with his cousin Canon Ketele at Lyme and whilst there he was asked by the Bishop to serve Honiton Parish. In due course, Fr. Jules Van Heede opened a temporary "tin" Church in Station Road (Harbour Road). When he left the area Fr. O'Toole took over the Mission. Other priests who served the area between 1910 and 1934 were Fr. Albert Hawkins (at Beer) and, in 1929, Fr. James Tymons (at Seaton).

In 1934 Bishop Barrett put the Parish into the care of the Augustinian Recollect Fathers under the direction of Fr. Mariano Ortiz O.A.R. Once installed, Fr. Ortiz bought a piece of ground at the corner of Manor Road from a Mr. Smith. This was the site for a new Church of St. Augustine of Hippo and on July 1st 1937 the foundation stone was laid by Bishop Barrett. The Church was opened for Public Worship later in the year, on the third Sunday in November.

In 1939 the Franciscan Sisters of Mill Hill took up residence in Seaton Parish. (It may be of interest to note that the life size crucifix in the Sanctuary, originally from France, was a gift from St. Mary's Abbey, Mill Hill.) On May 5th 1962 another new Church dedicated to St. Dympna (patron of handicapped children) was opened on a hilltop overlooking Seaton. In October 1976 Fr. Ortiz retired as parish priest of Seaton, but remained as chaplain of St. Dympna's, saying daily Mass. He was then 85 years old. Father John Currie became the parish priest. St. Augustine's Church was finally consecrated on the feast of Corpus Christi June 18th 1981.

Contact address of Priest:
The Presbytery, Manor Road,
Seaton, Devon. EX12 2AJ.
Telephone: (0297) 20476.

# Shaftesbury

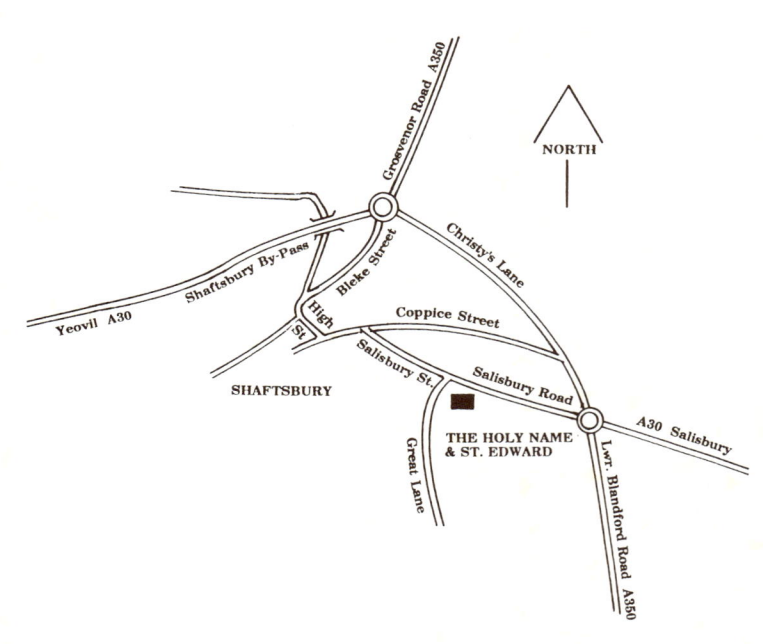

**The Holy Name & St. Edward, Salisbury Street.**

This Parish covers a beautiful part of North Dorset with views of outstanding beauty. It is a large area, extending over seven Anglican parishes. Many roads lead into Shaftesbury: the A350 Bournemouth to Warminster/Trowbridge; the B3081 Bruton/Gillingham to Ringwood; and B3091 from Sturminster Newton; also the A30 Yeovil to Salisbury which passes the front door of this Church. There is a long distance bus service, Bournemouth to Bristol, via the A350, and a local bus service. Ample car parking is available in the town.

St. Edward, the young king and martyr, murdered in 979 A.D. at Corfe Castle, was buried in Shaftesbury Abbey, hence the dedication to the Saint (apparently the only one in Shaftesbury). The Benedictine Abbey of Shaftesbury, now in ruins, was founded in 880 A.D. by the famous Saxon King, Alfred the Great. It became a final resting place for royal personages. In 980, the Benedictine Saint, Dunstan, organised a translation of Edward's body to the Abbey. Regard for the young martyr King spread, and many pilgrims flocked to his Shrine. When Shaftesbury Abbey, consecrated by Anselm, (later St. Anselm) Archbishop of Canterbury, in 1107, was dissolved at the Reformation, St. Edward's relics were hidden. Skeletal remains discovered during excavations in the 1930's are thought to be those of Saint Edward. His feast day is on March 18th.

# The Holy Name and St. Edward the Martyr

This Church, designed by Doran-Webb, was built in 1910 by the Sons of Mary Immaculate (FMI) whose Motherhouse was then in Shaftesbury. The latter is now The Royal Chase Hotel. Land for the Church was purchased when the Stalbridge Family (connected with the Duke's of Westminster) sold Shaftesbury. The Church is built in the late English style, of local Tisbury stone from Newtown Quarry. The same quarry provided stone, in 1960, for the stations of the Cross, carved by Peter Watts of Bath, a West Country artist of some renown. The interior of the Church contains other carvings also tastefully executed. The statue of Our Lady, Queen & Mother, is a replica of one in the Victoria & Albert Museum, completed in Italy. The stone carved reredos depicts St. Edward the Martyr, flanked by St. Michael, St. George, St. Boniface and St. Aldhelm, (the last, one of the Dorset saints.)

Contact address of Priest:
The Presbytery, 55, Salisbury Street,
Shaftesbury, Dorset. SP7 8EL.
Telephone: (0747) 52125.

# Shaldon

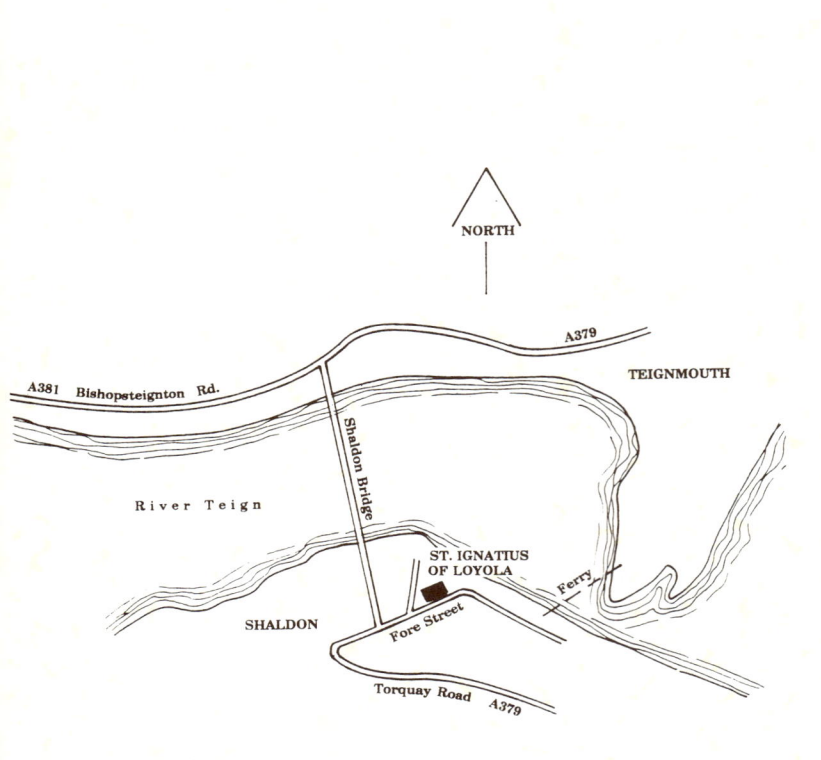

**St. Ignatius of Loyola, Fore Street.**

From Teignmouth cross the bridge over the River Teign; from Torquay follow the A379 north, turn right before the bridge; from Newton Abbot follow the A381 Teignmouth/ Newton Road and cross the bridge over the River Teign into Shaldon. Turn into Fore Street. The Catholic Church is not very far into the village, set back from the pavement behind a wall and wrought iron gate, opposite a butchers and a Spar shop. There is a bench on the patio outside the Church. Public transport operates between Exeter, Teignmouth and Torquay. Car parking in Shaldon in summer can be very difficult. Parking facilities are available by "The Green" and in "The Ness" car park.

The Church is dedicated to St. Ignatius, the founder of the Jesuits, patron of soldiers, scholars and those making a spiritual retreat. He was born in 1491 in the family castle in Loyola, Spain, the youngest out of eleven children. In his later youth he joined the army intent on a military career, but it was not to be. In 1521 he was gravely wounded in the siege of Pamplona, fighting the French invasion of Castile. As he began to recover he started reading the only literature available - a Life of Christ and a book of Saints. It had a profound influence on him. Soon after his convalescence he set off for Manresa, near the Abbey of Montserrat, to spend a year alone in penance and prayer. In 1523, he went on a pilgrimage to the Holy Land. Then he set himself on a course of many years study of latin, philosophy and theology. Eventually he was ordained a Priest, and in 1540 he received papal approval to found a new Religious Order, the "Society of Jesus". Ignatius died on 31st July 1556. He was proclaimed a saint by Pope Gregory XV (1621-1623). His feast day is kept on the anniversary of his demise.

# St. Ignatius of Loyola

This Church was formerly a Baptist Chapel, built in 1795. It was acquired for the Plymouth Diocese in 1931 by Mgr. Ignatius Morrissey, parish priest of Teignmouth and served from there. In 1948 a Father Henry O'Brien was made the priest in charge. Then in 1952 Shaldon became an independent Parish under the care of Fr. Thomas Horsfield. The Church was repaired and restored in 1988.

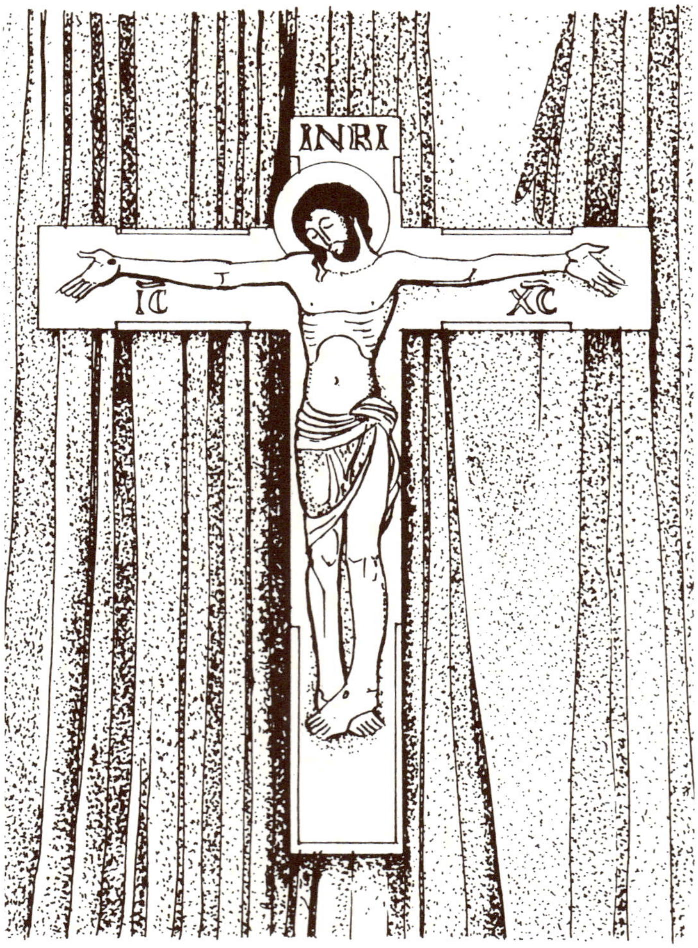
INRI
IC
XC

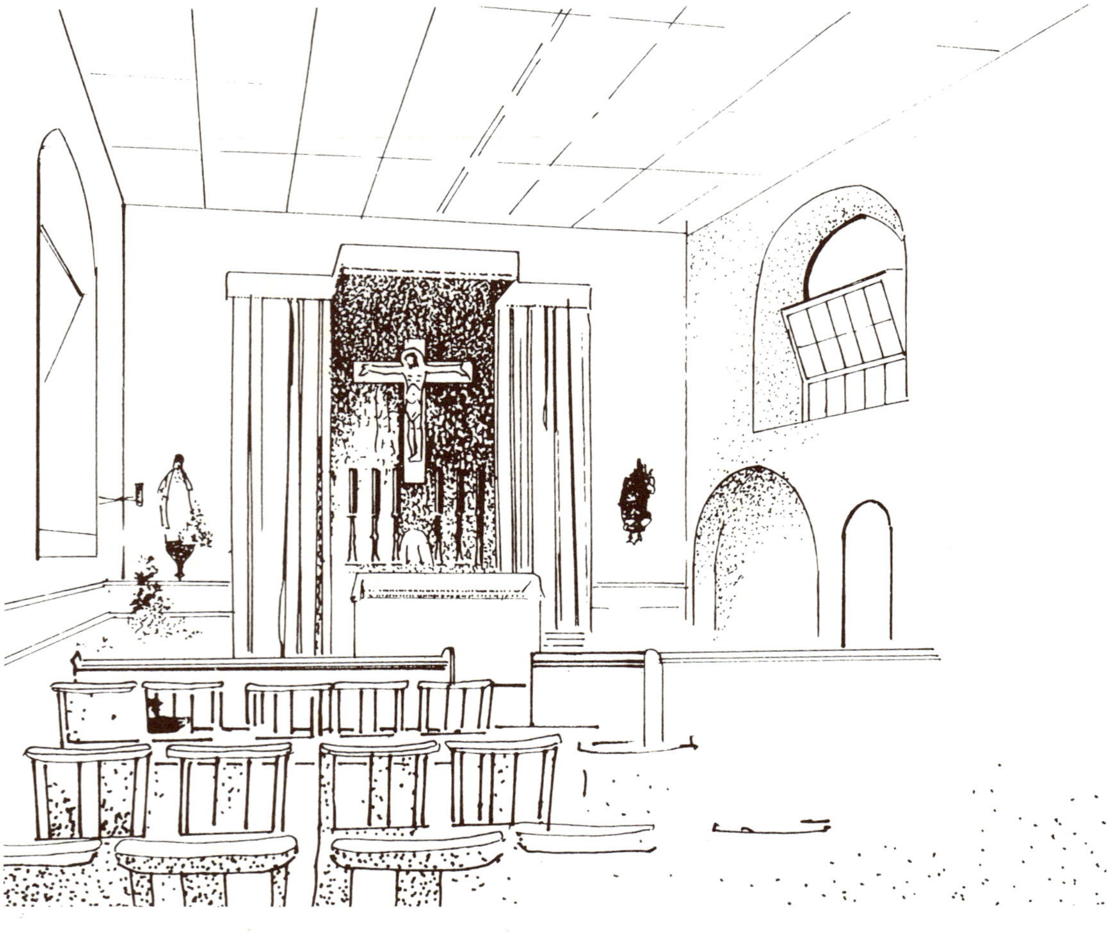

# St. Ignatius of Loyola

In the side chapel there is an embroidered banner remarkably comparable in style to the exquisite religious banner embroidery, some of it centuries old, exhibited at the Kreisker Church, St. Pol de Leon, Brittany, in August 1990. In another part of the Church there is a copy and explanation of the eighteenth century icon "The Protection (Pokrov) of the Mother of God". The historical origin of this icon dates back to the tenth century to the Russian Church of Blacherne, the scene of a vision. Here also in the Church of St. Ignatius there is a fine reproduction of the Murillo painting the "Education of the Virgin".

Contact address of Priest:
The Presbytery, 42, Fore Street,
Shaldon, Devon. TQ14 0EA.
Telephone: (0626) 873410.

# Sherborne

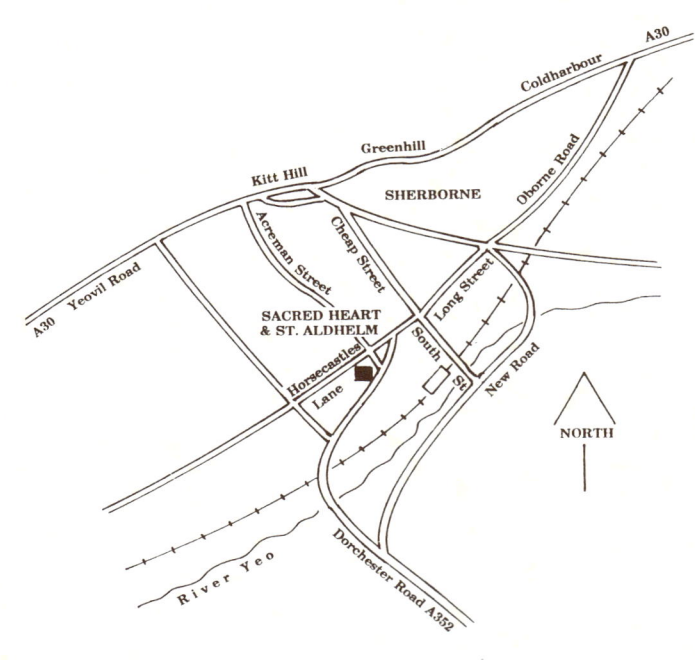

**Sacred Heart & St. Aldhelm, Westbury.**

From Dorchester take the A352 to Sherborne. From Shaftsbury take the A30 going west, entering Sherborne along Coldharbour, Green Hill, Kitt Hill. Turn left into Horsecastle's Lane, then take the third left into Westbury. The Church is adjacent to St. Antony's Convent School. From Exeter, Honiton, Yeovil follow the A30 east. From Yeovil turn right at the Post House Hotel and traffic lights. Turn left at the T junction, the School and Church are on the left. There are no car parking facilities. Trains from Sherborne Station run to London (Waterloo) and Exeter.

St. Aldhelm was formerly Bishop of Sherborne in Saxon times. He was born about 639 A.D., a relative of the Saxon King Ina of Wessex. He entered the monastic novitiate at Malmesbury, then went on to finish his learning at Canterbury. St. Aldhelm founded monasteries and built and repaired churches. He was a gifted administrator, an orator, a writer and musician. Apparently, some of his religious poetry was set to music, with harp accompaniment, to encourage church attendance! St. Aldhelm became Abbot of Malmesbury, then Bishop of Sherborne. He died in 709 A.D. at Doulting in Somerset. His feast day is 25th May.

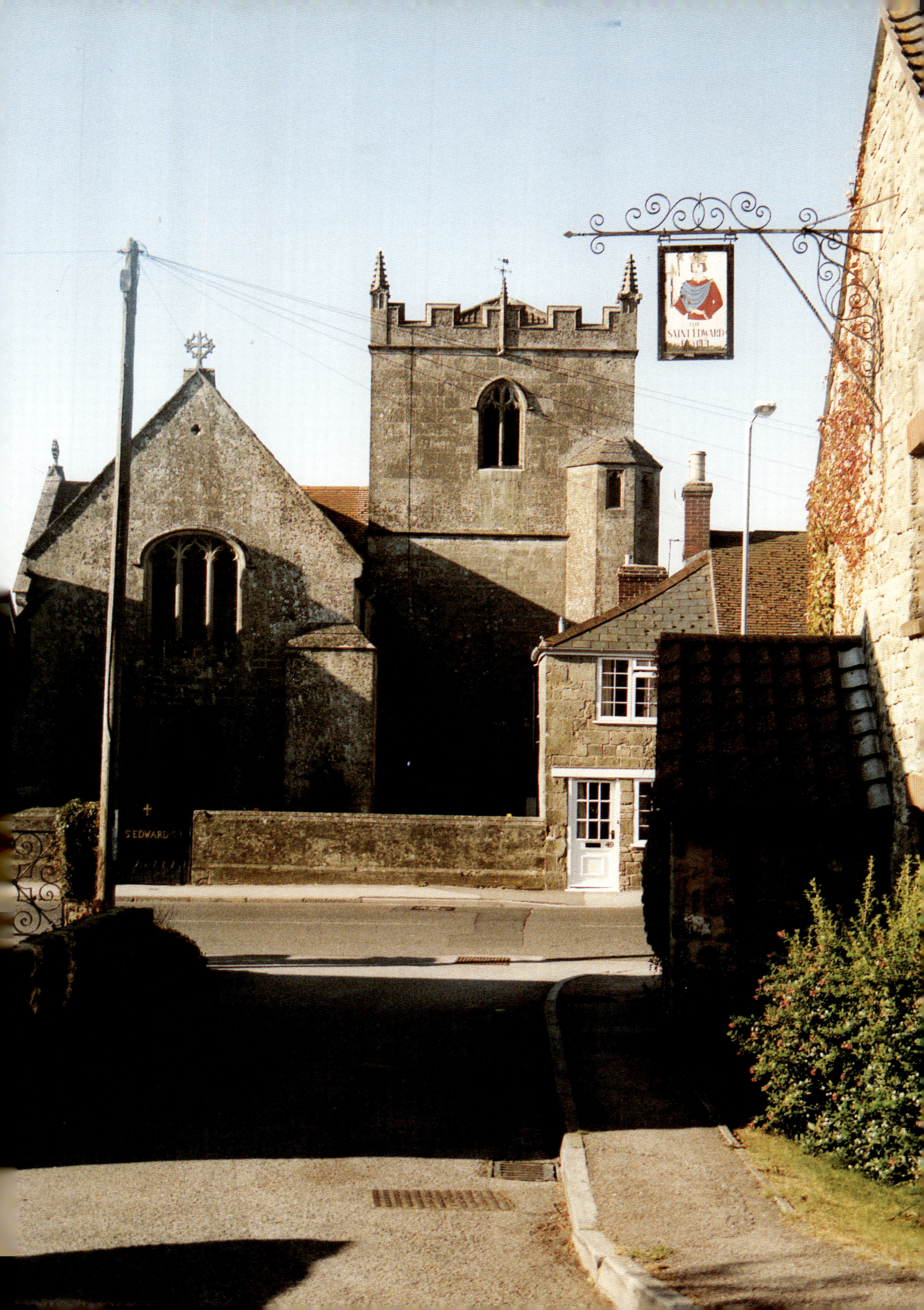
SAINT EDWARD

# The Sacred Heart and St Aldhelm

The Congregation of the Sisters of Christian Instruction was founded in Belgium in 1823 by Mother Agatha Verelle. It followed a constitution of love and service based on the Rule of St. Ignatius of Loyola. A subsequent successor of Mother Verelle, a Mother Ignatius Pollenus, inspired by St. Antony of Padua, arrived with a little community of sisters at "Mapperty House" (in time St. Antony's Convent) in 1891. They established a school and the first Catholic Parish in Sherborne since the Reformation. Plans for a "Victorian Gothic", Ham stone Church dedicated to the Sacred Heart & St. Aldhelm were approved by the Bishop of Plymouth in 1892. The building, designed by a priest/architect, Canon Scholes, was completed in 1894. His Lordship Bishop Vaughan presided over the solemn opening. Everything was financed by the Religious of Christian Instruction. In 1990 the Presbytery was given to the Diocese and in 1991 the Church was also similarly donated.

In the church there is a plaque which reads *To the Sacred Heart For the establishment of a Convent and Mission at Sherborne. A tribute of gratitude from the Religious of Christian Instruction, Ghent, Belgium, 17th June 1891.*

Contact address of Priest:
The Parish House, Westbury,
Sherborne, Dorset. DT9 3ER.
Telephone: (0935) 812021.

# Sidmouth

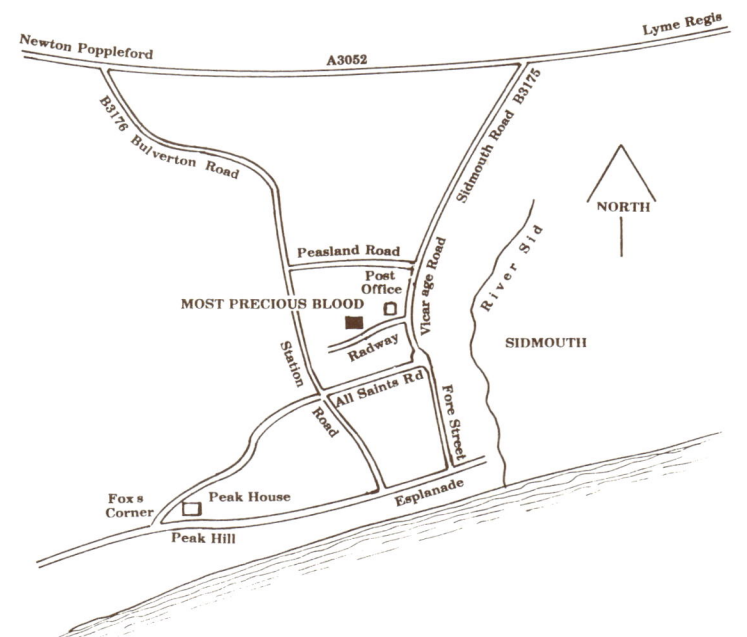

**Most Precious Blood, Radway.**

From Honiton follow the A375 via Sidbury and Sidford; from Lyme Regis follow the A3052 west via Colyford and Sidford; from Ottery St. Mary follow the B3176/5 south; from the M5 Exeter, junction 30, follow the A3052 east via Newton Poppleford and Bowd, then B3175 south into the seaside town of Sidmouth. From Station Road turn into All Saints Road. Turn left into Radway Place and left again by the General Post Office into Radway. The red brick Catholic Church is further down on the right easily recognised by its cross and tower, seventy five feet high. All the bus routes converge at All Saints Road bus stop. Car parking by St. Theresa's Hall, Connaught Road and Radway is very limited.

The Church is dedicated to the Most Precious Blood. In 1815 Blessed Caspar del Bufalo of the Missionary Society of the Precious Blood sought permission from the Vatican to celebrate a special day in honour of just such a dedication. In 1849 when Rome was freed from the republican revolutionaries by the French, Pope Pius IX (1846-1878), happily liberated from his enforced exile at Gaeta, announced a universal celebration of the above feast day.

JESUS MEETS HIS AFFLICTED MOTHER

# Most Precious Blood

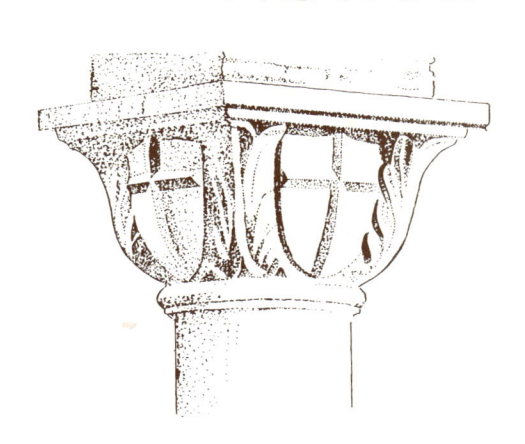

Catholicism in Sidmouth was revived in 1880 when Bishop William Vaughan welcomed refugee Jesuits from Lyons, France, into the Diocese. They found suitable accomodation, which they immediately made into a Jesuit College and Chapel, at Peak House. There they said the first Mass in Sidmouth since the Reformation. In 1883, however, they left the area to settle in Hastings. Another French Community, Sisters of the Assumption, had, by this time, founded a Convent in Cottingham House. They proceeded to build a new Convent in Sidmouth in 1884 and a Chapel in 1905, the latter always open for public use. In 1928 Bishop Keily appointed Fr. Alan Power as Parish priest of Sidmouth. Within two years Fr. Power managed to acquire land in Radway for a Church and presbytery. Funds were raised locally and donations made so that on April 8th 1935 the Bishop came to lay the foundation stone for the Church. On November 10th 1935 the Rt. Rev. John Barrett, Bishop of Plymouth, arrived again, this time, for the solemn opening of the Church of the Most Precious Blood.

Contact address of Priest:
The Presbytery, Radway,
Sidmouth, Devon. EX10 8TW.
Telephone: (0395) 513340.

# South Brent

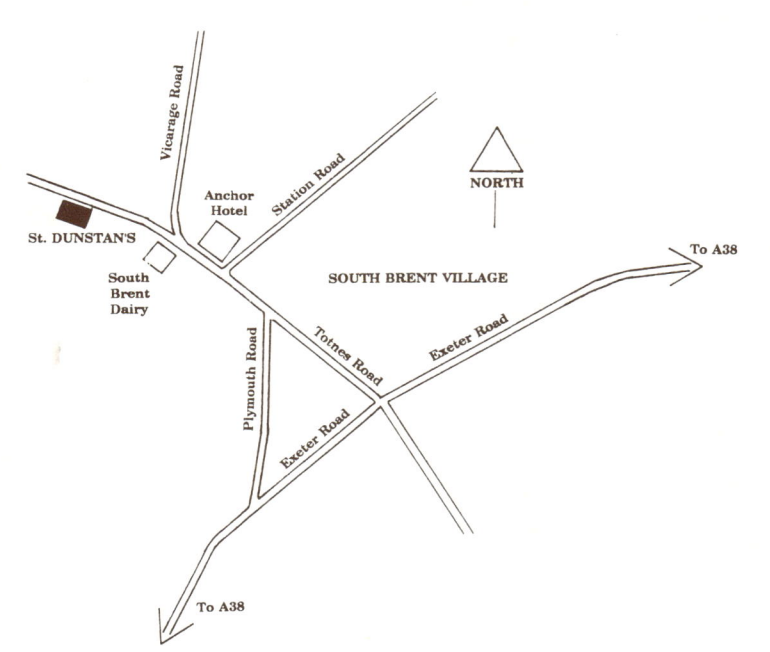

**South Brent   St. Dunstan's   New Park.**

From the A38 Exeter - Plymouth Road take the turning at Marley Head for South Brent. Go down Totnes Road into the village and bear right. Pass Station Road on the right, the Anchor Hotel on the corner. Keep going straight (past the Coop and the Home Bakery) to the South Brent Dairy on the left. Just beyond the Dairy there is a little lane which leads to St. Dunstan's Catholic Church and car park.

# St. Dunstan

The Church is dedicated to St. Dunstan, a Benedictine, and served from Buckfast Abbey. St. Dunstan was born in 909 A.D. near Glastonbury at Baltonsborough. He was the son of a noble family with royal connections. He became an important figure in the Church and also in English History. From the simple role of Benedictine monk he was made successively Abbot of Glastonbury, Bishop of Worcester, Bishop of London and, eventually, Archbishop of Canterbury. He was a man of God, of high ideals of conduct. During his life he spent some time in a monastery in Flanders. He was so impressed with the way of life there that on his return he became responsible for monastic reform, under the Rule of St. Benedict, in England. According to tradition, Dunstan had a talent for painting, music and metalwork. Many legends are attributed to him. In one, relating to his metalwork, Satan tempted him in the shape of a beautiful girl. The saintly Dunstan seized her nose with his long blacksmith's pincers so that the devil resumed his own guise and fled! Dunstan died a few days after the feast of the Ascension on 19th May 988 A.D.

St. Dunstan's was opened on September 14th 1937. The building is a salmon coloured, elongated hut situated in a well cared for garden. (On a hot June day the air is filled with a delightful aroma of roses and fresh grass.) Inside, the hut emits the ambience of a place of prayer. There are some interesting details: the stained glass behind the altar, the ornate crucifix over the sanctuary and the picture of the suffering Christ in the sacristy. The carved wooden altar rails came from the pre-Reformation Bridgettine Convent, Syon Abbey, in London.

The Stations of the Cross, by Powys Evans, are sombre tableaux painted on wood. Their most noticeable feature is the gaunt face of Our Blessed Lord, worn out with suffering and sacrifice, taunted with pain and the burden of the sins of men.

Contact address of Priest:
St. Mary's Abbey, Buckfast,
Devon. TQ11 OEE.
Telephone: (0364) 43301.

# South Molton

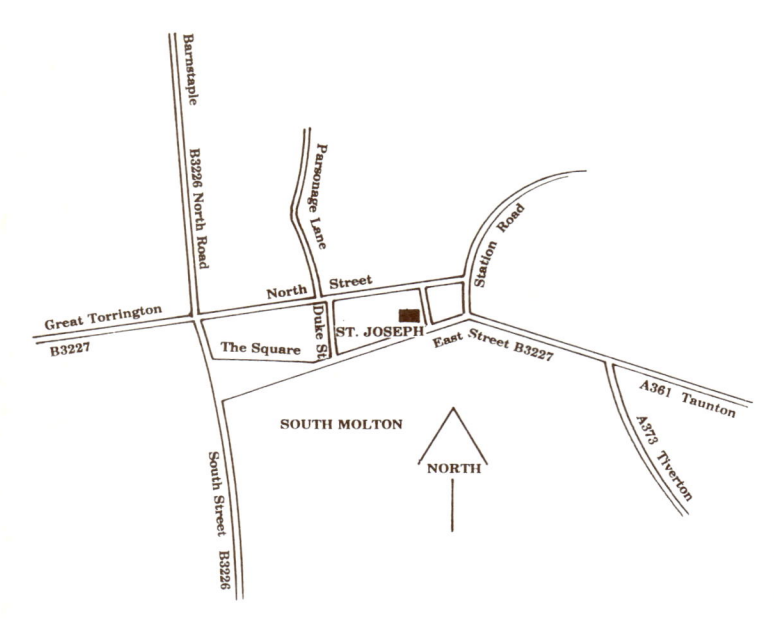

**St. Joseph, East Street.**

From Barnstaple follow the A361 east; from Tiverton follow the A373 north west; from Great Torrington follow the B3221 east into South Molton. St. Joseph's Church is on the left of the main street, East Street, going out of South Molton towards Taunton. The Church is situated well back from the pavement within its own small grounds behind a short iron gate and railings. The building has a pitched roof and the gable end faces the street. South Molton is on the Tiverton/Barnstaple bus route. Parking is possible in the street, at the roadside.

The Church is dedicated to St. Joseph, the foster father of Jesus, the Word Incarnate. Both St. Matthew's and St. Luke's Gospels give an account of the genealogy of Joseph's line. St. Matthew traces Joseph back through his father Jacob, to Matthan, through generations to Solomon, to David the King, to Jesse, through generations to Jacob, to Isaac, to Abraham our father in faith. St. Luke, in comparison, records Joseph as the son of Heli, of Matthat, through generations to Nathan, to David, to Jesse, through generations to Jacob, son of Isaac, son of Abraham, through generations to Seth, son of Adam. Many churches and hospitals are dedicated to St. Joseph. His feast is celebrated on 19th March and 1st May.

# St. Joseph

From 1950, for a period of seven years, Holy Mass was celebrated in a small "Upper Room" in South Molton, generally, inavoidably, amongst the odour of fish and chips. During the 1950's a former Methodist and Salvation Army Chapel was purchased. It was made into the Catholic Church of St. Joseph. The formal opening took place in 1957.

Contact address of Priest:
The Presbytery, Higher Church Street,
Barnstaple, Devon. EX32 8JE.
Telephone: (0271) 43312.

# Swanage

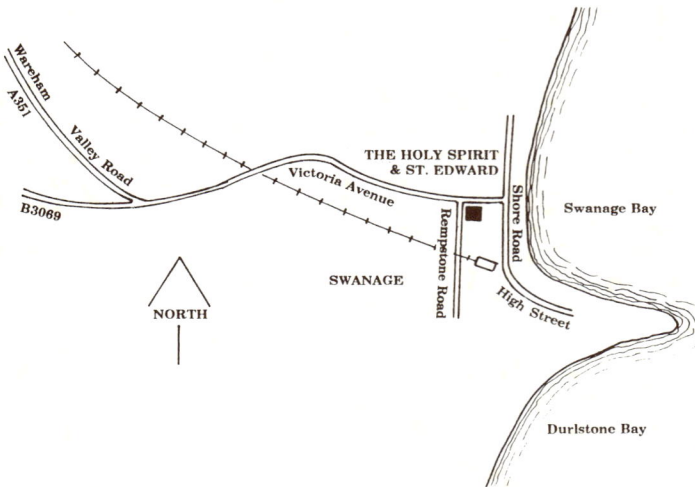

**The Holy Spirit & St. Edward, Victoria Avenue.**

Take the A351 from Wareham right through to Swanage. Follow the sign "To the Sea". The Church of The Holy Spirit & St. Edward is situated on the right, on the corner of Victoria Avenue and Rempstone Road, just before reaching the Sea Front. A Clock Tower, a useful landmark, is located on the Sea Front at the end of Victoria Avenue. There is a train service from London Waterloo to Wareham and from Wareham there is a bus (No. 143) running every hour to Swanage. Two car parks are available: one next to the Fire Station, the other next to St. George's Amusement Park.

The Church is dedicated to The Holy Spirit & St. Edward. King Edward succeeded his father, King Edgar of England in 975 A.D. Four years later he was assassinated at Corfe Castle, according to the order of his stepmother, Elfrida, who wished to put her son, Ethelred, on the throne. Edward was buried at Wareham without any regal pageantry or honour. In due time his body was translated from Wareham to the nunnery church at Shaftesbury, a royal resting place. In 1001, in a charter of Ethelred, Edward was proclaimed saint and martyr. Seven years after that his feast was observed throughout England. He did not die for religion, but was revered simply for having suffered an untimely death. He can only have been fifteen or sixteen years old. His stepmother, reputedly very beautiful, repented of her crime, and sought to make restitution by entering a convent at Wherwell (Hampshire).

# The Holy Spirit and St. Edward

250

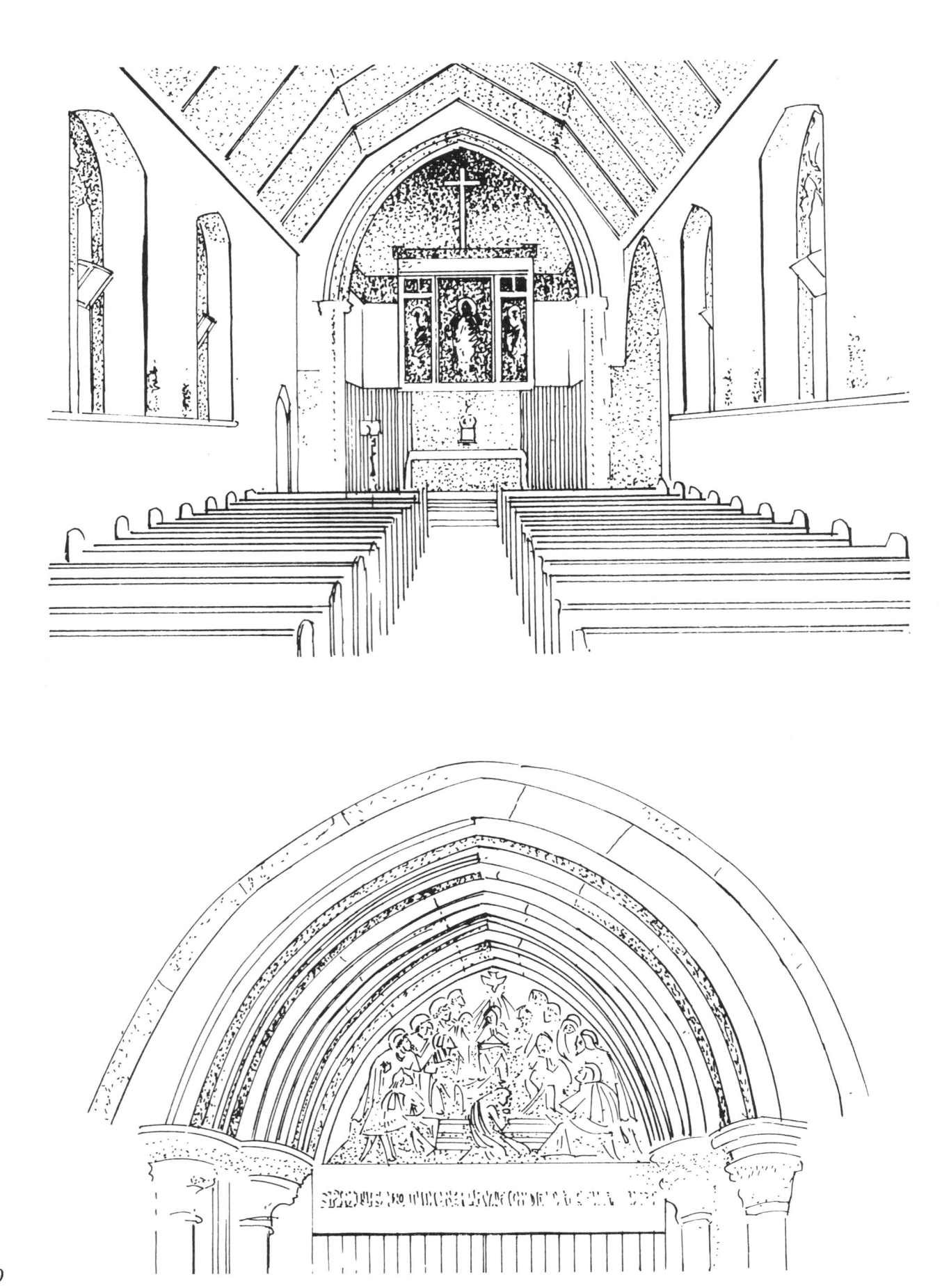

# The Holy Spirit and St. Edward

The interior of the Church contains some fine paintings. They include the canopy over the main altar, depicting the Blessed Sacrament being presented in Heaven by the Holy Angels; the Annunciation scene over the Lady Altar with its decorative Art Nouveau frieze; and the Triptych altar piece showing Edward the Martyr in the centre, flanked by St. Aldhelm, first bishop of Sherborne and St. Elgiva, the first Abbess of Shaftsbury. The Tryptych was painted in 1926 by Francis Henry Newbery, a famous artist of the day. He was born in Membury, Devon in 1853. Eventually he became Principal of the Glasgow School of Art. He married the talented Jessie Rowat who was gifted in applied art, especially embroidery. Francis Newbery exhibited at the Royal Glasgow Institute of Fine Arts, two Paris Salons, the Royal Scottish Academy, the Royal Academy and the Royal Society of Portrait Painters. Examples of his work went to galleries in Turin, Venice and Munich, Exeter, Newcastle, Paisley and Glasgow. When he retired in 1917 he moved to Corfe Castle in Dorset where he died in 1946.

The Church and presbytery were built about ninety years ago by the Canons Regular of the Lateran to house the Community and the Junior Seminary on its removal from Spetisbury. For many years a number of Canons were in residence, one of whom was the Parish Priest responsible for looking after Swanage. Subsequently the Juniorate moved on to Eton, and later to Datchet, and the Community gave way to two and then only one priest in the parish. Eventually, the Order left Swanage, and the Church and presbytery were handed over to the Diocese of Plymouth in September 1984.

Contact address of Priest:
The Presbytery, 1, Victoria Avenue,
Swanage, Dorset. BH19 1AH.
Telephone: (0929) 422491.

# Tavistock

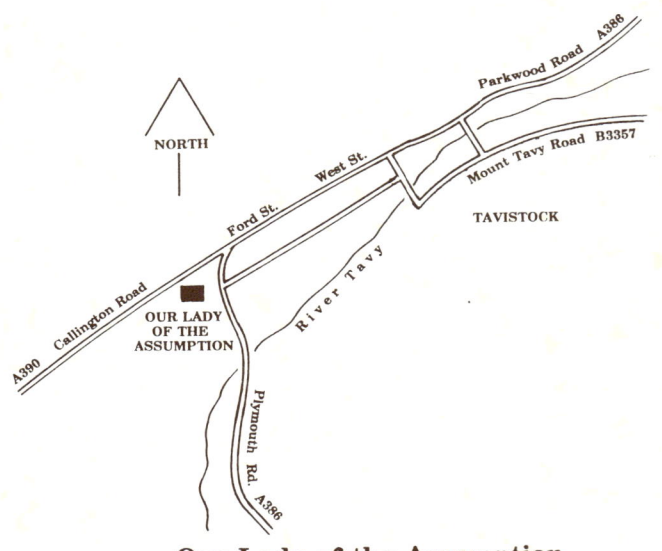

**Our Lady of the Assumption, Callington Road.**

From Plymouth follow the A386; from Dartmeet follow the B3357 via Two Bridges; from Okehampton follow the A386 south via Mary Tavy; from Liskeard follow the A390 via Gunnislake; from Launceston follow the A384 via Milton Abbot to Tavistock. The Catholic Church is located on the left going out of town on the Callington Road A390. It is a large stone building with a tall bell tower.

The dedication is to Our Lady of the Assumption. After the Ascension of Our Lord, Mary remained with the disciples. There is no record of her death, but both the Eastern and Western Church share the belief that she who was "full of grace", "highly favoured", the "Mother of Christ", bodily assumed into Heaven. There is a shrine honouring the "passing" of Mary in the Domitian Church in Jerusalem. The feast of The Assumption is celebrated on 15th August.

# Our Lady of the Assumption

The remains of Devon's once greatest religious domain, Tavistock Abbey, may be seen not too far away from the Catholic Church. It is situated beside Plymouth Road and the River Tavy, on the right going into the town. It was originally designed to house one thousand men, founded in 974 A.D. by Ordulf, the brother-in-law of Edgar King of Wessex. In March 1539 the Abbey like all the others in the Reformation was dissolved. It was given to Lord John Russell, later Duke of Bedford.

The Church of Our Lady of the Assumption (and St. Mary Magdalene) was built by William, eighth Duke of Bedford between 1865 and 1867. He used local stone and local labour, his own employees, the silver and tin miners. The Church was to be a Chapel of Ease for the Anglican Parish Church providing a place of worship for the miners who, in the nineteenth century, were discouraged from attending other churches because of their lower class status and their "stench of poverty".

The ediface certainly attempted to give the lower classes a taste of greater things. The scale is so large that when the stations were added, to be in proportion, they needed to be eight feet high! It has an enormous "state door", a suitable entrance for the past Duke of Bedford. The building fell into disuse in 1918, but was re-opened for public worship in February 1936. Then in 1947 it was closed again. When the Church came up for sale it was purchased by the Catholic Bishop of Plymouth, through the generosity of a benefactor, Mrs Reginald Rye, in memory of her husband who died in 1945.

The Church of Our Lady of the Assumption was solemnly reopened by the Rt. Rev. Francis Grimshaw, and Holy Mass was celebrated for the first time on Laetare Sunday, March 23rd 1952.

Contact address of Priest:
The Presbytery, Callington Road,
Tavistock, Devon. PL19 8EH.
Telephone: (0822) 612645.

# Teignmouth

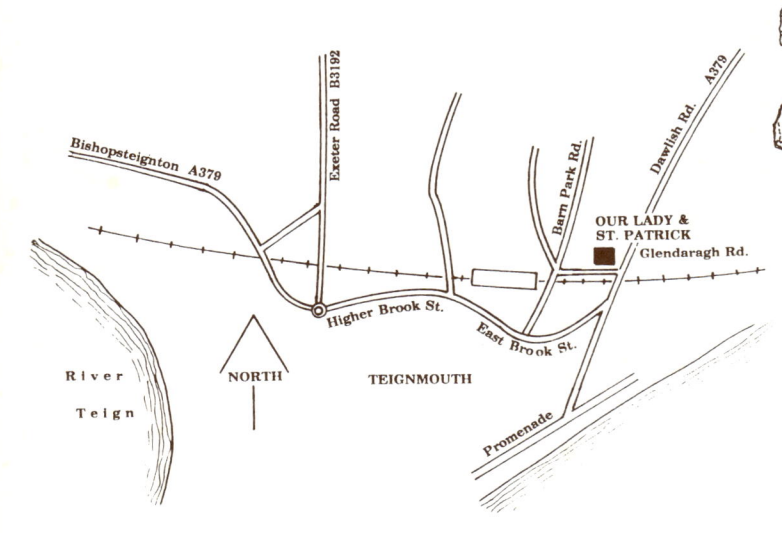

**Our Lady & St. Patrick, Glendaragh Road.**

The Church is situated at the end of Glendaragh Road, at the junction with the A379 Teignmouth, Dawlish, Exeter Road (via the coast). There is a bus service and Main Line British Rail Station nearby, Newton Abbot/Exeter route. Restricted car parking is available in Glendaragh Road. There is a public car park at Teignmouth Coach Station opposite the Church.

The Church is dedicated to Our Lady and the great fifth century Bishop and Apostle of Ireland, St. Patrick. Patrick was born in Britain. In his teens he was snatched by Irish raiders and put to work as a shepherd. During that time he came close to God in prayer. When, after six years, he returned to his family he longed to serve God in a ministerial way. Many, many years later he went back to Ireland as a missionary. Although not a literary man, some of the authentically spiritual (as opposed to the legendary) Patrick has been revealed to posterity through his autobiography and the famous poem (hymn) known as St. Patrick's Breastplate. His feast is celebrated on March 17th.

# Our Lady and St. Patrick

At one time Catholics in the Teignmouth area attended Mass at Ugbrooke. In 1840 a priest from Ugbrooke started a weekly Mass at the "Jolly Sailor Inn". Some years later, in 1845, a Church dedicated to Our Lady & St. Charles Borromeo was built in Teignmouth on land forming part of a tunnel over the railway. Eventually, the South Devon Railway Company required the land for improvements and the original Church was thus carefully dismantled and re-erected in Tothill Lane, now Beaumont Road, Plymouth. The present Church was built in 1878. The Parish has been served by both Jesuits and Redemptorists then handed over to the Plymouth Diocese. The Church of Our Lady & St. Patrick was consecrated on 7th October 1937.

Contact address of Priest:
The Presbytery, Glendaragh Road,
Teignmouth, Devon. TQ14 8PH.
Telephone: (0626) 774640.

# Tintagel

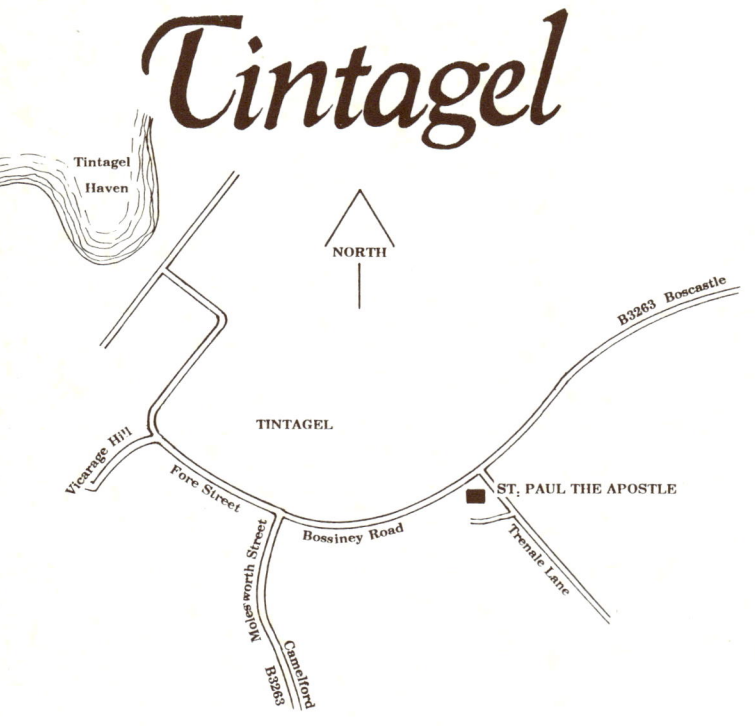

**St. Paul the Apostle, Bossiney Road.**

From Bude take the A39 to Camelford, follow the signs for Tintagel, B3266, then B3263. From Bodmin take the A389 heading for Wadebridge, turn right on to the B3266 to Camelford, follow Tintagel signs. From Wadebridge take the A39 to Camelford, follow Tintagel signs. From Launceston take the A30 towards Bodmin, turn on to the A395, Tintagel is signposted from the A39. From Boscastle follow the B3263 south to Tintagel. Notable landmarks in the vicinity are St. Materiana's Church on the cliffs and King Arthur's Castle (built on the site of a Celtic Monastery). The Church of St. Paul the Apostle is on the corner of Trenale Lane and Bossiney Road, opposite a garage. It is a small, white painted, square building with a tiled roof and gold coloured "fleche". Car parking is available at the rear of the Church for those attending services, otherwise in the village car parks.

The Church is dedicated to St. Paul the Apostle, recognised as such because of his missionary apostolate, one of the main characters in the spread and development of early Christianity. Paul spoke both Greek and Aramaic but was also fluent in classical Hebrew, and Latin, the language of Rome. As a fanatical pharisee he played an active role in the harassment and annihilation of Christians in Jerusalem. Then, on the road to Damascus, he received the experience which changed his life. From then on, with full missionary zeal, Paul laboured selflessly to carry the Gospel of Christ out to the far corners of the first century world: to Cyprus, to Asia Minor. He endured much hardship, an awful shipwreck at Malta, imprisonment in Rome, finally martyrdom during the persecution of Nero. The feast of St. Peter & St. Paul is kept on 29th June. The feast of the Conversion of St. Paul is on 25th January.

The Mission of Tintagel, like many others in Cornwall, was founded by the Canons Regular of the Lateran from Bodmin. The Church of St. Paul was built in 1968. Of particular interest inside the modern building is the Cornish serpentine statue of the Blessed Virgin, Stations of the Cross carved out of local wood, and the stained glass made by the monks at Buckfast.

On the left of the Church the windows depict Calvary, the spear of Longinus and the Holy Grail. It was King Arthur (of Tintagel) who,

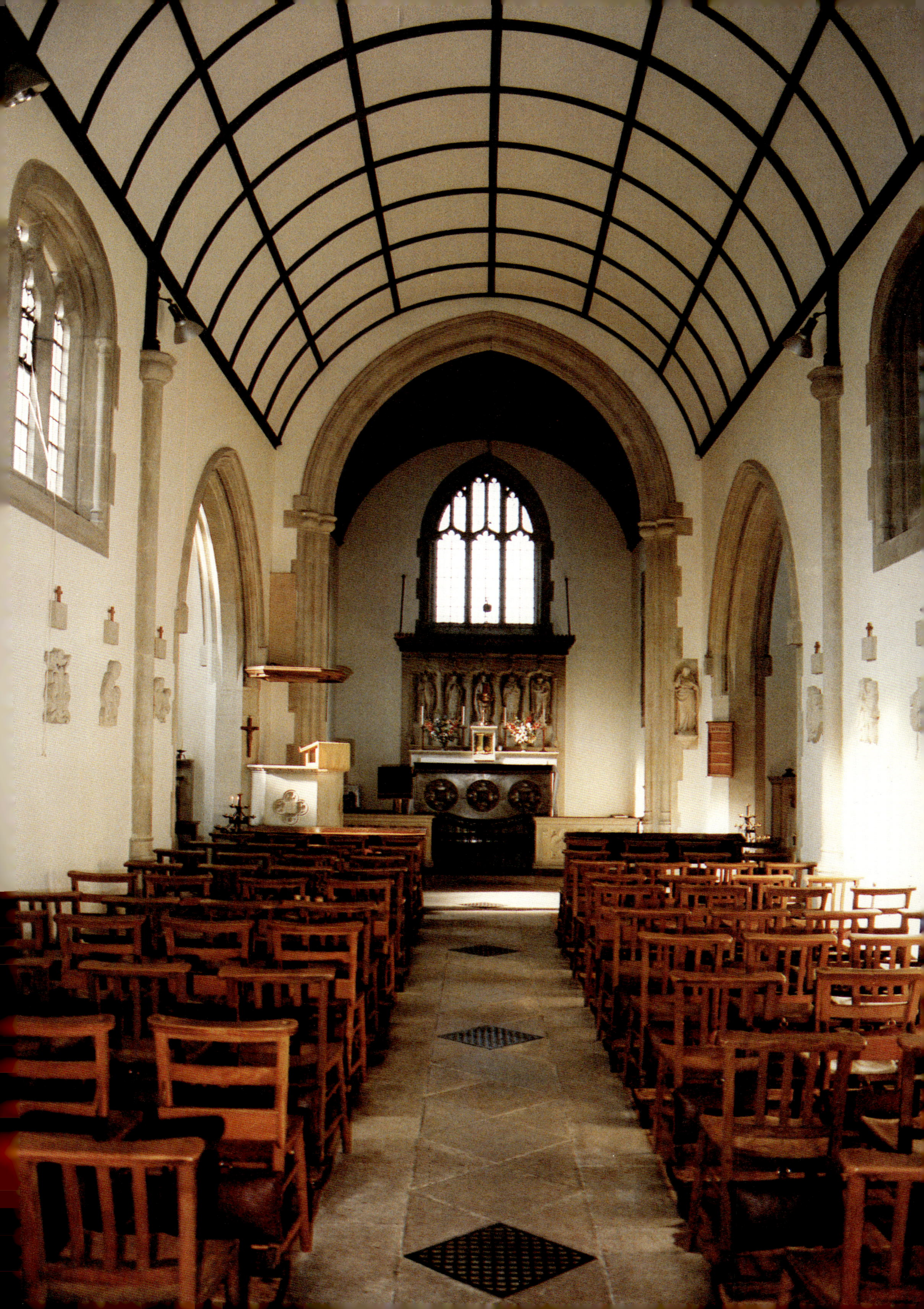

# St Paul

according to legend, sent his knights out to seek the Holy Grail, the Chalice used by Joseph of Arimathea to collect some of the Sacred Blood from the wounded side of Christ. Behind the altar there are two windows illustrating two coats of arms: on one side the five wounds of Christ, the symbolic banner used by the brave Cornishmen who defended their right to the Sacrifice of the Mass in 1549; the other relates to the coat of arms of the pre-Reformation Priory of Austin Canons, taken over by the CRL in 1881 when they took up residence in Bodmin. The three fish, seen in many parts of the Diocese, are possible reference to the ancient Priory's fishing rights.

On the right of the Church, the stained glass is again rich in visual imagery of Cornish tradition: Glastonbury Abbey, the Christmas bloom of the Glastonbury thorn, again, according to legend, brought from the Holy Land and planted by Joseph of Arimathea. Also is depicted the miracle of the multiplication of the loaves and the fishes, a preparation for the institution of the Sacrament of the Holy Eucharist and the Mass.

Contact address of Priest:
Chy An Pronter, Trewarmett,
Tintagel, Cornwall. PL34 0ET.
Telephone: (0840) 770663.

# Tiverton

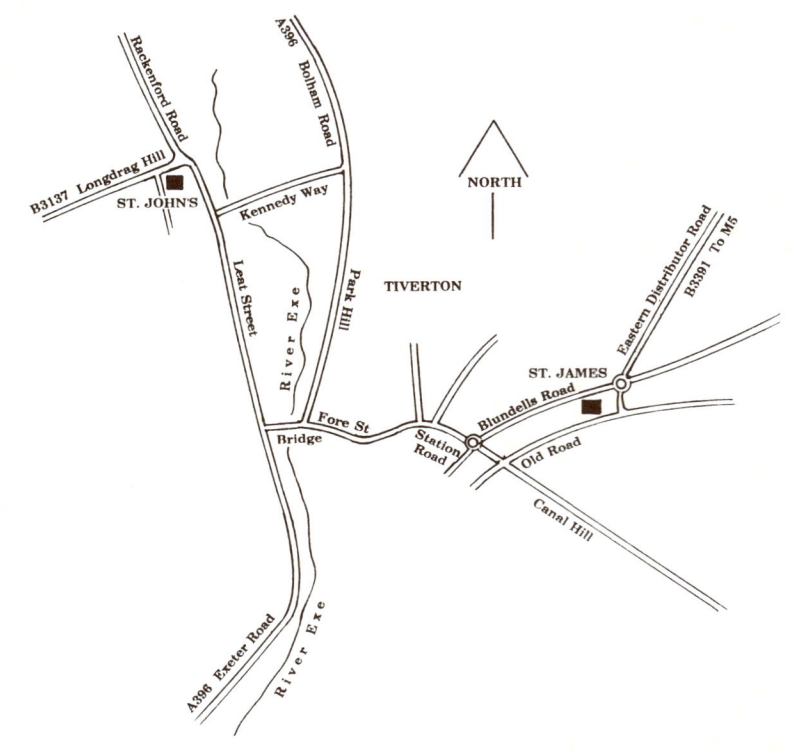

**St. James, Old Road.**

From Exeter follow the A377, A396; from M5, Junction 27, take A373; from South Molton follow the B3221 or A373; from Crediton follow the A396 north; from Minehead/Dunster follow the A396 south into Tiverton. The Church is situated in Old Road, located off the bottom of Canal Hill. Approaching from the M5 or Willand the Church is 100 yards from Horsdon Roundabout. British Rail operates from Tiverton Parkway about 4 miles away. Car parking is available at the Church.

The dedication is to St. James, the younger brother of St. John the Evangelist, the latter, the patron of the Parish of Tiverton from the 1830's. James and John, like their father Zebedee, were fishermen on Lake Galilee. St. James was one of the three disciples privileged to witness the miracle of the Raising of Jairus' Daughter to Life, also the Transfiguration on Mount Tabor and the Agony of Christ in the Garden of Gethsemane. James was the first of the twelve apostles to suffer martyrdom. King Herod Agrippa I, grandson of Herod the Great, had James arrested for being a leading Christian and put him "to the sword" in Jerusalem (Acts 12:2). There is an old tradition claiming that St. James preached the Gospel in Spain and that his mortal remains were taken to Compostela. In Medieval times the Shrine of "Sant Iago" was one of the most important centres in Christendom. There were certainly pilgrim boats sailing from seafaring parts of the "Plymouth Diocese" to the north western corner of the Iberian Peninsula, to the sacred tomb at Compostela. The feast of St. James is kept on 25th July.

# St. James

This Church was built in 1967. In the first seventeen years of its life it didn't look too much like a Church. It was built originally as a social centre to generate funds in order to finance the local Catholic School. Twenty five years later the School has been granted Voluntary Aided status and the Marley pre-cast concrete building has been renovated and re-ordered as a permanent Church and Hall.

Contact address of Priest:
The Presbytery, 40, Old Road,
Tiverton, Devon. EX16 4HJ.
Telephone: (0884) 252292.

# Tiverton

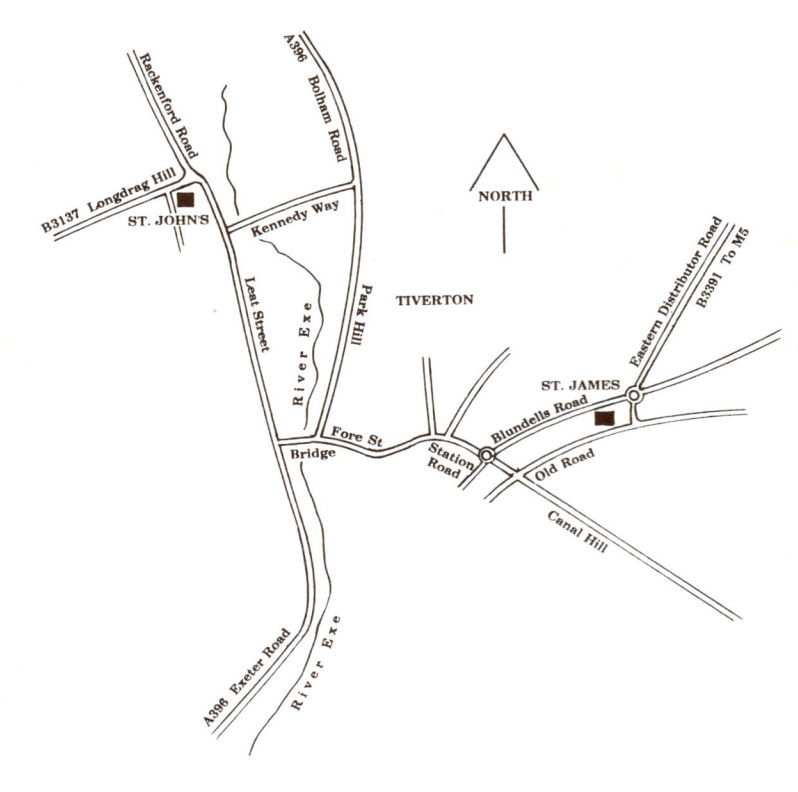

**St. John's, Longdrag Hill.**

Once in Tiverton follow signs for Witheridge. The Catholic Church of St. John is situated on an elevated corner site at the junction of Longdrag Hill and Rackenford Road. The Church, one of the oldest Catholic churches in Devon, is constructed of old weathered stone. Parking facilities are available outside the Church.

The dedication is to St. John, the Evangelist, patron of theologians and writers and all who endeavour to produce books. He was the brother of James, son of Zebedee, and initially a disciple of St. John the Baptist until he met the Messiah. St. John was possibly the youngest of the Apostles. Jesus held a very special regard for him. St. John and his brother were the two sent into Jerusalem to make the preparations for The Last Supper. At the Crucifixion on Mount Calvary Christ entrusted the care of His Holy Mother to St. John. On Easter Sunday SS. John & Peter were the two who raced first to the vacant tomb. Afterwards when the Risen Lord appeared to the Apostles on the shore of Galilee it was St. John who recognised Him before the others. Jesus called John and James "Boanerges", sons of thunder! Of ardent temperament he may have been but together with St. Peter he became one of the "pillars" of the Early Church . He preached in Asia Minor and later Ephesus and died at a great age, the last of the twelve apostles. The feast of St. John is kept on 27th December.

# St. John

In 1768 a wealthy Irishman, Joseph Nagle, from County Cork, bought the Manor of Calverleigh. Being a Catholic, he and his family had their own private chaplain at the Manor. Their priest also served the local Catholic Community in Tiverton. In 1795 certain members of the Chichester family joined the Nagles at Calverleigh Manor bringing with them their chaplain the Rev. Henry Innes. Over the years several French priests came to the Mission at Calverleigh. In 1823 a certain Abbe Jean Marc Moutier arrived at the Manor. He had been in England already for over twenty six years and had amassed quite a fortune through teaching French in the West Country.

The Abbe Moutier was instantly aware of the isolation of the Mission at Calverleigh, the real need for a Church in Tiverton amongst the people. He gave a very large sum of money to the Diocese for the purpose of providing a Catholic Church, Priest's House and School Room at Tiverton. The Heathcote family from Westexe kindly donated land for the project.

On 6th September 1836 the foundation stone for the Church was laid by Bishop Peter Augustine Baines O.S.B., Vicar Apostolic of the Western District. In May 1838, and for the next year, Mass was said, for the people of Tiverton, in the Schoolhouse. Then, on Whit Sunday, May 19th 1839, the Church of St. John the Evangelist was formally opened.

Contact address of Priest:
The Presbytery, 40, Old Road,
Tiverton, Devon. EX16 4HJ.
Telephone: (0884) 252292.

# Torpoint

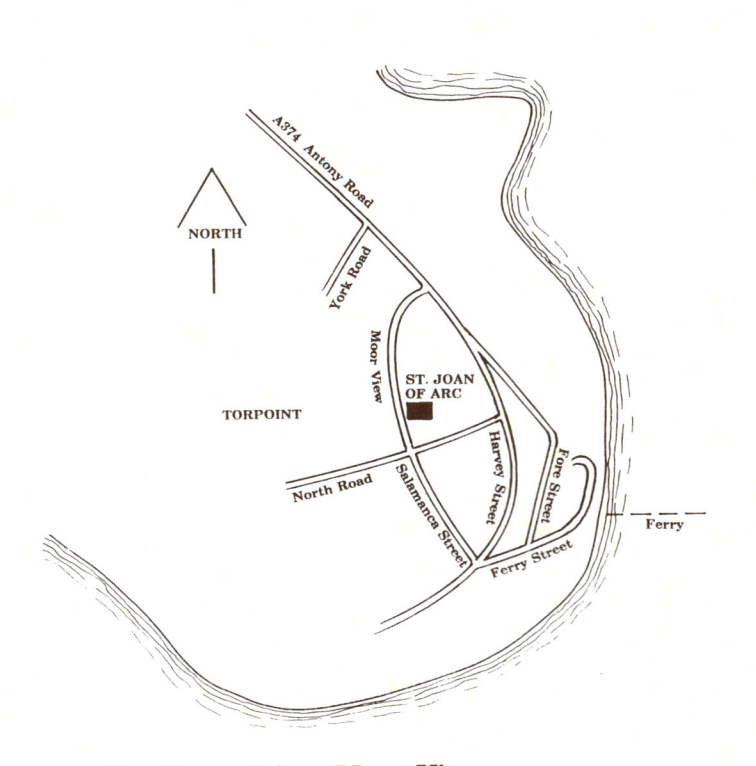

**St. Joan of Arc, Moor View.**

From Plymouth take the car ferry to Torpoint. Turn off Antony Road A374 opposite the supermarket into Moor View where the little church of St. Joan of Arc is found. Its external walls are covered in pebble dash render, the roof is tiled and there is a cross on the gable top. Parking is available in Antony Road Car Park.

There is a specific reason for the dedication to St. Joan of Arc. When Bishop Barrett attended celebrations in Rome for the canonization of this saint he vowed that the next church that he built in the Plymouth Diocese would be under her patronage. The next church in the Diocesan building programme was the one at Torpoint and, apparently, it was the first church in England to be dedicated to St. Joan.

The "Maid of Orleans" was born in 1421 at Domremy in Lorraine. Her father was a poor peasant farmer. Joan was the youngest of his five children. At the age of fourteen St. Joan became aware of "Voices" (St. Michael, St. Margaret of Antioch & St. Catherine of Alexandria) urging her to save France from the English armies. Her credibility was questioned then believed so that her presence was honoured at the fore front of the French troops. As towns became free from enemy control it made possible the coronation of Charles VII in 1429 in Rheims Cathedral. Later, however, Joan was taken prisoner at Compiegne and abandoned by the King. She was incarcerated at Rouen and tried for heresy and witchcraft. On 30th May she was led out to the stake, in the market place, to be burned alive. She was only nineteen years old and died with piety and great courage. Her feast is kept on the day of her demise.

# St. Joan of Arc

Before the Reformation, Torpoint did not exist as a parish, but there were parish churches at Antony, St. John and St. Germans. Nearly sixty years ago a few Catholic families in the area had to travel to the Cathedral or to Mutton Cove in Devonport for Mass each Sunday, in all weathers and without public transport. Midnight Mass was something of an adventure as there was no all night ferry, it meant finding accomodation on the other side of the river. Some years later a police boat was made available for the little Catholic Community returning from Midnight Mass. Eventually the Catholic population had grown sufficiently to promote the idea of a Mass centre in Torpoint. Priests came from Devonport and offered House Masses. Later, the British Legion Hut in Torpoint was used for the Eucharistic Celebration. As fervour increased a church building fund was initiated. In 1932 Bishop Barrett laid the foundation stone of the Church of St. Joan of Arc. The solemn opening took place in March of the following year.

Contact address of Priest:
The Presbytery, 1A Moor View,
Torpoint, Cornwall. PL11 2LH.
Telephone: (0752) 812347.

# Torquay

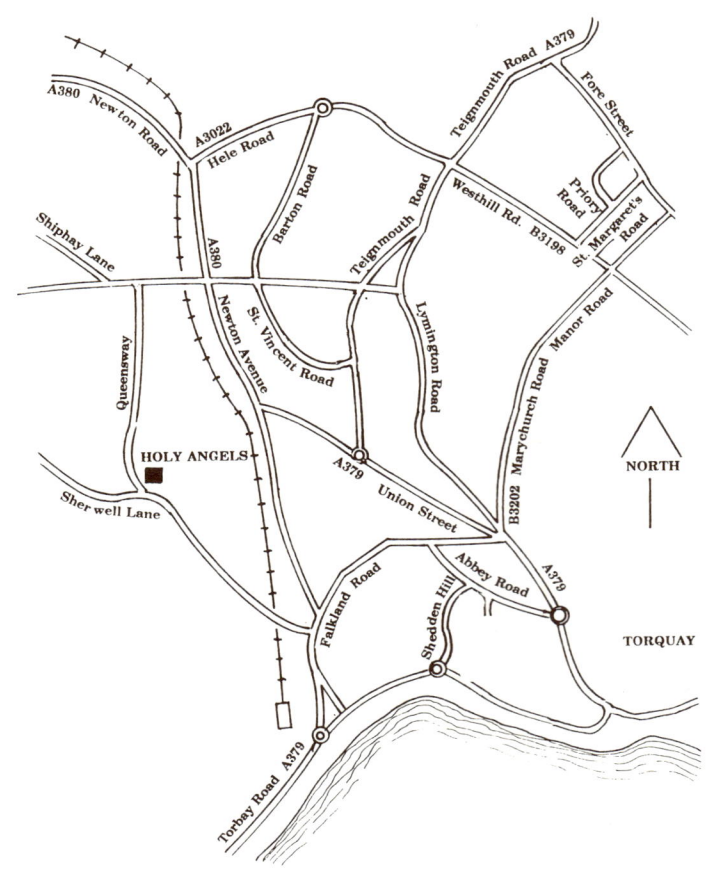

**Holy Angels, Queensway, Chelston.**

The Church of the Holy Angels is easily located at the bottom of Queensway just before Sherwell Lane. There are two useful landmarks: the Haywain Hotel, right beside it and St. Peter's Church opposite. Coming from Exeter take the main road to Torquay A380. At the third set of traffic lights fork right for Chelston into Avenue Road. Then turn right at the lights for Shiphay and then immediately left into Queensway. Car parking is available at the Church Hall and in Queensway itself.

The Church is dedicated to the Holy Angels. These innumerable Blessed Spirits are mentioned in various parts of the Old Testament. For example, the announcement of Samson's birth (Judges 13: 1-25), as a response to Sara's prayer (Tobias 3: 24,25) and a vision of the prophet Isaiah (Isaiah 6: 1-8). We hear Jesus refering to angels: "Everyone who acknowledges me before men, the Son of Man also will acknowledge before the angels of God; but he who denies me before men will be denied before the angels of God". As a conclusion to the Parable of the Lost Drachma Jesus says: "I tell you there is joy before the angels of God over one sinner who repents.." An angel came to Christ whilst He prayed in the Garden of Gethsemane. There are other instances when the Church reminds us of the reality of angels particularly during our communal prayers: "Glory to God in the Highest", the song of the Angels; "Hail Mary, full of grace", the salutation of the Angel Gabriel; "So we join the angels and saints in proclaiming your glory as we say, Holy, Holy..."; "Almighty God we pray that your angel may take this sacrifice to your altar in heaven..."

# Holy Angels

Holy Angels is a small red brick Church with a copper roof. It was built in 1938 when the old village of Chelston acquired a council estate and other developments. This was the last of the churches built by the Misses Robinson, a treasure of Italianate, encased in an outer shell of brick. There are some glorious stained glass windows, each one a different scene involving angels. "Veniam ad Visiones et Revelationes Domini". The original altar mural portrayed an artistic impression of the Mass, the sacrifice of Calvary, to the glory of God, in the presence of the Holy Angels. There are copies of the same mural elsewhere in two Diocesan churches. In response to Vatican II, there is now a modern altar decorated with a carved relief of Christ and his apostles at The Last Supper. Above the Stations of the Cross the dedication theme is emphasised with representations of Cherubim, Virtues, Principalities and Powers, Seraphim, some Holy Angels.

Contact address of Priest:
The Presbytery, Queensway,
Chelston, Torquay. TQ2 6BP.
Telephone: (0803) 607116.

# Torquay

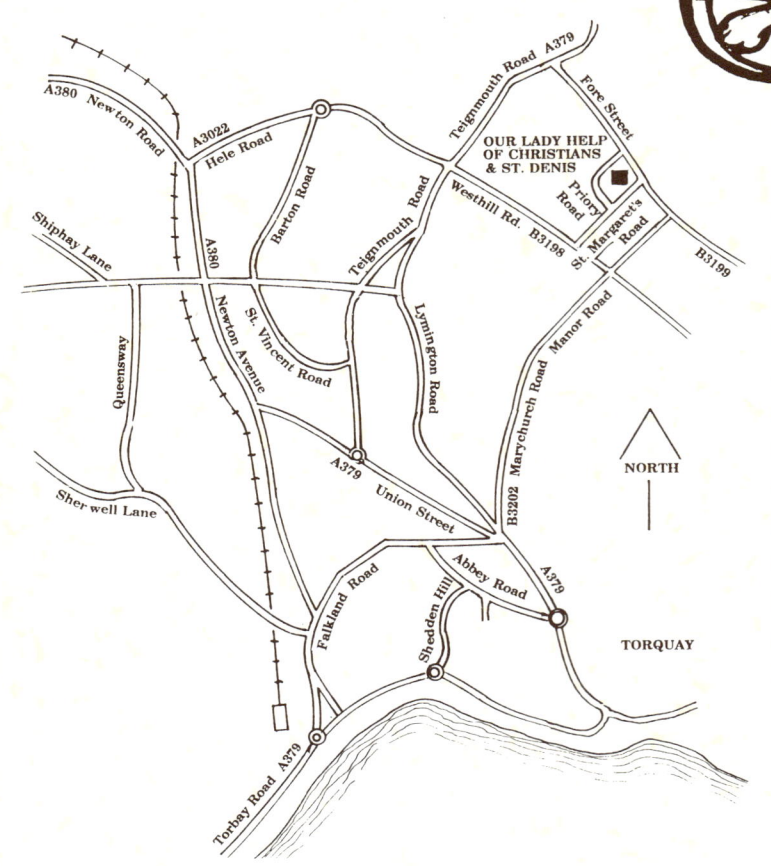

The Church is dedicated to Our Lady Help of Christians & St. Denis. The beautiful Marian title was used by Pope Pius VII (1800-1823). He instituted a special feast day in honour of "Our Lady Help of Christians" to commemorate his safe return from imprisonment by Napoleon and also in thanksgiving to God for the Papal States. St. Denis, Bishop and Martyr, Patron of France and of Paris, lived in the third century. He led a successful mission in Gaul, but jealous pagans put him in prison, and beheaded him. The seventh century Benedictine Abbey of Saint Denis was built on the site of his martyrdom.

**Our Lady Help of Christians & St. Denis, Priory Road, St. Marychurch.**

The landmark for locating the Church is the tall spire which can be seen on the approach to Torquay. Once within the town centre, from Castle Circus, take the St. Marychurch Road to the traffic lights at the junction of Westhill Manor Road and Warbro Road. Turn left, then immediately right to continue on the St. Marychurch Road. The first left turn after that is Priory Road. Coming from Newton Abbot turn left into Hele Road A3022 at the traffic lights at Lowes Bridge. Follow straight across Teignmouth Road into Westhill Road B3198, turn left into St. Margaret's Road, and left again into Priory Road. Car parking is available in the Church grounds and in adjoining roads.

# Our Lady Help of Christians and St. Denis

An ancient Church of St. Mary was built by Saxon monks on top of a hill. Around this holy building grew the village of St. Marychurch. In the nineteenth century only the tower was left standing. In 1864 a Dominican Order of nuns settled in Southampton Villa in St. Marychurch and founded an orphanage. They converted their drawing room into a Chapel for Mass. In 1867 on the feast of Our Lady Help of Christians Mr. William Potts-Chatto of the Daison made the Community an offer to build a votive Church in thanksgiving to St. Denis for the recovery of his son from a serious illness. A detailed account of the building in "The Story of Our Lady Help of Christians & St. Denis" compiled by the Dominican nuns makes fascinating reading.

Delays occurred at the onset of the building programme due to the architect, Mr. Joseph Hansom, going off to search for his son. The latter had disappeared to Rome to enroll in the Papal Zoaves following Garibaldi's invasion of the Papal States. However, on 24th May 1868 the Sister's Chapel was blessed by the Bishop. On August 5th in the same year, on the feast of Our Lady of the Snows, Bishop Vaughan blessed the foundation stone of the Church. The ceremony was attended by all the priests of nearby parishes and local Catholic laity including Mr. Cary of Torre Abbey. On August 19th 1869 the High Altar was consecrated.

The building is a magnificent specimen of late Gothic architecture. The entire structure exudes decorative skill in stone, rejoicing in richly carved capitals (no two pillars are alike), carved altars, a carved pulpit and a myriad of sculpted saints like those found in many pre-Reformation churches. There is a large Crucifix in the south aisle which was carved by the benefactor himself out of an enormous beam originally part of Notre Dame Cathedral in Paris.

The solemn opening of the entire Church of Our Lady Help of Christians & St. Denis took place in February 1881. Pontifical High Mass was sung by His Lordship Bishop William Vaughan who also delivered the homily on this auspicious occasion.

Contact address of Priest:
The Presbytery, Priory Road,
St. Marychurch, Torquay, Devon. TQ1 4NY.
Telephone: (0803) 327612.

# Torquay

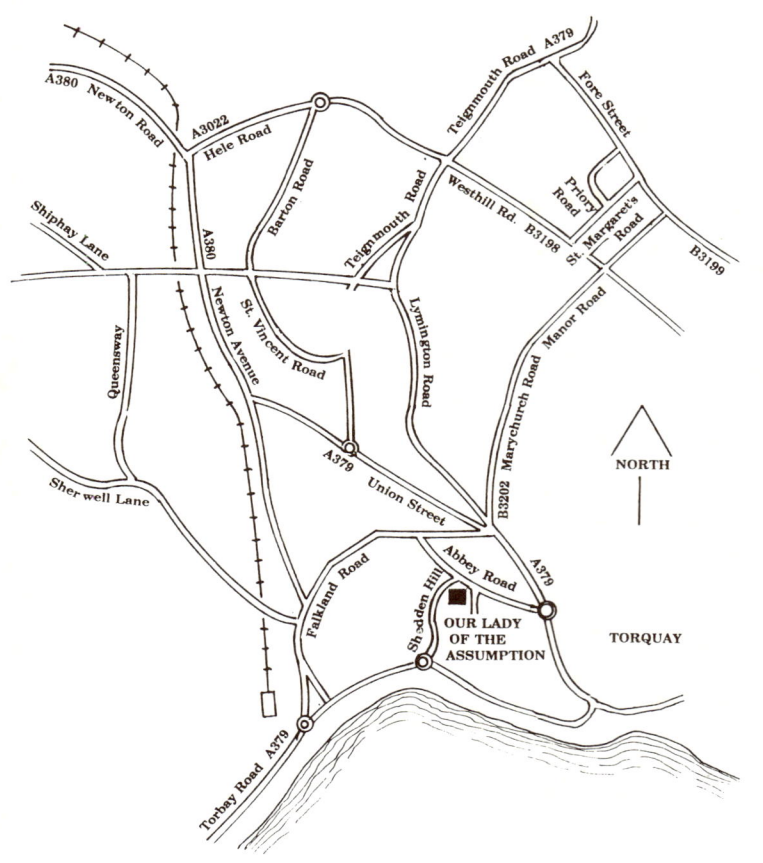

**Our Lady of the Assumption, Abbey Road.**

The Church is situated at the junction of Abbey Road and Warren Road. Follow the coast along Torbay Road A379 until it forks at the traffic lights. Turn up Shedden Hill, then turn right into Warren Road. Drive round the loop, then turn left into Abbey Road. There is a large government building nearby. Most town centre buses pass the Church. A small car park is available for parishioners.

The Church is dedicated to Our Lady of the Assumption. Belief in Mary's Assumption goes back to the early Church when a Marian tomb was venerated. There were, however, no relics of her body compared with the tombs of the apostles or other early Christian saints. Her Assumption was stated by St. Juvenal of Jerusalem at the Council of Chalcedon in 451 A.D. The conviction was generally accepted throughout the Church in the sixth and seventh centuries when Christian writers and those involved with the liturgy became concerned with Mary's Assumption. It was declared an infallible teaching of the Church by Pope Pius XII (1939-1958) in the Holy Year 1950.

# Our Lady of the Assumption

The Church of Our Lady of the Assumption, designed by the architect Hansom, was consecrated in 1854 by the first Bishop of Plymouth, the Rt. Rev. George Errington. The Church replaced the Chapel at Torre Abbey, owned by the Cary Family, where Catholics had attended Mass since 1660. In the 1850's the Catholic population had so escalated that a church was a necessity. The Carys provided the site and also helped generously with the building. In 1981 the interior of the Church was decorated and re-organized to comply with Vatican II liturgy. Fragments of the original Church furnishings have been incorporated where posssible in the new arrangement. For instance, the carved stone panel of Christ preaching to his Apostles, part of the original pulpit, is now framed in the modern Gospel lecturn. The Stations of the Cross are rectangular relief panels in handbeaten silver. They came from France in the 1850's and retain the original French inscriptions. Instead of being arranged in a conventional way the panels are fixed in the form of a continuous frieze on the south aisle wall.

The Church of Our Lady of the Assumption is the "Mother Church" for Torbay. An interesting booklet and guide to its history and treasures is available at the Church.

Contact address of Priest:
The Presbytery, 76, Abbey Road,
Torquay, Devon. TQ2 5NJ.
Telephone: (0803) 294142.

# Torquay

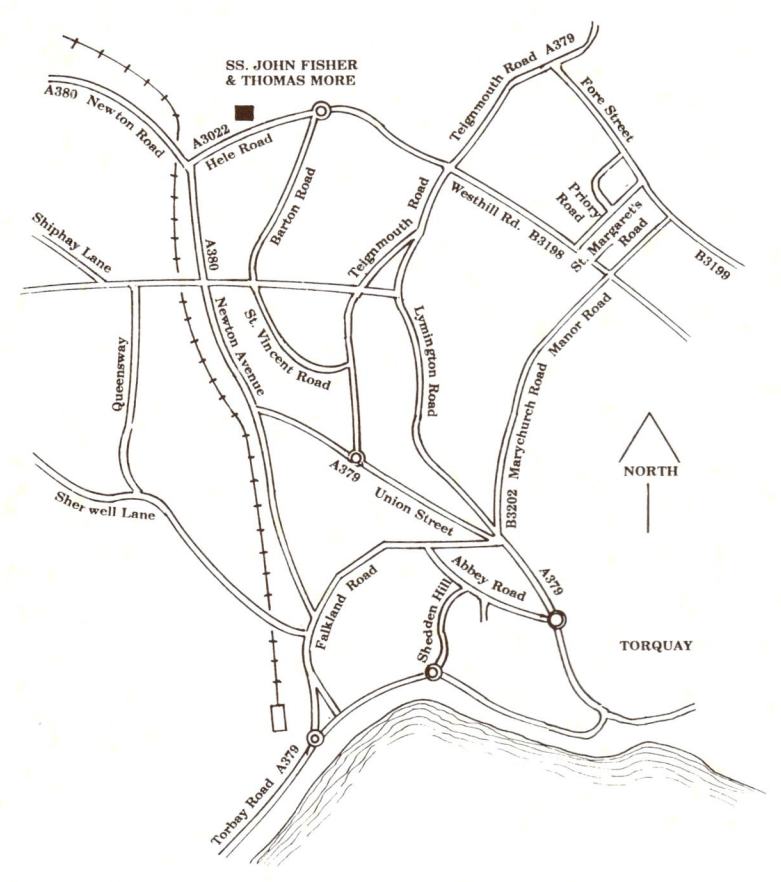

**SS. John Fisher & Thomas More, Hele Road.**

The Church, a small red brick building, is easily found on Hele Road, almost opposite "Suttons Seeds". Travelling from Torquay (on the Torquay to Newton Abbot Road A380) turn right into Hele Road A3022 at the traffic lights at Lowes Bridge. Travelling from Newton Abbot turn left at the traffic lights into Hele Road. Parking is available on the road outside the Church.

SS. John Fisher and Thomas More are the patrons of the Church. 1935 was the year in which they were canonized by Pope Pius XI (1922-1939), the same year as the Church was built, hence the dedication. Saint John Fisher was born in 1469, the son of a Yorkshire cloth merchant. He became a distinguished Cambridge scholar, then Chancellor of Cambridge University, and Bishop of Rochester. His life was a model of learning and holiness. His refusal to accept Henry VIII's new oath of succession cost him his head. Saint Thomas More was born in 1478, the son of a London judge. An eminent Oxford scholar he rose in public life to become Lord Chancellor of England. He was devoted to his Faith and his family. The royal oath which destroyed John Fisher also lost Thomas More his life: "the King's good servant, but God's first".

# SS John Fisher and Thomas More

The Church, designed by the late Joseph Walter of Paignton, is built in Romanesque style. Stained glass windows featuring the two patron saints are found above the doors at the back of the Church. There are also statues of SS. John Fisher and Thomas More on either side of the sanctuary.

The Rt. Rev. John Patrick Barrett, fifth Bishop of Plymouth, performed the ceremony of dedicating the foundations in April 1935. The solemn blessing and opening of the Church took place on Wednesday, 27th November 1935.

Contact address of Priest:
The Presbytery, Priory Road,
St. Marychurch, Torquay, Devon. TQ1 4NY.
Telephone: (0803) 327612.

# Torquay

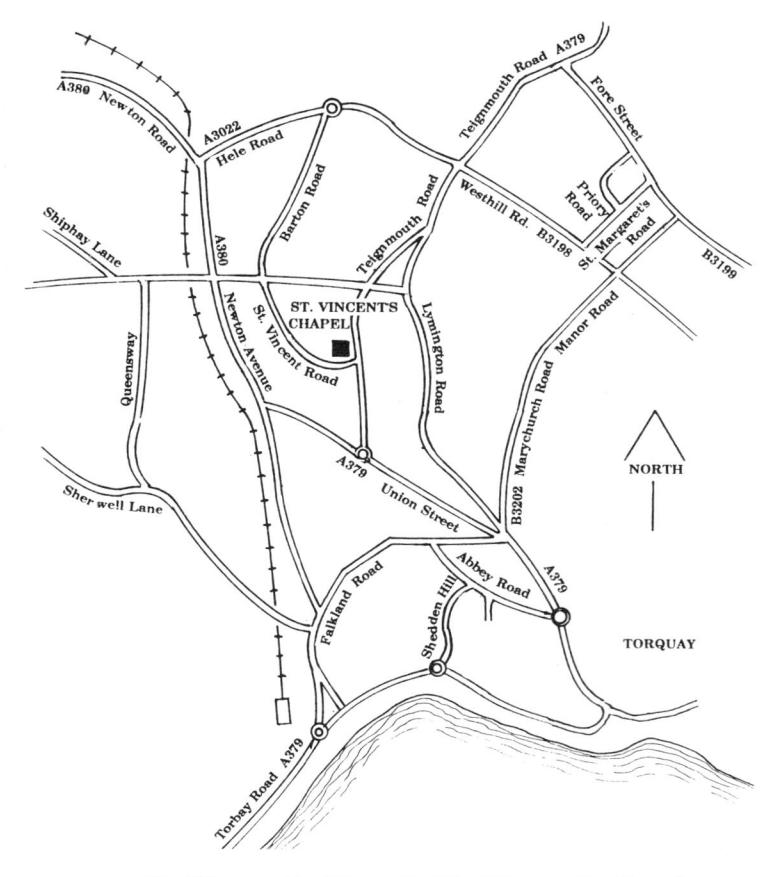

**St. Vincent's Chapel, St. Vincent's Road.**

St. Vincent's Chapel, built of grey limestone with Bath stone dressings and a redtiled roof, stands at the junction of St. Vincent's Road and Chapel Court. From Torquay town centre find the South Devon College of Arts and Technology at the junction of Union Street and Teignmouth Road. Drive up Teignmouth Road and take the second left turn into St. Vincent's Road. The Chapel is beside Mount Stuart Hospital. Car parking is available.

The Chapel's dedication to St. Vincent de Paul acknowledges the fact that the Sisters who ran the orphanage, then adjacent to the Chapel, were the Daughters of Charity of St. Vincent de Paul. St. Vincent was born in 1581, the son of a Gascon peasant family. He attended Toulouse University and was ordained a priest at the early age of nineteen. His entire life was given to spiritual work and practical charity. He founded a congregation of priests bound to live in community and devote themselves to poor country people. He also founded the Sisters of Charity, the first "unenclosed" female religious order wholly dedicated to the sick and poor. St. Vincent died in 1660, aged nearly eighty. Pope Leo XIII (1878-1903) named him patron of all charitable societies: one of the most well known is the S.V.P. active in most Parishes.

St. Vincent's is a Chapel of Ease to Our Lady of the Assumption Parish, Abbey Road, Torquay. It is situated in a pleasant garden furnished with benches conducive to rest and prayer. The setting provides a place of privacy and peace above the busy seaside town. The Chapel was solemnly opened on 25th April 1896, the gift of Mr. Vernon Benbow of Torquay, in memory of his wife. It was built for St. Vincent's Childrens' Home which at one time occupied that site.

The interior of the building is an artistic feast having been laboriously and lovingly decorated by the benefactor himself. The ceiling panels above the main body of the chapel each depict an invocation from the Litany of Our Lady:
*Regina Confessorum, Rosa Mystica, Vas Spirituale....*

In rich, dark hues over the Chancel, above the powerful words of the Sanctus, can be seen a glorious array of symbols refering to God. The Stations of the Cross, in the form of recessed carved stone relief panels, are portrayed without number or title, the individual scenes vivid enough reminders of the Passion of Christ.

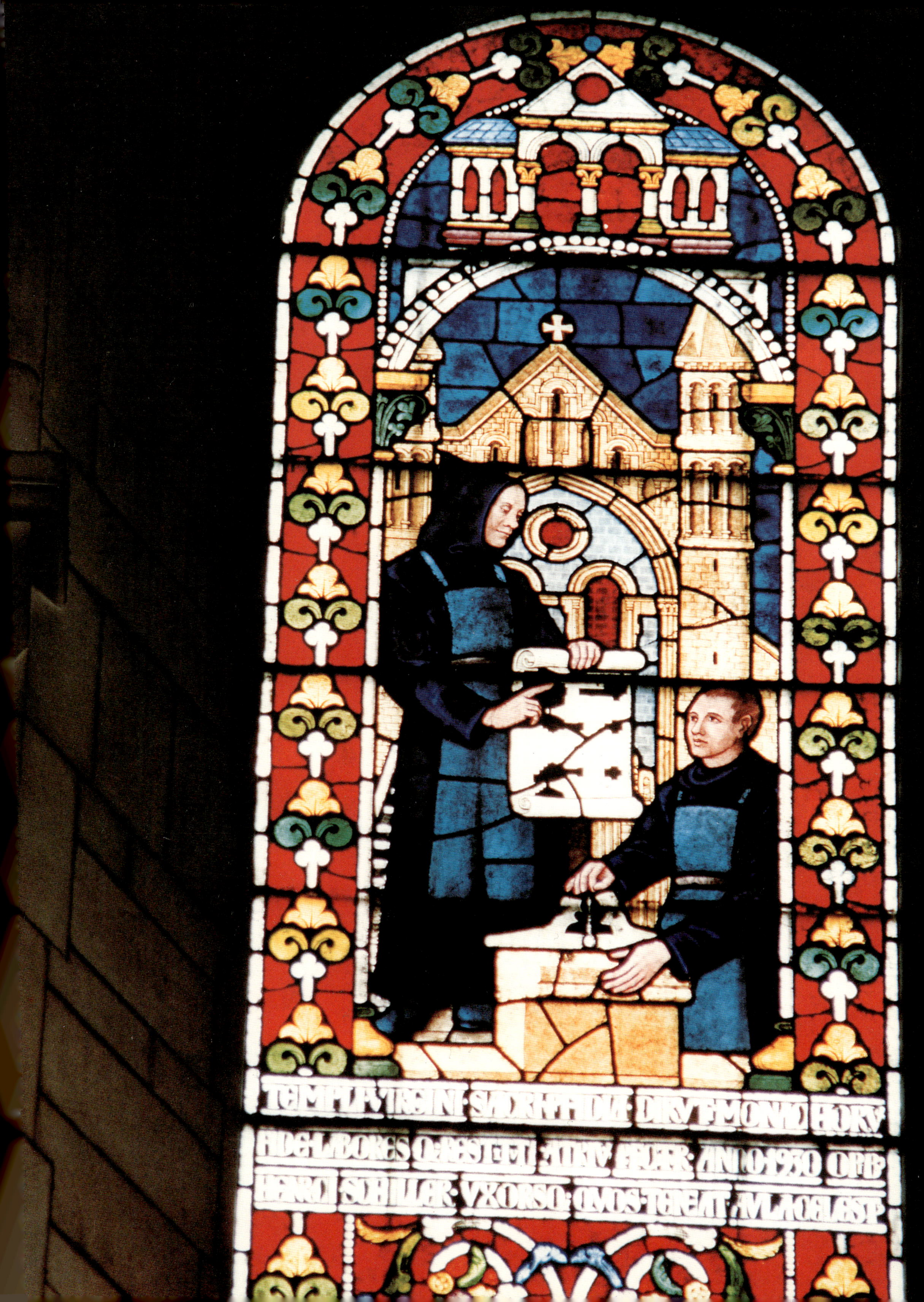

# St. Vincent's Chapel

## Caritas Christi urget nos

Contact address of Priest:
The Presbytery, 76, Abbey Road,
Torquay, Devon. TQ2 5NJ.
Telephone: (0803) 294142.

# Torrington

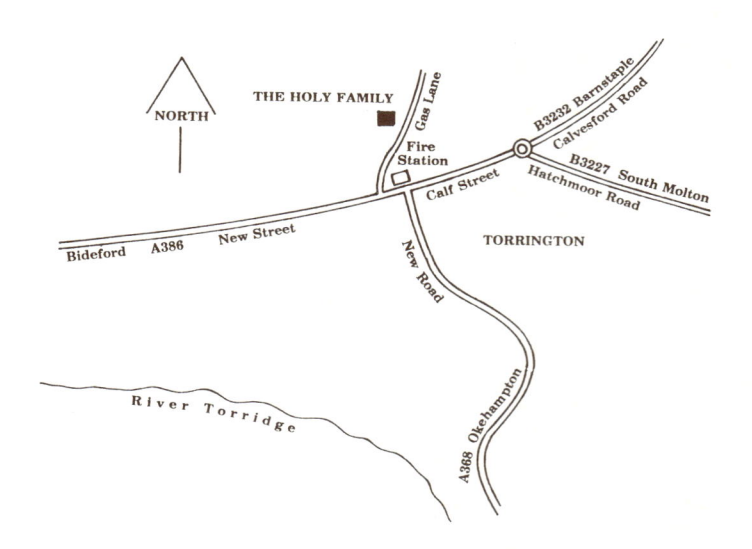

**The Holy Family, Gas Lane.**

The Church is easily located from the main Bideford /Torrington Road A386 (New Street, Calf Street). Turn left into Gas Lane, near the Fire Station and before the roundabout. The Church of The Holy Family, is at the end of the lane adjacent to the public tennis courts. It is in a beautiful setting overlooking the splendour of the countryside of North Devon. There is a large parking area within the Church grounds.

The Church, dedicated to the glory of God and in honour of "The Holy Family of Nazareth", was blessed and opened by the Rt. Rev. Cyril Restieaux, Bishop of Plymouth, on 25th March 1965. The feast of The Holy Family, Jesus, Mary & Joseph, is kept on the Sunday in the Octave of Christmas.

Mass has been celebrated in Torrington for around the last sixty years. During the 1930's it was said in the Public Library, then, in a room above a corn and seed merchants. During the later part of the War an influx of American Catholics created a need for more spacious accommodation, so the local cinema became the place for Mass. In 1950 a small hall behind a house in New Street was hired and converted into a temporary chapel. In 1964 the present site in Gas Lane was acquired with funds raised by the local Catholic community, and the Church built due to the generosity of a local benefactor.

# The Holy Family

Contact address of Priest:
The Presbytery, North Road,
Bideford, Devon. EX39 2NW.
Telephone: (0237) 472519.

# Totnes

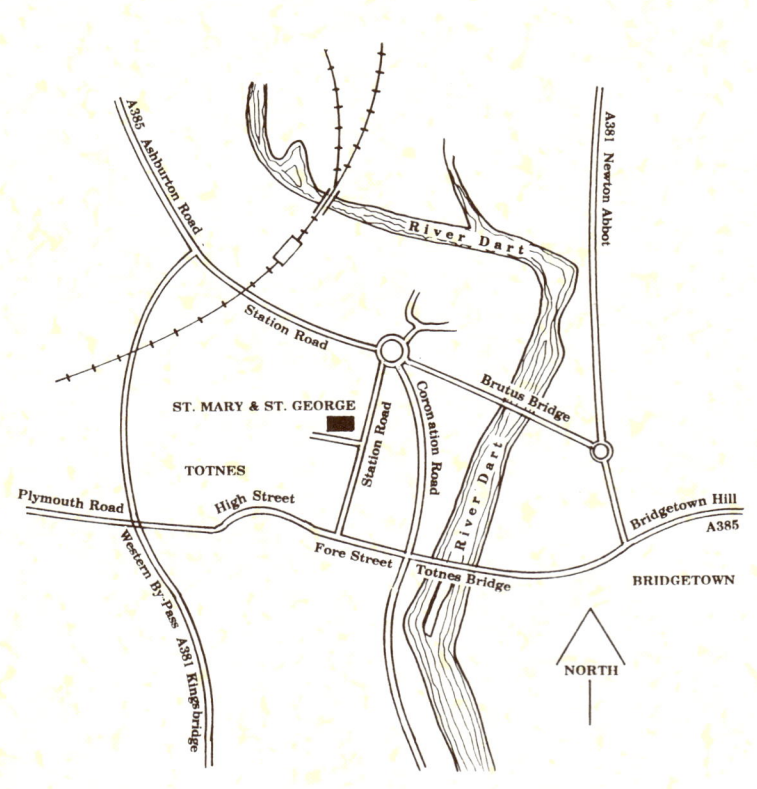

**St. Mary & St. George, Station Road.**

Several main roads lead to Totnes: the A385 Torquay/Paignton; A381 Newton Abbot; and the A384 Dartington which connects with the A38 Plymouth/Exeter Road. The Church is easily found near the junction of the town end of Station Road, almost adjacent to a large supermarket (Gateway) store and opposite the Conservative Club. Totnes is on the X80 bus route from Plymouth to Torquay. There is a Main Line Railway Station. Limited car parking is available at the Church and also in the Gateway car park.

The Church is dedicated to Our Lady & St. George, the patron of England. Historical evidence proves St. George's existence, but not a great deal is known about him. There was an ancient cult of St. George. Many dramatic legends survive, but much of his life is known only to God! About 303 A.D., he suffered martyrdom in Palestine at Lydda (Diospolis) possibly under Diocletian. His tomb was rediscovered there in 1868. St. George has been revered in England since the seventh and eighth centuries. The famous dragon legend may have started during the twelfth and or thirteenth centuries. During the Crusades the cult of St. George increased in fervour and he became the special patron of soldiers. His feast day is kept on 23rd April each year.

# St. Mary and St. George

The Parish was founded when Fr. Wilfrid Schneider of Buckfast Abbey opened a Catholic Church on a site in South Street in 1902. It was the first Catholic Church in Totnes since the Reformation. In later years the Parish was handed over to the Diocesan priests, one of whom, Fr. Russell, purchased "Crichel House" and land in Station Road in the centre of Totnes in 1940. The present Church is built on the former site of Crichel House. The site was first blessed after Mass on the feast of St. George 1985. On 9th March 1986 the new Church was dedicated by Bishop Budd.

The coat of arms on the outside wall is of the banner of St. George. It bears a large letter M for Mary as in the coat of arms of Pope John Paul II (1978- ). Inside the Church, set in one rear corner, is the Shrine of the Madonna, a statue carved from the trunk of a cedar tree. Mary and the Infant clasp "the serpent" turned rosary around her neck. At the foot of the Madonna is St. George slaying "the dragon", emphasizing the dedication of the Church to St. Mary & St. George, and the power of good over evil. A remarkable carved crucifix is placed on the Sanctuary wall. It depicts Christ giving us His blessing from the Cross: the pascal mystery of the Passion, Death and Resurrection portrayed. Most of the stained glass came from the old church except the window behind the tabernacle, from Buckfast Abbey.

The Stations of the Cross are worth seeing. The sculpted figures emerge starkly, vividly, from a background of flat, red brick. Some of the faces, "ghouls", waiting to disfigure and destroy the loving Christ. The crowd stare in masked mockery - "Behold the Man!" The tired, worn out, weakness of Pilate is so clearly demonstrated in his face. The Stations have no numbers, no titles. The journey nears its end with the twisted, torn, haggard Christ on the Cross. Could wood have so much fleshy feeling, emit so much emotion, provoke so much thought? The last scene for meditation leads to the joy of the Risen Christ, to the Tabernacle, in close proximity, at the end of the Via Crucis.

Contact address of Priest:
The Presbytery, 61, Fore Street,
Totnes, Devon. TQ9 5NJ.
Telephone: (0803) 862126.

# Truro

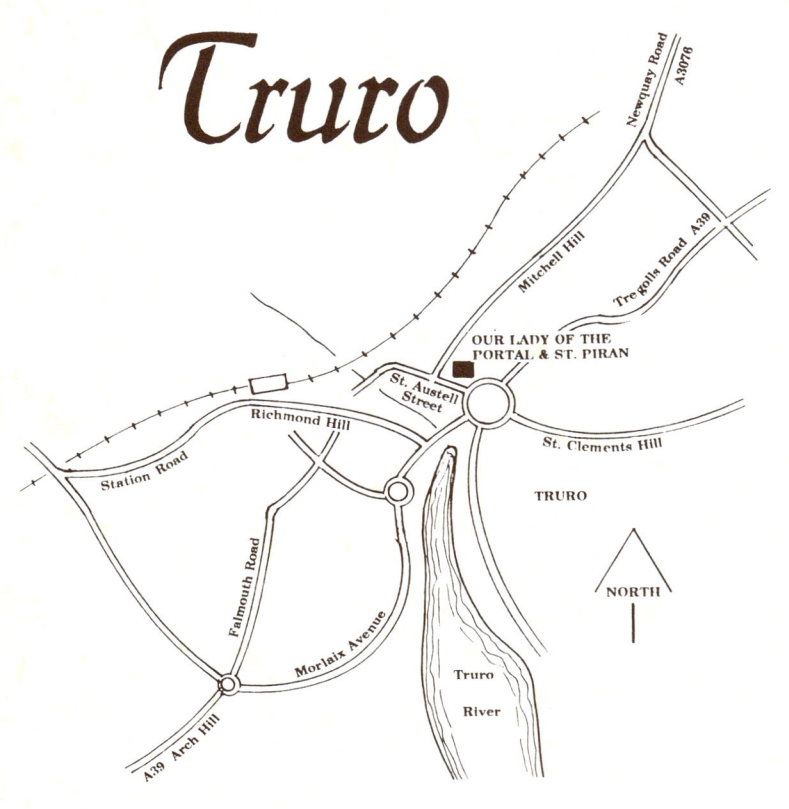

**Our Lady of the Portal & St. Piran, St. Austell Street.**

On entering Truro, from St. Austell A390 / A39, or from Bodmin A30 /A39, one arrives at Trafalgar Roundabout near the Police Station. The Church of Our Lady of the Portal & St. Piran is a large modern building on the corner of St. Austell Street adjacent to the Roundabout. The words "Catholic Church", in gilt lettering, are prominently displayed on the outside wall. Truro Railway Station is about 12 minutes walk from the Church. Limited car parking, including for disabled, is reserved at the rear of the Church, and additional spaces are available 100 yards up St. Austell Street in St. Clement's Car Park.

The dedication resurrected the medieval devotion to Our Lady of the Portal. A chapel dedicated to Mary once stood at the gate (porta) of Truro, recalling her who is "Gate of Heaven". In the fifteenth century Truro was the only place in England that had a church dedicated to Our Lady of the Portal. It was supported by its own Guild. The origins of the devotion came from Rome as far back as the sixth century. The third most important Marian shrine in Rome is the Church of Santa Maria in Portico. There King (!) James III founded a daily Mass, its intention the restoration of English Catholicism. One of the icons of Mount Athos, venerated since the ninth century, is that of Our Lady of the Portal. (The icon is part of the religious milieu of Byzantium preserved in a monastery on this Holy Mount in Greece.) Our Lady of the Portal also became a popular icon in Moscow when a seventeenth century replica was enshrined in one of the "portals" of the Kremlin. In 1964 devotion to Our Lady of the Portal was revived in Truro and the medieval Guild was firmly re-established on Sexagesima Sunday 1965.

The dedication to St. Piran invokes the patronage of a sixth century Celtic saint whose missionary activity covered the area of the parish. His name is recognised in the name of Perranporth in the north, and Perranwell and Perranarworthal in the south of the parish. This notable Cornish saint is the patron saint of tin miners.

# Our Lady of the Portal and St. Piran

In the nineteenth century a Catholic Church, dedicated to St. Piran, existed in Chapel Hill, Truro. It had been built in 1884/85 by Fr. John Grainger. Later it was served by the Canons Regular of the Lateran from Bodmin. As congregations expanded and more space was needed, some property known as "Polpeor" was purchased near the site of the Medieval Chapel of Our Lady of the Portal. Construction of a new Church began in January 1972, and the solemn blessing and opening took place on 17th May 1973.

On each side of the main altar there is an icon painting: one portrays the Old Testament Trinity, after the style of Rublev's Ikon of 1411, and the other shows the Annunciation. (Andrei Rublev was a monk in the monastery at Zagorsk, which became one of the most renowned centres for icon painting in Great Russia, under the spiritual and cultural direction of St. Sergius of Radonezh.) This Church in Truro may be the only one in the country with a well in it. A plaque in the floor over the well suggests "fons mariae matris pastoris et agni". Here also is a special Shrine to Our Lady of the Portal, and an unusual sixteenth century Basque statue of the Holy Mother feeding her Child.

Contact address of Priest:
The Presbytery, St. Austell Street,
Truro, Cornwall. TR1 1SE.
Telephone: (0872) 72291.

# Upwey

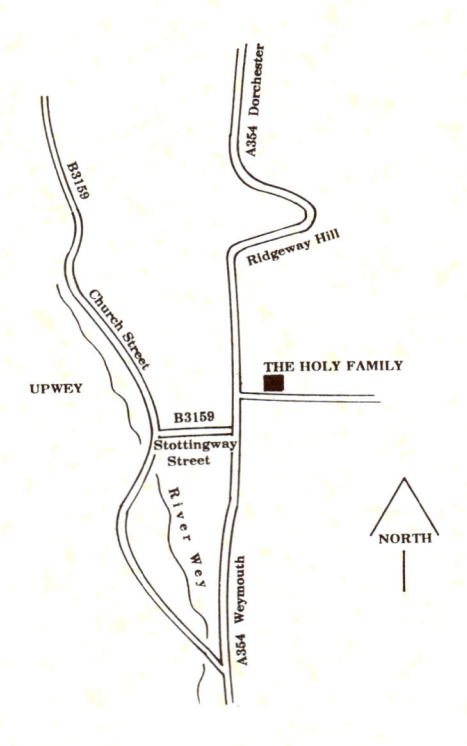

**The Holy Family, Chapel Lane.**

From Dorchester the A354 Dorchester Road leads to Upwey. After ascending from a hairpin bend at Ridgeway take the first turning on the left into Chapel Lane. The Catholic Church is 50 yards up on the left. From Weymouth sea front, near St. John's Church at the bottom of Dorchester Road, continue for 3 miles up the A354 to Upwey. Chapel Lane is on the right. A helpful landmark is the United Reform Church on the corner of the main road and Chapel Lane. A bus service runs along the main town routes to the end of Chapel Lane. Car parking is permissible in Chapel Lane or in adjacent Dorchester Road.

Father Robert, later Canon, Lyons had a great devotion to The Holy Family and his parish congregations consisted of one third children of various ages, hence the dedication to The Holy Family, the model for all Christian families. There are few details about the "holy house" in Nazareth, but we can imagine the tremendous joy, the love, the grace which must have existed there between Mary and Joseph with Jesus in their midst. The feast of The Holy Family is celebrated on the Sunday in the Ocatve of Christmas.

Towards the end of the second World War there was a small nucleus of Catholic families in Upwey with no bus service to either Weymouth or Dorchester, four or five miles away. There was also petrol rationing. In 1949 Father Lyons started a Mass Centre in a hut, belonging to the Womens' Institute, in Upwey. With the assistance of local families and against some local opposition, he went on to build a small Chapel which was consecrated in the Marian Year 1954.

# The Holy Family

Contact address of Priest:
St. Augustine's Presbytery,
38, Dorchester Road, Weymouth,
Devon. DT4 7JZ.
Telephone: (0305) 786886.

# Wadebridge

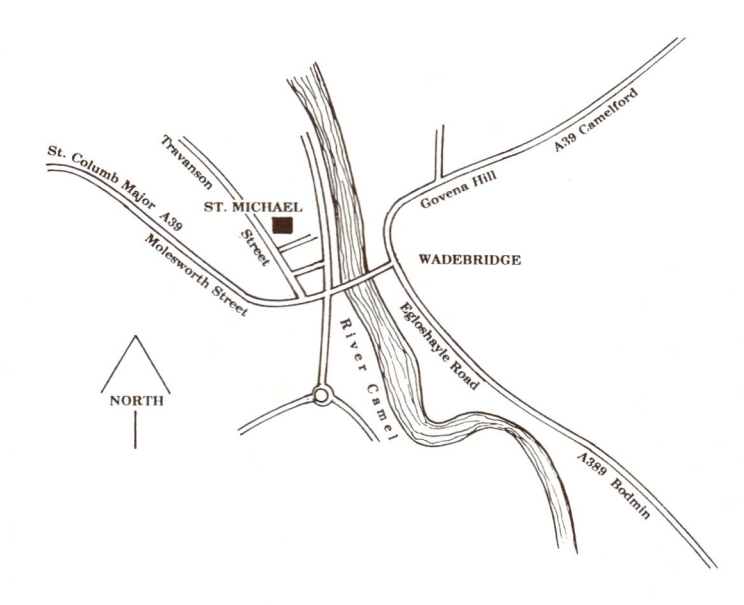

**St. Michael, Travanson Street.**

From Bodmin follow the A389, from Bude the A39 south, and from Truro the A39 north to the historic market town of Wadebridge. St. Michael's Church is a small, modern, block building with a tin roof situated about 200 yards down Travanson Street near Molesworth Court. Travanson Street is in the centre, a turning off Molesworth Street A39. Barclay's Bank is a landmark on the corner.

The Church is dedicated to St. Michael, the Archangel. The saint has received much devotion through the ages. St. Michael's Mount, the granite island, offshore from Marazion, 2 miles east of Penzance, was thought to commemorate an apparition there in the eighth century. Similarly, the tenth century Benedictine Abbey of Mont St. Michel in Normandy commemorated a vision. In Wales St. Michael was a popular patron in the eleventh and twelfth centuries and many churches in England were dedicated to him by the close of the Middle Ages. Church tradition has honoured St. Michael as a special guardian of souls in the fight against evil and especially at the hour of death. The feast of St. Michael together with SS. Gabriel and Raphael is celebrated on 29th September each year.

# St. Michael

This Church was opened in 1948.

Contact address of Priest:
Treban, Trevanion Road,
Wadebridge, Cornwall. PL27 2PA.
Telephone: (0208) 812429.

# Wareham

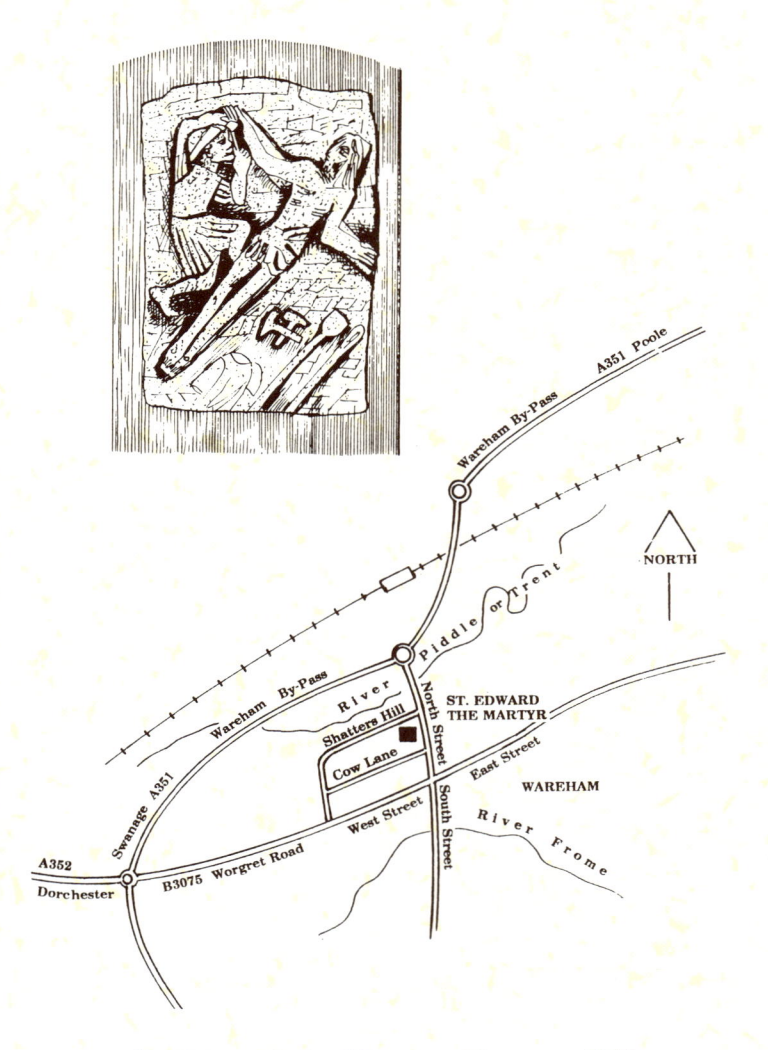

The patron of this parish is St. Edward whose cult was popular in pre-Reformation times. From boyhood he was prepared for a future role as King: he was trained in the regal arts of warfare and hunting and was spiritually enriched by the wisdom and example of his teacher, St. Dunstan. Edward was quite young when he succeeded to the throne of Wessex, but, unhappily for him, his stepmother Elfrida desired the throne for her own son Ethelred and she made plans to make it happen. One day, three and a half years into his reign, Edward went hunting as usual and then made a visit to Corfe Castle, to see his step-brother. Still in the saddle he was warmly greeted by Elfrida and she offered him a drink. As he lent forwards towards her he was cruelly stabbed in the back. The young monarch fell from his saddle and was dragged along by his horse as it panicked and bolted. Thus, Edward died. The Old Sarum Breviary recorded St. Edward's feast on March 18th as it is now.

**St. Edward the Martyr, Shatter's Hill.**
The A352 from Dorchester, the A351 from Swanage and the A351 also from Lychett Minster lead into Wareham. From the town centre, with the Town Hall on the right, and the Red Lion Hotel on the left, go up North Street. Turn left into Shatters Hill. The Church is a little way up on the left. As North Street joins Shatters Hill there is a large sign "Catholic Church". Car parking is available at the Church.

In 1888 a Religious Community of Passionists came and settled in Wareham in property known as the Westport Estate. Their new Retreat, opened on 8th May 1888, was dedicated to St. Michael. It was originally planned as a "Sanitorium". A Fr. Benignus organised the building of a Church and the foundation stone was laid on 19th April 1889 by the Duke of Norfolk. The solemn opening took place in November 1889 in the presence of The Father Provincial and Bishop Vaughan. Many important dignitaries attended: Baroness Boeslager, Lord & Lady Braye, Lady Heathcote, members of the Petre and Weld families and other "Honourable" personages. The Passionists left St. Michael's in 1901. Six years later the Church at Wareham was carefully dismantled, re-erected stone by stone at Dorchester under the title of Our Lady Queen of Martyrs & St. Michael.

# St. Edward the Martyr

The present Church of St. Edward the Martyr was built in 1933. Three hundred and fifty pounds came from Ireland, kindly donated by previous holiday visitors, for the purchase of the site. The sanctuary lamp was given by a Fr. James Player of Toronto C.S.B. who died 1st March 1931.

The ciborium bears the following intriguing inscription: *"Pray for the soul of Hugh Chyke Burgess of Wareham Parliament A.D. 1302 and of his posterity and kin."*

Contact address of Priest:
The Presbytery, Shatter's Hill,
Wareham, Dorset. BH20 4QP.
Telephone: (0929) 552820.

# West Moors

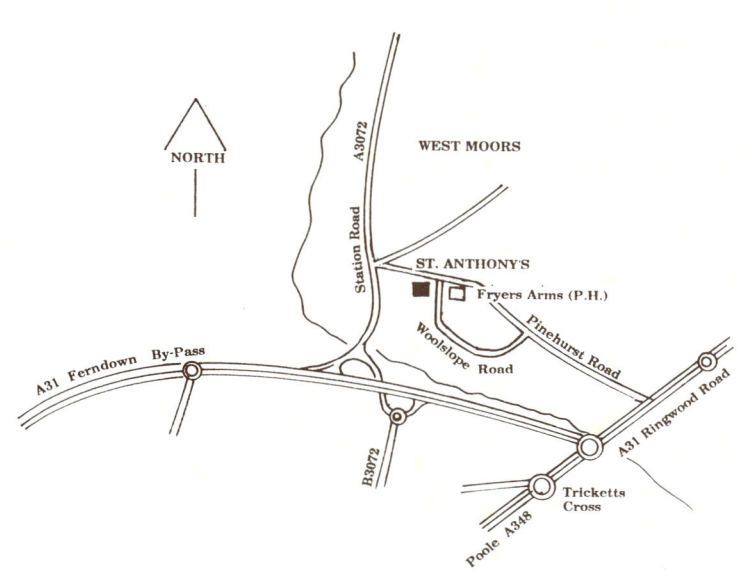

**St. Anthony's, Pinehurst Road.**

The Parish of West Moors covers the north east corner of Dorset. On the A31 from Wimborne turn off the Ferndown By Pass on to the B3072 "West Moors half a mile". Take the first right turn (Cemetery sign) into Pinehurst Road. Alternately, from Tricketts Cross Roundabout join the Dual Carriageway going towards Ringwood. Take the second turning on the left into Pinehurst Road. There is a sign "Catholic Church" immediately outside St. Anthony of Padua's. The Church is brick with a hall adjacent, set back in its own grounds with garden and car park. Landmarks close by include the Fryers Arms Pub and also a telephone kiosk and post box.

The patron of the Church is Anthony of Padua, born in Portugal, in 1195, of noble parentage. His vocation led him first to the Canons Regular of St. Augustine and then, after a time, on to the newly founded Order of Franciscans. With the latter he set off to become an African Missionary, but sickness forced him to return. At the tiny monastery at Sao Paolo, near Forli in Italy, his intellectual gifts of theology and oratory emerged. St. Anthony was sent to teach and preach in southern France and northern Italy. He was only 36 years old when he died, in Padua. His sanctity was readily proclaimed and canonization followed only a year after his demise. In 1946 he was declared a Doctor of the Church. St. Anthony's feast day is celebrated on 13th June. His relics remain in Padua.

# St. Anthony

The present Church replaces the old wooden building, which had become far too small, erected in 1928. When it was demolished the area was landscaped. The modern Church was built in 1975-76, solemnly blessed by Bishop Restieaux on Our Lady's Feast Day in December 1977 and consecrated on 8th December 1980.

The relics enclosed in the High Altar are those of St. Maria Goretti.

Contact address of Priest:
The Presbytery, 8, Pinehurst Road,
Wimborne, Dorset. BH22 0AP.
Telephone: (0202) 874811.

# Weymouth

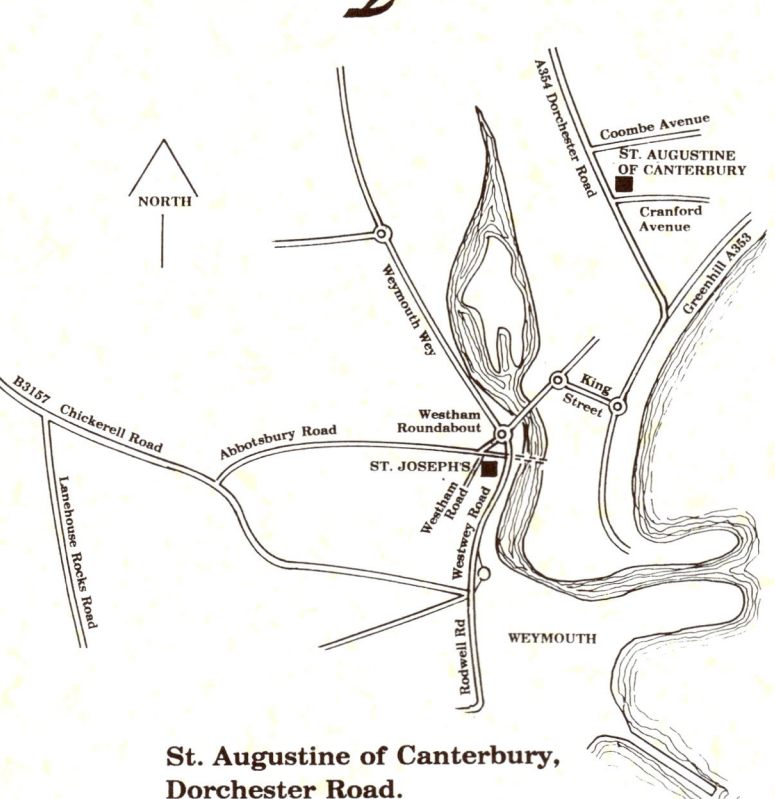

**St. Augustine of Canterbury, Dorchester Road.**

The A354 from Dorchester, the A352 /A353 from Wareham and the B3157 from Bridport all lead into Weymouth. From the promenade turn left at the "Clock" on the seafront esplanade. (St. John's C.of E. Church is also a landmark). Continue for approximately three eighths of a mile along Dorchester Road. St. Augustine's Church is on the right hand side, just past Fernhill Avenue. It has a classical facade in Portland stone facing the road, incorporating an imposing statue of St. Augustine of Canterbury in a niche above the entrance. The Church is situated on the main bus route, Dorchester to Weymouth, via the town centre. Car parking is possible in side roads nearby.

The Church is dedicated to St. Augustine of Canterbury, an Italian, a Benedictine monk, whose holy diligence led him initially to become Prior of the Monastery of St. Andrew on the Coelian Hill in Rome. In 596 A.D. Pope St. Gregory the Great (590-604 A.D.) chose Augustine and thirty or forty monks for the English Mission, the conversion of the Anglo-Saxons. Bishop Augustine, together with fellow religious, arrived on the shores of Ebbsfleet, Kent, in 597 A.D. Through hard endeavour, four years later, the King of Kent, Ethelbert, and many of his subjects sought Christian Baptism. Pope Gregory sent additional clergy, sacred vessels, chalices and ciboria, books and relics for the English Mission. Augustine went on to build the first Cathedral in Canterbury. He also founded a school there which became involved in book production. A sixth century manuscript, the "Gospels of St. Augustine" is kept at Corpus Christi College, Cambridge. Augustine became the first Archbishop of Canterbury, Pastor of all the English Southern Dioceses then established. He died in about 604 A.D. His feast is celebrated on 27th May.

# St Augustine of Canterbury

St. Augustine's is one of the oldest parishes in the country. It started in a modest way as a small mission when one or two priests lived in the vicinity and Mass was celebrated in parlours and various other places. A Baptismal entry exists for 1819. Three French priests were instrumental in setting up and maintaining the Mission in the 1820's.

In 1835, due to the persistence of one priest, a small Church, presbytery and hall were built. The official opening on 22nd October was marked by an article in the Dorset Chronicle headlined "Increase of Popery"! It related to the opening of a Roman Catholic Chapel of St. Augustine of Canterbury by the Rt. Rev. Dr. Baines of Bath, Vicar Apostolic of the Western District, assisted by Fr. Moutardier of Lulworth, Fr. O'Farrell and Fr. Hartley, the resident priest at Weymouth. In due course, St. Augustine's was enlarged and the house next door rebuilt as a presbytery. Through the years there have been many alterations, mainly internally.

Contact address of Priest;
The Presbytery, 38, Dorchester Road,
Weymouth, Dorset. DT4 7JZ.
Telephone: (0305) 787886.

# Weymouth

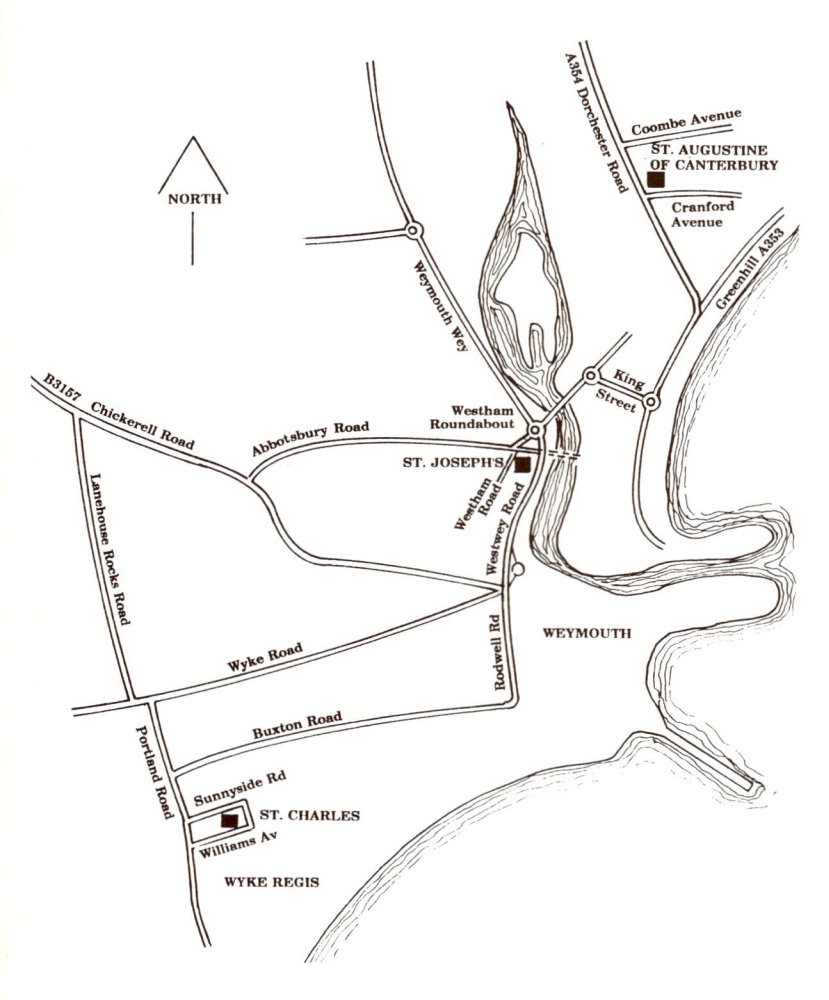

**St. Joseph's, Westham Road.**

From the old town, St. Joseph's Church can be approached by pedestrians (only) across the New Bridge. Plenty of parking spaces are available close to the east end of the bridge. Closer vehicular access up to the Church is also possible, with limited parking behind the Church. From Westham Roundabout go along Abbotsbury Road, then take the first left turning into Stavordale Road where the Church is situated on the corner. The front of the building is a tall, elegant Italianate gable, incorporating a campanile with an exposed bell. The canopy over the porch is proudly inscribed "Catholic Church". Symbols representing the four evangelists embellish a circular window above the canopy. Higher still there is a blue and white faience sculpture of Our Lady with the Holy Infant.

St. Joseph was chosen as patron saint of this parish, in memory of a benefactor of that name. St. Joseph, a simple carpenter, belonged to the house and family of the mighty King David and it was because of this that he had to travel with Mary from their home in sleepy Nazareth to Bethlehem in Judaea for the census demanded by Herod the Great. After Jesus' birth, Joseph took the Holy Family to Egypt. They probably followed a route which went from Jerusalem to the coast and then used the important Damascus to Egypt caravan trail, a little north of Gaza. After Herod's death Joseph took Mary and Jesus back to Nazareth, possibly via Bethlehem and then along the Joppa road to Lydda. From there he may have headed north across the Plain of Sharon and then across the Plain of Jezreel. A little way from the village of Nain he would have climbed north towards the foothills of Nazareth and home! In St. Luke's Gospel there is another record of a journey, a pilgrimage to Jerusalem, for the Feast of the Passover, made annually by Joseph and his family. After that there is no further Biblical reference to him. Many invoke the protection of the saint, the privileged foster father of the Word Incarnate. St. Joseph's feast is kept on 19th March.

# St. Joseph

The land on which the Church is built came on the market in 1933. The site was desirable but seemingly unattainable as the owner was opposed to purchases by Roman Catholics. A Messrs O'Halloran and Wilson approached the vendor and managed successfully to arrange for a sale. Two years later, on 19th March 1935, St. Joseph's was officially opened.

Our Lady's Grotto, situated beside the Church, was built in thanksgiving for the preservation of the Church during World War II.

Contact address of Priest:
The Presbytery, 1, Stavordale Road,
Weymouth, Dorset. DT4 0AB.
Telephone: (0305) 786033.

# Wimborne

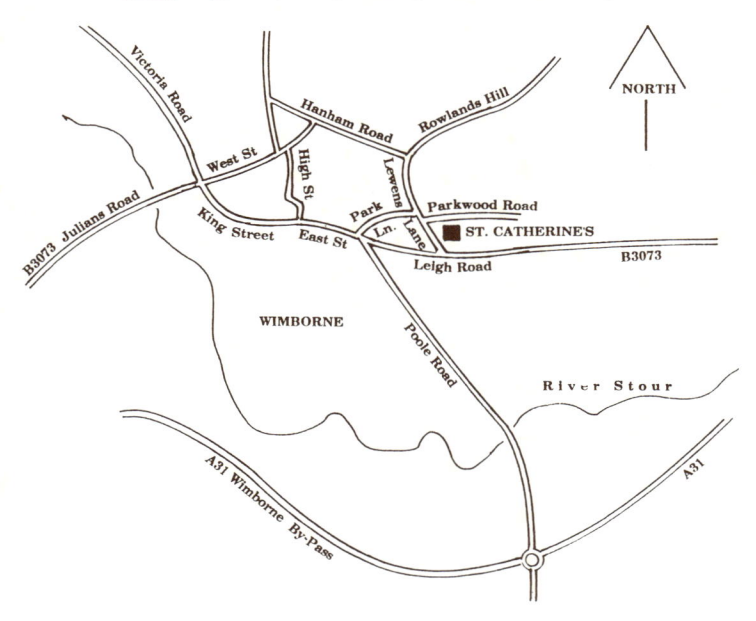

**St. Catherine's, Lewens Lane.**

From Ringwood follow the A31 west; from Cranborne the B3078 south; from Poole the A349 north; and from Dorchester the A35 and then A31 east to Wimborne. Having arrived in Wimborne the one way system can be confusing. There are parking facilities at the Church. For visitors who decide to use a car park in town, the Minster is an obvious landmark and reference point. With the Minster on your right, and then behind you, walk down High Street. Turn left into East Street. Go straight on (crossing the river) into Leigh Road. Continue until the roundabout, St. Catherine's Church is opposite on the left. There is a large notice outside: "Diocese of Plymouth Catholic Church of St. Catherine."

In the Middle Ages a small Chapel dedicated to Catherine of Alexandria existed on the same site as the present Church. Devotion to this saint seems to have started in the Holy Land on Mount Sinai. Although accounts vary, the fact remains that today there is still a monastery dedicated to St. Catherine. It is at the foot of Jebel Musa, the "Mountain of Moses" and was built at the beginning of the sixth century by the Emperor Justinian. In the centre of the monastery (which housed six to seven thousand monks in the first centuries of Christianity and three to four hundred during the Middle Ages) is the Church. Inside, near the central altar, is the "Crypt of St. Catherine". According to local tradition her cult can be traced back to the early fourth century when, during the reign of Maximinus, she left Alexandria in Egypt and retreated to a rocky valley in Sinai. There Catherine devoted her life to God and managed to escape Caesar's persecution. Ultimately, she was discovered and martyred. Approximately three centuries later some Sinai monks, in response to a dream, found her body on the mountain. It was reverently transferred to a golden casket in their Church.

# St. Catherine

The Catholic Church in Wimborne has been active in an unbroken line since 350 A.D. Right through the Reformation Mass continued to be said daily at Canford and Stapehill within the parish boundary.

The stone Church of St. Catherine replaces an earlier wooden building where Mass was celebrated for the first time on Christmas Eve 1926. The opening of the present Church took place in November 1933.

Inside there is an interesting stained glass memorial window dedicated

*"to the greater glory of God and in memory of the Rt. Hon. James Radcliffe 3rd Earl of Derwentwater and his wife Anna Maria daughter of Sir John Webb Bart of Canford in this parish, where the Faith was kept alive during the Penal Times - Feb.24th 1716 R.I.P."*

The Earl of Derwentwater was executed for his part in the 1715 Rebellion.

There is an ancient "link" also between the holy city of Rome and Wimborne. The Church "Santo Spiritu a Sassia" which stands on the site of a former hostelry, a house for pilgrims instituted in 726 A.D. by King Ina of Wessex, cherishes a picture of the Madonna thought to have belonged to King Ina. This same monarch donated land to his sister, St. Cuthberga, for the founding of Wimborne Minster in 713 A.D.

Contact address of Priest:
The Presbytery, 4, Lewens Lane,
Wimborne, Dorset. BH21 1LE.
Telephone: (0202) 883312.

# Withycombe

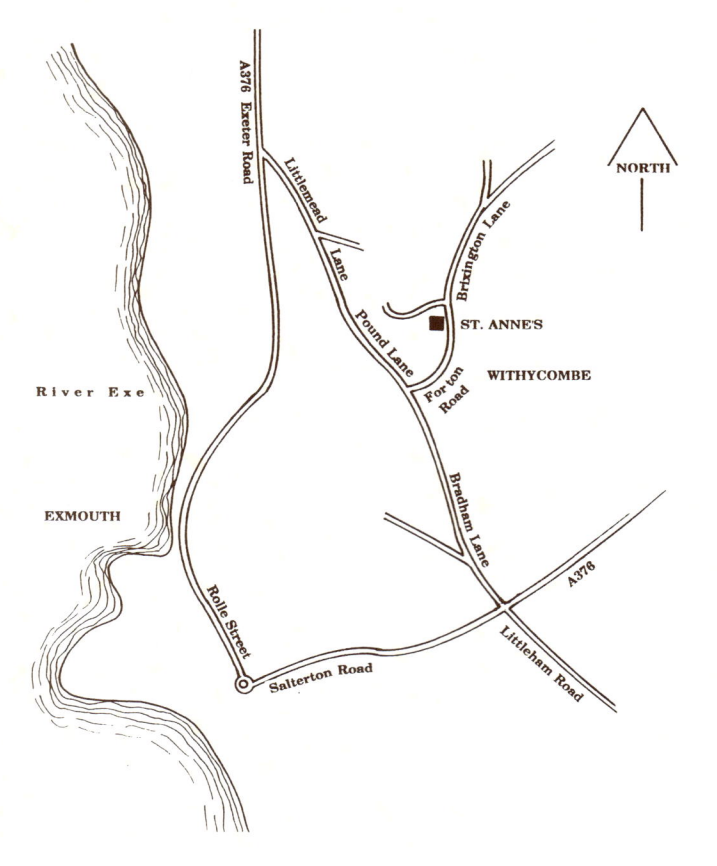

**St. Anne's, Brixington Lane, Exmouth.**

From Exmouth town follow Salterton Road A376 straight. Make a left turn into Bradham Lane and then a right turn into Forton Road. Go left into Brixington Lane. St. Anne's Church is nearly opposite Brixington Drive.

This church is one of the few in the Diocese which derives from the "Modern" movement in architecture, reminiscent of Le Corbusier's design for the chapel of Notre Dame at Ronchamp. The curved white wall of the church, seen against dark green trees, provides a dramatic background to the large cross standing starkly on the grass in front of the Church.

The dedication is to St. Anne, the mother of the Blessed Virgin Mary. Her name originates from the ancient Hebrew "Hannah" meaning "grace". According to tradition Anne came from Nazareth and was the wife of Joachim. She is mentioned in early apocryphal writings. Justinian built a Church dedicated to her at Constantinople and, apparently, relics were transferred from there to Jerusalem and Rome. Devotion to St. Anne spread during the Middle Ages. Her feast was celebrated in the tenth century at Naples, and from the beginning of the twelfth century at Canterbury and then Worcester. From 1382 her feast was generally observed in England. St. Anne has been the patron of different religious guilds. Her feast day is on 26th July, with St. Joachim.

# St Anne

The holy water stoop in the Church porch has been in existence since the fourteenth century. It was used in the Chapel of St. Margaret in Chapel Street, Exmouth around 1381. Later on it was built into the walls of a shop on the site of the Chapel. It survived the bombing of 1941. In 1964, when Exmouth Urban District Council were modernising the town centre, the water stoop was given to Canon J.P. O'Malley.

This is not the first time that the people of Withycombe have wanted to honour St. Anne. In 1415 they actually petitioned Pope Gregory XII (1406 -1415) for permission to build a church in her name. Their request was granted, but for some reason the construction never materialized. Over five hundred and fifty years later a copy of the Mandate was discovered in the Vatican Archives. So, finally, in 1968, the Church of St. Anne, Withycombe, became a reality.

Contact address of Priest:
The Presbytery, Raddenstile Lane,
Exmouth, Devon. EX8 2JH.
Telephone: (0395) 263384.

# Wool

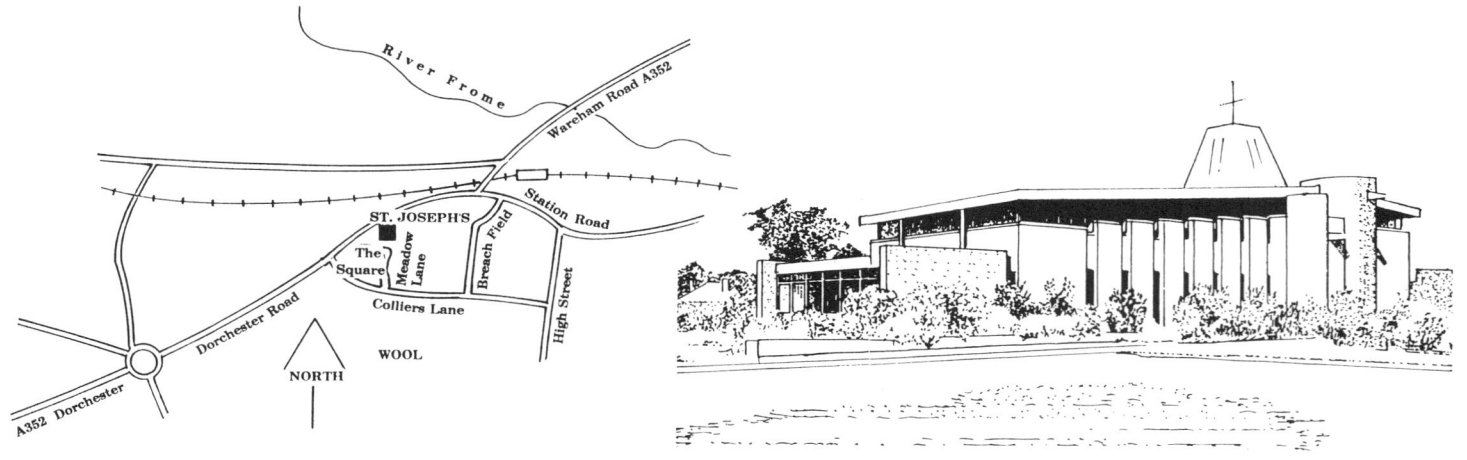

**St. Joseph's, The Square.**

From Dorchester follow the A352 east; from Wareham follow the A352 west; from Lulworth follow the B3071 north into Wool. The Church of St. Joseph is within walking distance of the Railway Station (Weymouth/ London line). From the Station turn right towards Dorchester, the Church is on the left, almost opposite the Ship Inn. Car parking is available in The Square, beside the Church.

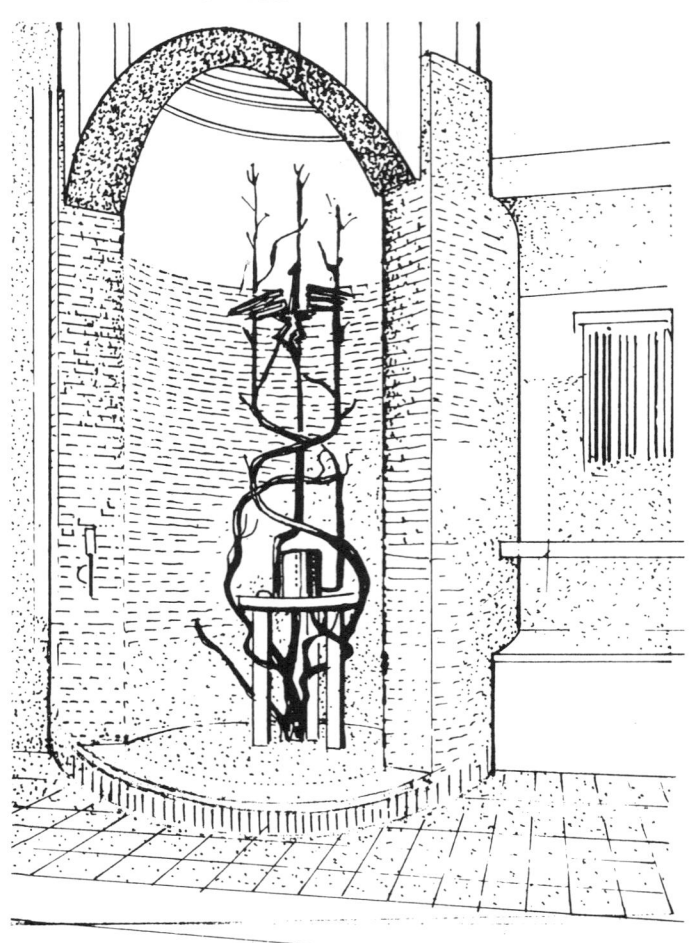

St. Joseph's is an exciting, massive, modern structure. It uses modern materials in a modern way, but the lines of perspective focus on the altar with all the insistence and conviction of an ancient basilica church. It is modern, but it has that elusive timeless quality which makes some churches memorable. According to an article in *The Architect*, November 1971, St. Joseph's Wool was inspired by principles laid down in a German Liturgical Commission Document of 1947. However, the Church was planned soon after Vatican II introduced the changes which are proving so difficult to implement in some earlier churches. At Wool, there is no token reredos. The plan meets the challenge of the new order boldly, and places the action of the Mass at the centre of a square, on a plain slab, below a square lantern rooflight. The Blessed Sacrament is given its special place, embraced in a circular space.

The Blessed Sacrament Chapel and the Baptistry are on opposite sides of the Crossing: the Blessed Sacrament is elevated by one step, the Baptistry lower by one step. The circular Chapel, a hollow round tower, is particularly apposite, its geometry, a traditional representation of God's Holy Presence. From below the sacred mensa, three thorn branches rise and intertwine, and near the top rests a pelican with outspread wings, a symbolic sculpture by Geoffrey Teychenne.

The antique organ although of unknown origin, was possibly built about 1783. It came from Lulworth Castle and has been carefully restored.

# St. Joseph

The history of the parish of Bindon and Wool can be traced back to the foundation of the Cistercian Abbey of Blessed Mary of Bindon in 1172. This Abbey served the parishioners for three hundred and sixty seven years until the Dissolution of the monasteries in 1539. Then it was partly demolished and used to construct Portland and Sandsfoot Castles. The Abbey ruins became the property of Humphrey Weld, Governor of Portland Castle in 1641. One of his descendants, a certain Thomas Weld, built a house from the old Cistercian ruins. In 1886 it became the Catholic centre for Wool with the lower rooms being used as a school and the upper part as a Chapel. Eighty years later larger accomodation was sorely necesssary.

In 1969 a new school was opened and work began on a new Church and presbytery. The solemn blessing of St. Joseph's took place on Friday, December 1st 1972. Bishop Cyril Restieaux officiated. Relics of SS. Felicis M. and Virginae M., formerly blessed by His Grace the Most Rev. Cyril Conrad Cowderoy, Archbishop of Southwark, were reverently placed in the Sepulchre on October 10th 1980 by the Rt. Rev. Cyril Restieaux, Bishop of Plymouth.

Contact address of Priest:
The Priest's House, The Square,
Wool, Dorset. BH20 6DV.
Telephone: (0929) 463334.

# Wyke Regis

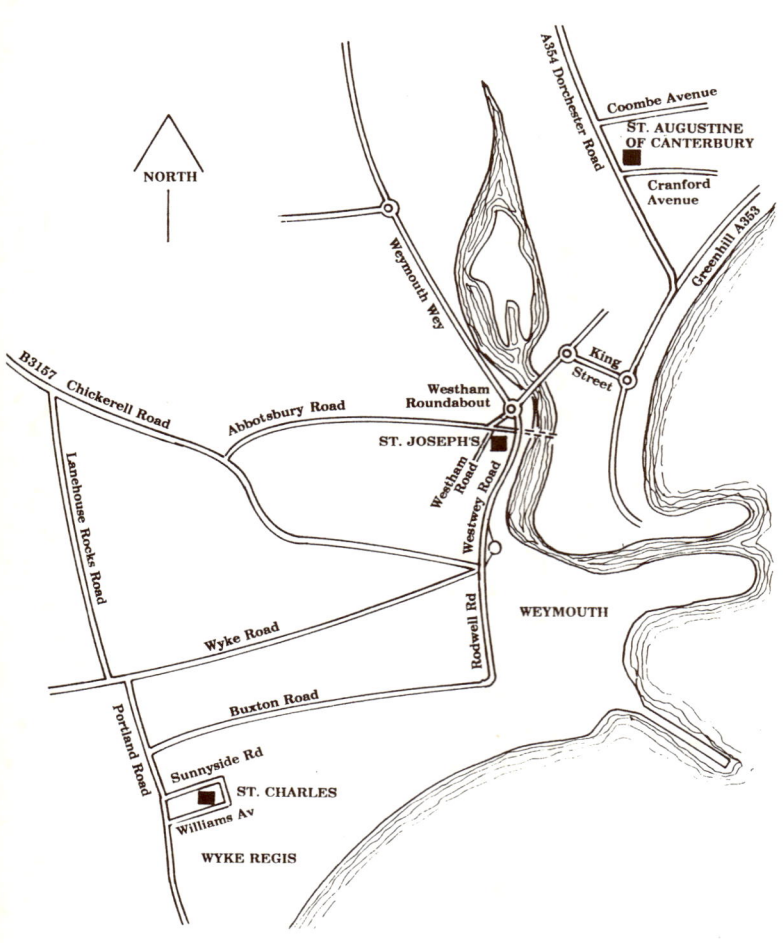

**St. Charles, Sunnyside Road.**

From Weymouth follow the signs to Portland and then the sign for Wyke Regis which leads into Wyke Road. Go straight. Turn left into Portland Road, signposted A354 Portland. Go past Buxton Road on the left. Take the next left into Sunnyside Road. The Catholic Church is signposted at the end of Sunnyside Road, a modern brick building with a metal cross on the roof.

The Church is dedicated to St. Charles who was born into a wealthy Italian family, in a castle on Lake Maggiore in 1538. At the age of twelve, he received the tonsure. At twenty two he had achieved his doctorate and diaconate and was invited to work for his mother's brother, the former Cardinal de Medici who had become Pope Pius IV (1559-1565). He was actively involved in the reassembly of the Council of Trent, the revision of the Catechism, the Missal and the Breviary and, as a patron of Giovanni Pierluigi da Palestrina, church music of the day. In 1564 he was ordained and then made Bishop. He rose in status to Papal Legate for all Italy, but his own life, in contrast, followed a path of simplicity and self discipline and generosity to the poor. St. Charles worked diligently for the Counter Reformation, particularly aided by the Jesuit and the Barnabite Religious Orders. He also became a benefactor of the English College at Douai. He had a special regard for John Fisher, the English Martyr, who had died some three years before his own birth. St. Charles held Fisher's picture in veneration. In Milan in 1580, he received a visit from Edmund Campion who was later to be remembered as one of the English Martyrs. St. Charles died at the age of forty six in Milan and, as Archbishop was buried there in the Cathedral. He is one of the patrons of Catechists. His feast is kept on 4th November.

# St Charles

The Church of St. Charles, Wyke Regis, was opened in 1955.

Contact address of Priest:
The Presbytery, 1, Stavordale Road,
Weymouth, Dorset. DT4 0AB.
Telephone: (0305) 786033.

# Yelverton

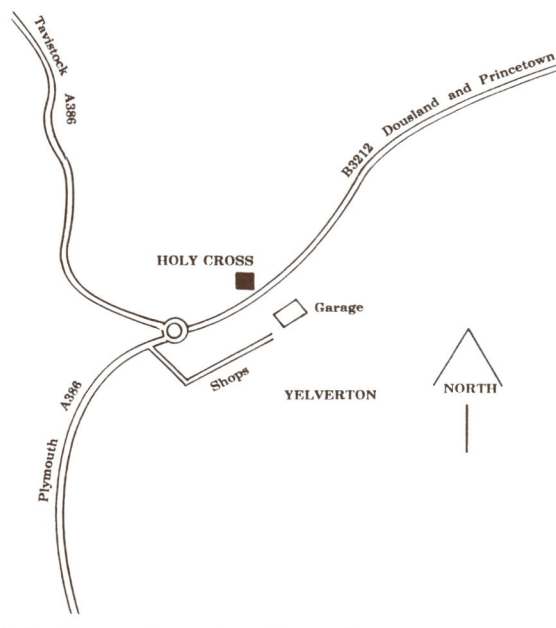

**Holy Cross, Dousland Road.**

Yelverton is on the B3212 road off the Plymouth/Tavistock A386. The local stone Church of the Holy Cross, with its crenellated tower, is easily found in the village opposite Westella Garage. The nearest bus route is the 83/84 Plymouth/Tavistock. Car parking facilities are available at the Church.

The Holy Cross is the dedication. Christ was crucified on a wooden gibbet, a cross. It was the punishment for a criminal according to Roman law (although the idea had been borrowed from the East). The Latin cross has been the symbol of Christianity, but persecution imposed a certain reluctance on the part of the First Christians to display openly such a sacred sign of their faith. One of the earliest depictions of the Crucifixion was a third century mocking caricature scratched on a beam on a building on the Palatine Hill in Rome. Near the end of the sixth century the Holy Cross, the Crucifix, began to be reverently displayed on public monuments. Between the sixth and twelfth centuries the depiction of the Crucified Jesus was one of triumph. Christ vested in a long sleeveless robe, wearing a royal diadem instead of the crown of thorns. After the twelfth century the Holy Cross was portrayed visually in all its horror. A later development was the addition of two figures at the foot of the Cross, the Blessed Virgin and St. John, as seen here at Yelverton in the Sanctuary. The feast of the Triumph of the Cross is celebrated on 14th September each year.

# Holy Cross

At one time Mass was said for the tiny local community, by the monks of Buckfast Abbey, at the Poor Clare Convent, Crapstone, also at the Oratory of Lady Seaton at Buckland. Then in 1917, due to the generosity of Lady Seaton, the first part of Holy Cross Church was constructed. In 1928 the Lady Chapel was added. Then a further extension was built and officially blessed by His Lordship Bishop Restieaux on 16th December 1978.

Contact address of Priest:

The Presbytery, Dousland Road,
Yelverton, Devon. PL20 6AZ.
Telephone: (0822) 853171.

COLOURED ILLUSTRATIONS

*Front cover*   Stone carving of St. Boniface.
                Lympstone, Devon.
*Back cover*    Grotto of Our Lady of Lourdes
                St. Brannoc's Holy Well,
                Church of St. Brannoc, Braunton, N. Devon.

*Facing page* 32  *Stained glass window. St. Catherine.*
                  Church of St. Mary & St. Catherine,
                  Bridport, Dorset.
              48  *View of the interior from the Gallery.*
                  Buckfast Abbey, Devon.
              64  *Our Lady Queen of Martyrs.*
                  Shrine of the Dorset Martyrs,
                  Chideock, Dorset.
              80  *Sixth Station of the Cross.*
                  The Church of the Most Holy Saviour,
                  Lynton, Devon.
              96  *View of the Interior.*
                  Christ the King,
                  Armada Way, Plymouth, Devon.
             112  *The Blessed Sacrament Chapel.*
                  Our Lady of Ilfracombe, Star of the Sea,
                  Ilfracombe, N. Devon.
             128  *National Shrine of St. Cuthbert Mayne.*
                  Launceston, Cornwall.
             144  *The Church of Our Lady.*
                  Marnhull, Devon.
             160  *View of the Abbey Church.*
                  St. Mary's Abbey, Buckfast, Devon
             176  *View of the Church of St. Paul.*
                  St. Budeaux, Plymouth, Devon.
             192  *St. Peter led to freedom by an Angel.*
                  Stained glass, Buckfast Abbey, Devon.
             208  *Stained glass - St. Francis Window.*
                  Plymouth Cathedral, Plymouth, Devon.
             224  *Embroidered Banner of Our Lady.*
                  Church of St. Ignatius of Loyola,
                  Shaldon, Devon.
             240  *View of the Church.*
                  The Holy Name & St. Edward the Martyr,
                  Shaftesbury, Dorset.
             256  *Interior of the Church.*
                  The Holy Name & St. Edward the Martyr,
                  Shaftesbury, Dorset.
             272  *Stained glass - Monastic Labour -
                  the building of St. Mary's.*
                  Buckfast Abbey, Devon.

# FURTHER READING

Axminster, *Some Account of St. Mary's Catholic Church Axminster*, Pamphlet.

Bainton, Roland *Penguin History of Christianity*, Volume I Penguin Books 1967.

Bideford, *Parish of the Sacred Heart 1882-1982* Publ. Associated Catholic Newspapers Ltd.

Carey, Rev. Edward D.D. Ph.D. *Saltash Catholic Parish 1884-1984*.

Carmelite Monastery Sclerder *The Bright Field*.

*Church of St. Mary Immaculate Falmouth A Brief Guide* Pamphlet.

Clegg, A. Lindsay *Church of Our Lady Queen of Martyrs & St. Ignatius, Chideock, Dorset*.

Daughters of St. Paul *Your Right To Be Informed* St. Paul Edition 1969.

Dawson, Lawrence H *A Book of Saints* George Routledge & Sons Ltd, London.

Diocesan Year Books: *1957, 1962, 1964, 1965, 1966, 1967, 1968, and 1970 to 1992 inclusive*.

Farmer, David Hugh *The Oxford Dictionary of Saints*. O.U.P. 2nd Edition.

Galbiati, Enrico & Paolo Acquistapace, Angelo Albani, Massimo Astrua of the MIMEP Assoc. *The New Testament, The Acts of the Apostles*. Edizioni Istituto S. Gaetano.

Hamilton Dom. Adam O.S.B. *History of St. Mary's Abbey of Buckfast*.

Hervey-Bathurst and J. Taylor *Catholic Wayside Guide* 2nd issue 1985.

Holy Trinity Church Dorchester *Bridging The Centuries*.

*In Diebus Illis* Retreat Notes, Wareham 1979.

Jarrold Colour Publications, *Plymouth Cathedral*.

*Lanherne Carmelite Convent*. Pamphlet.

*Lanherne Discalced Carmelite Convent*. Booklet

Martindale, C. (S.J.) *What Happened at Fatima*. London Catholic Truth Society.

Mausolff, A. & M *Saint Companions for Each Day*. St. Paul Publications 1954.

McDowell, Bart *Inside the Vatican* National Geographical Society 1991.

Merton, Thomas *The Waters of Silence* Hollis & Carter, London. 1950.

Meynell, Alice *Mary the Mother of Jesus* The Medici Society. 1925.

Monica Macadam & Norah West *A Short History of the Catholic Church in Sidmouth 1880 to 1985*.

Mostyn, General Sir David - KCB. CBE. *The Church of St. Michael & St. George Lyme Regis 1837-1987*.

National Geographic: *Byzantine Empire (Mount Athos)* December 1983.

Pax, Wolfgang *In The Footsteps of St. Paul*.

Pegg, John *Discover The Churches of Dartmoor* 1986.

Pepin, David *Pilgrims Guide To The South West* 1976.

Pettit, Paul *The New Shell Guides Devon, Cornwall & The Isles of Scilly*. 1987.

Pilkington, Francis *Ashburton The Dartmoor Town*. Publ. Penwell Ltd.

Rice, David Talbot *Art of the Byzantine Era*.

Rice, Tamara, Talbot *Russian Icons* 1963.

Short Historical Background Relating to *The Church of the Sacred Heart & St. Ia* Tregenna Hill, St. Ives.

Slader, John & Thorne Roger *Churches and Chapels in Devon* 1977.

Stephan, Dom John O.S.B. *Buckfast Abbey - Historical Guide*. 1923.

Stephan, Dom John O.S.B. *St. Brannoc's Chapel and Well, Braunton, N. Devon*. 1958

Stephan, Dom John O.S.B. *Buckfast Abbey - A Short Historical Guide*. Revised. 1968.

Stephan, Dom John O.S.B. *Buckfast Abbey - A Short Sketch*. 1930.

St. Therese of Liseaux *Autobiography - L'Histoire d'Une Ame* Translated by Ronald Knox. 1958.

Tilbrook, Richard *Buckfast Abbey* 1970.

The Architect *Wool Church - A Sum of Squares* November 1971.

The Church of The Assumption of Our Lady Torquay *A Guide to its History & Treasures*

The Daily/Sunday Missal 1975.

*The Icon* Editor Arnaldo Mondadori 1982.

*The Sisters of Christian Instruction Centenary In Sherborne 1891-1991*.

*The Story Of The Church Of Our Lady Help Of Christians & St. Denis* compiled by The Dominicans of St Mary Church.

Thompson, James *The Mouseman of Kilburn*. 1979.

*Ugbrooke* Beric Tempest & Co Ltd. St. Ives.